OUR DAILY WALK

F. B. Meyer

D1637847

Christian Focus Publications

Themes for each month

January	Our Daily Walk in Christ Jesus
February	Our Daily Walk of Life
March	Our Daily Walk of Fellowship
April	Our Daily Walk of Sincerity
May	Our Daily Walk of Communion
June	Our Daily Walk of Faith
July	Our Daily Walk of Service
August	Our Daily Walk of Wisdom
September	Our Daily Walk of Watchfulness
October	Our Daily Walk of Love
November	Our Daily Walk in the Holy Spirit
December	Our Daily Walk in the Light

© Christian Focus Publications
ISBN 1 85792 048 1

Published
in 1993
by
Christian Focus Publications Ltd
Geanies House, Fearn, Ross-shire
IV20 1TW, Scotland, Great Britain,
http://www.christianfocus.com

Reprinted in 1998

Cover Design
by
Owen Daily

JANUARY

OUR DAILY WALK IN CHRIST JESUS

As therefore ye received Christ Jesus,
the Lord, so walk in him
(Colossians 2:6)

Making a Fresh Start
January 1

'Put off con-cerning the former conver-sation the old man, which is corrupt ac-cording to the deceitful lusts. Be renewed in the spirit of your mind. Put on the new man, which af-ter God is cre-ated in right-eousness and true holiness' (Ephesians 4:22-24) 'Put ye on the Lord Jesus Christ' (Romans 13:14)

We can all start afresh! However far we have ascended, there is something higher; and however far we have fallen, it is always possible to make a fresh start. We need to take our place in the School of Christ and be taught by him (Ephesians 4:20, 21).

'The old man' which we must 'put off' is clearly our former manner of life. If we have not put it entirely away, let us do so now by an immediate act of faith in the living Spirit. It does not take long for a beggar to put off his rags and take away instead a new suit of clothes, and it need not take a moment longer to put away habits and thoughts, ways of speech and life which are unworthy of the children of God. Do it now, and look up to the Holy Spirit to keep renewing you in the spirit of your mind.

But more than this, let us 'put on the new man', which is the life of Jesus Christ, that ideal which is in the likeness of God, and which the Lord created for us by his blessed life and death and resurrection. But to enable us to live this life we need the daily help of the Holy Spirit. He entered our hearts at the moment of regeneration, and has been with us ever since. We may not have realised his entry, but we believe it because of the assurance of 1 Corinthians 6:19; Romans 8:9; Ephesians 3:16. For my part, I like to begin every day, before lifting my head from the pillow, by saying, 'Thou art within, O Spirit of Christ, though I feel thee not'.

If the Holy Spirit be ungrieved, he will witness to our sonship; he will enthrone Christ as king of our life; will keep the self-life in the place of death; will give us a hunger for the things of God; he will give power in witness-bearing. In order to have a strong and blessed Christian experience, the one thing is to see that we do not grieve the Spirit. I do not think that we can grieve him away, but we may greatly limit and restrain his gracious work by insincerity of speech, the nursing of an unforgiving spirit, any kind of over-reaching or fraudulent dealing, impurity of speech, or failure in love. We may be bound, so as not to be able to move our arms, by a number of cotton threads, quite as tightly as by a strong rope-thong. Let us take care not to grieve him by such inconsistencies.

Prayer: Fulfil in me, O God, those desires of goodness which thou hast cre-ated in my heart, and per-fect the work of faith, that Je-sus Christ may be glorified in me. Amen

Christ our Example
January 2

In the paragraph from which these words are taken, the wonderful description of our Lord's descent to share our shame and sorrow is cited by the Apostle, that it might become a living impulse and inspiration to ourselves, not to look upon our own things, not to hold them with a tight grasp, but to be willing to follow in the steps of Jesus Christ, who became the instrument through which God wrought out his redeeming purpose.

'Have this mind in you, which was also in Christ Jesus' (Philippians 2:5)

Guided by the Spirit of God, the Apostle opens the compasses of his imagination and faith, and places the one point upon the throne of the eternal God, and the other upon the cross of shame where Jesus died, and shows us the steps by which he approached nearer and nearer to human need and sin; that, having embraced us in our low estate, he might carry us back with himself to the throne of God; and that by identifying himself with our sin and sorrow, he might ultimately identify us with the glory that he had with the Father before the world was.

'Let this mind be in you.' Kepler, the great astronomer said, when turning his telescope to the stars: 'I am thinking over again the first thoughts of God'. But we can think earlier thoughts than have been written by the finger of God on the heavens and earth. We are able to think some of the thoughts that filled the heart of Jesus, when, before the foundation of the world, he stood forth as the Lamb to be slain.

Prayer: We ask, O Lord, that we may be so filled with these thoughts throughout the day, that our earthly life may be inspired with the spirit of Heaven. May we go to and fro about our business as those who have seen the face of God, and with the light of the other world upon our faces. Amen.

The apostle bids us think as Jesus thought; do not look exclusively upon your own interests; do not count anything of your own worthy to stand in the way, but always be prepared to deny yourself that through you God's redeeming love may pass to those that need his help. We must be willing to lay aside ambition and glory that we may be the better able to succour others. There is no other way to sit with Jesus on his throne; no other method of assisting him in his great mission. Many who would sit on the right and left of his throne will never reach it, because they refuse to bear his cross, to submit to shame and spitting, to misunderstanding and hatred. We must take the low seat, do the unnoticed tasks, refuse the honour which comes from human lips, or we can never be counted worthy to stand before the Son of Man.

Christ our Friend
January 3

'I have called you friends; for all things that I have heard from my Father I have made known unto you' (John 15:15).

I have read somewhere that when Michael Angelo was in the height of his fame, a boy named Raphael - destined to be his worthy successor - was introduced to him as a promising pupil. At first the lad was employed in the simplest duties of the studio, cleaning brushes and mixing paints, but as he developed the qualities of exactness, punctuality, and sympathy, he became entrusted with increasing responsibility, until the master made him his friend and confidant. So we come to Christ, first, as redeemed from the slavery of Satan, to be his servants, and he calls us his friends.

A friend will reveal himself. All the world may suppose that it knows a famous man, but after all, if he calls me his friend, I expect to get closer to him and hear from his own lips items of confidential information. Thus it is with the Lord Jesus. He manifests himself to those who love him, and keep his word, as he does not to the world.

A friend will interest his friends in his undertakings. It is a joy to Christ when those whom he loves are able to take a share in his worldwide redemptive schemes. For us, of course, it is a high honour, but it is as great a pleasure and delight to him as it is for some loving soul to have the pleasure of working with that other twin-soul, to which it is attached. It is wonderful that Jesus is glad to have us as his fellow-workers.

A friend will be interested in our failures and successes. Not otherwise is it with our Lord. When he sees some peril menacing us, does he not make the trial-hour one of special intercession? If we fail, he meets us with the same tender affection, not alienated from us, but only intensely sorry, ready to point out the cause of our failure and to encourage us to try again. *If we stand our ground*, he meets us as we come forth from the fight, glad for us, eager to refresh us in our weariness, careful to heal any wound that we may have received.

Such is the friendship of Jesus. He is always the same, his love never wanes, its manifestations are never remiss. Is it not worth while to make every effort so to keep his commandments that our entire abandonment to him may induce his entire abandonment to us?

Prayer: Heavenly Father, we pray that Jesus Christ may become dearer to us. May we love him as a personal friend, and hide ourselves in the hourly consciousness of his presence. May we have no taste or desire for things which he would disapprove. Let his love constrain us not to live unto ourselves, but to his glory. Amen.

Christ our Captain
January 4

The word translated in this passage 'Author' or 'Captain' might be rendered *File-leader*. It was thus used by Peter when he said, 'Ye killed the Prince (i.e. the File-leader) of life'. Our Lord is beheld stepping up from the grave in Joseph's garden, to which, apparently, the hatred of his foes had brought him; and as he passes forth, he is discovered to be the first, or leader, of an endless procession, which, in single file, is ever ascending from the grave to stand with him, and to follow him through all the subsequent ages.

In the earlier part of that great procession, we can see the glorious company of the apostles, behind them the goodly fellowship of prophets and the noble army of martyrs. Polycarp and Ignatius are there, Chrysostom and Augustine, Luther and Calvin, Wesley and Spurgeon. Our ancestors follow, and our parents. We are there, and our children will follow. We follow Christ our Captain through Gethsemane to Calvary; through death to life, through the grave to the Ascension mount.

When Isaiah anticipated Christ's advent, he said that God had given him to be a leader and commander to the people (Isaiah 55:4). He has the pre-eminence, not only because of his original glory, as Son of God, but since he has won it in his obedience as man. Never has the will of God been wrought out so perfectly as by our Lord; and in this we are called upon to obey and follow him. He was made perfect through sufferings, so shall we be; and as he is now crowned with glory and honour, so shall we be.

The only way in which Christ could bring us to share in his glory was to submit to suffering and death. In no other way could he act as the mediator of the divine life to us who are his brethren. Similarly, if we would become the mediators of help and blessing to others, we also must be prepared to suffer. We must learn to do despite to our own will and way. The way of the cross is the only path to the throne. We can only reach our highest by the constant saying 'no' to self-life. This will involve suffering and pain; but only so can we follow our Captain.

"For it became him, for whom are all things, and through whom are all things, in bringing many sons unto glory, to make the author (or Captain) of their salvation perfect through sufferings. For both he that sanctifieth and they that are sanctified are all of one: for which cause he is not ashamed to call them brethren' (Hebrews 2:10, 11).

Prayer: Teach us, O Lord, not only to bear, but to love thy cross. As we take and carry it, may we find that it is carrying us. Amen.

Christ our Light
January 5

'I am the light of the world; he that followeth me shall not walk in darkness, but shall have the light of life' (John 8:12).

It was the Feast of Tabernacles when our Lord uttered the words of our text, and it is supposed they were lighting the two great candelabra, which commemorated the fire-cloud that led the desert march. It was in direct allusion to the fiery pillar that our Lord used this metaphor. What that was to Israel, he is to his church.

The wilderness was a trackless waste to Israel. The people absolutely depended on the cloud to show their path, and to find a resting-place at night. When it gathered itself up from the Tabernacle on which it brooded, the people must strike their tents and follow. However desirable the site of their camp, they must leave it; however difficult the desert paths, they must traverse them; however uninviting the spot where it stopped, they must halt there, and remain as long as it tarried. To linger was to run the risk of wandering aimlessly in the desert till death supervened. Only where the cloud rested did the manna fall, the water flow, or the divine protection avail.

There are resting-times in our lives. God graciously arranges green pastures and quiet waters, and makes us to lie down. His voice sounds amid the turmoil of our existence, and bids us come aside and rest awhile. But often we fret against enforced rest, we persist in hurrying to and fro, and give way to bitter repining. When the cloud stays, remain where you are. When you do not know what to do, stop still until some indication points your path.

There are times for action. The trumpet is heard with its summons, to which we must give immediate attention. When the sleeper refuses to arise instantly at the whir of the alarm, he soon becomes so accustomed to it that it does not disturb him. So we shall gain keenness of hearing when we accustom ourselves to instant obedience. The peace and usefulness of our earthly life will be in direct proportion to our appropriation of the Lord Jesus for all the demands of our pilgrim condition. Nay, more, for as in the train the electric light comes on before the dark tunnel is entered, and lingers after it is passed, so the presence of Christ will precede and follow times of special need. 'I will make darkness light before them, and crooked things straight' (Isaiah 42:16).

Prayer: O send out thy light and thy truth, and let them lead me and bring me at last to my Father's house in peace. Amen.

Christ our Teacher
January 6

There was no doubt that Christ was a teacher come from God! Some teachers come evidently enough from man; they speak only of earthly things; their speeches are full of quotations; they imitate, in voice, manner, and method of stating truth, some commanding human teacher at whose feet they have sat. But there was a freshness, a self-witnessing truthfulness, a depth, an authority in the words of the Master, which bore the mint-mark of deity. Our Lord addressed Nicodemus as 'the teacher of Israel' (verse 10).

'We know that thou art a Teacher come from God: for no man can do these miracles that thou doest, except God be with him' (John 3:2).

Jesus taught with *authority* (Matthew 7:29). This was the verdict of the people. He needed not to quote Gamaliel or Hillel, because the conscience of his hearers said, He speaks the truth. He taught with *tenderness and sweetness* (Luke 4:22). To those who resisted his words, as the Pharisees did, his tongue was a sharp two-edged sword; but for the sinful, weary and heavy-laden, grace was poured on his lips. He taught with plenty of *illustrations* (Mark 4:34). From all quarters he gathered them, from the sky and the earth, from the vulture and the sparrow, from the lightning-flash and the sunrise, from the household candle and the temple lamp, from the woman's dough and the ripened corn, from the children's games and the housewife's jewellery, from the feasts of the rich and the bare larder of the poor. How picturesque and beautiful his talk was! The apples of gold were in pictures of silver. His speech was full of windows through which the light poured. What wonder that the people thronged around him, and hung with absorbing interest on his words.

But we must come to him as *Saviour*. Before we can understand his teaching, we must be converted, and become as little children. To us, he says, as to Nicodemus, 'Ye must be born again'. To reverence him as 'Teacher' will not avail, until the soul has cast itself in the dust before him, crying 'Have mercy upon me', for 'I am a sinful man, O Lord.'

Prayer: Give us grace to perceive thee, blessed Lord, to hear thy voice, and to receive the gracious teaching which comes from thine heart. Amen.

There is a marked gradation in the teaching of Jesus. He began by speaking about earthly things, and led his disciples on to understand heavenly things. He gave milk to babes, but those of understanding, hard and deep things, as strong meat. How differently he taught the woman at Sychar's well, and the disciples in the upper room.

Christ's Teaching about Blessedness
January 7

'Blessed is the man that walketh not in the counsel of the ungodly, nor standeth in the way of sinners, nor sitteth in the seat of the scornful: but his delight is in the law of the Lord' (Psalm 1:1, 2).

Our Lord lived inside the city of Blessedness, and in Matthew 5:1-12, he reveals to all men the eight gates by which that city may be entered. For myself, I cannot go in by the gate of Poverty of spirit, for I am not humble enough; nor by the gate of the Mourners, for I am not grieved enough for my own sins or the sins of others; nor by the gate of the Meek, for I often resent injury; nor by the gates of Mercy, or Purity, or Peace. But I may claim to enter by the fourth gate, for I *hunger and thirst after righteousness.* And as I go in, I find myself inside the city, and in the company of all holy souls that have entered by the other gates. For in the heavenly city, to enter by any gate is equivalent to having entered by all; and one grace which is inwrought by the Holy Spirit will ultimately lead on to all the rest.

What is Blessedness? According to our Lord's teaching, it is a condition or state of heart. Outward circumstances are not mentioned, unless it be reproach and persecution, as though they were matters of indifference. Blessedness is altogether independent of our outward lot, whether prosperous or perplexed, rich or poor. Blessedness begins and ends with a contented recognition of the royalty of Christ's kingdom; in the power of seeing the good in everything, and so inheriting the earth; in being satisfied, in obtaining mercy, in seeing God and being called his sons and daughters. Is it not worth while to strive to enter in at these wide-open doors? And if you can say that you really do yearn after better things, hungering and thirsting for more likeness to Christ, and more fitness for his kingdom; if that desire really represents the purpose of your life, you may account yourself as being already admitted within the gates of the blessed life.

We must not suppose that our Lord allocated the award of blessedness to the possessors of certain attributes with an arbitrary and royal prerogative. He simply declared what was true in the very nature of things. To be true, pure, merciful, and meek, is to have in your possession the seed-germs of the harvest of blessedness. If you turn from this wonderful enumeration of Christian qualities to Galatians 5:22, you will find all of them set forth in the list of the fruit of the Spirit. May he work in us and through us a well-balanced and full-orbed Christian character.

Prayer: Lord, take my lips, and speak through them; take my mind, and think through it; take my heart, and set it on fire. Amen.

Christ, the Teacher of Righteousness
January 8

Our Lord Jesus does not destroy, but fulfils, as the summer fulfils the promise of spring. Do not be afraid of him, as though he takes pleasure in dashing the cup from thirsty lips, and disappointing innocent and natural desires. He will certainly show himself hostile to every wrong means of gratification, but he will fulfil the desire of them that fear him in the best way, so that they will be satisfied for ever.

This is true religion. Christ *constructs*. He is more positive than negative; more Yea and Amen than Nay! He sends the pulse of the new sap into the trees, and as it passes the tip of every branch, the old dead leaves flutter silently to the ground. Give yourself to him, and ask him to fulfil in you the principles of righteousness. Christ fulfils the Law and the Prophets, which evidently stand for the authority and principles of the Old Testament (verses 17, 18). The *jot* was the smallest Hebrew letter; the *tittle* was a small part of a letter. What a contrast there is between the teaching of Christ and the attitude of some modern critics. They appear to take pleasure in destruction, in pulling down and overthrowing the foundations of faith, giving nothing in their place.

The righteousness which our Lord teaches is altogether different from that of the Pharisees, which was outward and formal, and essentially selfish, since by it they desired to earn admittance to God's favour. Christ, on the other hand, demands a righteousness which is inward, vital and spiritual. We stand before God in the imputed righteousness of his finished work, and then he imparts to us an inner righteousness through the indwelling of the Holy Spirit.

Notice how the Lord distinguishes between 'those of old time' (verse 21) and himself: '*I* say unto you'. What majesty is in those words! He counted it not robbery to be equal with God, yet he was meek and lowly in heart. How can we reconcile these statements except by the belief that he was Emmanuel - God with us?

'Whosoever shall break one of these least commandments, and shall teach men so, shall be called least in the Kingdom of Heaven: but whosoever shall do and teach them, he shall be called great in the Kingdom of Heaven' (Matthew 5:19).

Prayer: O Captain and Leader of the Holy War, may I have truth as the girdle of my loins, righteousness as my breastplate, salvation as my helmet, peace for my feet and faith for my shield. May I have no fellowship with unfruitful works of darkness, but reprove them by my consistent life and faithful words. Amen.

'Be not there-fore anxious, saying, What shall we eat? or, What shall we drink? or, Wherewithal shall we be clothed? ... Your Heavenly Father knoweth that ye have need of all these things' (Matthew 6:31, 32).

Let us trust God to care for us! This was the life that Jesus lived. He would not even make stones into bread; nor eat until his Father bade him and sent the angels to minister to him. He speaks out of his heart when he bids us trust our Father's care.

It is better to trust in God than to accumulate riches. The moth and rust destroy, thieves steal, all earthly goods are perishable and precarious. How many have placed their savings in stocks and shares, in banks and companies, and have lost every penny! Whilst others who have been unable to save and have lived to help their fellow-men, have found that God has made provision for them and carried them 'even to hoar hairs'.

Trust in God gives clearness of vision. When we are thinking partly of doing God's work in the world, and partly of lining our own nest, we are in the condition of the man whose eyes do not look in the same direction. There is a squint in our inner vision. We are endeavouring to serve two masters, and our judgment is therefore distorted. Who has not often experienced this? You have tried to ascertain God's will, or to form a right judgment about your life, but constantly your perception of duty has been obscured by the thought that, if you decided in a certain direction, you would interfere with your interests in another. Your eye has not been single, and you have walked in darkness. When, however, you feel so absorbed in God's interests that you are indifferent to your own, all becomes clear and you leave him to care for all results. 'Mind my business,' said Queen Elizabeth to one of her ambassadors, 'and I will look after yours.'

Prayer: Thou art our por-tion, our God, our Father. Thou art more than father and mother to those who trust thee. Thou lovest us with a tender pity that never fails or wearies. Encompass us with thy guard-ian care, and realise in us thy highest pur-pose. Amen.

Let us not think that God is niggardly and stinting in his gifts. He gives fish as well as bread when he feeds the crowds; colours as well as leaves when he clothes the flowers. You have been adopted into his family, and may call him 'Abba, Father'. Surely this act of grace shows a special love on his part. Would he have taken such care of the spiritual, and have none for the physical? The ungodly may worry about their maintenance; but a child of God may be sure that his needs will be supplied.

Christ's Teaching about Judging Others
January 10

Our Lord evidently does not, in these words, condemn that honest judgment which, for our own safety and for the good of society, we are compelled to form of men and women with whom we come in contact. Such judgments are inevitable. But he condemns that censorious and uncharitable judgment which is always finding fault, always neglecting the good and dwelling on the bad, always spreading unfavourable and inaccurate reports, which are often founded on very superficial and insufficient grounds.

'Judge not, that ye be not judged. For with what judgment ye judge, ye shall be judged' (Matthew 7:1, 2).

How true it is that we are measured by the measure we use for others. There is a remarkable Nemesis in life, which is the judgment-seat of God. The evils we inflict on others, like the Australian boomerang, which becomes almost a speck in the sky, come back to ourselves. If you are generous in your estimate of others, you will be estimated generously. If you are mean and stingy, others will treat you in the same spirit.

We are all would-be oculists! Nothing pleases us better than to try our hand at recovering motes of sawdust, as well as splints, from the eyes of others, while we are indifferent to the beams of timber which obstruct our own vision. Christ is always saying to us, 'Cast out the filthiness from the holy place'; and as his light falls deeper and deeper into our nature, it must reveal hidden evils which need to be put away. 'Let us be true to the inner light, and then with tender and chastened spirits, from which all consciousness of superiority has departed, we shall help others to be rid of their own obstructions.'

In verses 15-20, Christ gives us the infallible test. He suggests that in every age there will be those who care for the fleece more than for the flock, and who come into the fold under a most winsome and bewitching guise. Beware of such people, and judge them, not by their doctrine, but by their fruits. The devil is the most orthodox theologian in the world: 'I know thee, who thou art, the Holy One of God'.

Prayer: Make us merciful, O Christ, in our judgments of others. May we think no evil. May we forbear and forgive one another as thou dost forgive us. Amen.

'*By their fruits ye shall know them.*' You cannot judge what a man is by hearing him repeat a creed; but as you observe his character, his disposition, his behaviour; not in public, but in private; not for a day, but for a year, you can come to an almost certain judgment as to whether God or self be the ruling consideration of the inner being.

Christ's Teaching about Beneficence
January 11

'Thou shalt love the Lord thy God with all thy heart, ... and thy neighbour as thyself... But he said, And who is my neigh- bour?' *(Luke 10:27, 29).*

We cannot live alone. No one of us can be entirely independent of others. I am not only a centre, but I am part of another man's circumference; and every other man, woman or child I know is part of my circumference. We are members one of another. In other words, we all have neighbours; and a complete human life, which has windows opening to the infinite Creator, must have doors opening on the street towards our finite fellow-creatures.

When we talk about neighbours, we naturally think of those who live next door, and we are apt to reduce the divine command to those who reside in the same street. If these are very comfortable and well-to-do, it seems as though there is not much scope for helping them. This definition of *neigh-bours*, however, is altogether too narrow and contracted, as our Lord shows in the parable of the Good Samaritan. The lawyer asked who was his neighbour, and Jesus replied, *'Be a neigh-bour to someone else.'* And if it be asked what kind of people I am to neighbour, the answer comes: 'Make no distinction of race or creed; but wherever you come across a man who has been stripped, beaten, robbed, and is half-dead, don't wait for other men to succour him, but bind up his wounds; minister to him, and treat him as though you loved him with the natural love of brotherhood.'

A rich man might have paid an agent to patrol that dangerous road from Jerusalem to Jericho, and to look after those in distress, but it would not be so blessed in its effect on his own character, or on the men who were helped, as personal ministry would be. We ought to combine the two, because our personal experience of such cases will enable us to direct our agents, and live in their efforts, so that they may become our own. Perhaps the better policy is to get elected on the Council, or Magistrates' bench, so that we may put down the gangs of thieves which infest life's highways.

Remember that a gift of money is by no means the only way of helping your neighbours. What men and women need most is compassion, sympathy, your hand and heart-help. 'Silver and gold have I none' has been the confession of some of the greatest benefactors of our race. Above all, it was true of our Lord himself, who became poor that he might really help us, as he never could have done had he remained rich. Let him be our example, who came not to be ministered unto, but to minister.

Prayer: Show me, today, O Lord, that one of thy little ones to whom I am to give a cup of water in thy name. Amen.

Christ's Teaching about Resurrection
January 12

This crowning miracle of our Lord's life is generally described as the Raising of Lazarus. I am not sure that it might not with equal truth be called the Awakening of Martha, for it is certain that the Lord lifted this soul, whom we have been wont to count prosaic and matter-of-fact, to a most remarkable elevation of faith and hope, as they stood together in the shadow of a great sorrow.

In common with the majority of religious people, Martha believed in a general resurrection at some still future date, but she had not realised that *God lives in the present tense*, that the eternal is *here* and *now*, and that faith must learn to reckon on God's *I AM*. We are always putting the manifestation of the divine in the far past, or the far future. The heaven is high above the earth on which we stand; only at the horizon, behind us and before us, do heaven and earth touch. We all need to learn the lesson that here, in the prosaic commonplaces of life, Jesus Christ is the present and immediate answer to every need.

Christ's teaching about Resurrection differs widely from immortality. Plato believed in the immortality of the soul, but he had no conception of resurrection. Resurrection is the reunion of the soul with the body, when it shall be raised in a form identical with, though different from, the body laid in the grave, as the sheaf of corn is identical with, though different from, the seed corn cast into the soil amid the tears of autumn.

Martha could hardly understand all these marvellous disclosures, but she answered Yea to them, on the ground of what she knew Christ to be. He at least was the Messiah, and whatsoever he said, it must be so. So it is that we may still accept much, that we cannot understand, on the bare word of Jesus.

Christ always needed faith in some one, as the fulcrum on which to rest the lever of his mighty power, and he found it in Martha. What can he not do, even here and now, in the hearts of those who are slow to believe, and those who are dead in trespasses and sins? Believest thou this?

'Jesus said unto her, I am the resurrection and the life; he that believeth on me, though he die, yet shall he live: and whosoever liveth and believeth on me shall never die. Believest thou this? She saith unto him, Yea, Lord!' (John 11:25-27).

Prayer: O God of life and love, thou hast filled our hearts with joy unspeakable. We thank thee that Jesus is the resurrection and the life, and that those who believe in him shall never die. He lives, and they live, and we live! We thank thee, we praise thee, we bless thee. Amen.

'In that same hour he rejoiced in the Holy Spirit, and said, I thank thee, O Father, Lord of Heaven and earth, that thou didst hide these things from the wise and understanding, and didst reveal them unto babes: yea Father; for so it was well pleasing in thy sight' (Luke 10:21).

In that same hour. It was an hour of great congratulation for the little band of disciples. The seventy had returned with joy. They had tried the talisman of his name with demons and disease, and it had triumphed. Our Lord yielded to the gladness of his followers, and gave himself up to an unusual burst of happiness.

Notice his habitual mode of address to God. Twice he speaks to him as *Father.* Thus in joy, equally as in the sorrow of Gethsemane and the anguish of death, the Fatherhood of God was the Rock of Ages to the Man Christ Jesus, in the cleft of which he hid himself. Only Jesus knew what God was and could be to the lonely soul. As the mountain is reflected in the lake at its foot, so the Father saw himself perfectly reflected in Jesus.

Inscribed over the portico of an Egyptian temple are these words: 'I am he that was and shall be, and no man hath lifted my veil'. In this connection it is significant that when our Saviour died, the veil of the Temple was rent from the top to the bottom. Before that hour the knowledge of God had been confined to the few elect souls, and to these it came as through a glass darkly; but from that hour the innermost secret of God's love has been disclosed. And that unveiling of the Father's heart is typical of the work of our Lord for us all.

We must be child-like. The ways of God are revealed unto babes. The child is pure; is humble. It is to the transparent and simple heart that Jesus waits to give himself.

We must be prepared to say Yes to God. Our Lord was face to face with one of the great mysteries of Providence; why certain things are hidden from some and revealed to others; but he rolled the whole perplexity back on the Father, and was at rest. When in a deaf and dumb school, a visitor wrote on the blackboard: 'Why did God make you deaf and dumb, and me able to speak and hear?' One of the children took the chalk and wrote beneath: 'Even so, Father, for so it seemed good in thy sight'.

We must pass on to others what we know. He will not teach us merely for our own gratification, but that we may benefit others thereby.

Prayer: Teach us, O Lord, to pray. Pray in us by thy Holy Spirit. May our hearts be filled with his deep yearnings, and our lips become the medium by which he shall find utterance. Amen.

Power and Prayer
January 14

In our Lord's life there was no divorce between the life hidden in God and a ready response to the call of human need. As in Raphael's great picture of the Transfiguration, which combines the scenes of the mountain and the valley on the one canvas, so must it always be in true life. There must be the systole and the diastole - the heart must drive the blood to be aerated in heaven's ozone, and then pulsate to the extremities of hand and foot.

How many there are who seem to be possessed with evil spirits which are wrecking health and peace, and how many make the mistake of this man in bringing their relatives or friends to disciples who as yet have not been baptised with the power of the Holy Spirit, and have not entered into the secret place of power. Of course it is not possible for such to afford any real help, and the demon laughs them to scorn! We must learn our own inability to deal with the forces of evil that are sweeping through the world, unless we have received power from on high (Luke 10:17, 20; Acts 1:8).

Notice the way in which our Lord casts back the responsibility on the father. He said: '*If thou* canst do anything'; but Jesus answered: 'the *if* is not with *me*, but with *you*. It is not a question of *my* power but of *your* faith. Can you believe?' Then the father threw back the responsibility on the Master, saying in effect: 'I fear that I have not faith enough, but I trust thee to create it in me. *Help thou mine unbelief.*'

You and I often fail in our faith because of ignorance and besetting sin. There is the mighty ocean of power all around us, but for some reason we cannot tap it. It is like the electric current, which refuses to help us unless we have instruments precisely adapted to transmit the driving-power. Faith is absolutely necessary for the conveyance of God's power to meet the need and sin and sorrow of the world. But when we find it deficient, when our heart believes not, when we find ourselves face to face with Jerichos that are closely shut, and with mountains that seem to mock the tiny levers with which we propose to move them, then we must turn to Christ and say: 'I trust thee for faith, I trust thee to keep me trusting; I believe, help thou mine unbelief.'

'If thou canst do anything, have compassion on us, and help us. Jesus said unto him, If thou canst believe, all things are possible to him that believeth' (Mark 9:22, 23).

Prayer: We open our nature to let in thy blessed fullness, and if our capacity be small, we pray, O Lord, that it may be enlarged, that we may miss nothing that is possible to man. We are sure that we are never straitened in thee, but in ourselves. Amen.

Things to be left Behind
January 15

'Lay aside every weight, and the sin which doth so easily beset us, and let us run with patience the race that is set before us, looking unto Jesus' (Hebrews 12:1, 2).

Leave behind your past sins. They have been many and great, more than you can count. But if you have confessed and forsaken them, they have been put away, 'as far as the east is from the west'. Nothing could be more explicit than 1 John 1:9. It is useless to brood over the past. God has buried it in the grave of Christ. Go and sin no more!

Leave behind your bad habits that encumber you (R V marg.). You know what they are, and how they cling - ill-temper, jealousy, pride, evil-speaking, and many another! You have fallen again and again, overtaken by them, tripped up, your robes stained and torn. There should be some finality in your life, a mark on the grass from which you start to run the race. The command to put off the old man is in the definite tense (Colossians 3:8, 9). It bespeaks one sudden strong act of the will, God-nerved and God-empowered. This, then, is the hour when you must strike for liberty: 'Ye have died, and your life is hid with Christ in God.'

Leave behind your accomplished ideals. They were once far in front and above you. As you climbed they seemed almost inaccessible, and mocking voices rang out their defiance of your attempt. But by the grace of God things that once you dreamt of are now realised, and you are sitting on the peak that once seemed to laugh you to scorn. But you must leave it behind! Look up! Look forward! Are there not fresh ideals calling to you? Leave behind your attainments and strike your tents. One battle is fought, but a yet stronger foe bars the way immediately in front. It is suicidal to rest on your oars; to do so will expose you to the inevitable backward drift.

The best way to leave behind is to press forward. The Spirit of God bids us 'run with patience the race set before us, looking unto Jesus'. He is our forerunner, always before us, always leading us on. His crest like the plume of Henry of Navarre, is always in the very thick of the fight. Let the soul follow hard after him, and it will become almost oblivious to what it leaves behind. The boy who is running for the goal, in his eagerness to win the prize, strips himself of one and another article of clothing. He will not count their worth, so long as he may win the prize. So run that ye may attain! Apprehend that for which you were apprehended! Lay hold on the outstretched crown of life!

Prayer: Most gracious God, quicken me by thy Holy Spirit, that I may run in the way thou hast marked out for me. May I ever be kept looking off unto Jesus. Amen.

Glory to God in the Highest
January 16

Jesus was 'born a Saviour'. Being what he is, the King of Love, it is not wonderful that he entered into so close an identification with our human race that needed him so sorely. Could infinite Love have stood idly by? Every soul which enters into the human family helps to quicken or depress its vitality. How much our race owes to the great souls that have been born into it, but how much more to him who was in the form of God, and thought it not robbery to be equal with God! He laid aside the use of the mighty power, which as Creator he might have employed, and stooped to be born in a stable, that he might share the life of the humblest and poorest.

'Thou shalt call his name Jesus, for he shall save his people from their sins' (Matthew 1:21).

What love for men must have burned in the heart of Jesus! His zeal for mankind ate him up. There was a true enthusiasm for humanity in his heart. Why should there not be the same with us? Let us ask that the 'love of Christ - i.e. the very love which burnt within him - may also constrain us'. Let us be willing to subject ourselves to inconvenience, to limitations, to the wrapping of swaddling clothes, if only we may get near to others, removing all sense of distance and aloofness.

'Glory to God in the Highest' (Luke 2:14). Nothing has so augmented the glory of the Father as this stooping to death, even the death of the cross (Philippians 2:6-11). Men have turned to God with adoring reverence, as they could not have done if they had known him only in Nature. Whenever we seek the glory of God as our main end and purpose, it will always result in peace on earth. Live for the glory of God, and you will have peace in your heart, and your life will flow forth in goodwill and blessing for others.

Prayer: My Father God! Let the motto of my life henceforth be, 'Glory to God in the Highest', for only so can there be peace in my heart and goodwill towards men. May my heart be kept in unison with the angel's song. Amen.

The outburst of song from the shepherds, 'glorifying and praising God', as they wended their way back to their flocks, must have amazed all whom they met, and it bespoke the wonder that had transformed their lives. We are so ordinary and commonplace, so unemotional and impassive, we cannot forget ourselves, and are never carried beyond ourselves. David said that while he mused the fire burned! Let us muse on the love of God in descending to our world, in living our life, and dying for us on the cross. Then we shall burst out into songs, and shall come back to our ordinary life with the flow of a new spirit (Luke 2:20).

Walking not after the flesh, but after the Spirit
January 17

'There is therefore now no condemnation to them that are in Christ Jesus. That the requirement of the law might be fulfilled in us, who walk not after the flesh, but after the Spirit' (Romans 8:1, 4 RV)

The apostle here is dealing with the conditions of a holy life; and the condemnation to which he refers is that caused by the constant failure so graphically described in the previous chapter. From my own experience, I think that the introspection which is often induced by ill-health and weakness makes us very sensitive to the failure and shortcoming of the inner life. We know that we are accepted in Christ, and that our sins are forgiven us for his sake; but we are deeply conscious that in us (i.e. in our flesh) dwelleth no good thing (Romans 7:18).

The Reservoir of Eternal Life - 'the Spirit of Life in Christ Jesus'. We perceive what physical life is when a child comes bounding into our room in a very ecstasy of health and joy. We know what intellectual life is as we see the mind developing under the process of education. We know what the moral life of a stoic is, repelling by force of will the appeal of the senses. But above all these, there is *Life* which is resident in Jesus Christ, stored in him, abounding in him, which he longs to communicate to every soul that trusts in him. This was the witness of those who knew Jesus most intimately in his brief human life - that 'God hath given unto us Eternal Life, and this Life is in his Son'. 'He that hath the Son hath the Life; and he that hath not the Son of God hath not the Life'. This more than outweighs the down-pull of the self-life. The law of that life makes us free from the law of sin and death, for it has mastered death and the grave.

This Life is communicated and sustained by the Holy Spirit. We must be *one* with Christ; we must be *in* him, as the sponge is in the ocean. We must be *in* him, not only in our standing, but also in our *daily walk*. We must be *in* him as the branch is in the vine, and the vine-sap in the branch. And this must not only be a theory, but an hourly experience. We must abide in him and he in us. But how can this become our daily experience? There is but one way. Through the co-operation of the Holy Spirit, as we walk in him (Galatians 5:16). He is the essence of the Life which is in Christ Jesus. 'The Spirit of Life in Christ Jesus hath made me free from the law of sin and death.'

Prayer: Almighty God, I beseech thee to raise me from the death of sin to the life of righteousness by that same power that brought the Lord Jesus from the dead, that I may walk in newness of life through the aid of the Holy Spirit. Amen.

The Law of the Spirit of Life
January 18

The simplest child knows something of the law of gravitation. The word is from the Latin *gravitas*, which is the attraction of weight by weight. What gravitation is to matter, the down-pull of the flesh is to the spirit. There is not a single one of us, who is seeking to live the better life, that is not conscious of this down-pull. Indeed the laws of gravitation in the natural world have their counterpart in our inward experience. There is always a down-pull to the centre of gravity, i.e. to self - what *I* like, what *I* choose, what *I* prefer! The fall of the soul toward the flesh - or self-life - becomes increasingly rapid, so that every time we yield it becomes easier to yield, and the velocity becomes headlong. The child of God would fall with velocity equal to that of the depraved sinner if it were not for the law of the Spirit of Life which is in Christ Jesus which makes him free from the law of sin and death.

Overcoming the Earth-pull. You may see it in the soaring of the lark, singing as it rises, until you think it will split its tiny throat with song. One of the delights of an ocean voyage is to watch the gulls, as regularly, evenly, and easily they keep level with the progress of the boat. The bird does not float in the air; it balances itself; it measures its wings against its weight, and defies the earth-pull. But if the means of flight are maimed, it drops helplessly on land or water. Alas for the bird, though it be an albatross, that happens to alight on water covered by the oil discharged from an oil-driven vessel. When once its wings have become glued to its body, by immersion in that oil-bath, there is nothing for it but a miserable end!

The Spirit works according to Law - 'the *law* of the Spirit of Life'. Do not grieve him by any act of insincerity or hatred. If you are aware of the subsidence of his energy, go back till you have discovered where you dropped the thread of obedience to his gentle promptings. Pick it up by confession and restitution, and again you will become conscious of his mediation to you of a Law of Life that laughs at sin and death! Yours will be the wings of an eagle's flight, the soaring of a lark, sunward, heavenward, Godward! But you must take time to be holy - in meditation, in prayer, and especially in the use of the Bible.

'For the law of the Spirit of Life in Christ Jesus hath made me free from the law of sin and death' (Romans 8:2).

Prayer: Help me, O Lord, to find my life according to thy promise. I thank thee that thou hast implanted the germ of thine own nature. Leave me not, neither forsake me in the upward climb. Teach me to change my strength and mount up with the wings of eagles. Amen.

'I am the Vine, ye are the branches: he that abideth in me, and I in him, the same beareth much fruit: for apart from me ye can do nothing' *(John 15:5).*

Our Saviour's perennial joy was due to his unceasing endeavour to minister help and blessing to others. He saved others; he could not save himself. He said, 'I am the *true* Vine', i.e. the vine was made by him in creation to represent a certain phase or characteristic of himself. It is the reflection in the waters of materialism of eternal principles deep-seated in his own divine nature. The study of the vine is, therefore, specially precious in its teaching.

Behind the vine, as we know it, there is an immense pressure of energy. In the spring-tide, it seems as though the love of God were pressing for expression in the corn that supports life, in the oil that makes the face to shine, and in the grape that cheers. The vine cannot bear fruit of itself; it is only the channel along which the energy of God flows in its endeavour to gladden the heart and life of man. So Jesus is the channel through which the life and love of God reach us, that we may pass them on in loving ministry, and in so doing we are creating and storing up for ourselves infinite joy.

Let each of us learn to *abide in Christ*! With the heart open to him on the one hand, and open to men, women and children on the other. Then let us trust Christ to pour his love and grace into our hearts, that the pressure within may lead us to perform acts of tender sympathy and helpfulness of which we would not otherwise have been capable. Let us resolve to let no day pass without doing something at cost to ourselves, to make the burden lighter and the path easier for someone else. Our willingness for Christ to do these things through us will always meet a response from him; and his Spirit being in us will show us exactly what to say or do. It may be only a smile, a touch of the hand, or a word! Thus life will be filled with joy, and this will be perpetuated surely in that other life, when we shall awake and be satisfied. As we mingle with the throngs of happy spirits who have come out of great tribulation - the martyrs, prophets, apostles, and saints of every age - the greatest wonder of all will be that *we* are there. 'Lord, when saw we thee an hungered, and fed thee? or athirst, and gave thee drink? And he will say, Inasmuch as ye did it unto one of the least of these ... ye did it unto me.'

Prayer: May I never forget, O Lord, that the best and happiest life must be lived in communion with the needs, sorrows, and trials of others. Give me closer sympathy with thyself, who didst not please thyself, but whose blessed life was perpetually laid down for others. Amen.

The All-Sufficiency of Christ
January 20

It is hardly needful to explain that these are the first and last letters in the Greek alphabet. They represent all the intervening letters which they enclose as in a golden clasp. This majestic announcement refers to the eternal God. His nature underlies the whole created universe, all races of being, the entire work of redemption, the destiny of his children, and the ultimate victory of righteousness and peace. 'Of him, and through him, and to him are all things, to whom be glory for ever and ever'. Let us, for a moment, join with the ceaseless chant of heaven, saying, 'Holy, Holy, Holy, Lord God Almighty, which is and which was and which is to come'. We must never rush into his presence without due preparation and reverence of heart.

Jesus Christ is the Complement of our Need. From the alphabet of his being we may obtain all the letters and words which will make good our own deficiencies. It is a question whether some of us would ever have learnt the fullness of Jesus, if we had not been brought face to face with the infinite needs of our own nature and condition. You may engage your guide in an Alpine village, but you only realise all the qualities that lie hidden within him when you have crossed the glaciers, bridged the yawning chasms, and escaped the descending avalanche through his knowledge and care. So as we walk with Jesus we find in him the complement of our need.

Loneliness is an opportunity for Jesus to make himself known as the Living One (verse 17). When, like the beloved apostle on the Lord's Day in his lonely isle, you seem to hear songs and prayers on which you can only join in spirit, turn to the Lord himself, and reckon on him to bear you company. That loneliness constitutes a claim on him! Call upon his name out of the lowest dungeon. He will not hide his ear at thy breathing or thy cry. He will draw near in the day when thou callest upon him, and will say, Fear not! He will plead the causes of thy soul; he will redeem thy life. The site of Polycarp's death is still visible above the Smyrna coastline and harbour; but Jesus stood there with him, enabling him to be faithful unto death, and encircling his brow with the crown of life. Be thou faithful unto death; the First and the Last is with thee! 'Yea, though I walk through the valley of the shadow of death, I will fear no evil, for thou art with me!'

'I am the Alpha and the Omega, saith the Lord God, he which is and which was and which is to come, the Almighty' (Revelation 1:8 RV).

Prayer: Be thou, O Lord, the Alpha and the Omega of every year, month, day, hour, and act of my life. Let all things be begun, continued and ended in thee. Amen.

'For if by one man's offence death reigned by one; much more they which receive abundance of grace, and of the gift of righteousness, shall reign in life by one, Jesus Christ' (Romans 5:17).

It would take a lifetime - nay, it will demand eternity - to explore the treasures of this paragraph from which our text is taken. Let us not, however, stand gazing into heaven, but avail ourselves of the privilege offered us during our earthly life of reigning through the one, even Jesus Christ. Do not postpone the fulfilment of this promise! We may have to wait for the future life to unfold depths of meaning which now transcend our thought; but any fair reading of this radiant verse compels us to appropriate it for *here* and *now*.

But, '*how can these things be?*' Ah, a master in Israel asked that question of Christ! This blessed life of victory is only possible to those who have been born from above. By nature we were born *from below* into the first Adam, who was 'a living *soul*'. We must be born *from above*, into the second Adam, who becomes to all who trust in him a life-giving *spirit* (1 Corinthians 15:45). That which is born of the flesh is flesh, and cannot of itself rise into the Spirit; the Holy Spirit must stoop to lift it into union with himself. But he will do this for you, if only you will lift your heart to Christ in simple faith and surrender.

The difference it will make! Each life has been planned by God with the intention of training it for high service here and beyond; and whatever happens in life, there is always an abundance of grace awaiting our use. But how often we are as blind to it as Balaam was to the Angel that stood on the wayside! We make our plans! We lie awake half the night in a fever of anxiety! We go to this friend or that! But we do not claim that abundance of grace which is intended to meet the need of the hour. It is only as we *receive* it by a childlike faith that we can *reign* in life. That word 'abundance' in its Latin original speaks of ocean waves. Stand on the shore and look out on that infinite expanse, and do not be content with scooping up enough to fill an oyster-shell!

What will result? A royal life! If a throne means power - we are strengthened with might by his Spirit in the inner man. If it means *victory* - we are more than conquerors through him that loved us. If it means *largesse* - we have always all sufficiency in all things, and abound to every good work.

Prayer: Heavenly Father, I thank thee for the trials and pains that are ever working for my good, and making me a partaker of thy holiness. May I receive the abundance of thy grace, and reign in life here and hereafter. Amen.

Dislocated Limbs
January 22

The Greek word here rendered *perfect* really means 'to put in joint, to complete'. In his original creation man's *will* was intended to register the will of God, to say Yes to it, and to pass the divine impulses and commandments to the rest of our being. Sometimes on board ship, before the phone made it possible for the captain to speak to every part of the ocean liner, I have heard him quietly utter his orders to a subordinate officer beside him, who in turn repeated them in a loud voice through a speaking-trumpet or tube. That intermediary may represent the will which was intended to receive its directions from the Will of God, and pass them throughout the economy of our being. Such was our Lord's attitude throughout his earthly life. He said: 'My meat is to do the will of him who sent me'; I seek not my own will, but the will of him that sent me'; 'Nevertheless, not as I will, but as thou wilt.'

But in the Fall, the dominance of God's will and the loyal response of man's will became disorganised; and the human will instead of functioning in harmony with the Will of God, began to obey the will of the flesh in its grosser or more refined forms. Not what God wills, but what *I* will, has become the working principle of the great majority. Thus it has come about that the will, by constant misuse, has become dislocated, warped, 'out of joint'. Tennyson says: 'Our wills are ours to make them thine!' Just so, but they are too stubborn for some of us to manage. Hence the suggestion that we should pass the matter over to the 'God of peace, who brought again from the dead our Lord Jesus'.

Sometimes at football, or on the ice, a player may lose his balance, or be tripped up, and in the fall his shoulder may become dislocated. His arm is still in the body, but out of joint, so that it hangs useless by his side, until the surgeon by one strong wrench forces the bone back into its proper place. Is not that true of us? We are in the Body of Christ by redeeming grace, but we need to be *set*, i.e. to be brought into articulated union with the will of God in Christ Jesus. Let us humbly ask the great surgeon of souls, by the pressure of his strong and gentle hands, here and now, to joint our wayward wills with the will of God, and then to work in us and through us that which is well-pleasing in his sight!

'Now the God of Peace ... make you perfect in every good thing to do his will, working in you that which is well-pleasing in his sight, through Jesus Christ' (Hebrews 13:20, 21).

Prayer: Gracious Father! I yield to thee my will and desires, my members and faculties, the life of my body, the thoughts of my heart, and the aspirations of my spirit; perfect, I pray thee, that which concerneth me. Amen.

The Garden of the Cross
January 23

'In the place where he was crucified, there was a Garden' (John 19:41).

It was in a garden that Paradise was lost, and in a garden it was regained! The sweet flowers of spring waved their incense-cups around the cross, on which their Creator, to whose thought they owed their beauty, was dying for man's redemption.

Amid all the anguish of this human world, nature pursues her unbroken routine. Spring with its green, summer with its glory, autumn with its gold - these in perennial beauty carry on their unbroken succession through all the days of human sorrow. Sometimes her unchanging order almost drives men to madness. It seems as though she has no sympathy with man in his stern battle for existence! Yet surely it is better so! Our tears and strife and storm are transient, whilst the order of creation will be the basis of that 'new heaven and earth' for which we wait. Yes, there were flowers at the foot of the Saviour's cross, and they have blossomed at the foot of every cross since his!

Where there is a cross, there will be a garden. Of course, the cross must be properly borne. We must suffer for others, not careful about ourselves. We must take the cup from the hands of the Father, even though it is presented by the hands of a Judas! We must suffer silently. No man or woman, who really suffers deeply for another's salvation, talks about it, save to God. Suffer for others in your Gethsemane-garden, and when you have been crucified after that fashion, then look for a garden in bloom. Set up a Calvary in your own heart! Let the cross there be a splint from the cross of your Saviour! Bring thither your self-love, your ambitions, your moods and vagrant, selfish thoughts. Fasten your self-life, vain and proud as it is, to the cross of Jesus, and let it remain there. Then in the garden of your character will arise a profusion of the rarest and sweetest flowers. If the world shuns your company, if you go lonely and unappreciated through life, yet you may find that the Lord Jesus will walk in the glades of your garden in the cool of the day, as he did in Paradise.

Your heart's a garden God has sown
To give your life the work it needed.
Some day he'll come to pluck his flowers,
So mind you keep your garden weeded.

Uttermost Salvation
January 24

The *attraction* of the divine nature. We draw near because we are drawn. As the sun is ever exerting a drawing power on each planet and each particle of stardust in the solar system, so God is ever attracting us to himself. To all eternity we shall be ever drawing nearer to him, though there will be ever an infinite distance to traverse. When Jesus was lifted up on the cross he began to draw all men unto himself, and that magnetic attraction has continued through the centuries.

There is no reason for us to be afraid of God. He is Love! He is a consuming fire to our sin, but his nature is essentially lovely. Moses exceedingly feared when he ascended Sinai, amid the trembling of the mountain and the heavy clouds that enclosed the divine light. But, as we learn from the 12th chapter of this epistle, when we approximate to God, we encounter three circles. The innumerable *Hosts of Angels*, including the cherubim and seraphim, with their burning love and purity! The *Church of the First-born*, the purest and noblest of elect spirits! *The Spirits of the Just made perfect*, inclusive of our own beloved ones that have passed over. Surely where these are, we may venture without fear. The God in whom they live and move and have their being cannot be other than infinitely beautiful to know and love. Lord, thou hast been the dwelling-place of all generations, and thy secret place shall be our home for ever. 'Draw us, and we will run after thee!'

Our fears are met by the risen and living Saviour. First, he will ever live to make intercession for us; but next he will go on sanctifying us lower down, even to the uttermost. To the depths of our nature, he will carry his gracious work. Salvation has three stages. It begins with deliverance from the penalty of the past. Our sins are blotted out. The penalty is remitted or turned to benediction. Then we are saved lower down. The process of purification goes deeper and deeper into our nature. Finally, our body is renewed through the resurrection-grace of Christ. And surely there is a sense in which the grace of Christ will ever sink deeper, giving us a profounder realisation and participation in the things that will open before us in the eternal progress. Here we see in a glass darkly, there face to face. Here we know in part, there we shall develop in the knowledge and love of God. Salvation to the uttermost!

'He is able to save to the uttermost them that draw near unto God through him, seeing he ever liveth to make intercession for them' (Hebrews 7:25).

Prayer: I draw near to thee, Almighty and Ever-living God, in the Name of Jesus Christ, my High Priest and Mediator, who hath passed into the heavens, where he ever liveth to make intercession for sinners. Forgive and accept me for his sake. Amen.

Grace Abounding!
January 25

'God is able to make all grace abound toward you; that ye, always having all sufficiency in all things, may abound to every good work' (2 Corinthians 9:8).

Abundance is characteristic of God! Go forth on a spring morning, and look on the flowers with which he has carpeted the woodlands. Daisies and buttercups, primroses and cowslips in myriads, bear witness to the prodigality of his thought and power - his thought to fashion, his power to produce. But this profuse carpeting of the earth's nakedness is equalled in the heavens! There, depth opens beyond depth, lighted and inlaid with constellations, and the wonders of the sky answer to those of the earth. How multitudinous is God's creation!

But what shall we say of his grace? His joy is unspeakable, his peace passeth understanding, his love is beyond knowledge! Get great thoughts of God, who holds the ocean depths as a drop in the hollow of his hand, and weighs the mountains as grains of dust in his scales. Lie upon that bank of flowers, and consider their multitude; sweep the skies with a telescope and see if you can tell the stars; number the sand-grains upon the shore, and count the shells strewn along the strand; and when you have considered the gifts of his hand, ascend to the wealth of his heart. Study the infinite map of God's nature; compare it with the need of your little life, and then remember that the Father loves you infinitely, so much so that for *your* salvation and *mine* he gave his only-begotten Son. He has set his love upon you, and will certainly deliver you! He will set you on high because you have known his name. All the resources of eternity and infinity are at his disposal, and he can make all grace abound toward you, that always having all sufficiency in all things, you may abound to every good work.

It is a very wonderful text! Count the number of universals in it. *All* grace - *always*! *All* sufficiency! *All* things! God *abounding* to us that we may *abound*. The word translated, 'abound', might be rendered literally 'to flow or pour over'. 'My cup runneth over.' Our Lord said: 'I am come that they might have life, and have it *overflowingly*'; 'Where sin *overflows*, grace much more *overflows*' (John 10:10; Romans 5:20).

Let us remember that God does not pour in unless we pour out. If we are filled with the presence and grace of Christ in our hearts, we must give ourselves out to others.

Prayer: Give me grace, O Lord, to see the beauty lying at my feet in the common places of life; and to feel that thou art as near, and that life is as wonderful today, as when men beheld thee in the days of thy flesh. Amen.

Knocking at the Door!
January 26

Christ knocks at the door when his judgments are in the earth. That God has arisen 'to shake mightily the earth' is hardly doubtful. This is a day of the Lord of Hosts, when judgments are abroad upon all that is proud and haughty, upon the cedars and the oaks, upon the high mountains and the uplifted hills. But it is at such a time that he draws near to reassure us (Isaiah 2:11-21; Joel 3:16).

'As many as I love, I rebuke and chasten: Be zealous therefore and repent. Behold I stand at the door, and knock' (Revelation 3:19, 20).

On the eve of the overthrow of the cities of the plain, he came to the door of Abraham's tent, partook of his fare, and gave promises of assurance to himself and Sarah which unfolded the divine purpose. Standing before the Lord, Abraham was prepared for the tragedy of the morrow and was permitted an intimacy in which he seemed possessed by a passion for God's rectitude and righteous dealing.

Do not fear the things that are coming, but open to him who knocks for admission. He has come to spend the dark hours in your fellowship, as a mother runs to her child's cot, when a sudden thunderstorm sweeps the sky.

Christ knocks when we are preparing for some great task. You are going forth on one of his errands, and expect misunderstanding or opposition, or you are uncertain as to your reception. Like Moses, you say, 'Send by whom thou wilt send, but let it not be by me.' With Jeremiah, you plead, 'I am a child, I cannot speak.' Like the apostles, you have to face a world in arms. At such a time, he waits at the door to encourage and inspire. On the night following the upheaval in the Sanhedrin, where Paul was nearly torn to pieces, the Lord stood by him, and said, 'Be of good cheer!'

Prayer: Come nearer to us than the nearest. Enter our hearts, saying, Fear not,

Christ knocks when bereavement enters our homes. We all know what it is to be full of longing 'for the beloved ones, whom we cannot reach by deed or token, gesture or kind speech'. The ship's masts have sunk below the rim of the horizon, in the sunset, and we turn back to homes out of which all light has gone. It is then that you may surely expect a gentle knock at the door, and he who came to Bethany when Lazarus died, that he might mingle his tears with those of the sisters, will certainly come to the door of your heart, and knock for admission that he may help to fill the gap.

I am with thee, I will help thee. Give us all that we need to enable us to fight the good fight, and finish our course with joy. Amen.

Christ Pleading for Admission
January 27

'Behold, I stand at the door and knock; if any man hear my voice, and open the door, I will come in to him, and will sup with him, and he with me' (Revelation 3:20).

Do not forget the majesty and glory of him who asks for admission! In the following verse, he declares that he is able to give the right of sitting with himself on his throne. He *stands*, that some day we may sit! O child of two worlds, shut your ear to the chatterings and noise of this passing age, and listen to him who stands at the door of your life and knocks!

Of course, we know that the Saviour never withdraws himself from hearts that are really his own. He *abides* in them, as they abide in him. But with us there may be ebbs as well as flows. The current may drop from feet to inches. The light may linger in the sky, while clouds obscure the face of the sun. The heat of the body may remain, but the extremities may become chilled. It is under these circumstances, that the Lord of all worlds comes to the door of our poor tenement, and stands, and knocks, and asks for admission!

Prayer: We thank thee, O God, that thy love has come to us in a human Form, that it shines from the face of the Man Christ Jesus, and speaks to us in gentle tones we can understand. We thank thee that he stands at the low doorway of our hearts, and knocks, and waits to come in and dwell with us for ever. We humbly ask that the Holy Spirit may open our eyes more fully to behold him, and our hearts more ardently to love and welcome him. Amen.

We may expect his knock when our love is cooling. Once our hearts beat quickly when we heard his approaching step; now, when he is at hand, we keep him waiting on the doorstep till his head is filled with dew, and his locks with the drops of night. Do we not all know what it is to be 'neither hot nor cold'? Somehow our heart has gone dead! It is then that we may expect to hear the knock of Christ. He only asks us to admit him and he will restore the soul to love, and love to the soul.

We may expect his knock when we must go forth from this world. The moment comes when the post will present us with a letter like that received by Christiana: 'The Master expecteth thee to stand in His Presence, in clothes of immortality, within ten days'. The same summons will come to Mr Honest and Mr Ready-to-halt; to Mr Despondency and to Miss Much-afraid; to Mr Stand-fast and Mr Valiant-for-truth. But in each case there will be the accompanying knock of Jesus, saying, 'Fear not, I will be with you. I have called you by your name, you are mine' (Isaiah 43:1).

Day-Break on the Beach
January 28

The previous evening had been full of interest and hope. Those seven fishermen had long been separated from their craft, and thinking probably that they were not to see their Master again, they betook themselves, with considerable zest, to the shore of the lake. They entered the old familiar boat, and that night they caught nothing! It was the last fishing expedition they were to have. They were to navigate other waters, use other nets, and sail under other skies. The greatness of their disappointment was to block the door in that direction and open it in another. No longer fishermen on the shores of Galilee, but shepherds, pasturing their flocks on the celestial mountains, whence views are to be obtained, in fair weather, of the eternal city.

'When the morning was now come, Jesus stood on the shore: but the disciples knew not that it was Jesus' *(John 21:4).*

Has your life been a disappointment? Did you start out, years ago, with a good heart and hope! Perhaps the winds were soft, the starlight brilliant, and there was a chance of the moon breaking through. But the sky soon clouded over, and the years have gone wearily! It isn't that you have been idle, but for some reason everything has miscarried; and now there seems nothing for it but to land on the shore of Eternity, as Paul did on the shore at Malta. But do not be too sure of this! When the morning breaks on that coastline, it is more than likely that you will see Jesus standing on the beach. He will know the time of your arrival, and will come down to meet you, as he did for the first martyr, Stephen, and has done for a multitude beside.

It is very pleasant, as in the big ship, you emerge from the night, to see familiar faces greeting you, or even one dear face with a smile of welcome awaiting your coming! It may happen to be the landing-stage at New York, Bombay, Melbourne, or Liverpool, but what a difference it makes. And when the Day of days shall break, and the shadows flee away, and the little boat of our life grates on the shore, it will be good indeed to see Christ standing there, with his outstretched hand to welcome, to help us disembark, to lead us to the prepared place on which he has expended thought and care. 'I go to *prepare* a place for *you...* I will come again to *receive* you unto myself.'

> *Suffice it if - my good and ill unreckoned,*
> *And both forgiv'n through his abounding grace -*
> *I find myself by hands familiar beckoned*
> *Unto my fitting place.*

'That disciple whom Jesus loved saith unto Peter: It is the Lord' *(John 21:7).*

Love will see most quickly. James was there, full of practical common sense; Thomas also, who doubted, but afterwards believed; Peter, who wanted to die with Jesus, but afterwards denied him; and the rest of them; but it was John whom Jesus loved, and who afterwards became the Apostle of Love, that first recognised the Master, whether by the intonation of his voice, or the thoughtfulness of his inquiry, or the readiness of his help, does not appear. The intuitions of love are as sure as they are swift. Whether there be prophecies, they shall fail; whether there be tongues, they shall cease; whether there be knowledge, it shall vanish. None of these things will help as much when we come to that last hour. But *love will never fail*, and those who have loved will see most quickly, most certainly, most satisfyingly.

It is love that unites us, and we believe that Jesus is as eager for the hour to come when we shall be with him where he is, as we are to get there. Do you not believe that the friend who has come to the landing-stage to greet you, after a long voyage, is even more eager than you are to see that breadth of water dwindle from miles to furlongs and furlongs to yards? Do you think that Peter thought the water cold, when he plunged in, or that he would spoil his fisher's coat? Will not the chill of the river be forgotten when at last we see Jesus just beyond?

In that fair morning we shall recognise and help each other. The disciple whom Jesus loved said unto Peter, 'It is the Lord', *and gave him the preference*! Surely John would have been excused by all the rest, if he had immediately cast himself into the sea and had met Jesus first! But no! He knew how Peter had suffered, how he longed for the chance to do something to obliterate the past, how he would prize the few extra moments of private fellowship; and so he said, 'It is the Lord', knowing full well what an effect would be produced on his impulsive friend.

That probably is the etiquette of Heaven! We sometimes suppose that there will be such a throng there, that we shall not be able to get near the Lord. But the greatest saints will always be the humblest and the kindest. They will come to the outer ranks, where some of us may have to stand, and say, 'Come, take my place!' John will say to Peter, 'It is the Lord.'

Prayer: Impart unto me, O God, I pray thee, the spirit of thy love, that I may be more anxious to give than to receive, more eager to understand than to be understood, more thoughtful for others, more forgetful of myself. Amen.

Descending and Ascending
January 30

This is an amazing verse! Why did our Lord descend? In the council-chamber of eternity, when the creation and fall of man were foreseen, it was agreed that he should deliver man; but how could this be effected, unless he had experienced conditions of human life? Mere power, though it were that of omnipotence, would not have availed. Even perfect love might have failed in absolute sympathy, for lack of actual experience. 'Forasmuch, then, as the children are partakers of flesh and blood, he also himself took part in the same, that he might be a merciful and faithful High Priest' (Hebrews 2:14, 17).

'He that descendeth is the same also that ascendeth up far above all heavens, that he might fill all things' (Ephesians 4:10).

How low did he descend? He bowed the heavens, and came down, and darkness was under his feet. Down to the Virgin Mother and the manger-bed; down to Joseph's home in despised Nazareth, and the carpenter's shop; down to hunger and thirst, to agony and bloody sweat, to the cross and passion; down to death and burial even in a borrowed tomb; down to the dim shadow-world of Hades, to the spirits in prison, and if there be any lower depth, *thither!*

But he ascended from these low depths, with the keys of death and Hades at his girdle. He ascended on high, leading captivity captive, and as he passed upward, he annexed each province as he went. This same Jesus who descended is now ascended, with no change in his nature, that he may fill all hearts, all lives, all homes, with the grace and love and help that he exhibited during his earthly ministry. When I saw that, only the other day, I said to myself, 'Jesus Christ is literally in this room. It is true that he is at the right hand of God, but this is only to allow him the more easily to fill my heart, my need, my life. He is the very same as when Martha and Mary welcomed him to their home in Bethany. I will read the Gospels again, not so much as a record of the past, but as a mirror of the living present' (Hebrews 13:8).

Is there one person who reads this page, in loneliness, poverty, sickness, sorrow, and pain, that can fail to get this comfort? Read the Gospels again as the Diary and Day-book of the living Saviour! He that descended is the same also that ascended; and he ascended that he might fill the lowest depths of human need. Though ascended to the right hand of the Majesty on high, he is the same loving, tender Saviour as when the children flocked around his knees, and his tears brimmed over at the grave of his friend.

Prayer: I bless thee, O Son of God, that there is no need for me to go up to heaven to bring thee down, or into thy grave to bring thee up. Thou art here, in this hour, and at this place. Amen.

Turning Things Upside Down
January 31

'Ye turn things upside down! Shall the Potter be counted as clay; that the thing made should say of him that made it, he made me not... He hath no understanding' *(Isaiah 29:16 RV marg.).*

Will you let your Saviour frame your life and make it what he will? All power is his in heaven and on earth. Do not resist his moulding touch, or say that he has no understanding of your peculiar difficulties or temperament. Let him appoint your place in life, and endow you with the wisdom and strength needed for the right discharge of its responsibilities.

By the Holy Spirit he forms in us his own life, leading us to walk in the way that pleases him best, not following our own desires and wishes, but his; yielding to him our will and obeying his instruction.

Prayer: Great Potter, fashion us! Wise Artificer, frame us! Pierced hands, guide us where we should go. We will not be perverse children, but submit to thy wise understanding and trust where we cannot see, committing the keeping of our souls to thee in well-doing, as unto a faithful Creator. Amen.

FEBRUARY

OUR DAILY WALK OF LIFE

We shall also walk in newness of life
(Romans 6:4)

The Purpose of Life
February 1

'To this end was I born, and for this cause came I into the world, that I should bear witness unto the truth' (John 18:37).

This was our Lord's answer to Pilate's inquiry, and to a certain extent each of us may appropriate his words. Wordsworth's immortal lines suggest that we stood before God to receive our commission, ere we became clothed with this body of humiliation. Whether or not the poet is right in his surmise that 'not in utter nakedness or forgetfulness do we come from God, who is our Home', we need not argue. It is enough that God, who hates nothing that he has made, sent us forth to realise an ideal, to fulfil a purpose, to bear witness to some phase of truth! Shall we not ask ourselves, as in his presence, whether we are fulfilling the divine purpose of what the apostle calls 'our high calling' (Philippians 3:14).

God created each soul with a purpose. The potter takes in hand a lump of clay with a distinct design. He means, when he places it on the horizontal wheel, to make of it a vessel to adorn a temple or palace, or he has in mind to serve some household use. The revolving wheel on the one hand, and his skilful manipulation on the other, will evolve and complete his purpose. 'Cannot I do with you, as this potter?' saith the Lord.

'Thou hast made me and fashioned me. Thou didst choose the time and circumstances of my birth, my parentage and heredity, my mental equipment and my physical frame. From the first thou didst know the constitution of my body, which thou didst fashion in secret, and curiously work in the lowest places of the earth.'

To our humble challenge: *'Why hast thou made me thus?'* God does not always give an audible reply. His answer is often voiceless, it steals in upon the soul insensibly, and we *know* that we are fulfilling his purpose. If you are engaged in some unwelcome task, which evidently is your duty; if you are shut up as companion with some uncongenial charge; if you are called to minister to people who seem unresponsive or unsympathising ask that the Saviour and you may be yoked together, that his will may be done through you, that his love and kindness may bear and forbear in you, and that you may witness to the truth, as it is in Jesus.

Prayer: O God, some of us shrink from our life-work, from those with whom we have to associate, from unwelcome toil and irksome tasks. Enable us to see thy plan, and to trust thee who art working out thy plan in our lives. May the love of Christ constrain us no longer to live unto ourselves but to him. Amen.

The Mystery of Regeneration
February 2

Marvel not! said Jesus to Nicodemus - but notwithstanding, it is difficult not to marvel at the wonder and mystery of the new birth. Birth, as in the case of the little chick, is emergence. It is the emergence of a tiny creature from darkness and confinement into the great world, with its over-arching blue, its mantle of green, and its abundant wealth. So the mineral may be born into the vegetable, the vegetable into the animal, the animal into the human, the human into the divine. But in each case the process is the same. We are born *from above*. (See marginal reading of AV and RV in verses 3 and 7.) In other words, the kingdom above us must stoop down and take us into union with itself.

'Jesus said unto him, Except a man be born from above, he cannot see the Kingdom of God. Nicodemus said: How can a man be born when he is old?' (John 3:3, 4).

This new birth from above is the heavenward side of faith. Just as the outstretched hand has two sides to it, the palm and the back, so the act by which we are incorporated into life eternal has two sides to it - the angels speak of it as being born into the life of God; we describe it as trusting Jesus Christ for salvation. If we are believing - trusting in him - we are born from above. 'He that believeth on the Son *hath everlasting life.*' To them that receive him, Jesus gives the *right to become* the sons and daughters of God. '*Now* are we the sons of God.'

This is the mystery of the new birth. 'Thine eyes did see my substance, yet being unperfect, and in thy book all my members were written, which in continuance were fashioned, when as yet there was none of them.' 'Such knowledge is too wonderful for me. It is high, I cannot attain to it.' It doth not yet appear what we shall be, but we know that when he, the first-born from among the dead, shall appear, *we shall be like him*!

It is a marvel, that in some mysterious manner we awake to find ourselves attached by the ties of birth and nature to this wonderful world. What are we! Whence came we! What is the true significance of this discipline of pain and weariness intersected with joy and gladness - we cannot tell! But is it not more marvellous that we should find ourselves belonging to that eternal world through Jesus Christ our Lord; that he is the ladder linking this world to his own, and that where he is, we shall be also?

Prayer: We thank thee, O Saviour, that thou hast taught us to know thee, and to love thee; but we thank thee most of all for adopting us into thy family, and making us the sons and daughters of the Lord God Almighty. May we walk as children of light, and go through the world fulfilling the ministries of heaven. Amen.

The Fountain of Life
February 3

'Whosoever drinketh of the water that I shall give him shall never thirst; but the water that I shall give him shall become in him a well of water springing up into eternal life' (John 4:14).

One morning, when the land was carpeted with flowers of spring a woman awoke in the little town of Sychar that lay in the lap of the twin mountains, Ebal and Gerizim. She little realised that that day would revolutionise, not her own life only, but that of untold thousands. Throughout its happenings her story would be embalmed in the history of the race, and she would take the first step which, as tradition says, ended in martyrdom.

Her nature was passionate and intense. The well was deep! She had sought to satisfy her heart with human love, but in vain, and she had ceased to believe in love. Her character was gone, and her neighbours would not tolerate her presence at the ancient well, so that she had no alternative but to carry her pitcher hither in the sultry noon, instead of the cool of the late afternoon, when the women came to draw their water.

She was not destitute of religion. There was the ancient tradition of Jacob's faith, for he had lived within sight of these hills and had drunk at that well. She believed in this ancestral religion, which had existed in its sublime simplicity before the division arose between Jew and Samaritan, and had listened to many discussions as to the rival claims of the temples at Jerusalem and Gerizim. She also believed that some day the long-looked for Messiah would appear, and explain all things. In the meanwhile, however, she was sick and weary at heart. Her daily lonely visit to the well seemed to epitomise her inner experience. 'Give me, stranger,' she seemed to say, 'anything that will appease this soul-thirst, and restore to me the years that the locust and cankerworm have eaten. Then I shall cease to thirst and come all the way hither to draw!'

Is she not the type of myriads? Some among my readers have drunk of all the wells sunk by human hands, and have found them brackish and empty. They have turned from them all with the ancient verdict: 'Vanity of vanities, all is vanity.' Is it thus with you, my friend? Then it may be that he who came far out of his usual way to find and help this distraught soul, is near to you also, waiting to open those hidden springs of which, if a man drink, he shall never thirst again.

Prayer: O Christ, who didst sit at Jacob's well, give me to drink of the water of life, and to hear thy voice, which is as music; let that spring of which thou didst speak to the woman, rise up within my heart unto eternal life. Amen.

Spring up, O Well!
February 4

True religion is the union of the Spirit of God with the human spirit and this is effected in and through Jesus Christ. 'He that is joined to the Lord is one Spirit.' Jesus is the mediator between God and man. He reveals the Father, unites us with the Father, and comes with the Father to make his home with us (John 14:21-23).

'He that is athirst, let him come: he that will, let him take the water of life freely' (Revelation 22:17).

Continuing our thought in yesterday's reading, it is thus that our religious life becomes a springing-fountain. The woman spoke of 'the well', our Lord of 'the spring in the well'. She spoke of the fatigue of drawing-up, he of the rising-up. With too many, religion is not spontaneous, but derived. They must have religious services, or a rousing preacher, or books of religious stimulants. We all profit by outside helps, but we must not depend upon them. Learn the habit of being still before God, till his love rises yearningly and earnestly within you.

Whatever impedes the uprising of the fountain must be abandoned. A curious thing once happened at a training college. The house was full of students, when suddenly the entire water supply failed. After every effort had been made to trace the failure, a plumber was sent for, who went at once to the junction between the main supply and the house pipe. On opening this a big toad was discovered, which had filled the orifice and made it impossible for the water to pass through. It had come in as a tiny tadpole, had lodged in the joint, living on the water, until, full-grown, it sealed the passage.

Prayer: O Saviour of men! I am nothing better than common earthenware; but may I be cleansed and purified, and then filled with thy heavenly treasure. Dip me deep into the water of life, and give refreshment through me to many parched and weary hearts. Amen.

Something like this may happen in our lives. Hidden sin may grow within, unchecked, until it chokes the incoming love of God. Jesus knew that in the woman's heart there was unconfessed sin, which blocked her reception of the living water. In mercy, he uncovered the evil thing, the obstacle was removed, the fountain of life immediately arose. She ceased her arguments, and became a disciple. She forgot her prejudices, and leaving behind the water pot, started off to the town, telling everyone she met that at last she had found the Messiah. Presently she returned with the whole town behind her, and Jesus knew that harvest-time had arrived!

God's Guiding Hand in our Lives
February 5

'The Lord is my Shepherd: I shall not want' (Psalm 23:1) 'When he putteth forth his own sheep, he goeth before them, and the sheep follow him: for they know his voice' (John 10:4).

Do you need guidance as to your path? Look unto Jesus; it is always possible to discern his form, though partially veiled in mist; and when it is lost, be sure to stand still until he comes back to find and re-establish the blessed connection. Do not look to impressions which often contradict one another, which rise and fall with variable fickleness and are like eddies upon a flowing current; do not seek for guidance from friends who will differ from each other, and not two of which will give the same advice on the same grounds, but look away to Christ; throw on him the responsibility of making you know the way you are to take; leave it to him to make it so abundantly clear that you cannot do other than follow; even tell him that you will stand still until he puts his arms under you, and carries you where he would have you be. Do not get anxious or flurried. Put the government of your life upon his shoulder, and leave him to execute his plan.

Sometimes he guides us to the rest of the green pastures, and the quiet of the still waters. In other words, we are left through happy months and years to fulfil the ordinary commonplaces of life, content to fill a little space, and receiving great increments of spiritual force for future service. At other times, we are guided from the lowland pastures up into the hills. The way is sunny, above us the precipitous cliffs, beneath the dark turbid stream; but this is well; we would not always be lying in the pastures or walking softly by the waters. It is good to climb the heights with their far view and bracing air.

Prayer: Tell us, O Lord, where thou art leading thy flock today, that we may follow upon thy track. We do not ask thee to come our way, but to teach us thine. Amen.

In the late afternoon the shepherd may lead his flock back into the valleys, through the dark woods, where the branches meet overhead and the wild beast lurks in ambush, but we know that in one hand he has the rod or club, with which to belabour anything that may attack; and in the other the crook to drag us out of the hole. He would not lead us into the dark valley which he had not explored, and whose perils he was not prepared to overcome. Darkness, sorrow or death do not prove that we have missed his guidance, or have taken the wrong path, but rather that he accounts us able to bear the trial by faith in himself.

The Christian Ideal
February 6

An ideal is a mental conception of character after which we desire to shape our lives. It is the fresco which we paint on the walls of our soul, and perpetually look at in our lonely hours; and since the heart is educated through the eye, we become more and more assimilated to that which we admire.

Our ideal should be distinctly beyond us. We must be prepared to strain our muscles and task our strength, attempting something which those who know us best never thought us capable of achieving. Like St Paul, we must count the ordinary ambitions of men as dung, must forget the things which are behind and press forward to those before.

We should choose as an objective some *ideal which is manifestly*, in our own judgment or that of others, *within our scope.* It is a mistake to set before our minds an ideal which is altogether out of harmony with the make-up of our nature. Therefore we should learn to say with the apostle, 'I follow on to apprehend that for which I was apprehended by Christ Jesus.' Be sure that God created and redeemed you for a definite purpose. Discover that purpose, and set yourself to make it good.

Our ideal should give unity to life. Happy is the man who is able to prosecute his ideal through each hour of consciousness, and who can say: 'This one thing I do!' Such people are the irresistible ones. Those who know one subject thoroughly, or who bend all their energies in the prosecution of one purpose, carry all before them. The quest for a holy character may be prosecuted always and everywhere. In every act and thought we may become more like Christ.

The Christ idea is the highest ideal. 'That I may gain Christ, and be found in him.' But such an ideal will only be realised at the cost of self-denial. You must put aside your own righteousness to get his; you must be willing to count all things loss; you must ignore the imperious demands of passion. So shall you be prepared for the hour when even 'the body of your humiliation' shall be transformed to the likeness of the glorious body of Christ. His working is on your side; in you and for you he will subdue all things to himself.

'One thing I do, forgetting the things which are behind, and stretching forward to the things which are before, I press on toward the goal unto the prize of the high calling of God in Christ Jesus' (Philippians 3:13, 14).

Prayer: Thou, O Christ, art all I want. May thy grace abound towards me, so that having all sufficiency in all things, I may abound unto every good work. Amen.

Vision and Purpose
February 7

'I said, What shall I do, Lord' (Acts 22:10) *'Not that I have already obtained, or am already made perfect: but I press on toward the goal' (Philippians 3:12-14).*

When the apostle Paul was suddenly brought into the presence of the Eternal, the whole course of his life was changed. In that flash of light he saw the exalted Saviour, and learnt that he was antagonising the purposes of redeeming grace, and that vision altered the whole of his purposes and actions. From that great hour he forgot the things that were behind, and endeavoured to apprehend that for which he had been apprehended by Christ Jesus. It was his ambition to build his life on the pattern shown him on the mount.

Years after, as he reviewed his life-work, the churches he had founded, the cities he had evangelised, the epistles he had written, surely he might have reckoned that he had apprehended; but ever as he climbed, he envisaged heights beckoning beyond his attainments. Is not that the case with us, as we compare the vision of God's purpose with what we have realised? Oh, give us back the years that have gone, that we may do better, be more accurate and successful in the transmission to living fact of those fair ideals, which called to us years ago! The vision in the sanctuary may never be perfectly realised by these bungling apprentice-hands. Yet God accepts and forgives the mistakes, as the mother accepts the cobbled stitches of her little girl who tries to help her with her sewing. 'Not that we have already attained, or are already perfect, but we follow on', and God forgives and accepts our poor patchwork!

What must we do to achieve our ideals? We must be more often in the sanctuary, in fellowship with Christ, to whose image we are to be conformed. With the Psalmist we must say: 'Whom have I in heaven but thee, and there is none on the earth that I desire beside thee'. As we look on him, we shall be changed into his likeness. As he is, so shall we become. Martyrs on the night before their agony; reformers hesitating at their tasks; scholars wondering whether their long self-denial was worthwhile; fathers and mothers; teachers and workers; preachers and missionaries - all these have stood in the sanctuary of God, until they have seen the vision and ideal. They have reckoned that what God had taught them to long for, he was prepared to enable them to effect. 'All things are possible to him that believeth.'

Prayer: Grant unto me grace, O Lord, that I may both perceive and know what things I ought to do, and may also have grace and power faithfully to fulfil the same. Amen.

Faithfulness in Daily Life
February 8

The common drudgery of daily life can be a divine calling. We often speak of a young man as 'being called to the ministry'; but it is as fitting to speak of a carpenter being *called* to the bench, the blacksmith to the forge, and the shoemaker to his last. 'Brethren,' said the apostle, 'let every man wherein he is called, therein abide with God.'

'With goodwill doing service, as to the Lord, and not to men' (Ephesians 6:7).

Remember that your life has been appointed by God's wise providence. God as much sent Joseph to the drudgery and discipline of the prison as to the glory and responsibility of the palace. Nothing happens to us which is not included in his plan for us; and the incidents which seem most tiresome are often contrived to give us opportunities to become nobler, stronger characters.

We are called to be faithful in performing our assigned duties. Not brilliance, not success, not notoriety which attracts the world's notice, but the regular, quiet and careful performance of trivial and common duties; faithfulness in that which is least is as great an attainment in God's sight as in the greatest.

In every piece of honest work, however irksome, laborious, and commonplace, we are fellow-workers with God. We must help God to give men their daily bread. It is for him to cause the growth of the corn, but man must reap and thresh, grind out the flour, make and distribute the bread. The tailor is God's fellow-workman, helping him to clothe the bodies which he has made to need garments of various textures. The builder co-operates with God in housing his children. The merchant helps to bring the products of the east to refresh and enrich the toiling masses of the west. God uses man in a thousand ways to serve the children of men.

Take up your work, then, you who seem to be the nobodies, the drudges, the maid-of-all-work, the clerk, or shop assistant. Do it with a brave heart, looking up to him who for many years toiled at the carpenter's bench. Amid the many scenes and actions of life, set the Lord always before your face. Do all as in his presence and to win his smile; and be sure to cultivate a spirit of love to God and man. Look out for opportunities of cheering your fellow-workers. Do not murmur or grumble, but let your heart rise from your toil to God your Maker, Saviour and Friend. So the lowliest service will glisten, as grass blades do when sun and dewdrops garnish them.

Prayer: Be not far from me, O Lord, this day; and through all its hours may I be found doing those things which are well-pleasing in thy sight. Amen.

Changing our Strength
February 9

'*They that wait upon the Lord shall renew their strength*' (*Isaiah 40:31*).

It is more than probable that these lines will be read by some who have lost heart. They are fainting beneath the long and arduous strain of life, and ready to give up in despair. It seems as though God had forgotten to be gracious, and in anger had shut up his tender mercies. To all such Isaiah says: God is not tired; you think he is because you are. Wait upon the Lord, and *change* your strength (see margin).

The question is not as to altering your environment, but altering your courage, your power of endurance, your assurance of victory; then, notwithstanding every hindrance and difficulty, you will mount up on wings like eagles, you will run without being weary, you will walk without being faint.

The inevitable order. Mounting up - running - walking! We should have supposed that it should have been *walking* in the beginnings of religious experience; then the walk breaking into the run; and finally the runner leaping on wings into the azure, like the eagle a black speck against the blue! But experience confirms the prophetic order. Isaiah is right! We mount, we run, we walk!

Let us claim the promise - 'They that wait on the Lord shall change their strength'. Too often in the past we have depended on the stimulus of services, sermons, conventions which have made the embers glow again on the heart's altar. We have gone back to our homes, to our daily calling, with a new zeal and impulse that has lasted for weeks or months. Then we have found ourselves flagging again; we have run and got weary; we have walked and become faint.

To all such comes the word: if you would once more mount up and run and walk, you must change your strength. Time tells on us! Moods influence us! Circumstances impede us! Satan blows cold blasts on our heart-fires and cools them! Sins pile up their debris between us and God! From all these let us turn once more to Jesus and wait on him. 'My soul, wait thou only upon the Lord, for my expectation is from him.' Look not back, but forward! Not down, but up! Not in, but out! Never to your own heart, but keep looking to Jesus, made near and living by the grace of the Holy Spirit. So shall you change your strength, as you wait upon the Lord.

Prayer: Thou knowest, Lord, how often I am sorely let and hindered in running the race which is set before me. May thy bountiful grace and mercy come to my help, that I may finish my course with joy, and receive the crown of life. Amen.

The Water of Life turned to Wine!
February 10

Do not forget the necessity of obeying the inner voice of Christ, which may be recognised by these three signs - it never asks questions, but is decisive and imperative; it is not unreasonable nor impossible; it calls for an obedience which costs us some sacrifice of our own way and will. 'Whatsoever he saith unto you, *do it!*'

Do as you are told. It was a severe test to obedient faith to fill up those big jars, which stood in the vestibule of the house. Each would contain about twenty gallons, and as they were probably nearly empty, it would be a long and tedious business to fill them, especially at a time when guests required other attention. 'They filled them up to the brim!'

'Whatsoever he saith unto you, do it. Jesus saith unto them, Fill the waterpots with water. And they filled them up to the brim' (John 2: 5, 7).

In your obedience, *always give Christ brimful measure.* It may be a very small thing he asks you to do - to teach a class of children, to pay a visit to some sick man or woman, to write a letter, to speak a word of comfort, to hold out the helping hand, to give a glass of cold water, but see to it that your response is hearty and brimful! The jar is your opportunity! A very common and ordinary one! An act that may seem needless or inconvenient; but out of it may come the greatest achievement of your life! When the Lord calls you into co-partnership, be sure not to say: 'Please do not ask me!' Nay, serve him to the brim! He never asks you to do one small act for him, without being prepared to add his almighty grace to your weakness, thereby perfecting the act. It is an amazing thing that he should want our help. Let us give him to the brim, and, as we do so, we shall see a wonderful and beautiful thing, which is 'hidden from wise and prudent, but revealed to babes'. 'The servants who drew the water knew.'

Prayer: Enable me to do not only what I like to do, but what I ought. Cause me to be faithful in a little, and in common tasks to learn thy deep lessons of obedience, patience, and conscientiousness. Amen.

Many of us realise that this miracle is constantly taking place. We fill our waterpots to the brim with water; but at the end of days of careful preparation we sadly review the result, and say to ourselves; 'After all, it is very poor stuff, *only water* at the best!' But as we pour it out in service to others, we know that the Master has been collaborating with us, and has *turned the water into wine!* There are secrets between the Lord and those who obey him! It is blessed when we are workers together with Christ. He knows, and you know. A smile passes between you and him, and it is enough! The best wine is always kept in reserve!

The All-Sufficiency of Christ
February 11

'The glorious Lord will be unto us a place of broad rivers and streams... The Lord is our King; he will save us' (Isaiah 33:21-22).

The Revised Version translates our text 'Jehovah will be with us in Majesty'. The reference can only be to our Saviour, who is the divine vice-regent of the world. Through him it was created, by him it has been redeemed, in him its government is vested. He is King of kings, and Lord of lords. His are the glories of the cross, of victory over death and hell, of the ascension, of Pentecost, of the millennial reign, of the judgment seat!

And this glorious and transcendent Saviour is willing and eager to be the complement of our deficiencies and needs. We look around, and some of us, as we compare our lot with others, lament, even if we do not audibly complain, at our disadvantages. Others, whom we have known from childhood, seem to have all that heart could wish - a happy married life, a spacious and beautiful home, hosts of friends, buoyant health, opportunities of travel and enjoyment that are denied to us. We have been plagued all the day long, and chastened every morning. We have spent a shut-in, cloistered life. The bare necessities of life have been our only portion, and a sense of anxiety as to our future has haunted our dreams.

But we are not alone in this experience. When every one went to his own home, our Lord Jesus spent the night on the Mount of Olives. The birds had their nests, and the foxes their holes, but the Son of Man had nowhere to lay his head, but, like Jacob, was wont to make a stone his pillow. You are not singular, therefore, if your life is barren and lonely, for many of God's noblest saints have lived from hand to mouth, wandering in deserts and mountains, in dens and caves of the earth, being destitute, afflicted, and tormented.

Remember that such experiences are designed to bring into prominence what the glorious Lord is prepared to be and do. In mathematics we speak of the complement of a curve - that which is needed to make a curve into a perfect circle. So Jesus is willing to complete our lives, however, imperfect and ineffective they may be. He is able to compensate for all deficiencies, and to become in your experience 'a place of broad rivers and streams'. A river to intercept dreaded evil, and a stream to refresh and fertilise the drooping thirsty heart.

Prayer: Be to us, O glorious Lord, a place of broad rivers and streams; our Judge, our Lawgiver, our King, our Saviour. Make the wilderness of our life a pool, and the dry land watersprings. Amen.

Every-Day Religion
February 12

There is no doubt that if every Christian person were to begin to live up to the New Testament ideal, avoiding always what Christ would not be, and seeking to be always what he would be, there would be little need for preaching, for the beauty of the Christian character would in itself be sufficiently attractive to win men for Jesus Christ.

Let us examine ourselves by the suggestions in this chapter, from which we have selected our text (verses 8-18). Have we the mind of Christ, which makes us willing to be of no reputation, and to stoop even to the death of the cross, for others? Are we compassionate, sympathising in the joys and sorrows of others? Do we love the brethren, not always liking them perhaps, but treating them kindly, and making their interests more important than our own? Are we tender-hearted and pitiful towards the afflicted and distressed? Are we courteous, with true Christian politeness which differs from the world's code of manners? How do we reply to injury? Do we bless when we are cursed, or do we retaliate with hot and indignant words? Are we willing to leave our vindication to God?

Do you want a happy life and good days. Then leave God to vindicate and deliver you. Set yourself against evil, and live at peace with all, as much as in you lies. The one thing for all of us to be really anxious about is to *enshrine Jesus Christ in our hearts as Lord* (RV). Is there a door in your heart opening on a throne-room which is reserved for Jesus only? Have you written on that door such words as these: 'Other lords have had dominion over me, but henceforth he only is my king'? *Be ready to give a reason for the hope that is in you.* This is what Peter, on one memorable occasion, failed to do; and we shall fail also but for the help of the Holy Spirit, who will teach us what we ought to say (John 14:26). *Have a good conscience* - one that can look God and man in the face, and is not conscious of wilful violation of what is right and good. Follow the gleam; obey the inner light; listen to the still small voice, which is ever saying: 'This is the way, walk ye in it.'

'Sanctify the Lord God in your hearts; and be ready always to give an answer to every man that asketh you a reason of the hope that is in you with meekness and fear. Having a good conscience' (1 Peter 3:15, 16).

Prayer: Help me, O God, so to live that those who are associated with me, directing or serving me day by day, may long to have the love and joy which they see in me. Show me how to apply to the common things of daily life the heavenly principles of the risen life. Amen.

God's Partnership with Man
February 13

'Come now, and I will send thee unto Pharaoh... And God said, I AM THAT I AM: Thus shalt thou say unto the children of Israel, I AM hath sent me unto you' (Exodus 3:10, 14).

Prayer: Accomplish thy perfect work in our souls, O Father. As yet we are bound with many chains; we tarry among things seen and temporal; we are exposed to the storms of the outer world, and are wrestling with its ills. But we are not dismayed, for we are more than earth and dust, we are akin to thee, O Spirit of the Lord, and can experience thy heavenly influence. Fill us with faith and love and hope. Amen.

Nothing is more needed today than God's partnership as a realised fact in Christian experience. Many of us may assent to what is written in these lines, and then put it aside, as a dream which is too ethereal to be of practical service. But when the apostle said that 'our fellowship, i.e. our *partnership*, is with the Father, and with his Son Jesus Christ' it is surely meant that we should enter upon our inheritance. 'I AM...' says our great Partner: 'fill in your need, and I will meet your demand, according to the riches of my glory in Christ Jesus'. Let us tear out the order-forms from God's service-register, fill them up, and present them for delivery. Not one of them would be dishonoured. And if it happened that we had wrongly diagnosed our need, he would erase the demand based on our imperfect knowledge, and substitute what we would ask if we knew. There is nothing more certain than that the more we ask of God, the more pleased he is to do exceeding abundantly beyond all that we ask or think.

Our Lord made use of this incident when he was challenged by the Sadducees to adduce proof of the future life from the books of Moses. He answered by quoting this paragraph of the burning bush, calling special attention to the fact that Moses referred to God as the 'God of Abraham, of Isaac, and of Jacob'. He said that the use of the present tense - I AM - proved that God is not the God of the dead but of the living, and that all live unto him.

What a comfort there is in this thought, that our beloved who have passed from us are in-breathing the same atmosphere as we are. We all eat the same spiritual meat and all drink the same spiritual drink. We see in a mirror darkly, but they face to face; but this identity of fellowship, of partnership with the 'I AM', the ever-present God who fills heaven and earth, is a proof and a pledge that they have not altered essentially. They are drinking of the same stream higher up and nearer its source: 'One family we dwell in him.'

God's Partnership in our Affliction
February 14

Many are the afflictions of the righteous, but the Lord delivereth him out of them all. There is the *affliction of ill-health*, which compels us to stand aside and leave our tasks to others. The languor of sleepless nights, the inactivity and loneliness of the long days, the fear of being burdensome to others. The anxiety as to how this or that interest may fare in inexperienced hands. The sense of helplessness and weakness. These are the ingredients of that cup which many have to drink!

There is the *affliction of poverty*, when every door seems closed against our appeal; when hundreds of applicants are answering the same advertisement; when the cruse of oil has been drained of its last drop, and the barrel scraped bare; when the rent is overdue, the boots are wearing out in vain journeys, and the faces and the clothes of the children begin to tell the tale of privation - then the iron seems to enter our soul!

There is the *affliction of uncongenial companionship*. 'Woe to them that sojourn in Meshech, and dwell in the tents of Kedar!' To how many the Psalmist's words would express their precise position: 'My soul hath long dwelt with him who hateth peace; I am for peace, but when I speak, they are for war.' There is even profounder suffering, when a man or a woman is mated for life with one who is out of Christ, or is the one Christian disciple in an irreligious family. It was with a deep knowledge of human nature that the apostle urged his converts not to be unequally yoked with unbelievers.

There is also the *affliction of temptation*. Jealousy, pride, discontent, self-will - these assail us from without, and too often they find a response from within, as though there were an accomplice in hiding.

Such are some of the problems and afflictions which darken our experience. The mistake is that we face our troubles without God's fellowship, consciously realised. We carry our burdens, without casting them upon the Lord, and claiming the grace which waits to help us in our hour of need. We do not realise that he has come down to deliver us, because he knows our sorrows. In all our afflictions, he is afflicted.

'In all their affliction he was afflicted, and the Angel of his presence saved them; in his love and in his pity he redeemed them: and he bare them, and carried them all the days of old' (Isaiah 63:9).

Prayer: O God, we have no help but thine, nor do we need another arm save thine to lean upon. Teach us how to gain strength from thee hour by hour, in the glance of an eye, the breathing of a sigh, the brief ejaculation, may we take into ourselves that strength which thou hast stored for us in Christ Jesus our Lord. Amen.

'Be not conformed to this world; but be ye transformed by the renewing of your mind' (Romans 12:2). 'But we all, with open face beholding as in a glass the glory of the Lord, are changed into the same image' (2 Corinthians 3:18).

In our texts the word rendered '*transformed*' or '*changed*', is the same as is used in Matthew 17:2; and this must have been in the mind of the apostle when he said, 'Be ye transfigured' and 'we are transfigured into the same image'. How can this transformation be effected? First, from within, by the renewing of the mind; and second, by beholding the glory of the Lord.

The renewing of the mind. This is no matter for emotion or ecstasy, but of bringing our minds into close and constant contact with the truth as contained in the Holy Scripture. You have not to study yourself in the mirror, to see whether you are becoming transfigured; but as day by day you steep your mind in God's Word, without your realising it, you will become transfigured. Moses wist not that his face shone. It was for the crowd that waited for him at the mountain foot to see it, not for him.

Our Lord said, 'Abide in me and I in you'. This is somewhat mystical and profound; but he said again, 'If ye abide in me and my words abide in you' - that is surely within our reach. 'It is not too high, not too deep, not too inward, not too mystical,' said Dr Whyte on one occasion; 'and when the Master asks that his words shall abide in me, he can mean nothing else than that I shall often recall and recollect his words, and shall repeat them to myself at all times.'

Prayer: O Lord Jesus Christ, grant me such communion with thyself, that my soul may continually be athirst for that time when I shall behold thee in thy glory. In the meanwhile, may I behold thy glory in the mirror of thy Word, and be changed into the same image. Amen.

As a man thinketh in his heart so is he; and if we think those thoughts of self-giving, which characterised our Lord's forecast and determination on the Mount of Transfiguration - if we are animated by the resolve to present ourselves as living sacrifices, holy and acceptable to God; as we steep our minds in his mind - the transfiguring glory of that high resolve will insensibly pass into our faces, thus irradiating our meanest actions, our simplest speech.

Beholding and reflecting the glory of the Lord. The mirror again is Holy Scripture. We find there the reflection of our Lord's highest glory, which is patent, not in his creative but in his redemptive work. As we gaze on him who, for our salvation hid not his face from shame and spitting, but became a willing sacrifice on our behalf, we shall be changed.

The Love of Christ for us!
February 16

The Lord Jesus stripped himself of everything save love, that he might more readily meet each human soul on its own level. Being in the form of God, and equal with God, he emptied himself, humbled himself, and became obedient unto death, even the death of the cross, for our sakes. He stripped himself of all, that he might give to us fair clothing instead of the fading fig-leaves of apologies and excuse. He descended so low as to put the everlasting arms beneath the most hapless and hopeless. He desired to get so low, that none could get lower. He was set on proclaiming his gospel so that even the dying thief might enter Paradise, and that not one prodigal in all the human family should think that he had sunk too low or gone so far as to be excluded from the hope of salvation. 'He is able to save to the uttermost all that come unto God by him'.

'Let this mind be in you, which was also in Christ Jesus ... who made himself of no reputation, and took upon him the form of a servant, and was made in the likeness of men' (Philippians 2:5, 7).

Surely it is inexcusable that any soul of man should evade the love of God, when the Son of his love has made so great an effort to acquaint us, not only with its height and breadth and length, but with *its depth*. Why are we so cold, so unmoved, so inert? The apostle speaks of the love of Christ constraining him, of the love of God shed abroad within us and flooding our heart. How is it that, with God's love so near, so close, so easily within our reach, we are so apathetic and irresponsive?

The cure is, in part, the consciousness that God's love is all around us, which we cultivate by meditation. 'Thy omnipotence,' says St Augustine, 'is not remote from us even when we are remote from thee'; and we may say as much of his love. Even when we feel cold and distant, we are beset by God's love behind and before, and his grace is overshadowing us with infinite tenderness. Do not try to kindle love by thinking of the cross as far away back in the past, but by musing and meditating on Christ's love as being as tender and real as when he said to his mother, 'Behold thy son' and to John, 'Behold thy mother'.

Prayer: May the Holy Spirit so fill my heart with the consciousness of the love of Christ my Lord, that there may be no room in my life for anything inconsistent with his love. Amen.

Jesus knows the need of our heart, and is even now close at hand to lead us by the Holy Spirit into the realisation of his love. Let us open our nature to the blessed Comforter, and he will not be slack in his response. 'The fruit of the Spirit is Love.'

Serving the Lord
February 17

'I beseech you therefore, brethren, by the mercies of God, to present your bodies a living sacrifice, holy, acceptable to God, which is your reason- able service' (Romans 12:1).

The first thing for all of us to do is to present ourselves to God as alive from the dead, and our bodies as living sacrifices. The path of blessedness can be entered by no other gate. It is only as we refuse to be conformed to this world, and yield ourselves to be transformed by the free entrance of the Holy Spirit into our minds, that we can learn all that God will do for us. We are nothing; he is all. And he is prepared to be and do all things in us, if only we will lie open to him as the land lies open to the summer sun.

Those who really live the yielded life, do not need to ascertain God's will by signs. They recognise it by the whisper of his voice and the touch of his hand. It is as we refuse to be moulded by the world, and give ourselves up to the transfiguring Spirit of God, that we prove what is his good, acceptable and perfect will. But more than that, we begin to live for others, and draw by faith from the fulness of God, that we may minister to them aright.

First, we understand what the will of God is; then we present our bodies that it may fulfil itself through us; then we discover that it means goodwill to men, and we become the happy channels of heavenly ministry to those around us in one of the spheres enumerated in verses 6-8 of this chapter. It is impossible to cherish jealousy, because the Head may use this member or that; it is equally impossible to be proud, because we have nothing that we have not received. Let us always remember that each has a special ministry to fulfil, and that we shall find in our daily lot the opportunity of fulfilling it. How many resemble the land- owner of the Eastern story, who sold his property in order to go in search of diamonds, and lo! the man who purchased his property found it full of diamonds. Indeed, it was the famous Golconda region. In the daily drudgery of life you will find your heavenly opportunity. How many who are pining for a great mission, will never be permitted to enter it, because they despise the low and narrow door of humble service to those in their immediate neighbourhood.

But we can never realise these divine ideals of service merely by an external obedience. We must be constrained by a holy love to our Lord and to one another. What a despair these ideals would be apart from the Holy Spirit. That holy love comes from him.

Prayer: O God work in me, not only to will but to do of thy good pleasure; and may I work out in daily life what thou dost work in. Amen.

The Cry of the Oppressed
February 18

This prayer is so indefinite that it will suit any emergency, and yet brimful of faith that God will undertake all responsibility. Are you oppressed with the sense of failure, with temptation, with the consciousness of sin? Or oppressed with poverty, or debt, or the fear of unemployment, or with inability to find work? Or cast down with bitter persecution within or without your home? Or sorely beset and hindered by ill-health, the hopelessness of recovery? All these cases of oppression are included in this petition, and may be handed over to your faithful Creator, with the certainty that he is as willing as he is able to undertake for you. He is never weary of hearing your cry; the everlasting arms are never tired; and our God neither slumbers nor sleeps.

'O Lord, I am oppressed, undertake for me' (Isaiah 38:14).

What may we expect from a prayer so simple, yet so comprehensive? *We shall know God.* 'What shall I say, he hath both spoken unto me, and himself hath done it' (verse 15). Hezekiah had been a religious man, had maintained the temple services, had enjoyed the close friendship of Isaiah, yet it was in none of these things that he had met God face to face. But when he turned his face to the wall, and poured out his soul-anguish, he touched God, knew him after a fresh fashion, heard him speak, saw him work. Only through sickness, loneliness, and the pressure of overwhelming sorrow, do some men rightly learn to live, and discover that unseen and most real world, where the life of the spirit unfolds to God as a flower in spring.

At the pit we learn God's love (verse 17). How can we measure God's love? They say that a man's fist is the measure of his heart. Come and stand beneath the stars! There is God's hand! Now judge his heart! It is illimitable! By that love he has put our sins behind his back into the ocean depths! With that love he has drawn us out of the pit of our sins! By that love he bears with our cold response and languid petitions! Through that love he will bring us to glory! His is a love that will never let us go!

Prayer: I pray thee, O my Father, to shut me up to a simpler and more confiding faith. May I trust more than I know, and believe more than I see; and when my heart is overwhelmed within me, lead me to the rock that is higher than I. Amen.

Take the hand of Jesus to steady you; look down into the hole of the pit from which you have been redeemed, and then look up to the throne of God to which he passed at his ascension, and recall his own words: 'Where I am, there shall ye be also'. Trust him to undertake for your little life!

'Jacob said: All these things are against me' (*Genesis 42:36*). *'What shall we then say to these things: If God be for us, who can be against us? Nay, in all these things we are more than conquerors, through him that loved us'* (*Romans 8:31, 37*).

Thy complaint is very bitter, thou Prince of Israel! What ails thee so sorely? Is there none to comfort?

'I do well to be sorrowful! The days of my years have been few and evil! Driven from my father's home; a stranger in a strange land for thirty years; in constant dread of my brother; compelled by the misdeeds of my sons to flee the country; bereaved of my beloved Rachel; lamed through my resistance to God's angel - I had already suffered to the uttermost; but now we are straitened by famine and want; Joseph is not, Simeon is detained in prison as a hostage, and they are demanding Benjamin, the son of my old age and my right hand.'

Let us beware of passing hasty judgments on God's dealings with us. He cannot work out his fair design without some cross-stitches on this side of the canvas. The black clouds are only his water-cisterns, and on the other side they are bathed in sunshine. Do not look at your sorrows from the lowlands of your pilgrimage - but from the uplands of God's purpose. No chastening for the present is joyous but grievous, nevertheless afterward ... dwell on that *afterward*! If Jacob had not been led along this special path, he would never have come out on the shining tableland, where God himself is Sun.

Prayer: Help me, O Lord, to believe that what seem to be my losses are really gains, and that each ounce of affliction is adding to the weight of glory, not hereafter only, but now! Amen.

'*In all these things we are more than conquerors!*' These are brave words, thou strenuous soul, how darest thou reverse the findings of the patriarch? Hast thou sounded the depths? Hast thou been in the pit?

'Ay! I have most certainly been there! I have experienced tribulation, distress, persecution, famine, nakedness, peril, and sword; thrice beaten with rods, once stoned. In journeyings and perils, in hunger and thirst, in cold and pain. But nothing has succeeded in separating me from the love of Christ; and I am persuaded that neither life nor death, things present nor things to come ... shall ever separate us from the love of God, which is in Christ Jesus our Lord.'

Yes! thou great apostle and lover of Christ, thou art right! In all these things *we are more than conquerors*, through him who has loved us - our Saviour, Jesus Christ!

Joy in the Hour of Trial
February 20

We are bidden to count our trials as pure joy, since our patient endurance leads ultimately to the finished product of a holy character. All the trials and afflictions that beset us are seen and shared by our heavenly Father. God did not save Israel from the ordeal of affliction, but passed through it with them (Exodus 3:7-9; Isaiah 63:9). Evidently there was a wise purpose to be served by those bitter Egyptian experiences. So with ourselves. There is a reason for our trials which we do not understand now, but we shall do some day, when we stand in the light with God. Afflictions are not always chastisement, though in some cases that may be so; but more often we are in grief through manifold trials, that the proof of our faith, being much more precious than of gold that perisheth, may be found unto praise and honour and glory at the revelation of Jesus Christ.

'Count it all joy when ye fall into divers temptations. Knowing that the trying of your faith worketh patience' (James 1:2, 3).

Let us therefore rejoice, and magnify his lovingkindness. What a theme is here for praise! Sweet psalms and hymns have floated down the ages, bearing comfort for myriads, because those who wrote them passed through searching discipline. And it may be that we who have passed through great tribulation will be able to contribute notes in the heavenly music that the unfallen sons of light could never sing. The Psalter of eternity could not be complete without the reminiscences, set to music, of the grace that ministered to us in our earthly trials, and brought us up out of the furnace of pain.

Then we shall tell how God's glorious arm went also at our right hand, as at the right hand of Moses; of how the stony paths became soft as mossy grass; of how he led us out of the scorching heat into green pastures and waters of rest; and how he provided for us to make for himself a glorious name. Yes, we will make mention of the Lord, according to all that he shall have bestowed upon us, according to his mercies, and according to the multitude of his lovingkindness. We will tell the story of how the Angel of his presence saved us; how, in his love and pity, he redeemed us; and how he bare and carried us all the days of old. We shall have a great story to tell! 'My heart and my flesh fail, but thou art the strength of my heart and my portion for ever!' 'None of them that trust in him shall be desolate.'

Prayer: Give me, O Lord, a steadfast heart, which no unworthy affection may drag downwards; give me an unconquered heart, which no tribulation can wear out; give me an upright heart, which no unworthy purpose may tempt aside. Amen.

The Refiner's Fire
February 21

'He shall sit as a refiner and purifier of silver; and he shall purify the sons of Levi, and purge them as gold and silver' (Malachi 3:3). ' That the trial of your faith, being much more precious than of gold that perisheth, though it be tried with fire, might be found unto praise and honour and glory at the appearing of Jesus Christ' (1 Peter 1:7).

Nothing is harder to bear than the apparent aimlessness of suffering. They say that what breaks a convict's heart in gaol is to set him to carry stones from one side of the prison to the other, and then back again! But we must never look upon the trials of life as punishments, because all penalty was borne by our Lord himself. They are intended to destroy the weeds and rubbish of our natures, as the bonfires do in the gardens. Christ regards us in the light of our eternal interests, of which he alone can judge. If you and I knew what sphere we were to fulfil in the other world, we should understand the significance of his dealings with us, as now we cannot do. The refiner has a purpose in view, of which those who stand beside him are ignorant, and, therefore, they are unable to judge the process which he is employing.

Dare to believe that Christ is working to a plan in your life. He loves you! Be patient! He would not take so much trouble unless he knew that it was worthwhile. 'We do not prune brambles, or cast common stones into the crucible or plough sea-sands!' You must be capable of some special service, which can only be done by a carefully-prepared instrument, and so Christ sits beside you as the refiner, year after year, that you may miss nothing.

Whilst the fire is hot keep conversing with the refiner. Ponder these words: 'He shall sit as a refiner and purifier of silver'. The thought is especially suitable for those who cannot make long prayers, but they can talk to Christ as he sits beside them. Nicholas Hermann tells us that, as he could not concentrate his mind on prolonged prayer, he gave up set times of prayer and sought constant conversation with Christ! Speak to him, then, in the midst of your daily toil. He hears the unspoken prayer, and catches your whispers. Talk to Christ about your trials, sorrows, and anxieties! Make him your confidant in your joy and happiness! Nothing makes him so real as to talk to him aloud about *everything*!

Prayer: Let the fire of thy love consume in me all sinful desires of the flesh and of the mind, that I may henceforth continually abide in Jesus Christ my Lord, and seek the things where he sits at thy right hand. Amen.

The Ladder to Heaven
February 22

Bethel was a bleak moorland in the heart of Canaan. The hillsides and level downs were strewn with huge boulders. As he fled northwards, Jacob suddenly found himself overtaken by the swift eastern night while he was traversing this desolate moor. There was nothing for it but to lie down on the hard ground, taking one of the big stones as a pillow for his head. As he slept, he dreamed; and in his dream his mind wove together his last waking thoughts in fantastic medley. It seemed as if the big slabs of limestone came together, and built themselves into a gigantic staircase, reaching from where he lay to the starry heights above him; and on that staircase angels came and went, peopling by their multitudes that most desolate region, and evidently interested in the sleeper who lay beneath.

Let us think of that mystic ladder which is Jesus Christ our Lord, by which he descended to our humanity and ascended to the throne of God. He is 'the Way' by which 'the sons of ignorance and night' can pass upward to the eternal light and love. Where are you? It may be on a moorland waste, in a ship's cabin, a settler's hut, in a humble cottage, in the crowded city, lying on a bed of pain in the hospital ward! Wherever you are, Jesus finds you out and comes just where you are. The one pole of the ladder is the gold of his Deity, the other the silver of his Manhood, which is placed against your life. Transmit to him your burdens of sin and care and fear. 'Surely the Lord is in this place, and I knew it not'. 'We have a Mediator between God and man, the Man Christ Jesus.' None of us is outside God's loving thought and care. There is always a linking ladder between ourselves and heaven, and God's angels still pass to and fro, sent forth to minister to the heirs of salvation. Let us see to it that we wait at the foot of the ladder to claim our share in the blessings which they bring to earth.

'Behold a ladder set up on the earth, and the top of it reached to heaven; and, behold, the angels of God ascending and descending on it' (Genesis 28:12).

'Hereafter ye shall see Heaven open, and the angels of God ascending and descending upon the Son of Man' (John 1:51).

Prayer: We thank thee, O Father, that from whatever place thy children seek thee, there is a ladder reaching up beyond the stars to heaven; that Jesus is the way to thyself, and we may come to thee in him; nay, thou dost come to us, and dost send thine angels to minister to our need, so that heaven is near to earth, with sympathy, help and succour. Amen.

The Lesson of the Thorn-Bush
February 23

'The angel of the Lord appeared unto him in a flame of fire, out of the midst of a bush ... And God called unto him, and said, Moses, Moses, and he said, Here am I' (Exodus 3:2-4).

Prayer: Some of us sorely need thee, O God; we have been disappointed many times in the things we thought would yield us profit and satisfaction. When we are most absorbed in our necessary business, may thy presence be manifested in us. May we realise that we are not wandering aimlessly upon the trackless desert, because thou art leading us. May every common bush be aflame with God. Amen.

Moses was an old man of eighty years! For forty years - the spring-tide of his life - he had basked in court favour. The son of the palace, though born in a slave-hut! According to Stephen, renowned in deed and word, eloquent in speech, learned in the highest culture of his age, accustomed to lead victorious armies in the field, or to assist in raising pyramids or treasure-cities in peace - all that the ancient world could offer was at his feet (Acts 7:22; Hebrews 11:24-27). But this had been followed by forty other years - of exile, poverty, and heart-break. Instead of the riches of Egypt, he was engaged in tending the sheep of another and the years slowly passed away in obscurity. He was a disappointed and perplexed man. His own record was that when a man's life reaches four-score years, it is labour and sorrow, and he welcomes the cutting off of the web (Psalm 90:10).

One afternoon suddenly a common thornbush seemed wrapt in flame. The blaze was pure and clear, and as he watched, 'Behold! the bush burned with fire, and the bush was not consumed.' Small wonder that he arose from the shelter which screened him from the sun, and drew near to 'see this great sight'. Then was heard that inner voice, familiar to all pure and humble hearts, which bade him realise that the fire was no ordinary flame, but the pledge and sign of God's presence.

We must not suppose that there was more of God in that common bush than in the surrounding landscape. It was simply the focusing of his presence which had always been there, as it is always everywhere. God is as near to each reader of these pages as he was to Moses at that moment. Take this to heart, you most forlorn, most down-hearted, most helpless soul! Be of good cheer! God comes to you, though humbled and scorched, and at the end of yourself! He wraps you around, interpenetrates you, and concentrates himself on your need, saying: 'I AM' - leaving you to fill in his blank cheque, and to claim what you most need. 'For the mountains shall depart and the hills be removed, but his kindness shall not depart from you.'

Songs from a Dust-heap!
February 24

This cheery summons to awake and sing is addressed to those who dwell in the dust! The world is filled with them - those who dwell in the dark cells of disappointed love and faith, or who have failed in their life's purpose, or who, like Bartimaeus, are blind and reduced to beggary. Hope has been painted as blind-folded, her head downcast, her lyre broken in her hand. Sitting on the axis of the earth, which is making its difficult way through the storm and cloud, she presses her ear to the one unbroken string, as though catching at the music of a better time. It is thus that in many lives string after string has become broken and failed, and they have come down to sit in the dust of death and despair.

'Thy dead shall live!'... 'Awake and sing, ye that dwell in the dust; for thy dew is as the dew of herbs' (Isaiah 26:19).

It may be that you have lost all sense of God's nearness and love - not because of any known sin, but through physical weakness, mental exhaustion, or the loneliness of sorrow and suffering. It may be that you have been seeking an experience of God, instead of God himself. You have been seeking him *without*, whilst he is *within*.

It may be that you are perplexed by the mystery of unanswered prayer. 'O my God, I cry in the day-time, and thou hearest not; and in the night season, and am not silent.' Yet no answer comes back from the infinite, and your prayers seem like vessels lost at sea.

It may be that your life has not realised its early ideals. As the years go forward they carry us into disillusionment and heart-break. Life has its prizes and rewards, but they are not for us!

To all such we pass on Isaiah's words: 'Awake and sing, for thy dew is as the dew of light'. The dew is used here of the grace and love of God. Instead of *dust* there will be *dew*, which steals so gently and silently over the earth. The more dry and sapless a patch is, the more tenderly does the dew caress it! Even to graveyards it extends its gracious operations, bidding them awake and sing with the certainty of resurrection.

Sing! because your moods, which the psalmist called 'down-sittings', do not affect your standing in Christ. We are all subject to fits of despondency. 'The Lord hath chastened me sore, but he has not given me over unto death. Open to me the gates of joy, that I may enter into them, and praise the Lord!'

Prayer: We thank thee that many evils that we dreaded have not come to us. Storms have expended themselves outside the circle of our lives. Thy mercy has been greater than our sin, thy supplies larger than our need, thy grace more abundant than the pressure of temptation. Amen.

'Who is this that cometh from Edom ... glorious in his apparel, travelling in the greatness of his strength? I that speak in righteousness, mighty to save' (Isaiah 63:1).

We can never speak of our Lord as we would! We select the richest metaphors of Scripture, the ideals of poets, the masterpieces of the rarest art; but none of them suffice. We steep our thought with fragments from the diaries and autobiographies of the saints. We meditate on his words till our hearts begin to burn! But we come back to the light of common days, and the summons of daily tasks, knowing that we have him, but what he is neither tongue can tell nor heart conceive. We wait therefore, with some impatience, till the veil will part asunder and we shall see him as he is.

The wistful yearning after Christ, which has characterised every age, has broken out again and again in transcendent expression, but among all the imaginings of sanctified and glowing souls, it is hard to find one more suggestive and inspiring than this pre-vision of Isaiah. He is standing on the foothills of the Judean table-land, looking due south towards Edom, when he is startled by an unexpected and extraordinary spectacle. A mighty conqueror is descried in the distance, of commanding appearance, traversing slowly and majestically the desert-wastes. His back toward Edom, his face toward the Judean frontier. He is clearly alone. Whether he had led an army, or had completed his work without an army, is not immediately apparent; but he approaches, travelling in the greatness of his strength. It is only natural that the astonished seer should challenge him with the cry: 'Who is this that cometh from Edom?' Across the intervening space the answer comes: 'I that speak in righteousness, mighty to save!'

Clearly, then, he is no enemy, but an ally, and much more! The word *save* suggests that there is no reason for fear, but every reason to hope. Notice the special aspect of Jesus Christ which appears in this scene. It is not Jesus on the cross, but in his resurrection and ascension glory. He it is who stands sentry between us and the power of the flesh, for which Edom stands. He is not simply the forgiver of sin, but the conqueror over all sin. He is more than a conqueror for himself - he is responsible for all who trust him.

Prayer: O Lord Jesus Christ, thou captain of salvation, who discernest the malevolence and working of evil spirits against my soul, deliver me, I entreat thee, amid the manifold temptations and trials by which I am beset, make a way for me to escape, succour me by thy mighty power, and cause me to become more than a conqueror. Amen.

The Exalted Lord
February 26

We live in troubled times, but always in human history, when outward events seem most distracting and distressing, God's servants are drawn in to the secret place of the Most High, and are shown the reassuring vision of God's overruling providence, and the ordered regularity of his eternal reign. When the land was passing through dark distress, and revolution was imminent, Isaiah beheld the stability of God's throne.

'In the year that king Uzziah died I saw the Lord sitting upon a throne, high and lifted up' (Isaiah 6:1).

'It was high and lifted up', far above all other authority, power, or dominion in heaven, on earth, or under the earth! It was crowned with love - 'above it stood the Seraphim'. Seraph is derived from *fire*, and the Seraphim stand for radiant love. If the throne stands for stability, for judgment, and for power, then above all these attributes, and overarching him who sits there, is *love*. This is the loftiest conception possible to mortals - love supreme. The Lamb that was slain is in the midst of the throne.

The one man who was chosen out of all Israel to see was Isaiah. In all humility he ascended the temple steps, hustled by the crowds that went there as a mere religious form. Any of them appeared to need a revealing vision more than he did, but it was the man who had seen, who now saw the Lord; it was the one saint in all Israel who appeared to be most in touch with God, who was brought into still closer touch. The rest saw only the temple, the high altar, and the ritual, but *he* saw the 'skirts of glory' filling every cranny of the holy place.

Let us not be satisfied with the outward and sensuous, with ritual however splendid, with sermons however magnificent! Those who are humble and persistent in their quest for God will hear notes which other ears cannot catch, will detect a presence that evades ordinary sight, will enter the realm of the spirit which is closed to the outward observer.

The world may be full of tumult; the floods have lifted up their voice, but the Lord on high is mighty, and he shall overcome, for through death, resurrection, and ascension he is Lord of lords and King of kings!

Prayer: We cannot understand the meaning of the darkness and tumult around us, but we know that thou art love, and that thou dost reign. May we see thee raised above principality and power, might and dominion. Glory and blessing, honour and power be unto thee, O Son of God, who art the Man amid the sapphire throne. Amen.

Practising the Presence of God
February 27

'The Lord is at hand. In nothing be anxious; but in everything by prayer and supplication, with thanksgiving, let your requests be made known unto God' (Philippians 4:5, 6).

The word *anxiety* comes from the same root as *anger*, and suggests the idea of choking. Worry chokes the life of faith. It does not help us to overcome our difficulties, but unfits us for dealing with them. No weapon that is formed against us shall prosper; every tongue that shall rise against us shall be condemned; our bread shall be given, and our water sure. God will perfect that which concerneth us, and his goodness and mercy shall never cease. Roll thyself and thy burden on the Lord, and *leave them there*. Too many take them back again!

In the darkening autumn evenings, we light our lamps earlier, or turn on the switch, and lo! there is a burst of light which had been waiting to be called upon. So let us keep a smile upon our faces. As we put off our heavy and rain-soaked clothes in the vestibule, so let us leave our anxieties with God, until we have to resume our destined path.

The Lord is at hand! Let us often repeat these words, amid the commonplaces of life, as well as when anticipating his near advent! Say it when Euodia and Syntyche are giving you trouble! Say it when you are irritated and think that there is no reason why you should accept rebuffs and slights so meekly! Say it when you are worried and anxious! Say it, till you come again into that presence, which is as the light of the morning when the sun riseth. Practise the presence of God! Hold fellowship with him! Even in business, or in the midst of daily toil, often lift your heart for a moment into the atmosphere of his presence! There is a great difference between faith and its intellectual expression. We must rise above the intellectual into spiritual fellowship with God. It is not for us to excite a transient feeling of love toward God. This will soon evanesce. Our business is the absolute surrender of the heart to him. Not the rapture of the mystic, but the consciousness of the spirit, which is aware of an unimpeded union with the life of the infinite. To be ever - tranquilly, joyously, and strenuously - at one with the blessed will of God - that is the heavenly Paradise, and each of us, by his grace, may walk with him in happy fellowship, as Enoch did of old, and then we can make *known* our requests.

Prayer: We ask not, O Father, for health or life. We make an offering to thee of all our days. Thou hast counted them. We would know nothing more. All we ask is to die rather than live unfaithful to thee. Living and dying we would be thine. Amen.

A Faithful Creator
February 28

The more one ponders these words, the more wonderful they appear! That God is faithful is as clear as noonday. He is faithful in the return of the seasons and the orbit-order of the stars; faithful in holding back the flood, that it should not overflow the world and destroy the homes of men; faithful to every living creature that he has made, providing for its exact sustenance. Even the odd sparrow, which Christ must have seen thrown in by the dealer, when his mother bought four others, does not fall to the ground without his notice.

God is the faithful Creator in the heavens above and in the earth beneath. We are not surprised, therefore, to find his faithfulness the theme of holy writ; but why does Peter lay emphasis on his faithfulness as Creator, when ministering to the special circumstances of suffering believers? Is not this the reason? We are apt to concentrate our thoughts on the birth, the cross, the grave, the intercession of our Lord, and to forget that behind all these, deep in the nature of God - the almighty Creator - there are ever-welling fountains of faithfulness, love, and tenderness. We are summoned to go back beyond the story of redemption to the infinite silence of eternity, when each of us was a distinct thought in the mind of God. In his book, all our members were written, when as yet there was none of them. Whether we have realised that eternal purpose is open to serious questioning, but every one of us has a right to look into the face of God and say, 'Thine hands have made me, and fashioned me; give me understanding that I may learn thy commandments'.

We may not question God's dealings with us. They are immutably wise and right. But we may claim that in some way he should make good our deficiencies, so that though sorrowful, we should be always rejoicing; though poor we should make many rich; though having nothing, we should scatter our wealth, as though possessing all things. There is no reason why our life should be a failure, no reason why we should not minister richly to others, no reason why, by his grace, we should not be more than conquerors! We may humbly make this claim on the almighty Creator, and he will not allow his faithfulness to fail!

'Wherefore, let them that suffer according to the will of God, commit the keeping of their souls to him in well-doing, as unto a faithful Creator' (1 Peter 4:19).

Prayer: Help us to commit ourselves to thee in well-doing, O God, our faithful Creator. May we find a solace for our own griefs and disappointments, in sympathy and ministry to others. Amen.

The Banishment of Pain
February 29

There are few lives in the world that escape pain. Beneath the outer surface of our physical frame there is a network of nerves, every fibre of which may become the source of suffering. We hardly realise that health is due to the combined action of thousands of delicate fibres, each moving in perfect accord with all the rest; but if one of these minute chords is jarred or out of tune, there ensues the discord of pain.

Our minds and hearts are as susceptible to suffering as our bodies. Probably there is more suffering generated in the world through the derangement of the soul than of the body. A wounded spirit, who can bear? The sensitive network of our affections, of our hopes and fears, of our attitude towards God or our fellow men, and our self-consciousness, are capable of inflicting suffering, so acute and imperious, as to be an agony which can make us almost oblivious to physical pain.

Pain has a purpose. It is a danger signal, which compels us to refrain from the things which have caused it, or to have recourse to the physician for alleviation. In the moral world, God has made the way of transgressors hard, and sown their paths with thorns, so as to dissuade and turn evil-doers from their wicked ways. In the spiritual world, the sharp sting of remorse, the scourge of conscience, the agony of conviction, when, like Peter, we have denied our Lord, are of inestimable value in reminding us that we have run off the line and are tearing up the track.

Our Lord Jesus suffered pain. He was a man of sorrows and acquainted with grief. He was moved with compassion as he beheld sorrow and suffering, and was constantly relieving pain and healing disease. In this he gave an evident sign that one day he would abolish it.

Why did the seer at Patmos affirm that pain should be no more? Because pain arises from dislocation, and in that fair world, every limb and joint will work without fret or friction. Because pain is the result of sin, and sin shall be no more. Because pain was induced by the fruit of the knowledge of evil, and we shall eat of the tree of life, whose leaves shall be for the healing of the nations. Then there will be songs instead of sighs, and anthems instead of heartbreak.

Prayer: Grant, O Lord, that we, and all whom we love, and all weary and tired souls, may rest in peace, and may finally enter into the city where there shall be no more sorrow, nor crying, nor pain, nor sin, for the former things shall have passed away. Amen.

MARCH

OUR DAILY WALK OF FELLOWSHIP

Enoch walked with God: and he was not;
for God took him
(Genesis 5:24)

Can two walk together, except they be agreed?
(Amos 3:3)

Walking in God's Ways and Paths
March 1

'Shew me thy ways, O Lord; teach me thy paths' (Psalm 25:4). 'He will teach us of his ways, and we will walk in his paths' (Micah 4:2).

There is a clear difference between a *Way* and a *Path*. The one is filled with the throb and stir of the world's life; the other is comparatively lonely and unfrequented. The roll of vehicles and noisy traffic fills the one, whilst the other is, for the most part, trodden by the individual, being too narrow and quiet for the crowd. It is a great comfort that God has paths as well as ways.

God's ways are the great principles on which he acts, the mighty thoroughfares of creation, providence, revelation, human history, and final judgment. On these his goings-forth have ever been of old, even from everlasting. To know them is the passionate desire of the purest and loftiest natures. Moses prayed: 'Shew me now thy ways, that I may know thee', and God graciously granted his request, for to Moses he made known his *ways*, but to Israel only his *acts*. There is need for us all to know God's ways, especially in this momentous era; because only so can we enter into his rest. In the Old and New Testaments the same warning is repeated: 'They shall not enter into my rest, because they have not known my ways' (Psalm 95:11; Hebrews 3:10). We can look out calmly on this troubled world when once we have learned to know the divine programme of gathering up all things in Christ, who is the head; when we walk with him who is the way to God (John 14:6).

Prayer: Be with me, Lord, as I step out on the untrodden way of this month. I know not what it may bring of joy or sorrow, of temptation or service; but I humbly commit myself and my way to thee. Make the best that thou canst of me for thy glory. Amen.

The paths of the Lord may be taken to describe his personal dealings with the individual, who through sickness, or the care of others, or by lonely duty, is isolated from the ordinary worship of the church, and shut away from fellowship and Christian ministry. All such may expect and reckon upon the saving help which will come through God's private communications.

God is faithful to the soul that utterly trusts him. He always comes on time - not a moment before, not a moment too late. Remember that all his paths are mercy and truth. Dare to believe that he is coming along a secret pathway to bring the assurance of his mercy and grace to help in this time of need.

Knowing and Following
March 2

Some people do not seem to desire to advance in the knowledge of God. They have not seen the heavenly vision. Religion to them consists in saying, over and over again, the same prayers that they have used for years, and reading a prescribed portion of Scripture. This is better than nothing, but they cannot appropriate David's comparison between himself and the hunted deer that pants for the water-brook, or our Lord's blessing for those that 'hunger and thirst after righteousness'.

'Then shall we know, if we follow on to know the Lord' (Hosea 6:3).

But with others, there is a longing for a further advance. Like the apostle, they are pressing toward the mark, though it seems to evade them and to recede! They are like the blind man, on whom our Lord wrought the miracle. First, he saw men as trees walking, dimly appreciating the glory of perfect vision; but, presently, as those dear hands touched him again, he saw clearly. Is there one who reads this page who does not long for this clear vision, this knowledge of God! Let us not desist in our quest, but follow on! When the last lesson is learned, the last and deepest surrender taken, the final act of faith accomplished, the partition will remove, and we shall know what Pascal meant when he wrote: 'The world hath not known thee, but I have known thee. Joy! Joy! Joy! Tears of Joy!' 'Now we see through a glass, darkly; but then face to face: now I know in part; but then shall I know even as also I am known' (1 Corinthians 13:12).

God has a way of his own for each of us. 'His going forth is prepared as the morning; and he shall come unto us as the rain.' Some are smitten by a sudden sense of the reality and vision of the eternal world, that hides behind the veil of sense. Others, as they partake of the bread and wine of communion, have such a vision of the love of Jesus, that they are more than satisfied. At any time a heavenly door may open before the knock of the seeker; or, we may suddenly look up and see his face, and exclaim with St Paul: 'The Lord is at hand!' We shall see his hand beckoning to us, and we shall arise and follow into that world of reality and love that is so near, but sometimes seems so far!

Prayer: Lord Jesus! Give us this second sight, we beseech thee! Lift us up, by thy strong arm, above the mists and darkness of the valley, to walk with thee on the high level of thy manifested presence and glory. Amen.

The Viewpoint of the Sanctuary
March 3

'It is good for me to draw near to God' (Psalm 73:28).

The good Asaph was greatly troubled about the prosperity of the wicked of his time. He refrained from speaking to others on the matter, lest it should impair their religious life; but the iron went deep into his soul! Here were people, who seemed always at ease, though they set their mouths against the heavens, while he, though he cleansed his heart, and washed his hands in innocency, was plagued all day long. It was in a very perturbed and distressed condition of mind, therefore, that he went one day into the sanctuary of God. It was there that God spoke to him and unveiled the future, and showed the glorious contrast between the wicked and himself, when time had given place to eternity, and heaven had corrected the uneven balance of earth.

Each of us has, or should have, a sanctuary - the house of God, or it may be a quiet room, or some sacred spot in the woods or garden or beside the sea. Greatly is the soul to be pitied that has no sanctuary, where it can shelter from the rush and noise of life. Like Abraham, we need to have some place where we can stand before the Lord (Genesis 18:22, 23).

Let us remember the injunction to build according to the sanctuary pattern (Exodus 25:8, 9, 40). We must not drift aimlessly through life, at the mercy of every current and every gust of wind; nor must we be content to be our own pattern-makers, or mere copyists. Before we enter upon some change or fresh objective in our life, let us ascend into the sanctuary of God's mountains, and get to know his mind and will. Be sure that he has a plan and programme for each of us, extending even to the cords and tassels of our life; and if we are true to the leadings of his Spirit, we shall be led out and on to things that eye hath not seen, nor heart conceived.

Prayer: Grant unto me, O Lord, the blessedness of the one whom thou choosest, and causest to approach unto thee. Amen.

Frances Ridley Havergal writes: 'I am struck with the possibilities of the Christian life! In my own case, what once were far-off possibilities are now actualities; while a new horizon opens before me of possibilities which also in God's time shall become actualities.'

Forget the past! Your failures and sin; the fading laurels of past successes; the bitter memories of abortive efforts. Leave them with God. Let the dead bury their dead! Work out your life-plan knowing that God is able and willing to make the necessary grace abound toward you.

God's Condescension to Man
March 4

A certain writer ridiculed the idea that the Almighty Ruler, who inhabits the stellar spaces, can have any knowledge of such a cheese-mite as man. He says, 'Put yourself in the planetary space, a mere dot, and do you think that the Almighty Maker can have discernment of thee!' But bigness is not greatness! The infant in the cradle is worth more to the parents and the nation than the royal palace in which he was born. The age which discovers the telescope, with the infinite abyss above, discovers also the microscope, with the infinite abyss beneath.

How absolutely different is the outlook of the Psalmist! He stands under the eastern heavens, blazing at midnight with myriads of resplendent constellations, and cries: 'O Jehovah, my Lord, how excellent is thy name in all the earth, who has set thy glory above the heavens! They are *thy* heavens, the work of *thy* fingers; as for moon and stars, *thou* hast ordained them. How great *thou* art!' Then he turns to think of man, and says: There must be something more in man than a superficial gaze is competent to discover. He must surely possess an unrealised dignity and worth, since the great God, the Maker of these worlds, stoops to call him *friend.*

But the question arises: How can God find pleasure in visiting, i.e. in having fellowship with a race so full of evil as ours? Granted that he might have fellowship with Moses or Elijah, with Daniel or John, but how can he stoop to intercourse with ordinary people like ourselves? What is Zacchaeus, that the Son of Man should visit at his house - is he not a publican? Yes, but of late he had been restoring his ill-gotten gains, and Jesus sees in him the possibility of a son of Abraham! What is Simon Peter, that Christ should visit him? Ah, but he will one day become the rock-man, the foremost leader of the church! So does Christ our Lord see what we may become, and he stands at the door of our life, seeking admission. Let us heed his knock and bid him come in.

'When I consider t h y heavens, the work of thy fingers, the moon and the stars, which thou hast ordained; what is man, that thou art mindful of him, and the son of man, that thou visiteth him?' (Psalm 8:3, 4).

Prayer: O God, may our whole nature be consecrated for thine indwelling and use. Let there be no part in us dark, but may the clear shining of thy presence dispel all shadows, and fill us with peace and joy. Amen.

Standing Before God
March 5

'Who is able to stand before this holy Lord God?' (1 Samuel 6:20).

The phrase 'to stand before God' designates a high-toned religious life; it includes the knowledge of God, the faculty of executing his commands, and the power of interceding for others. The phrase was a favourite one with Elijah, as expressing the spirit of his great career, and we surely desire that the spirit and attitude of our life may be designated thus. But if this is to be something more than a vague wish or idle dream, there must be a close adhesion to great principles.

Amongst many it is the general tendency to follow the practice of the majority. We drift with the current, and allow our lives to be settled by our companions or our whims, our fancies or our tastes. If we have a momentary qualm, in contrasting our lives with the standards of primitive simplicity, of which Scripture, or the biographies of the saints are full, we excuse ourselves by saying that so long as the main purpose of life is right, the details are unimportant. But what we are in the smallest details of our life, that we are really and essentially.

What a revolution would come to us all, if it became the one fixed aim and ambition of our lives to *stand before God*, and to do always those things that are pleasing in his sight. It would not make us less tender in our friendships, or less active in our service. It would not take the sparkle from the eye; the nerve from the grasp; or the warm glow from the heart. But it would check many a vain word, arrest many a silly jest, stop much selfish and vainglorious expenditure, and bring us back to whatsoever things are true, honourable, just, pure, lovely and of good report.

We must hold lightly to the things around us. It is difficult to say what worldliness consists in, for what is worldly to some people is an ordinary part of life's circumstance to others. But all of us are sensible of ties that hold us to the earth. We may discover what they are by considering what we cling to most; what we find hard to let go, even into the hands of Christ. Whatever it is, if it hinders us from living on the highest level; if it is a weight that impedes our speed heavenward, it should be laid deliberately on God's altar, that we may be able, without let or hindrance, to be wholly for God.

Prayer: May the Holy Spirit enable us to realise in daily life our true position in thy purpose. May we in heart and mind thither ascend, and with him continually dwell. May our affections be set on things above, not on things of earth. Amen.

The Secret Place of Prayer
March 6

In prayer there must be deliberateness - the secret place, the inner chamber, the fixed time, the shut door against distraction and intruders. In that secret place the Father is waiting for us. He is as certainly there as he is in heaven. Be reverent, as Moses when he took the shoes from off his feet! Be trustful, because you are having an audience with one who is infinite sympathy and love! Be comforted, because there is no problem he cannot solve, no knot he cannot untie!

God knows even better than we do what we need and should ask for. He has gone over every item of our life, every trial, every temptation - the unknown the unexpected, the glints of sunshine on the path, and the clouds of weeping. He listens to our forecast and requests, and rejoices when they accord with his infinite foreknowledge; or he may give us something better and more appropriate to our case.

'He will recompense thee.' If he does not remove the cup, he will send an angel to strengthen; if the thorn remains unremoved, he will give more grace. You may be sure that, in some way or other, your heavenly Father is going to meet your particular need. It is as certain as though you heard him say, 'Go your way, your prayer is heard; I will undertake, trust me, leave all in my hand!' When you have once definitely put a matter into God's hands, leave it there. Do not repeat the committal, for that suggests that you have never made it. Your attitude thenceforward is to look into God's face, not to ask him to remember, but to say, 'Father, thou knowest, understandest, carest! I know whom I have trusted, and am persuaded that thou wilt not fail.'

There is a prayer which is without ceasing; but surely that is not the reiterated request for the same thing, but the blessed interchange of happy fellowship. Use not vain repetitions, as do the heathen, who think that they will be heard for much speaking, but count him faithful that promised! This reckoning of faith is probably the loftiest attribute of prayer, for faith is the quiet assurance of things not yet seen!

'When thou prayest, enter into thy closet, and when thou hast shut the door, pray to thy Father which is in secret' (Matthew 6:6).

Prayer: Lift us into light and love and purity and blessedness, and give us at last our portion with those who have trusted in thee, and sought in small things as in great, in things tempered and things eternal, to do thy holy will. Amen.

The Model Prayer
March 7

'After this manner therefore pray ye: Our Father which art in heaven, hallowed by thy Name' (Matthew 6:9).

The Lord's prayer is a temple reared by Christ himself - the embodiment of his ideal, and as we repeat these simple and wonderful sentences, we cannot but think of the myriads who have been moulded by them, and have poured into these petitions their hearts' desires.

Our Lord was not always insisting on prayer, but was constantly praying to his Father himself. His disciples knew his habit of getting away for secret prayer, and they had on more than one occasion seen the transfiguring glory reflected on his face. Happy would it be for us if the glory of fellowship and communion with God were so apparent that men would come to us saying, 'Teach us to pray' (Exodus 34:35).

Prayer must be simple. The Jewish proverb said, 'Everyone who multiplies prayer is heard', but our Lord forbade senseless repetitions by his teaching of the simple, direct, and intelligible petitions of this prayer.

Prayer must be reverent. The tenderest words, the simplest confidences, the closest intimacy will be welcomed and reciprocated by our Father in heaven. But we must remember that he is the great King, and his name is Holy. Angels veil their faces in his presence. Let us remember that 'God is in Heaven, and thou upon earth; be not rash with thy mouth and let not thine heart be hasty to utter anything before God'.

Prayer must be unselfish. Our Lord so wove intercession into the structure of this prayer that none can use it without pleading for others. Sorrow or sin may isolate us and make us feel our loneliness and solitude, but in prayer we realise that we are members of the one body of Christ, units in that great multitude which no man can number.

Prayer must deal with real needs. Daily bread stands for every kind of need, and the fact that Jesus taught us to pray for it, suggests that we may be sure that it is God's will to give.

Prayer must be in faith. We cannot but believe that we are as certain to prevail with God, as the good man of the house with his friend; and if among men to ask is to get, how much more with him who loves us with more than a father's love (Luke 11:9-13).

Prayer: O God our Father, help us to live in the spirit of prayer today. Breathe thy Spirit into us as we kneel before thee, subduing the selfishness that makes discord, and uniting our hearts in the fear of thy name. Amen.

Turning Passion into Prayer
March 8

When we read that Elijah was a man subject to the same passions as ourselves, we are apt to suppose that we have the clue to the driving force of his life. But Scripture shows that the results of his wonderful career were achieved, not by his passion, but by his prayer! Elijah, though capable of the same vehement earnestness with which we are all endowed, refused to accomplish his life-work by the employment of lower energies, but set himself to obtain the results he desired, through prayer. He was a man of like passions with ourselves, but he prayed earnestly. He turned his passion into prayer.

'Elijah was a man of like passions with us, and he prayed fervently' (James 5:17 RV).

There was no salient element of a strong nature of which his was destitute. There was the passion of *patriotism*, as when he was prepared even to witness the sufferings of his people, if these would bring them back to God; of *tenderness*, as when he bore the dead body of the child to his room; of *righteousness*, as when he slew the false prophets; of *love for nature*, as when he fled into the wilderness to die; of *devotion to God's glory*, as when he cried, 'I have been very jealous for the Lord God of Hosts'. All these passions dwelt strongly within his breast, but if he had relied on them alone, his life work would have faded as the mirage on the glistening sand.

There is a marvellous contagion in vehement feeling. As a tiny pith-ball, light as a feather, by continually impinging on a suspended bar of iron, will make it move, so one soul can move others. The brain is able to create waves of thought, and the heart waves of emotion. But we must learn to secure through God results which some try to achieve by the energy of their own nature. Let us pray more. Let us seek to be filled with a passionate love to our Lord Jesus, and to the world of men - with a love so hot that the most passionate words of St Bernard or Faber may not seem extravagant. Then let us divert the glowing metal into the mould of prayer - which may express itself in an intense silence of intercession, or with strong cryings and tears. At least let us not dare to be tepid and apathetic in the midst of this wonderful universe which is electric with living energy! (Revelation 3:15, 16).

Prayer: O Christ, who baptizeth with fire, kindle in our hearts the flame of thy love, that we may not be lukewarm or cold. We would not trust in the force of our emotions, lest they fail us, but in the power of prayer and of thine intercession for us. Amen.

'Peter said unto him, Lord, why cannot I follow thee now? I will lay down my life for thy sake' (John 13:37).

Peter's impulsive spirit could ill brook delay - 'Lord, why cannot I follow thee now?' Easier far is it to rush into the battle, when excitement and passion may be trusted to render us oblivious to pain and discomfort, than to stand at our post through the long cold nights of sentry duty.

He made the mistake of miscalculating the might and power of the Adversary. It was the hour of the power of darkness. The moment was at hand in which the prince of this world would make the supreme effort to hold his own, and refuse to be cast out.

He miscalculated his own strength, and relied upon the fervour of his emotion. He had no conception of how much need there was for something more than the strong fervour of passionate affection.

He miscalculated the weapon by which to overcome. He had a literal sword, and thought that it would be sufficient to draw it and smite with all his might, as he did, cutting off the ear of Malchus. He expected that with his fervent passion for Christ on the one hand, and cold steel on the other, he would be able to follow wherever Jesus led. But it is not possible for human enthusiasm to sustain the soul, when it comes to close grips with the great Adversary of the Kingdom of God.

Prayer: Lord, we would follow thee whithersoever thou goest, but we are weak and helpless, and our own strength will fail in the final test. May we not trust in our own resolutions or vows, but in the saving strength of thy right hand. Amen.

He miscalculated the help that comes through prayer. So confident was he that he slept instead of praying. Thrice the Lord came to remind him of the urgent need for watching against the hour of trial, but his words were unheeded, because the advice seemed needless. Why should he pray when he had already made up his mind!

Then the crash came, and he went out a broken-hearted man! Ah, we too have failed in like manner. We have brandished the cold steel of strong resolve. But the disillusioning process has set in, and we have sorrowfully proved that it is not by flesh and blood that we can enter the Kingdom. Let us not forget our Lord's comforting words to Peter, 'Thou shalt follow me afterwards'.

Broken Cisterns
March 10

What an infinite mistake to miss the fountain freely flowing to quench our thirst, and to hew out broken cisterns, in which is disappointment and despair. Many such may read these words - each with soul-thirst craving satisfaction; each within reach of God, whose nature is as rock-water for those that are athirst, but they are attempting the impossible task of satisfying the craving for the infinite and divine, with men and the things of sense.

There is the cistern of *pleasure*, engraved with fruits and flowers, wrought at the cost of health and peace; the cistern of *wealth*, gilded and inlaid with costly gems; the cistern of *human love*, which, however fair and beautiful, can never satisfy the soul that rests in it alone - all these, erected at infinite cost of time and strength, are treacherous and disappointing.

At our feet the fountain of God's love is flowing through the channel of Jesus Christ, the divine Man. He says to each of us: 'Whosoever drinketh of the water that I shall give him shall never thirst'. We must descend to the level of the stream, if its waters are to flow over our parched lips to slake our thirst. We must come back to Calvary, take our stand at the foot of the cross, hear again the words of him who died there for us, saying, 'I thirst', that he might be able to give the water of life freely to all who come to him.

You who are weary of your toil, drop your tools, and come back to God. Forsake the alliances, the friendships, the idolatries, the sins which have alienated you from your best Friend. Open your heart, that he may create in you the fountain of living water, leaping up to eternal life. 'The Spirit and the Bride say, Come! And let him that heareth say, Come! And let him that is athirst, Come! And whosoever will, let him take the water of life freely.'

> 'I came to Jesus, and I drank
> Of that Life-giving stream;
> My thirst was quenched, my soul revived,
> And now I live in him.'

'They have forsaken me the fountain of living waters, and hewed them out cisterns, broken cisterns, that can hold no water' (Jeremiah 2:13). 'If any man thirst, let him come unto me, and drink' (John 7:37).

Prayer: Teach us, O Lord, the art of so living in fellowship with thyself that every act may be a psalm, every meal a sacrament, every room a sanctuary, every thought a prayer. Amen.

'Notwithstanding, lest we should offend them ... thou shalt find a piece of money; that take, and give unto them for me and thee' (Matthew 17:27).

Peter had been fairly well-to-do. He had his house and boat and nets. There was no lack in the fisherman's house. But when Jesus said, 'Come after me', he left all, and there was an immediate cutting off of the former sources of supply, so that when the tax gatherer came, there was nothing to meet his claim. Our Lord maintained that he personally was under no obligation to meet the demand. As a child, to use his own words, he was free; but he immediately identified himself, as he always does, with his troubled disciple. We can never leave anything for Christ, without his recognition, and his being ready to defray whatever cost may accrue from obedience.

The identification was so absolute between the Master and his disciples, that he refrained from providing two coins, which might have indicated some severance of interest. Was it not his intention to put beyond all controversy that he and his are one, and that in every act of his on our behalf, in his willingness to meet the demands made upon us, there is no severance of interests, no mere patronage, but an absolute identification with all that concerns us.

There are profound lessons here. Demands are constantly knocking at the door of life, which we find it hard, sometimes impossible, to meet. There are needs of food and clothing, of the rent collector and the tax gatherer. But is not Christ aware? Is he not faithful? Will he let us go under in the struggle? Never! Whatever demand made on the servant is assumed by the Master - *That take*, he says, *and give unto them for me and thee.*

As he enters the wilderness of temptation, he reminds us - it is '*for me and thee*'. As he hangs upon the cross, and passes forth from the grave, radiant with triumph, he turns to us and says: 'This victory over death and the grave is *for me and thee*'. Yes, and through all the ages that are yet to be, amid the marvels of unfolding new worlds, nothing shall accrue to him of which he will not say, 'That take, and give, or use, for me and thee'. Only remember, we must *take*, and *give*. We must appropriate the unsearchable riches of Christ, we must *impart* them, or they will not profit us.

Prayer: We thank thee, our Father, for our union with the risen Christ. May we share more largely in his glorious life, and live as the heirs of God and joint-heirs with Christ. Amen.

The Possibility of the Impossible
March 12

You are asking me to perform the impossible; I am sure that I can never become a great tree, said a tiny mustard seed, which is the smallest of all seeds, as it lay on the soft mould where it had dropped. Suddenly it was caught up with a spadeful of earth, and buried, it seemed, fathoms deep - in reality, but a few inches! There it lay in darkness and neglect. After some weeks, a tiny green shoot appeared above the ground, and looked up to where the great parent-tree was growing; it whispered softly to itself, 'Perhaps I shall be able to do it after all'. 'Do what?' 'Perhaps I shall become a great tree in which the birds may shelter.' 'But a few weeks ago you said it was impossible.' 'Ah! then I had no idea that Mother Nature would work in me as she has done; if she goes on pouring herself into me as she has been doing of late, there is nothing that I cannot do; yet not I, but her life which dwelleth and worketh in me.'

There is no need to explain or enforce the meaning of the allegory. Our Lord had bidden his disciples forgive 'until seventy times seven', and they had replied that such a thing would be impossible, without a great increase of faith. 'No,' said the Master, 'you do not need quantity but quality.'

All God's fullness will flow through the tiniest channel that faith opens out on his almighty power. Faith is the open heart towards him, and through the channel of faith Christ lives in and through us. Hudson Taylor heard God say, 'I am going to evangelise inland China, and if you will walk with me, I will do it through you'. D L Moody said that the beginning of his marvellous ministry was the remark made in his hearing: 'The world has yet to learn what God can do through a man wholly yielded to him'. It is not what we *do*, but what God does through us, that counts; and his mighty power, passing through the tiniest aperture of faith, keeps hollowing it wider.

'Lord, increase our faith. And the Lord said, If ye have faith as a grain of mustard seed, ye would say unto this sycamore tree, Be thou rooted up, and be thou planted in the sea; and it would have obeyed you' (Luke 17:5, 6 RV).

Prayer: Most gracious Lord, thou didst truly say, 'Without me ye can do nothing'. We know that this is so by our past failures, when we have wrought in our own strength. Help us to use the little faith we have that it may become the channel for thy wondrous power. Amen.

Maimed: but Fuller Life
March 13

'If thy hand cause thee to stumble, cut it off: it is good for thee to enter into life maimed, rather than having thy two hands go into Gehenna, into the unquenchable fire' (Mark 9:43 RV marg).

Our Lord calls all who love and would follow him to present themselves as living sacrifices, even though in the process they should be exposed to salt with its searching sting, and fire with its consuming flame (verse 49). In such moments he reminds us of something which he sees to be hindering our highest ideals, and there is only one alternative - though it be dear as right hand or foot, we must cut it off! Of course it is best to retain the members and faculties of our body in purity and righteousness; they are most important assets to the working-force of a successful life. No one has a right to perform an amputation, unless it is the only alternative to death, or the uselessness of Gehenna, which was the rubbish-heap of Jerusalem.

Our Lord well advised, when he said, 'Cut it off!' The one swift, irrevocable blow is the easiest in the end. It may be a friendship which is causing us to stumble; or an evil habit, sapping our nervous energy; or a form of amusement, which may be innocent enough in itself - but whatever hinders us in our spiritual progress, if we cannot master it and keep it in bounds, must be yielded to the knife. We often expose ourselves to more anguish in our effort to retain and restrain, than to remove absolutely and for ever.

Maimed lives are nevertheless strong and full. Notice those words: 'Enter into *life* maimed'. Some lay the emphasis on their losses, sacrifices, and privations; others dwell upon *life*, and refuse to consider the straitness of the gate through which they press. True, they are maimed, but by the forfeiture of the lower they gain the higher, and by the way of the cross enter into the joy and glory. There are great compensations for us all, if we dare to follow the ideals that beckon to us from the snow-capped pinnacles above. Surrender all that impedes and hinders your highest life, and fountains will burst forth in an abundance that will make the desert blossom and sing. Is not this better than to be a castaway from the hands of Christ as unclean and useless?

Prayer: Most blessed Lord, may we drink so deeply of thy Spirit that we shall be willing to surrender all that hinders us in following thee absolutely and always. Amen.

Divine Deliverance
March 14

It is supposed that this psalm, like the preceding one, was composed by Moses, 'the man of God', and that each may be applied to the flight of Israel from Egypt.

To 'abide under the shadow of the Almighty' reminds us of the words of our Lord, when he said, 'How often would I have gathered thy children together, as a hen doth gather her brood under her wings, and ye would not'. Bunyan says that the hen has four calls - the call when night is near; the call for food when she has found some dainty; the call of peril when the hawk is nigh; and the call of brooding love, when she wants to feel her nestlings under her wings. Today God is calling to each of us, saying: Come my children, make the secret place of my presence, of my environment, of my constant keeping, your home; for he that dwelleth in the secret place of the Most High shall abide under the wings of God. When night is nigh, when money and food are scarce, when the hawk is in the air ready to pounce on us, when loneliness or desolation oppresses, let us hear the brooding cry of God our Father, and nestle beneath his shadow.

God is prepared to keep us in *all* our ways. Many of us believe that somehow God will bring us out at last, but we have no expectation that he can keep us in blamelessness of soul; we expect to be brought to heaven, but that we shall be battered, and beaten, and despoiled on the way. But surely our God can do better for us than that! He can keep us from yielding to passionate temper, jealousy, hatred, pride, and envy, as well as to the grosser forms of sin.

The promise is clear: 'He shall give his angels charge over thee, to keep thee in *all* thy ways' - the business ways, the social ways, the ways of service into which God may lead us forth, the ways of sacrifice or suffering. Let us simply and humbly ask for the fulfilment of the promises in this psalm. He will answer your prayers. He will be with you in trouble. He will satisfy you with many years of life, or with living much in a short time, and he will show you the wonders of his salvation.

'I will say of the Lord, He is my refuge and my fortress; my God; in him will I trust' (Psalm 91:2).

Prayer: Lord, be thou within me, to strengthen me; without me, to keep me; above me, to protect me; beneath me, to uphold me; before me, to direct me; behind me, to keep me from straying; round about me, to defend me. Amen.

'And they were all filled with the Holy Ghost, and began to speak with other tongues, as the Spirit gave them utterance' (Acts 2:4).

On the day of Pentecost all who were gathered together in the upper room were filled with the Holy Spirit - women as well as men, obscure disciples, as well as illustrious apostles. Deacons called to do the secular business of the church must be men filled with the Holy Ghost. That he was a good man, full of the Holy Ghost, was a greater recommendation of Barnabas than that he had parted with his lands.

The majority of Christians have seemed to suppose that the filling of the Holy Spirit was the prerogative of a few - they have never thought of it as within their reach; and the church has been paralysed for lack of the only power that can avail in the conflict against the world, the power which was distinctly pledged by her ascending Lord. Pentecost was meant to be the specimen and type of all the days of the years of this present age, and we have fallen far below this blessed level, not because of any failure on God's part, but because the church has neglected its privilege.

We must desire to be filled for the glory of God. We must seek the Spirit's power, not for our own happiness and comfort, nor even for the good that we may be the better able to effect; but that 'Christ may be magnified in our bodies, whether by life or death'.

We must bring cleansed vessels. God will not deposit his precious gift in unclean receptacles. We must be washed in the blood of Christ from all conscious filthiness and stain, ere we can presume to expect that God will give us what we seek.

We must appropriate him by faith. There is no need for us to wait, because the Holy Spirit has been given to the church. We need not struggle and agonise in the vehemence of entreaty, but have simply to take what God is willing to impart. He gives the Holy Spirit to them that obey him (Acts 5:32).

We must be prepared to let the Holy Spirit do as he will with and through us. There must be no reserve, no holding back, no contrariety of purpose. Let us believe and reckon that we are being filled with new power and joy which shall be for the glory of God and the service of man.

Prayer: We pray, O God, that the Holy Spirit may so infill us, that sin and self may have no dominion over us, but that the fruits of the Spirit may abound to thy honour and glory. Amen.

Our Eternal Destiny
March 16

There is a contrast, and yet a similarity, between this parable and that of the tares. In the latter we learn that it is impossible in the present age to separate the evil from the good in the professing church of Christ; in the former we see that with an inevitable pressure, we are all being drawn towards the discrimination of the judgment seat of Christ.

What a confused mass of dead and living things are brought to shore by a net - weed, mud, shells, unwholesome things as well as those which are good for food, lie in a confused heap together. So it is with the professing church. It embraces every variety of character - good fish amid a certain amount of rubbish, and there is no society of men and women in which this mixture does not obtain. Our Lord teaches that when the great net of the gospel dispensation has been drawn in to the shores of eternity, then, with unerring judgment, the angels will begin their work of separation.

The distinction which separates the good and the bad is determined by the service we can render in God's kingdom. He wants those who will co-operate with him in the work of redemption, who are living unselfish and consecrated lives, through which his Spirit may work for the highest purposes of salvation. Those who he rejects are the selfish, worldly, and sense-bound natures, who refuse to be the implements and instruments of his redemptive purpose.

To which of these two classes do we belong? Are we willing to be identified with Christ in his cross and shame? Do we delight in mercy, self-sacrifice and holy service? If so, we may anticipate the future without fear. But if, on the other hand, we are shut up within ourselves, even though it be the enjoyment of religion, without tears for men's sorrows, or yearning for their salvation, we may question whether it may not be our lot to be cast away on the rubbish heap (1 Corinthians 9:27).

'The kingdom of heaven is like unto a net, that was cast into the sea, and gathered of every kind: which, when it was filled, they drew up on the beach ...and gathered the good into vessels, but the bad they cast away. So shall it be in the consummation of the age' (Matthew 13:47-49 RV marg).

Prayer: O Lord, we acknowledge thy dominion over us; our life, our death, our soul and body, all belong to thee. Grant that we may willingly consecrate them all to thee, and use them in thy service. Amen.

God Wrestling with Man
March 17

'Thy name shall be called no more Jacob, but Israel: for as a prince hast thou power with God and with men, and hast prevailed' (Genesis 32:28).

This story of the angel wrestling with Jacob is an instance of God's earnest desire to take from us all that hinders our best and highest life, whilst we resist with might and main. There was much evil in Jacob that needed to be laid aside, and so the love of God drew near to him in the form of an angel to wrestle with him. At first he held his own but whatever it is that enables a soul whom God designs to bless to stand out against him, God will touch. It may be as *natural* as a sinew, but if it robs us of spiritual blessing, God will touch it; it may be as *small* as a sinew, but its evil influence will compel the Almighty Lover of our souls to take notice of it, to cause our scheming to miscarry, and the sinew of our strength to dry up.

Then Jacob abandoned the posture of defence and resistance, and clung to his Adversary. It is good when we come to this attitude, for there is nothing which God will not do for the soul that clings to him in absolute weakness (2 Corinthians 12:7-9).

Prayer: We thank thee, O God, that our backslidings and transgressions, our failures and inconsistencies, cannot turn aside thy compassionate love. We would yield ourselves to thee. Make us as rock to the seducing influences of the world and of the flesh, but soft as clay to the least touch of thy hands. Strive mightily in us by thy Holy Spirit, and perfect that which concerns us. Amen.

Three things happened: *The changed name*, which indicated a changed character. Israel means 'prince with God'. The supplanter, cheat, and weak vacillator became royal! There is only one road to royalty, it is the path of self-surrender and faith. *Power*: as a prince hast thou power with God, and with men thou shalt prevail (RV marg). He who would have power and authority with his fellows must first secure it by yielding to God. *The Beatific Vision*: 'I have seen God face to face'. Our moments of vision come after the night of wrestling. The price is high, but the vision more than compensates. Our sufferings are not worthy to be compared to the glory which shall be revealed. Such is life! As the dawn of heaven breaks we see the Angel of Love, and as Christ meets us we awake to the royalty of the sons of God.

Consecration
March 18

The fact that we have been bought with a price, not with corruptible things, as silver or gold, but with the precious blood of Christ, lies at the foundation of all consecration (1 Peter 1:18). In consecration we do not make ourselves Christ's but recognise that we are his by an unalienable right. In the slave market human beings were sold like cattle; but this institution is set forth as the first step in our devotion to the service and person of Jesus Christ, the Lord who bought us. Slaves pass from one master to another. Among the Hebrews an Israelite would sometimes sell himself into slavery until the year of Jubilee, or until one of his kinsmen redeemed him (Leviticus 25:47-50). So our kinsman, Christ, bought us back from sin and guilt and condemnation; he says, as he buys us: 'Ye shall be for me, ye shall not be for another.'

'Know ye not that your body is a sanctuary of the Holy Ghost which is in you, which ye have from God? and ye are not your own; for ye were bought with a price; glorify God therefore in your body' (1 Corinthians 6:19, 20 RV marg).

Our Lord's claim upon us is built on his own supreme sacrifice. 'He gave himself for us,' says the apostle Paul, 'that he might redeem us from all iniquity' (Titus 2:14). He gave himself up to the death of the cross, that we might reckon ourselves to be dead unto sin. The apostles constantly speak of themselves as 'the slaves of Jesus Christ'. Oh, that we might all live like this, counting nothing as our exclusive possession, but believing that all we have has been given to us to use in trust for our Lord and Master. He assigns to us each and all the work that we can do best. Some are called to work for him in the high places of the church, and others to toil in lowly obscurity, but everything is important in the great house of the Master, and all he requires is faithful service. I shall never forget when I first entered into the realisation of the ownership of my Lord; that I was his chattel, and had no longer any option or choice for one's enjoyment or emolument. The life which was commenced then has been one of perfect freedom, for this is the enigma of his service, that Christ's slaves are alone free; and that the more absolutely they obey him, the more completely do they drink of the sweet cup of liberty!

Prayer: O Lord, I give myself to thee. I am born to serve thee, to be thine, to be thy instrument. I ask not to see - I ask not to know - I ask simply to be used. Amen.

Risen with Christ
March 19

'If then ye were raised together with Christ, seek the things that are above, where Christ is, seated on the right hand of God' (Colossians 3: 1 RV).

If! Some one will say, 'Ah, there's the rub! I'm afraid that is not true of *me*; my life is sinful and sorrowful; there are no Easter chimes in my soul, no glad fellowship with the risen Lord; no victory over death and hostile powers.' But if you are Christ's disciple, you may affirm that you are risen in Him! With Christ you lay in the grave, and with Christ you have gone forth, according to the thought and purpose of God, if not in your feelings and experience. This is distinctly taught in Ephesians 2:1-10 and Romans 6. The whole church (including all who believe in one Lord Jesus) has passed into the light of the Easter dawn; and the one thing for you and me, and all of us, is to begin from this moment to act as if it were a conscious experience, and as we dare to do so we shall have the experience.

Notice how the apostle insists on this: 'You *died*, you were *raised* with Christ, your life is *hid* with Christ. Give yourself time to think about it and realise it.'

The cross of Jesus stands between you and the constant appeal of the world, as when the neighbours of Christian tried to induce him to return to the City of Destruction. This does not mean that we are to be indifferent to all that is fair and lovely in the life which God has given us, but that the cross is to separate us from all that is selfish, sensual, and savouring of the lust of the flesh, the lust of the eyes, and the pride of life (1 John 2:15-17).

Set your mind on things above (verse 2). 'As a man thinketh in his heart, so is he.' With many of us there is little attempt to guard our thoughts. The door of our heart stands open, with none to control the ingress or egress of the tumultuous throng of thoughts that wander in and out. If only we would ask the Holy Spirit to control our thoughts, so that we might think only the things that are true and of good report, a wonderful change would pass over our life (Philippians 4:7, 8).

Realise that Christ is your life - he is in you! See to it that nothing hinders the output of his glorious indwelling. Never mind if the world of men misunderstands you. Some day your motives and reasons will be manifested (Colossians 3:4).

Prayer: Grant, most gracious God, that we may love and seek thee always and everywhere, and may at length find thee and for ever hold thee fast in the life to come. Amen.

Stooping to Rise
March 20

We wake up from the unconsciousness of infancy to find ourselves in a world of revolt, and learn that so far as the memory of man reaches back into the past, this conflict has been recognised as existing between man and himself, man and his fellow, man and God. Is there no help? Will not God some day bring peace and good will into these troubled scenes? Yes, indeed! This paragraph tells us that the time will come when every knee shall bow, every tongue confess that Christ is Lord, and that God will be glorified. And this is being effected by Christ through means that we did not expect.

'Being found in fashion as a man, he humbled himself, and became obedient unto death, even the death of the cross. Wherefore God also hath highly exalted him' (Philippians 2:8, 9).

When our Lord stooped to live visibly amongst men, he refused to avail himself of the homage due to his original nature. He had been in the form of God, but was content to veil his glory, to assume the form of a servant, to be made in the likeness of men. In the cradle of Bethlehem, in the home of Nazareth, in the voluntary limitations of his earthly ministry, in his obedience to the death of the cross, there was the hiding of his power. He refused to use the attributes of his intrinsic Deity, that he might manifest the love of God, that he might bear away the guilt of the world, and work out and bring in an eternal righteousness. Therefore he is exalted and bears evermore the name of Jesus - the Saviour of the world.

Prayer: Our heavenly Father, give us the patience, the tender pity, the humility of Jesus our Lord; who, though he was rich, for our sakes became poor. Make us obedient even to the death of the cross. Help us not to save ourselves, that we may save others. Amen.

The apostle says, let this same mind be in you ; think these thoughts; follow in the steps of Jesus. We must show a holy emulation as to who shall stoop the lowest, and follow the Master the closest. The most urgent matter for each of us to consider is not whether we are orthodox in our creed (though that is not unimportant) but whether at any cost we have the mind which was in Christ, whether at any cost to ourselves we are manifesting the love of God to those around us.

A New Beatitude
March 21

Our Lord put within the reach of his noble forerunner the blessedness of those who have not seen and yet have believed; of those who trust him though they are slain; of those who wait the Lord's pleasure; and of those who cannot understand his dealings, but rest on what they know of his heart. This is the beatitude of the unoffended, of those who do not stumble over the mystery of God's dealings with their life.

This blessedness is within our reach also. There are times when we are overpowered with the mystery of life and nature. The world is so full of pain and sorrow, strong hearts seem breaking under an intolerable load. God's children are sometimes the most bitterly tried. For them the fires are heated seven times; they suffer, not only at the hand of man, but the heavens seems as brass to their cries and tears. The enemy of souls has reason to challenge them with the taunt, 'Where is now your God?'

You and I have perhaps been in this plight. We have said, 'Hath God forgotten to be gracious? Has he in anger shut up his tender mercies?' We are tempted to stumble;

Prayer: Forgive our sins, our faithless tears, and our repining murmurs. Lift us on the tide of thy love into fuller, richer, deeper experiences. May we know what it is to have Christ in us, the hope of glory. Amen.

we are prone to fall over the mysteries of God's dealings with us. But it is then that we have the chance of inheriting the new beatitude. If we refuse to bend under the mighty hand of God - questioning, chafing, murmuring at his appointments - we miss the door which would admit us into rich and unalloyed happiness; we fumble about the latch, but it is not lifted. But if we will quiet our souls like a weaned child, anointing our heads and washing our faces, then light will break in on us from the eternal morning. The peace of God will keep our hearts and minds, and we shall enter upon this blessedness of which our Lord speaks.

The Meaning of the Cross
March 22

Faith is not simply an intellectual experience of a statement of fact, but it is our personal trust and confidence in him of whom the fact is true. We are not saved merely because we believe that Jesus Christ died for us on the cross but because *we trust in him* who died. It is the personal touch between Christ and ourselves that causes his life to pass into our nature, making us sound and healthy, as well as secure and safe.

What does the cross mean to you and me? Does it not mean that there our Lord gave himself absolutely to the Father's will. Never in any way did he make himself the origin and fountain of his action, but was ever the empty channel through which God poured himself. 'He humbled himself, and became obedient unto death, even the death of the cross.' It seemed as if he went down lower and lower, on rung after rung of the ladder until he reached Hades, giving up everything only to follow the will of God; but out of the lowest depths God raised him to the eternal throne.

In each one of us there is strong self-will. You say, 'I am resolved to be a good man or woman, to live a noble life, to give up bad habits - I will!' But it can never be accomplished in that way. It is only when we are willing to see ourselves, our own energy, our good self as well as our bad self brought to an end on the cross of Jesus, that we shall be able to enter into and live his eternal life.

At this moment I would summon you to stand beneath the cross and to see there one who entirely yielded up his own will. More than that I want you to see your self-life nailed there, and turn from it to God in adoration, saying that you are prepared to be weak and helpless so far as your own energies are concerned, that he may put forth in your life the mighty energy of that power which raised Christ from the dead. It is only when we are weak that we are really strong; it is only when we surrender ourselves to the power of the cross, so that we realise that we have been crucified with Christ, that we are able to share in his eternal victory over the devil and the power of evil.

'Let this mind be in you, which was also in Christ Jesus' (Philippians 2:5).

Prayer: O God, thou hast revealed thyself to us in thy Son, Jesus Christ our Lord. We love him, because he endured the cross, and despised the shame in order to save us. May we follow him by the way of the cross, bearing his reproach, sharing his griefs, obedient even unto death, that we may also live and reign with him here, and more perfectly at last. Amen.

The Power of Christ's Resurrection
March 23

'Like as Christ was raised up from the dead by the glory of the Father, even so we also should walk in newness of life' *(Romans 6:4).*

The keynote of this inspiring paragraph is life in union with the risen Christ. Behind us lies the death of our Lord, which severed for his people their fellowship with the world. As the voice of praise or blame cannot reach the dead, but are arrested at the fast-closed ears, so it is intended that the murmur of the world should not affect us, but that we should be set only on the will of God.

It is not wise, however, to dwell always on the negations of the Christian life. It is true that they are always present, but to dwell on them is to miss the power by which self-sacrifice and self-denial become easy. Do not live on the *dying* but on the *risen* side of the Saviour's work. Behold him as he goes forth upon his upward way to the throne of glory. Seek to experience union with him in the likeness of his resurrection (Philippians 3:10).

There ought to be a finality in our experience. It is good for us to recognise the break with our past life. It must be clearly defined; we must have done with it for ever. It is possible that we may be tempted, and come temporarily beneath the dominion of old sins; but in principle, like the Israelites, we have passed from Egypt, never to return to it, and the Red Sea of Christ's redemption severs us from our former condition. We do not reckon ourselves to be dead to sin in the sense that our nature is henceforth incapable of sinning. If we think thus, we shall soon be disillusioned, and find that tendencies and strivings are within us which prove the contrary. But we must reckon that we *have* died to sin, and whenever temptation comes, that it has no claim upon us. Nelson turned his blind eye to the signal to retreat from action, and we are to turn blind eyes and deaf ears to the tempter.

The apostle says that we are to present our members as instruments of righteousness to God. Do not look at the tempter, but at Christ; yield the eyes, ears, heart and mind to him, that he may make the best possible use of them; and that which becomes the habitual practice of the outward life will inevitably affect the soul and spirit.

Prayer: Constrained by thy love, O Lord, we would here present ourselves, spirit, soul and body, not to live unto ourselves, but unto thee who didst die and rise again. Amen.

Foolish Excuses
March 24

In this parable our Lord seems to show that the temptations of life lie in three directions.

Our Property. So long as we are pilgrims and strangers, with no settled piece of land to call our own, with no stake in the country, with no accumulation in the bank, we reach out our hands towards the city that hath foundations (Hebrews 11:10, 13). But when we buy a field, we are often preoccupied and engrossed with it, and all it stands for. We must lay it out for building, or plan the crops we are to raise; we think how we can sell it again at some advantage; we hope the railway company may need it. And so, though we may be outwardly punctilious in our religious observance, yet our affections are not set on things above (Colossians 3:1-4).

Our Activities. There is nothing wrong in having a team of oxen; on the contrary, it is a great and noble thing to plough up the virgin soil, and to make corn grow for the sustenance of the toiling millions of our fellow men. The oxen of Christ's time have their counterpart in the machinery of today - the traction engine and the motor car. All these things marvellously preoccupy our minds. Men become so deeply interested, that they have no time or energy for anything else. They may not give an absolute negative to the invitations of Christ, but their urbane and polite excuse covers a practical refusal - 'I pray thee have me excused.'

Our Home and Family Life. Our Lord said no word against these. Did he not honour a wedding feast with his presence and first miracle? But he knows that we are apt to set aside the claims of the spiritual life when we are surrounded by all the joys and comforts of material happiness.

The excuses which were offered were very shallow - the land would not have disappeared if its owner had postponed visiting it for a day; the cattle had surely been proved already, or they would not have been bought. As to the newly-married wife, there was no reason why she should not have accompanied her husband, there was plenty of room for both. Let us respond to the love which Christ offers to us, lest we be refused by him at the last (Hebrews 12:25).

'Come; for all things are now ready. And they all with one consent began to make excuse' (Luke 14:17, 18).

Prayer: We beseech thee, our most gracious God, to preserve us from the cares of this life, lest we be too much entangled therein. Amen.

Music and Dancing!
March 25

'As he came and drew nigh to the house, he heard music and dancing ... And he was angry, and would not go in' (Luke 15:25, 28).

The elder brother heard the sounds of music and dancing as he drew nigh to the house. They were the chord of the house, because they were the chord which was ringing through the heart of the master and father. Every household is more or less attuned to the spirit of those who are at its head. There is a warning here for us not to carry our moods and worries home, lest we lower and depress the tone of all the inmates of our family circle!

The father's joy at the return of his younger son was highly infectious. As the Greek suggests, there were three grades of servants in the house - evidently a great household - and the whole of them were abandoned to exuberant joy. Not a girl who did not smarten up and dress herself in her best; not a lad who did not polish his buttons. The effect was the more remarkable as contrasted with the dark clouds which, during the last few years, had enveloped them all, the reflection of the sorrow of the master.

Prayer: Take from my heart, heavenly Father, all hatred and malice, all envy and jealousy, and everything which would cause a breach between me and others; that nothing may prevent the inflowing of thy love to my heart, and its outflowing towards others. Amen.

But ought there not to have been a similar outburst of joy in respect of the elder brother? Not that he had come back, but that *he had never gone astray*! Not that he was a forgiven wastrel, but that he had never transgressed at any time his father's commandment! But no fatted calf was killed in his honour; no music and dancing celebrated his adherence to the home! Was this quite fair?

But there were compensations. 'Thou art ever with me, and all that I have is thine.' 'If children, then heirs; heirs of God, and joint heirs with Christ.' All things are ours in him. Like Enoch, we may always walk with God and have fellowship with him. The prodigal may have his music and dancing, but is it not better to have a life cultured in love, radiant with peace and joy, unbroken in its even tenor and happiness? No! we will not grudge him one hour of exultation, but give us God's best and sweetest gift - an unclouded heart, rest, serenity, peace, the daily love of God our Father shed abroad within us, as we live in his dear presence!

The Morning Cometh
March 26

Six times these words are repeated, and the one lesson that rings out is that God counts his periods, not as man does from night to night, but from evening till morning. 'Not first the light, and after that the dark; but first the dark, and after that the light.' God saw that each night would end in daylight, and that the end of all the nights and all the days would be the eternal day in which there can be no darkness at all. This is what St John saw: 'There shall be no night there, for the Lord God giveth them light' (Revelation 22:5). The sun of materialism sets in a black ocean, unlit by the star of hope. But as long as God is, we believe that he will make a new heaven and new earth; and from out of what seems disappointing and hopeless he will bring a fairer creation than before. Creation shall participate in the glorious liberty of the sons of God. Watchman, what of the night? The morning cometh! The darkness will finally pass away before the radiance of the dawn, and this because God is God; he is Love and Light and his word creates.

'And the evening and the morning were the first day' (Genesis 1:5).

So it is with the individual. Life may be dark. Sin is darkness; sorrow is darkness; ignorance is darkness, and these three may be part of your daily lot. But the night is far spent, the day is at hand. For you the morning star is in the sky. The education of your soul is like that of a child at school. How hard and difficult those first days, but when the rudiments were mastered; when the discipline had played its part, then were reaped the harvests of sowing, and darkness was turned to day. Be of good cheer! Even in death there is nothing to fear. 'That night they caught nothing; but when the morning was now come, Jesus stood on the shore.' The dark waves, as they break around the boat of your life, are bearing you onward to the morning meal upon the golden sands, where you will find that Love has gone before you with its preparations! It shall be evening and morning and lo! the day without night.

Prayer: O God, the darkness and light are both alike to thee, and the night shineth as the day. Help us to follow thee even through the valley of the shadow, and to trust thee whatever be our lot; until the day dawns, and the shadows flee away. Amen.

'Teaching them to observe all things whatsoever I have commanded you: and, lo, I am with you alway, even unto the end of the world' *(Matthew 28:20).*

There is an added beauty and meaning in these words when we translate the Greek into literal English: *I am with you all the days.* How fresh and vital and inspiring they are! Though familiar household words, they refresh us like the breath of a spring morning laden with the ozone of the sea.

We shrink back from the mysteries of life, and dread its pain, less for ourselves than for those who are so closely twined into our life. We need wisdom, strength, guidance, a brother's love, a Saviour's intercession - but all is here, if only we can appreciate and receive the benediction of the wonderful fact of *the perpetual presence of Christ.*

There are conditions which we must fulfil.

Obedience. If a man keep my words ... I will manifest myself unto him. The path of your life is marked out by the providence of God, either in the levels of ordinary existence, or in some special mission and calling. As you bravely tread it, you become aware of a glorious presence coming to meet you, and walking by your side.

Purity: 'the pure in heart *see* God'. This is the finding of the Holy Grail, of which Tennyson sang!

A quiet heart. I do not say a quiet life - this may be impossible, but a heart free from care, from feverish passion, from the intrusion of unworthy ambition, pride or vanity. The habit of meditating on God's Word helps to induce the quiet heart and devout spirit which realises the Lord's presence. The Bible is like the garden in which the Lord God walked in the cool of the day; read it much and prayerfully, and you will meet him in its glades.

Recollection. There will be times when the sense of his presence will be wafted into your soul. At other times, it is a great secret to say: 'Thou art here, O Lord! I do not feel or enjoy thee. My heart is desolate, but thou art beside me!' Faith, not feeling, is the realising faculty. Without it, you would not have perceived his presence, though you had been beside St John on Patmos; with it we may find him as near in London today, as in Palestine, long years ago!

Prayer: Lord Jesus, thou art with us all the days. Give us eyes to see thee and ears to hear thy voice, that thou mayest become more real than the dearest and closest of our friends. Amen.

The Soul's Amen
March 28

Jeremiah was conscious of the special current of divine energy which was passing into and through his soul. The word had come to him 'from the Lord', and he felt it as a burning fire which he could not contain. He must needs give vent to it, but when it has passed his lips, and he has time carefully to consider it, he answers the divine message by saying - 'So be it, O Lord'!

'Then answered I, and said, Amen, O Lord' (Jeremiah 11:5 RV).

The soul's affirmation. Let us guard against mistakes. It is not always possible to say 'Amen' - Yes - to God, in tones of triumph and ecstasy. Sometimes our response is choked with sobs that cannot be stifled, and soaked with tears that cannot be repressed. It was probably so with Abraham, when he tore himself from Ur of the Chaldees; when he waited weary years for his son; when he climbed the steep of Moriah. These words may be read by some who suffer year after year constant pain, by those whose earthly life is tossed upon the sea of anxiety, over which billows of care and turmoil perpetually roll. It is not improbable that these will protest as to the possibility of saying 'Amen' to God's providential dealings, or they will ask: Of what avail is it to utter with the lips a word against which the whole heart stands in revolt?

In reply, let all such remember that our blessed Lord, in the garden, was content to put his will upon the side of God. He knew it was enough if, in the lower parts of the earth to which his human nature had descended, he was able, unflinchingly to affirm, 'Not as I will, but as thou wilt'.

Dare to say 'Amen' to God's providential dealings. Say it, though heart and flesh fail, and you will find that if the will doth acquiesce, the heart comes ultimately to choose; and as the days pass, some incident, some turn in the road, some concurrence of unforeseen circumstances, will suddenly flash the conviction on the mind and reason that God's way was right, the wisest, and the best. 'What thou knowest not now, thou shalt know hereafter', is the assurance of our Guide. Dare to trust him, and in the strength of that trust to say, 'Amen, O Lord'.

Prayer:
For all things beautiful, and good, and true;
For all things that seemed not good yet turned to good;
For all the sweet compulsions of thy will
That chased, and tried, and wrought us to thy shape -
We thank thee, Lord.

The Child in the Midst
March 29

'He called to him a little child, and set him in the midst of them, and said, Verily I say unto you, Except ye turn, and become as little children, ye shall in no wise enter into the kingdom of heaven' (Matthew 18:2, 3 RV).

Our Lord desired to show wherein true greatness consists. First of all, it begins with *Humility*. Without this, no one can be his disciple (verse 4). A child is naturally humble, until parents and friends begin to spoil it by directing its attention to itself. For us, as for the proud Naaman of old, our flesh must become as a little child. Some people are rather proud of their humility, and expect to be praised for it, but that is not the genuine humility of which Christ speaks.

The next qualification for greatness is *Love*. We must recognise and welcome Christ-like souls, however lowly their lot. What a contrast between the boy, whose pitiful case is described in the previous chapter (17:14-18) and this little child. But to each the Lord Jesus proved himself to be a loving friend. The one he restored to sanity and health, the other he gathered in his arms. Probably the child was standing or playing quite near to him, so that it only needed a very slight gesture to bring him to the Master's side, and he became the text of the sermon that followed. We must not despise one of the least, for they are the objects of Christ's special regard. Our Lord draws aside the veil from the eternal world, and shows that the youngest and weakest ones are they to whom the loftiest angels are allotted as their guardians. The holy ones of the Presence Chamber, who always behold the face of God, are set to watch over the children.

The third step to true greatness is in the disposition which is unsparing of self, and thoughtful for all others. We dare not put a stumbling-block or an occasion to fall before one of Christ's weakest disciples; we must be prepared to cut off the right hand, or pluck out the right eye rather than grieve the Holy Spirit of God. Our attitude about many things which might appear perfectly harmless must be determined by the effect of our influence upon others.

Prayer: Give unto us, O Lord, true humility, a loving and friendly, a holy and a useful manner of life; bearing the burdens of our neighbours, denying ourselves, and studying to benefit others, and to please thee in all things. Amen.

The Perfecting of Christ
March 30

For the long and steep ascent of life, our Father has given us a companion, a captain of the march, a brother, even Jesus our Lord, who passed through the suffering of death, and is now crowned with glory and honour (Hebrews 2:9-11). He has passed along our pathway, and climbed our steep ascents, that he might become our merciful and faithful friend and helper. In this sense he was perfected, and became unto all them that obey him the author of eternal salvation.

As regards his nature, it was impossible for him to be otherwise than perfect. In him all the fulness of the divine nature dwelt without let or hindrance. But since the children partook of flesh and blood, he also himself partook of the same; it behoved him in all things to be made like unto his brethren. To each of us he says: 'I have trodden this path before thee, and know every inch of the way'. Christ is the Great-Heart, the companion for all pilgrim souls.

But if we are to walk with him and realise his eternal salvation, *we must learn to obey*. This is the lesson taught to the scientist by nature. He must be exact, minute, microscopic in his attention and obedience to details. If he should fail in one tiny point, his best-conceived plans and experiments must fail. Exact obedience is essential to the engineer. The slightest inadvertence will clog and stop the mightiest machine that human ingenuity ever invented. It is, however, in the spiritual sphere that disobedience brings the greatest and most momentous catastrophes. We must learn to obey, even in the dark! Not ours to make reply, or to question God's dealings. He withholds his reasons, but demands our obedience.

The strength to obey is God-given. There appeared an angel from heaven to strengthen Christ, and to each of us treading dark and hard paths, that angel comes still. But you never know the angel till you reach your Gethsemane. It is because our Lord learned these things by experience, that he is perfected to impart eternal salvation to every soul of man.

'Though he were a Son, yet learned he obedience by the things which he suffered; And being made perfect, he became the author of eternal salvation unto all them that obey him' (Hebrews 5:8, 9).

Prayer: Eternal Saviour, who knowest each step of this difficult pathway of life, we come to thee for thy gracious help; enable us to obey thy promptings, and in every hour of mortal weakness and fear stand beside us to be our very present help. Amen.

The Life-Giving Stream
March 31

'Every thing shall live whithersoever the river cometh' (Ezekial 47:9). 'And he showed me a river of water of life, bright as crystal, proceeding out of the throne of God and of the Lamb.' (Revelation 22:1 R.V.)

In this wonderful chapter in Ezekiel the influence of restored Israel is compared to a life-giving stream issuing from the divine dwelling place (47:1). When the waters rise in the heart, they flow out, as our Lord promised, in ever-deepening, widening rivers of blessing to mankind (John 4:14; 7:37-39). The *ankles* may mean the steps of daily life; the *knees* our prayers and intercessions; the *loins* our affections and passions. Our influence for God should perpetually deepen and extend. In every life, there must be the unfathomable depth of fellowship with God - 'a river that cannot be passed' (verse 5).

Prayer: O God our Father, the Ocean of Love to whom all streams tend, but in whom there is no ebb! The depth of our need calls to the depth of thy grace, but thy grace is deeper than our need. May we drink deeply of the river of the water of life and overflow in blessing to the thirsty world around. Amen.

APRIL

OUR DAILY WALK OF SINCERITY

I am the Almighty God;
walk before me and be thou perfect
(Genesis 17:1)

The Choice of a Life-Work
April 1

'I am but a little child: I know not how to go out or come in ... Give thy servant an understanding heart' (1 Kings 3:7-9).

We shall never rightly choose our life-course until we are determined to put first things first. Wealth, honour, fame, the surpassing of our rivals, are not the chief things to be considered, or our judgment will be impaired and our vision distorted. It was because Solomon desired and sought the kingdom and glory of God, that he gave him also the things for which he did not ask (1 Kings 3:13; Matthew 6:33).

Impressed by the greatness of his responsibilities, the young king had gone to Gibeon to worship God. He wished to fulfil his opportunities to their highest measure, and to serve his fatherland, but he realised his inefficiency. Do you feel like this? You realise the wonderful opportunities and responsibilities of life in this marvellous age, and long to be of service to God and your fellows, but what can you do? You are but as a little child, and 'know not how to go out or come in'. 'Going out' stands for the active life in the world of men; 'coming in' for the hours spent in the home, in recreation and society. It is like the systole and diastole of the heart's action, which should be alike consecrated to God and of service to man.

Solomon asked for an *understanding* heart, that he might discern between good and bad. We all need this faculty, that we may discriminate between things that look very much alike, but are different in nature and direction (Hebrews 5:14; Philippians 1:9, 10; marg RV). It is not an enduement of intellectual power, but of moral taste and discernment. It has been said, that the difficulty in life is not to discriminate between white and black, but to choose between the different shades of grey. In our fellowships, recreations, literature, business - we are in urgent need of the understanding heart which listens for and heeds the voice of God.

Solomon offered a thousand burnt-offerings upon the altar (1 Kings 3:4). We are required to present our *bodies as living sacrifices unto God*, which is our reasonable service. Our career is often determined by our circumstances, or by our special gifts and talents, and, on the whole, we succeed best in doing what we like best. But if we yield ourselves to do God's will, he will direct our paths.

Prayer: O God, make us diligent in business, fervent in spirit, serving the Lord. May we prove all things, and hold fast to that which is good. Amen.

God's Requirements
April 2

Micah was a man of the people, and a true patriot. In his day, the political outlook was dark in the extreme, and the prophet felt that one thing only could save his country, and that was a deep and widespread revival of religion. To the inquiry of the people as to whether Jehovah desired the sacrifice of animals, or little children, who were immolated by the heathen people around in order to rid their consciences from sin, the answer came that God required something more spiritual and searching: 'He hath shewed thee, O man, what is good, etc.'

'What doth the Lord require of thee, but to do justly, and to love mercy, and to walk humbly with thy God' *(Micah 6:8).*

Let us make this threefold message our own.

To do justly, giving not a fraction less than can be rightly claimed from us. Every one of us must acknowledge the righteous claims of our home-circle, and of our neighbours, and we must adjust these claims, giving each his due.

Let us love mercy. There are some who have perhaps forfeited all claim on our mercy - the prisoner, the fallen, the helpless, our enemies - we must help all these not grudgingly, but cheerfully and willingly. Do not try to love mercy till you begin to *show* it. Dare to step out into a life of selfish beneficence, and as you do so, you will come to love it. St James insists that pure religion as much consists in visiting the widow and fatherless in their affliction as in keeping oneself unspotted from the world.

Let us also walk humbly with God - not lagging behind, nor running before, but walking with him, hand in hand. All down the ages, from Enoch onward, there have been those who walked with God in unstained robes. It is not in sacrifices, or rites, or church-going, or almsgiving, though these will follow afterwards, but in holy and humble living, that the heart of true religion is realised.

Is that all? No! What is to be done for those who have tried and failed, who are conscious of guilt and sin? In the closing verses of this book is the answer. There we learn that God will not only forgive, but will subdue our iniquities. He will turn again and have compassion upon us, and cast all our sins into the depths of the sea. He delighteth in mercy! Who is a God like unto thee?

Prayer: O Lord, may thy all-powerful grace make me as perfect as thou hast commanded me to be. Amen.

The Divided Heart
April 3

'Where your treasure is, there will your heart be also. If thine eye be single, thy whole body shall be full of light' (Matthew 6:21, 22). 'A double minded man is unstable in all his ways' (James 1:8).

The closing paragraphs of Matthew 6 are full of instances of a divided heart. The Greek word for *care* means that which divides. Some are divided by *anxiety*. The anxious soul cannot take a strong straight course, any more than a man can sleep who is wondering whether he has bolted the front door or wound up his watch. Some are divided by *contrariness* - a most difficult and complicated disposition of soul. We would like to be pleasant, helpful, agreeable, and amiable, but are conscious of cross-currents that restrain and make us awkward and disagreeable, and we find ourselves rent between two strong influences, the one to be Christlike and gracious, the other to be distant and angular. Others are divided by *fitful* and *passionate impulses*. Happy are they who can hold them well in check. Even St Paul tells us that he was conscious of these two wills - the better self which longed to do the will of God, and the lower, selfish, passionate self which brought him into subjection. St Augustine tells us that, though the prayers of Monica, his mother, greatly affected him, he was constantly swept back from his ideal by an outbreak of passion.

Bunyan also illustrates the same condition, saying that two selves were at war within him. The devil came and said, 'Sell him!' But he resisted even to blood, saying, 'I won't!' But, as the tempter continued urging 'Sell him!' Bunyan finally yielded, and suffered an agony of remorse, as on the one hand, he accepted Christ as his only hope, and on the other was prepared to barter him away.

A divided heart lacks the first element of strength - it is unstable. The men who leave their mark on the world are those who can say: 'This one thing I do'. But we need more than concentration, we need consecration. We must not only be united in ourselves, we must be united in God. Let us make the prayer of Psalm 86:11, our own: 'O knit my heart unto thee, that I may fear thy name'. Yield yourself to God that he may disunite you from the world, and weave you into his own life.

Prayer: O faithful Lord, grant to us, we pray thee, faithful hearts devoted to thee, and to the service of all men for thy sake. Amen.

The Child Heart
April 4

Our Lord bids us seek the child-heart! Not to be childish, but childlike! It is recorded of the illustrious soldier, Naaman, that after he had washed in the Jordan waters, his flesh came to him as that of a little child. It is a noble combination - the stature and strength of the full-grown man united with the winsome purity and sweetness of a little child. It is not possible for any one of us to attain these two qualities unless we are prepared to pay the price. The orders of rank in the kingdom of heaven are diametrically opposed to those of our earthly kingdoms. Here men are ever striving to rise above their fellows; but in Christ's kingdom they stoop to serve, and in stooping become crowned!

'He called to him a little child, and set him in the midst of them, and said, Verily I say unto you, Except ye turn, and become as little children, ye shall in no wise enter into the kingdom of heaven' (Matthew 18:2, 3 RV).

The King of Glory girded himself with a towel, and kneeling down washed the feet of his disciples, and the nobles in his kingdom are those who have become willing to be the servants of all!

Simplicity, humility, and freedom from self-consciousness are the natural traits of early childhood; alas! that they so quickly learn from us to seek for notice, patronage, and the first place! How happy that little one was as he nestled to the Saviour's heart! Three times over in this chapter the Master speaks about 'these little ones'. How dearly he loved the children, and each time must have pressed the child closer to himself! It was thus that like came to like!

It is the childlike hearts that agree on earth in the symphony of prayer. One may go east and the other west, but beneath the touch of the Spirit of love, they will be of one accord, i.e. in attuned fellowship with each other and with Christ (verses 19, 20). The child-spirit, also, will be willing to forgive and forget (verses 15, 21, 22).

Prayer: Grant, O Lord, that I may become as a little child in thy kingdom. May my heart be filled with thy love, my lips with gentle, helpful words, and my hands with kind, unselfish deeds. Amen.

The Cry of the Heart for Forgiveness
April 5

'Have mercy upon me, O God, according to thy loving-kindness; according to the multitude of thy tender mercies blot out my transgressions' (Psalm 51:1).
'I have blotted out as a thick cloud thy transgressions, and as a cloud thy sins: return unto me; for I have redeemed thee'

This staircase has been trodden by myriads of penitent souls. Few of God's elect saints have passed through life without having painfully climbed its stairs. On the wall opposite the pallet in the cell where St Augustine died, this first verse was set out where his eyes could constantly see it.

The Psalmist uses three words for the forgiveness he craves - that his *transgressions* might be blotted out, like the legends scribbled over the ancient Gospels of the palimpsest; that his *iniquity* should be washed away, as the soil from linen; and that all traces of his past *sin* should be forgiven and cleansed away, even as leprosy in the case of Naaman was so obliterated that his flesh became as a little child. How tenderly Jesus responded to the agonised cry of the leper for cleansing: 'I will, be thou clean!'

How wonderfully these petitions of the soul burdened with the sense of sin are answered! Do you ask to be purged with hyssop? Listen to the voice of God saying: 'I even I, am he that blotteth out thy transgressions for my own sake, and will not remember thy sins'.

Prayer: Let there be no doubt with any one of us that thou dost forgive, even to the uttermost, all those who draw nigh in penitence to thee; that so, those of us who are sad because sinful, may have this day the joy of the Lord. Amen.

He purges us with the blood of Christ, who through the eternal Spirit offered himself without spot to God. Do you ask to be made white as snow? 'These are they who have washed their robes, and made them white in the Blood of the Lamb.' Do you ask to hear joy and gladness? 'It is meet to make merry and be glad, for this, my child was lost and is found.' Do you desire to offer a sacrifice of praise and thanksgiving to God? Give him your broken and contrite heart; think not that he will despise it! The fragrance of a broken box of alabaster fills heaven and earth to this day!

The Blessedness of the Cleansed Soul
April 6

In the last chapter of the book of Revelation there is a very interesting change from the Authorised to the Revised Version, which accentuates a line of thought which cannot be too often emphasised. The AV reads 'Blessed are they that keep *his commandments*, that they may have the right to the tree of life'. The RV reads, *Blessed are they that wash their robes*. May we not be thankful that this is the condition, rather than the absolute keeping of his commandments, which might induce legalism and pharisaism into our character and experience. We are very conscious of our sin day by day, but as we wash our robes and make them white through the blood of the Lamb, we may approach the tree of life and eat of its fruit.

There are two other references to the tree of life in this wonderful chapter. In verse 2, we are told that it yields each month the food appropriate for the month; in verse 19, we learn that each of us has a distinct and individual part in that tree. Its leaves are for our healing, and its fruit is suited to every phase of human experience. The tree of life was originally planted in Paradise together with the tree of knowledge (Genesis 2:9). As the latter fed the soul-life of our first parents, with knowledge of good and evil, so the former stood for the life of the spirit nurtured and fed by the Spirit of God.

When we learn of its monthly yield, are we not reminded that whatever each passing experience of human life may require, it will be met out of the fullness of the divine supplies. January days with their new resolves and hopes! February days with storms and frosts! May days with the flowers of hope! June days with warmth and light. September days of fruition! December days of sickness or old age! But whatever month or day there is always a supply of adequate and suitable grace to be obtained from the fellowship of our dear Lord. He is the completement of every need, and perhaps we are led through these varying experiences in order to give the opportunity of learning phases and utilizing resources in our Saviour, of which, otherwise, we should have known nothing.

'Wash me throughly from mine iniquity, and cleanse me from my sin' (Psalm 51:2). 'Blessed are they that wash their robes' (Revelation 22:14 RV).

Prayer: Give us grace, O Lord, to come to thee for daily cleansing, and for all our needs in the various circumstances through which we are called to pass, that by our holy living we may glorify thee in our daily life. Amen.

The Bible as a Safeguard
April 7

Thy word have I hid in mine heart, that I might not sin against thee' (P s a l m 119:11).

The prayer: 'Teach me thy statutes' occurs eight times in this wonderful psalm. It may be said to be its keynote. God's statutes are the path of purity. If a young man will take heed to them, his way will be cleansed. The passage of the Word of God through the heart, like the running of clean water through a pipe, will purify it. Constant study of the Bible is the condition of soul-health.

Consecration is closely associated with Bible study (verse 10). Holiness is *wholeness* - that is, the whole-hearted devotion of a whole nature to God, the consecration of every power to his service. This leads us to lean hard on God, and to seek his companionship and fellowship. Verse 11 tells us of a good thing laid up in a good place, and the result. In the midst of a London season, and amid the stir and turmoil of a political crisis, William Wilberforce wrote in his diary: 'Walked from Hyde Park Corner, repeating the 119th Psalm in great comfort;' John Ruskin said, 'It is strange that of all the pieces of the Bible which my mother taught me, that which cost me most to learn, and which to my child's mind was most repulsive, the 119th Psalm has now become, of all, the most precious to me in its glorious passion for the law of God.'

The study of the Bible enables us to bear witness for God (verse 13). An inspector on one of our railways once told me that he had a vision of God whilst studying his Bible and kneeling in prayer. From this he went to his duties on the station platform. At one end of the train, a man offered him some whisky, but he was able to answer, 'I have had a better drink than that', and pointed him to the water of life (John 4:14; Revelation 22:17). At the other end of the train, another man asked him for a *testament*, the slang phrase for a pack of cards, and my friend was able to pass on to him a Pocket Testament! It is when the word of God fills the heart that it overflows through the lips and actions, and it is what flows over from us that really helps and blesses our fellow-men. '*Out of him* shall flow rivers of living water.' Let us live in fellowship with God through his word. This will light up our life with gladness, amid many sorrows. Wait not for heaven, but here and now, day by day, be joyful in heart and life (14-16).

Prayer: Open thou mine eyes, that I may behold wondrous things out of thy law. Amen.

The Assurance of Salvation
April 8

Salvation is a great word. It is conjugated in three tenses:

The Past Tense. We were saved at the moment when we first trusted Christ. This salvation is a distinct and definite matter, which is ours at the moment we exercise simple faith in Jesus. 'Being now justified by his blood, we shall be saved from wrath through him' (Romans 5:9).

The Present Tense. 'To us who are *being saved*, Christ is the power of God', such is the accurate rendering of 1 Corinthians 1:18. We are being saved perpetually from the love and power of sin. The disinfectant of Christ's presence is ever warding off the germs of deadly temptation. The mighty arm of the divine Keeper is always holding the door against the attempts of the adversary. The water is always flowing over the eye to remove the tiny grit or mote that may alight. 'We are being saved by his life' (Romans 5:10).

The Future Tense. We are being kept by the power of God unto a salvation which waits to be revealed in the last time (1 Peter 1:5).

Salvation is a great word. It includes the forgiveness that remembers our sin no more; deliverance from the curse and penalty of our evil ways; emancipation from the thrall of evil habit; the growing conformity of the soul to the image of Christ, and the final resurrection of the body in spiritual beauty and energy, to be for ever the companion and vehicle of the redeemed spirit.

'If thou shalt confess with thy mouth the Lord Jesus, and shalt believe in thine heart that God hath raised him from the dead, thou shalt be saved' (Romans 10:9).

Prayer: O blessed Spirit of God, we pray thee to give us the assurance of being the children of God, the sons and daughters of the Lord God Almighty; and so prepare us for the glory to be revealed to us, and for that great hour when the whole creation, which now groans and travails in pain, shall be delivered from the bondage of corruption into the glorious liberty of the children of God. Amen.

Our Glorious Standing!
April 9

'There is, therefore, now no condemnation to them which are in Christ Jesus' (Romans 8:1).

The characteristics of this glorious standing.

It is present: 'Now'. If we are in Christ, we need not wait in doubts and fears for the verdict of the great white throne. Its decisions cannot make our standing more clear, or our acceptance more sure, but we shall learn there the meaning of God's dealings with mankind, and triumph in the successful vindication of his ways. We can never be more free from the condemnation of God's righteous law than we are at this present.

It is certain: 'There is no condemnation'. You must catch this accent of conviction, and be able to speak with no faltering voice of your assured acceptance with God, if you would enter upon the rich inheritance of this chapter, to which these opening words stand as the door of passage. The shadow of a peradventure cannot live in the light of that certainty of which the apostle speaks.

It is invariable. There are some who live on a sliding scale between condemnation and acceptance. If health is buoyant and the heart is full of song, they are sure of their acceptance with God; but if the sun is darkened and the clouds return, when the heart is dull and sad, they imagine that they are under the ban of God's displeasure. They forget that our standing in Christ Jesus is one thing; our appreciation and enjoyment of it quite another. Your own heart may condemn you; memory, the great recorder of the soul, may summon from the past evidence against you; the great accuser of souls may lay against you grievous and well-founded charges; your tides of feeling may ebb far down the beach; your faith may become weak and lose its power and grip; your sense of unworthiness may become increasingly oppressive - none of these things can touch your acceptance with God if you are complying with his one all-inclusive condition - 'no condemnation to them which are *in Christ Jesus*'. This mystic union with the Son of God is only possible to faith working by love (1 John 3:23, 24).

Prayer: We commit ourselves to thy care and keeping this day; let thy grace be mighty in us, and sufficient for us, and let it work in us both to will and to do of thine own good pleasure, and grant us strength for all the duties of the day. Amen.

The Indwelling of the Spirit
April 10

It is of the utmost importance to know that we have been born from above of the incorruptible seed of God's implanted nature. How can we be quite sure that we are the sons and daughters of the Lord God Almighty? The beloved apostle gives us many assurances in the first epistle of St John.

'Ye are not in the flesh, but in the Spirit, if so be that the Spirit of God dwell in you. Now if any man have not the Spirit of Christ, he is none of his' (Romans 8:9).

If we are the children of God *we shall be content to be unknown of the world* (1 John 3:1). The leaders and rulers of society may view us with contempt, as they did our Lord, but we shall refuse to enter into any alliance with the children of the world, and shall lose our taste for the things that used to appeal to us.

We shall be very sensitive to the leading of the Holy Spirit, as Philip was when he tore himself away from the revival in Samaria, to go to a lonely spot in the desert, and there await the arrival of the Ethiopian statesman. There was no hesitation in his obedience to the command: 'Arise, and go toward the south ... and he arose and went' (Acts 8:26-40). Are we being obedient to the call and command of our Lord to tell the good tidings of the gospel to those who have never heard? Or do we make all sorts of excuses for our apathy?

We shall certainly love the brethren (1 John 3:14). We may begin by loving them with our strength, and by sacrificing ourselves on their behalf, but we shall pass through the different phases of self-sacrifice until at last we come to love with the Spirit of Christ.

We shall be very sensitive for the honour of our Lord, and when men speak ill of him we shall hasten to avow our discipleship and devotion.

Prayer: O God, make me increasingly conscious of the indwelling of thy Holy Spirit; may he witness with my spirit that in spite of all my sins and shortcomings, I am still thy child. Amen.

We shall be very sensitive about sin. Directly we have offended against the law of love, we shall be restless and unhappy until we have confessed and been forgiven and cleansed. We shall hasten at once to our merciful and faithful High Priest that he may remove the stain. An old Puritan once said that a sow and a sheep might fall into the same miry pit; the one would wallow in it, whilst the other would never rest until it was extricated and cleansed!

The Sevenfold Work of God's Spirit
April 11

'The Spirit of the Lord shall rest upon him, the spirit of wisdom and understanding, the spirit of counsel and might, the spirit of knowledge, and of the fear of the Lord' (Isaiah 11:2).

We have in this chapter a wonderful forecast of our Saviour's person and work; and probably no other single paragraph in the Old Testament seems to sum up so perfectly the sevenfold work of God's Holy Spirit. The stock of Jesse might seem to be cut down to its roots, but it would yield the Messiah. The mother of our Lord was so poor that she could only offer the two pigeons of the humblest and poorest, as the expression of her thanksgiving at his birth, but he was conceived of the Holy Spirit, and in his baptism was anointed and empowered for service by the same Spirit.

Notice the beautiful alternative rendering of verse 3 in the Revised Version. 'His delight shall be in the fear of the Lord.' In the margin the literal meaning of 'delight' is 'scent'! The phrase might be translated: 'He shall draw his breath in the fear of the Lord'. Our Saviour, though living in this world, was never infected by evil surroundings. Let us seek to live like this - in the world, but not of it! We know instinctively when we inhale the foetid air of certain places and society. What a difference there is in the pure ozone of the ocean or the breath of the hills! If our lot is to be cast amid the murky atmosphere of the great city, let us be more careful to inbreathe the pure air of Holy Scripture and prayer.

Prayer: Lord Jesus, tenant of our hearts; fill us with thy Holy Spirit, and fit us for that new life when all evil passions shall be subdued, and the knowledge of thy redeeming love shall flow over the world as the waters cover the ocean-bed! Amen.

The Holy Spirit of God anoints for service by descending *upon* us, and then builds up within us his sixfold grace. We all need wisdom in the spirit, and understanding in the intellect; we all need counsel and direction as to our life purpose, and might to execute the divinely-given plan; we all need to become students in the knowledge of God, and in devout reverence. Why should we not make each of these the subject of our special dealing with the Paraclete, who gives freely to all who will yield their wills, minds, and lives to his control (Galatians 5:22). Then all creation will respond to us; there will be a new beauty in heaven above and earth beneath, the preface and augury of that new creation which shall emerge when our Saviour returns to bring in the millennium of blessedness and peace.

God's Challenge to Man
April 12

In this mighty chapter, God seems to draw near to the perplexed and stricken soul, who sits brooding over the problems of human life, and points out that mysteries equally insoluble are above his head and under his feet; that he lives and moves amongst them. Man frets and despairs over a mystery forced upon him by sorrow and loss. He cannot interpret it, and is shaken to the heart; but the whole universe teems with mystery. Man cannot explain the creation of the world, the separation of sky and earth, the reflex influences of the one on the other. Light and darkness, wind and rain, snow and ice, storm and sunshine; the instincts of the animal creation - these defy man's absolute understanding.

But who frets at the inscrutable mystery which enshrouds these natural phenomena! We use all of them, and make them serve our purpose.

We cannot be surprised therefore, if we discover similar mysteries in God's dealings with ourselves. He does not answer our questions by always telling us his secret reasonings. His thoughts and ways are as much higher than ours, as the heavens are higher than the earth, and we could not more understand his reasons than tiny children can the mysteries of human life. But behind all mystery the Father's heart is beating, and a Father's voice is pleading, that we should trust him. 'Little children, you cannot understand, but you are infinitely dear to me; I have many things to say to you, but you cannot bear them now; "what I do, thou knowest not now, but thou shalt know hereafter." Trust me, and "let not your heart be troubled, neither let it be afraid".'

'Where wast thou when I laid the foundations of the earth? Declare if thou hast understanding' (Job 38:4).

Prayer: O God, there are so many mysteries in the world, and in human life, and our eyes grow tired with straining into the darkness. Help us to believe in thy unchanging love, and to trust where we cannot see or understand. Amen.

'The Lord's portion is his people' (Deuteronomy 32:9).

'According as he hath chosen us in him before the foundation of the world, that we should be holy and without blame before him in love' (Ephesians 1:4).

We do not become God's property when we consecrate ourselves to him, but only awake to see that we are already his, and assume that manner of life which they should live who are not their own, but have been bought with a price (1 Corinthians 6:19, 20). The three symbols of God's care of his own, as enumerated by Moses in his Song, are exquisitely beautiful.

'He kept him as the apple of his eye' (verse 10). Almost instinctively we raise our hand to protect the eyes if anything threatens us, and it is thus with God's care to us. How carefully the eye is preserved from impurity and evil by the strong bony socket in which it is set, by the eyebrows and lashes which catch the dust and grit, by the eyelid closing over, and the tear-water washing it. Thus the soul which God loves may pass through the evil of the world without taint or soil, because of his gracious keeping power.

'As an eagle' (verse 11). When the young eaglets are able to fly, but hover about their nest, unwilling to venture from the cliff, the mother-bird breaks up their eyrie home, drives the fledglings forth on to the air, compels them to use their wings, flutters beneath to catch them if they are inclined to fall, and bears them up on her strong wings until they can fly alone. So it is in life that sometimes God has to break up the happy conditions to which we have been accustomed from our birth, and drive us forth. But it is for our good since only so can we acquire the glorious powers of sustained flight on the wings of the wind.

Divine leading (verse 12). God teaches us to go as a mother her little child; his hand leads and guides our tottering steps (Hosea 11:3, 4).

The epistle to the Ephesians gives us a list of the blessings, like a string of pearls, which God our Father, the Owner and Lover of our souls, heaps upon us, and is waiting for us to appropriate and use (1:3). His love to us is no passing fancy, but the carrying out of an eternal purpose. He redeems us from the love and power of sin; he abounds towards us with the riches of his grace; we are kept and sealed by the Holy Spirit; and ultimately, shall be presented before him, without blemish, to the praise of his glory.

Prayer: What can I lack if I have thee, who art all good? Verily the heart is restless, until it rest in thee alone. Amen.

Weighed in the Balances
April 14

Our Lord's ministry began with an octave of blessedness, but it ended with a sevenfold woe, which he pronounced on the religious leaders of his time. He did not threaten, but pronounced the inevitable outworking of their evil ways.

Men often quote the punishment that follows sin as indicating some harsh or vindictive sentiment on the part of the divine Being. They do not understand that, whereas human sentences are often arbitrary, God's judgments are natural, i.e. they are the inevitable result of wrong-doing. The penalty is part of the constitution of the universe. The final judgment of the great white throne will only announce the penalty which man's sin has produced.

God is merciful as well as just, but if a man will tamper with explosives, he does not save his face or limbs. Our Lord was not animated by personal invective when he pronounced the terrible judgments of this chapter. There were tears of sorrow in his voice as he said, this temple is no longer my Father's house, but 'your house which is left unto you desolate'.

We read of the 'Wrath of the Lamb', but it is the counterpart of love; not vindictive wrath, but the bitterness of disappointed love! Notice the gleam of light at the end of this chapter. Jesus seemed to hear the welcome which would be accorded to him in that day when he shall finally appear to vindicate and save his brethren according to the flesh (verse 39).

'O Jerusalem ... how often would I have gathered thy children together, even as a hen gathereth her chickens under her wings, and ye would not!' (Matthew 23:37).

Prayer: O Lord, make us, we implore thee, so to love thee that thou mayest be to us a Fire of Love, purifying and not destroying. Amen.

My Guest-Chamber
April 15

'The Master saith, Where is my guest-chamber, where I shall eat the passover with my disciples?' (Mark 14:14 RV).

There has evidently been a previous understanding between our Lord and the good man of the house, who was probably a devoted friend and follower. Jesus knew that his death was being plotted by the chief priests and that Judas desired to betray him that very night. He wanted to take part in the Passover supper, and therefore did not tell the two disciples, whom he sent to prepare the supper where it was to be held, lest any should overhear, and his arrest should take place. The locality of that last gathering with his disciples was revealed to the two by the sign of the man bearing the pitcher of water when they reached Jerusalem, and only to the remainder of the party when they actually arrived.

Our Lord knew what treachery meant in the home circle. You may be experiencing this. Your familiar friend, in whom you trust, may be absolutely unreliable - a sieve through which your secret confidences filter, or an adder waiting to sting! But Christ experienced this also, and suffered as we all do, from the feeling of restraint in the presence of one who is unsympathetic and critical (John 13:31).

Jesus knew what devoted friendship means. What he could not confide to the band of apostles he was able to make known to the good man of this house. They had evidently conferred together and arranged that this room should be at the Master's disposal, furnished and prepared for his reception.

Our Lord asks us for the use of our guest-chamber. He still stands at the door and knocks, saying, 'If any will open the door, I will come in and sup with him, and he with me'. There is a room in each heart, which he covets for himself. The Revised Version inserts the word '*my*'. We are his by right of creation and redemption; let us be his by choice. Having given the guest-chamber of our heart to him, may we go on to give our spare room to his disciples, and our loving hospitality to those who go forth for the sake of his name (3 John 5-8).

Prayer

Is there a thing beneath the sun
That strives with thee my heart to share?
Ah, tear it thence, and reign alone,
the Lord of every motion there.

Amen.

Keeping Step!
April 16

A yoke is for two! All through his earthly life Jesus was saying: 'Come, take my yoke!' *What was his yoke*? It was surely his desire to do the Father's will. This was the watchword of his life (John 5:30; 6:38). So persuasive was his appeal, that the sons of Zebedee left their father and boat; Andrew and Simon their fishing-nets; and Matthew his toll-booth to become his disciples. Women forsook their sins, and men their ambitions, in order to become his humble friends, and followers. Saul, the proud young Pharisee, heard his appeal, and abandoning everything that might lead to high honour and worldly success, counted it his highest glory to be associated with Christ in redeeming a lost world.

'Come unto me; Take my yoke upon you, and learn of me; For my yoke is easy, and my burden is light' (Matthew 11:28-30).

But this association or fellowship requires *agreement*, identity of purpose. 'Can two talk together except they be agreed?' (Amos 3:3). Hence there can be no fellowship between light and darkness; between the Christian soul and the unbeliever (2 Corinthians 6:14-18; 1 John 1:6, 7).

The yoke means subsoil ploughing. The salvation of a lost world or of one human soul is no child's play. Christ saw before him the hard surface of mankind, the spirit of man caked over by long years of neglect and resistance. Before salvation can be effected, the subsoil has to be turned up, and the thoughts of many hearts revealed (Jeremiah 17:9,10).

The yoke means fellowship. The divine and the human united in feeding the five thousand; in turning the water into wine; in the raising of Lazarus! There has never been an island redeemed from cannibalism to service for Christ, or a paralytic cleansed and healed, apart from the cooperation of the divine and human.

Yoke-bearing anticipates the harvest. So we plough the furrow in hope, knowing that one day the harvest will be ripe, and one like unto the Son of Man will thrust in his sharp sickle and reap. What joy to share in that harvest-home!

Prayer: The fetters thou imposest, O Lord, are wings of freedom. Put round about my heart the cord of thy captivating love. Bind me to thyself as thou bindest the planets to the sun, that it may become the law of my nature to be led by thee. Amen.

'Be content with such things as ye have; for he hath said, I will never leave thee, nor forsake thee' (Hebrews 13:5).

Such things as ye have - plus! The Greek literally means that there is within us an undeveloped power only awaiting the call, and there will be enough. I may be speaking to people who wish that they had more money, or more brains, or more influence. They dream of the lives they would live, of the deeds they would do, if only they were better circumstanced. But God says No! You have present within the narrow confines of your own reach the qualities that the world is wanting. Use them, and be content with the things that you have. You have never explored the resources of your own soul.

'Such things as ye have' - Moses had only a rod, but a rod with God can open the Red Sea. David had only five pebbles, but these with God brought down Goliath. The woman had only a little pot of oil, but that pot of oil with God paid all her debts. The poor widow was scraping the bottom of the barrel, but with God the handful of meal kept her child, herself, and the prophet until the rain came. The boy had only five tiny loaves and two small fish, but with Jesus they were enough for five thousand men, beside women and children. Estimate what you have got, and then count God into the bargain! He never lets go your hand. He will never leave nor forsake those that trust in him!

Therefore be content! The most glorious deeds that have blessed and enriched the world have not been done by wealthy men. Our Lord had none of this world's goods; the apostles had neither silver nor gold; Carey was only a poor cobbler; Bunyan a travelling tinker; Wesley left two silver spoons. It is not money, but human love and God that is needed. Therefore do not be covetous; do not hoard, but give! Be strong and content. With good courage say: 'The Lord is my Helper; I will not fear' - for life or death, for sorrow or joy!

Prayer

The soul that to Jesus has fled for repose,
He cannot, he will not, desert to its foes.
That soul, though all hell should endeavour to take,
He'll never, no never, no never forsake!

Amen.

Praise and Prayer
April 18

What raptures there are here! It reminds one of a lark at dawn filling regions of air with music which threatens to rend its tiny throat. The psalmist is in fellowship with God. He is enjoying his prayer and praise so much that it seemed to him as though all flesh must wake up to enjoy it also. His iniquities and transgressions are purged away. He feels that God is causing him to approach into his secret place, and all nature takes on a new radiance and beauty.

'Praise waiteth for thee, O God, in Sion; and unto thee shall the vow be performed. O thou that hearest prayer, unto thee shall all flesh come' (Psalm 65: 1, 2).

The personal pronouns for God - thou, thee, thy, occur at least twenty times in thirteen verses! We remember that Wordsworth speaks of a presence that rolls through all things: 'A sense sublime of something deeply interfused, whose dwelling is the light of setting suns, and the round ocean, and the living air, and the blue sky - a motion and a spirit.' The poet was a lover of the meadows, and the woods, and the mountains!

To many of us, also, nature seems but the slight covering or garment, which only partially conceals the glory and beauty of God's presence. The bush still burns with fire. The mountain-heights are filled with the horses and chariots of angelic guardians. 'The heavens declare the glory of God, and the firmament sheweth his handiwork.' There is no voice or language that the ordinary sense of man can detect, but when our hearts are clean, and our ears open, we realise that we are in touch with him whom some day we shall see face to face, but who even now reveals himself to the pure in heart (Matthew 5:8).

Prayer: O God our heavenly Father, renew in us the sense of thy gracious presence, and let it be a constant impulse within us to peace, trustfulness, and courage on our pilgrimage. Amen.

Love's Confidence!
April 19

'His sisters sent unto him saying, Lord, behold he whom thou lovest is sick' (John 11:3).

The lapse of years made it possible for the apostle to draw aside the veil which curtained the happy friendship and fellowship of Christ in the home at Bethany. It was the one green oasis in the rugged wilderness through which he passed to the cross!

There were diversities in that home - Martha, practical, energetic, and thoughtful for all that could affect the comfort of those she loved and served; Mary, gifted with spiritual insight and tender sympathy; Lazarus, probably a man of few words, quiet and unobtrusive, but Jesus loved each one (verse 5).

The sisters never doubted that Christ would speed at all hazards to save Lazarus after the breathless messenger had brought the tidings of his sickness. Anything less than infinite love would have rushed instantly to the relief of those troubled hearts; divine love alone could hold back the impetuosity of the Saviour's tender heart until the Angel of Pain had finished her work. He wanted to teach his disciples never-to-be-forgotten lessons, and also he was eager for the spiritual growth of the faith of the sisters.

This chapter might be more truly known as 'The Raising of Martha', for our Lord enabled her, matter-of-fact and practical as she was, to realise that he was the resurrection and the life. He insisted that *her faith* was an essential condition in the raising of her brother to life. The emphasis is on the word '*thou*' (verse 40). Our Lord always needs the cooperating faith of some true heart to be with him when he works a miracle, and he chose the least likely of the two sisters to supply the pivot on which he could rest the lever of his divine help. As she withdrew her objections to the removal of the stone, her faith suddenly became capable of claiming the greatest of Christ's miracles.

He calls to us also to help our brethren. In many cases those who have received life from Christ are still bound about with grave-clothes - old habits and evil associations cling to them and impede their progress, and he bids us 'Loose him and let him go'. He asks for our cooperation in the emancipation of those who have been held fast in the power of the evil one.

Prayer: O God, we rejoice that we can turn to thee in the midst of great anxiety and commit all our troubles to thy sure help. As thou art with us in the sunlight, be thou with us in the cloud. Sustain us by thy near presence and let the comforts which are in Jesus Christ fill our hearts with peace. Amen.

Life Abundant: Grace Abounding
April 20

Notice that word '*Receive*'! We first receive forgiveness, or reconciliation, then abundance of grace (verses 11, 17). We cannot merit or earn either one or the other; all that we have to do is to *take* what God offers, by an act of the will which accepts and appropriates. If men are lost, it is because they refuse to receive the grace and love of God, secured to us, in spite of our failure and sin, through the second Adam. We must believe that we have received, even when we are not conscious of any new experience (John 1:12). It is a blessed thing, when our emotional life is at a low ebb, and we feel out of sorts, to receive, to inbreathe, to drink in the 'abundance of grace', and to know that life is working in us in power.

'For if by one man's offence death reigned by one; much more they which receive abundance of grace, and of the gift of righteous- ness, shall reign in life by one, Jesus Christ' (Ro- mans 5:17).

There is no limit to the abundance of God's supply - it *abounds*! The apostle keeps using that word, which really means 'running over' (verses 15, 17, 20). And the result of receiving more and more out of God's fullness, is that we reign, not in the future life, but in this. Ours becomes a royal, a regnant, a triumphant life.

This glorious life in which we are daily victorious over sin, daily using and scattering the unsearchable riches of Christ, daily helping others up to the throne-life, is within the reach of every reader of these words. God wants you to enter upon it; he has made every provision for it, and is at this moment urging you to enter upon it. The only thing for you to do is to receive the abundance of his grace and the gift of righteousness. Open your heart and life and he will fill it; dare to believe that he has filled it, even though you don't feel it; and go forth to live a royal life, distributing the largesse of his royal bounty!

But we must pour out as God pours in! Only so will he be able to trust us with his fullness. Our love to others, our willingness to help them, our forgivingness and patience must go to the point of self-exhaustion, if we would know the abundant life and the grace that flows over.

Prayer

For souls redeemed, for sins forgiven;
For means of grace, and hopes of heaven,
Father, what can to Thee be given,
Who givest all?

Amen.

'Now when Daniel knew that the writing was signed, he went into his house; and his windows being open in his chamber toward Jerusalem, he kneeled upon his knees three times a day, and prayed, and gave thanks before his God, as he did aforetime' (Daniel 6:10).

The chosen hour. It was at the time when Daniel's enemies appeared to have accomplished his downfall and death - 'when the writing was signed' - that this heroic statesman knelt down and prayed, and gave thanks to God. These are times when prayer is the only way out of our perplexities.

George Muller said: 'Our very weakness gives opportunity for the power of the Lord Jesus Christ to be manifested. That blessed one never leaves and never forsakes us. The greater the weakness, the nearer he is to manifest his strength; the greater our necessities, the more have we ground to rely on it that he will prove himself our Friend. This has been my experience for more than seventy years; the greater the trial, the greater the difficulty, the nearer the Lord's help. Often the appearance was as if I must be overwhelmed, but it never came to it, and it never will. More prayer, more faith, more exercise of patience, will bring the blessing. Therefore our business is just to pour out our hearts before him, and help in his own time and way is sure to come.'

The chosen direction. 'His windows open towards Jerusalem.' There the holy temple had stood, and the altar of incense; there God had promised to put his name and meet his people. When we pray, our windows must be open towards our blessed Lord, who ministers for us in heaven, mingling the much incense of his intercession with the prayers of all saints (Hebrew 7:25; Revelation 8:3).

The chosen attitude. 'He kneeled upon his knees.' It is most appropriate to kneel before God in homage and worship. St Paul bowed his knees, even though his hands were chained, to the Father of our Lord Jesus Christ (Ephesians 3:14). But we can pray also as we walk, or sit, or ride. Nehemiah flashed a prayer to the God of heaven before he answered the king's question, but he also prayed before God day and night. Let us contract the habit of praying and giving thanks three times a day. At even, morning, and noon, let God hear your voice.

Prayer
Thee we would be always blessing,
Serve thee as thy hosts above;
Pray, and praise thee without ceasing
Glory in thy perfect love.

Amen.

The Midnight Wrestle
April 22

Such is our mortal life! We meet angels before we encounter our Esaus! Their unseen squadrons must be counted on as one of our permanent assets.

'Oh purblind souls! We may not see our helpers in their downward flight, nor hear the sound of silver wings, slow beating through the hush of night.' But they are surely present (Psalm 34:7; Hebrews 1:14). If we accustom ourselves to their presence and help, we may presently come, like Jacob, to an experience of the eternal, before which all else will dwindle into insignificance. When our Rachels and Leahs, the babble of the children, the lowing of the herds are away; when the only sound is the low murmur of the brook, or the sigh of the night wind; when the sense of loneliness steals over the spirit, and the starry hosts expand overhead, it is then that we may come into personal contact with one, whose delights from of old were with the sons of men. He is the Word of God, but he is also the Saviour, the Lover and Friend of man.

In our first meeting, he will wrestle with us to break down our stubbornness; he will touch the sinew of our strength till we can hold out no more; he will withdraw from us till we insist that we cannot let him go; he will awaken a mysterious longing and urgency within us, which he alone can satisfy. And as the memorable interview ends, he will have taught us that we prevail best when we are at our weakest, and will have whispered in our ear, in response to our entreaty, his own sublime name - Shiloh - the Giver of eternal peace!

Why should you not meet that Angel, and let him make you a prince?

'Jacob went on his way, and the angels of God met him ... And Jacob was left alone; and there wrestled a man with him until the breaking of the day' (Genesis 32:1, 24).

Prayer: Be not weary of me, good Lord. I am all weakness, but thou art almighty, and canst put forth thy strength perfectly in my weakness. Make me truly to hate all which thou hatest, fervently to love all which thou lovest - through Jesus Christ. Amen.

The Guidance of the Holy Spirit
April 23

'They assayed to go into Bithynia; and the Spirit of Jesus suffered them not. And a vision appeared to Paul in the night; There was a man of Macedonia, standing beseeching him, and saying, Come over into Macedonia, and help us' (Acts 16:7-10).

The Spirit of Jesus often shuts doors in the long corridors of life. We pass along, trying one after another, but find that they are all locked, in order that we may enter the one that he has opened for us (Revelation 3:7, 8). Sometimes in following the Spirit's guidance we seem to come to a blank wall. The little missionary band found themselves facing the sea. They had not contemplated crossing to Europe, but there seemed no other course open. They walked to and fro on the sea-wall or landing-stage looking over the restless waves, and noticing the strange costumes of sailors and travellers who had gathered in the thriving sea-port, which bore the name famous to all the world for the Siege of Troy.

It was with such thoughts in his heart that St Paul slept that night in his humble lodging, and in his dreams, a man from Macedonia, like one he had seen on the quay, stood and beckoned to him (verse 10 RV).

Where it is possible for the judgment to arrive at a right conclusion, on the suggestions that may be supplied by the divine Spirit, we are left to think out the problems of our career. Within your reach are the materials needed for formulating a correct judgment; use them, balance the pros and cons, and looking up to God to prevent you from making a mistake, act. When once you have come to a decision, in faith and prayer, go forward, not doubting or looking back.

Prayer: O God, since we know not what a day may bring forth, but only that the hour for serving thee is always present, may we wake to the instant claims of thy holy will; not waiting for tomorrow, but yielding today. Consecrate with thy presence the way our feet may go; and the humblest work will shine, and the roughest places be made plain. Amen.

A small door may lead to a vast opportunity. St Paul might have been discouraged by his reception in Europe. He looked for the man whom he had seen in the vision, but the only trace they could find of the worship of God was the gathering together of a few women. How startled they must have been by the sudden appearance of these missionaries, but a mighty work for God began in the life of at least one of them 'whose heart the Lord opened'. Let us not despise the smallest opening, for we can never tell into what a wide place it may conduct us.

Spiritual Dimensions
April 24

The cube was evidently a favourite unit of Hebrew measurement. The Holy of Holies was a cube, and so was the New Jerusalem, the Holy City, which St John saw in a vision, 'coming down from God out of heaven'. We are reminded of the length, and breadth, and depth, and height of the love of Christ which passeth knowledge (Ephesians 3:18). Ought not this to be the measurement of every well-ordered life?

There must be *Length* - i.e. the issuing forth of the soul as it leaves the things that are behind and reaches forth to those that are before. We must never be satisfied with that whereunto we have already attained, or think that we are perfect.

But with length there must be *Breadth*. Our life must reach out on the right and left to help others. The cross stands for unselfishness, and those who claim to have been crucified with Christ must live, not to themselves, but *to him* who died for them and *through him* for all that he cares and loves. The world is full of lonely, weary and desolate lives, to whom Christ would send us if we were ready for his use.

There must also be *Depth*. We must dwell deep! The apostle says *rooted* - i.e. we must strike our roots into the subsoil; *grounded* - we must have our foundations in the very depths of a life hidden with Christ. From his life we must arise as fountains spring from the depths of the hills. Tree roots need to spread as far underground as the branches above.

There must be *Height*. Our ideals should always be rising. We must fix our affections on things *above*, not on things on the earth. Let us by thought and prayer thither ascend and dwell where Christ sits on the right hand of God (Colossians 3:1-4).

'And the city lieth foursquare ... the length, and the breadth, and the height of it are equal' (Revelation 21:16).

Prayer: O eternal God, sanctify my body and soul, my thoughts and my intentions, my words and actions; let my body be a servant of my spirit, and both body and spirit servants of Jesus; that doing all things for thy glory here, I may be partaker of thy glory hereafter, through Jesus Christ our Lord. Amen.

Cultivating Cheerfulness
April 25

'A merry heart is a good medicine (causeth good healing); but a broken spirit drieth up the bones' (Proverbs 17:22). 'Rejoice alway; pray without ceasing; in everything give thanks' (1 Thessalonians 5:16, 17 RV).

A happy and cheerful heart is a matter of cultivation. We cannot afford to abandon ourselves entirely to our moods. There are times when we feel depressed and sad, for no special reason, except that the mood is on us! It is at such times that we need to anoint our heads, and wash our faces, that we may not be consumed by our fretfulness, or impose our depression upon others, for nothing is worse than to be a wet blanket (Matthew 6:16-18).

On the other hand, there is nothing more objectionable than to be always in the presence of a comic person who thinks that every occasion must serve for frolic. After a time one gets as tired of funny stories and perpetual punning as of gloom, but while avoiding this extreme, we must not fall into the other of wearing a lugubrious expression and giving way to a moodiness of spirit, which cannot be accounted for.

We may alter our dispositions and moods by a resolute action of the will. We can refuse to look miserable, to speak mournfully, to be pessimistic, to pass on depression. In a spirit of unselfishness we can put on a cheerful courage, array ourselves in the garments of joy, anoint ourselves with the spirit of praise and thankfulness, and go forth into the world to shed sunbeams rather than shadows on the path of life. Do not nurse your sorrow of heart, lest your spirit and the spirits of others be broken.

We can promote a cheerful heart by dwelling on the bright things of our lot; by counting up the mercies which are left, rather than dwelling on what we have lost. When the heart is full of the light and love of God, can it be other than cheerful? How can this be obtained except by a living union with Jesus Christ. In him there is an infinitude of supply of peace and joy, sunshine and light. Let us open our hearts to him, and put on these things as we array ourselves each morning in our garments (Isaiah 61:3, 10).

Prayer
*Through all the changing scenes of life,
in trouble and in joy,
The praises of my God shall still
My heart and tongue employ.*
Amen.

The Days of Noah
April 26

We do well to give heed to the description given of the 'days of Noah', for our Lord said, that as it was in those days, so shall it be in the days that close the present age (Matthew 24:37-39).

The world of that time had made great progress in the arts and civilization of life. But, as it has happened repeatedly all through human history, great luxury produced infamous immorality, cruelty, and widespread indifference to the claims of God. Things took place in those olden times which have their counterpart in the great cities of our time. In its feverish atmosphere sin of every kind abounded, and in mercy to the race, there was no alternative than to bring that wicked generation to an end. 'They ate, they drank; they married, and were given in marriage, and knew not, till the flood came and carried them all away'.

Amidst all this, Noah lived an unblemished and righteous life. He walked in daily converse with God (Genesis 6:8, 9). His Almighty Friend was able to reveal to him his intentions. 'The secret of the Lord is with them that fear him, and he will show them his covenant.'

Keep near to God, that you may hear the accents of his still small voice. Our happiest experience is when we walk with him in unbroken fellowship, and he takes us into covenant with himself. Through any one individual, whose heart is perfect toward him, God will save others. We too shall cross the flood of death and enter the new life of resurrection, but we must be quick to detect his voice, and our hands deft to fulfil the revelations of our divine Teacher and Friend.

'By faith Noah, being warned of God of things not seen as yet, prepared an ark to the saving of his house; by the which he condemned the world, and became heir of the righteousness which is by faith.' (Hebrews 11:7.)

Prayer: Lead me, O Lord, in a straight way unto thyself, and keep me in thy grace unto the end. Amen.

Love of Hospitality
April 27

Our text refers to that memorable scene when Abraham was sitting at the door of his tent, probably inclined to slumber in the heat of noon. Suddenly he saw three men apparently waiting for alms and help. Plenty of travellers had come to his door before, seeking help and hospitality which he had given freely. But though the heat was great, though he may have been disappointed again and again in the recipients of his bounty, he felt it better to be disappointed a hundred times than to miss the chance of showing hospitality and welcome. Therefore he sprang to his feet, called to Sarah for help, and the two of them quickly ministered to the three unknown men. How thankful he must have been that he had not refused to entertain them, for two of them were angels, and the third was the Son of God!

In our crowded lives, where room is scarce, it is less easy for us to care for the people who may be cast as strangers amongst us, but there is a hospitality of the mind that we can all exercise, when we open our hearts to some story of sorrow. None of us are quite aware, except we have suffered in that way, how much it helps some people to be able to pour out their burdens and sorrows. It is much to have a hospitable mind, to have a sympathetic ear, and to make room in our heart for the story of human pain, sorrow, and loneliness, which some, who are comparative strangers, may want to confide in us. We may rebuke ourselves that our hearts do not more nearly represent the hostel or inn into which sad or weary souls may creep for shelter. Although you cannot say much, there may always be the open door of your heart where the lonely and desolate may enter and find in you a fire of sympathy, kindness, and goodwill. Thus cold hands may find warmth, and souls that are frozen for want of love and sympathy may be sheltered and refreshed, and we shall find that in showing love to a stranger we have been ministering to our dear Lord himself, who said, 'Inasmuch as ye did it unto one of the least of these my brethren, ye did it unto me.'

Prayer: Help me, blessed Lord, to bear the infirmities of the weak, to succour those that are overborne in the fight of life, and to bear the burdens of others. Amen.

A Changed Occupation
April 28

The trade between the Orient and the vast populations on the Mediterranean, passed through the Lake of Galilee, making a highly profitable trade for Capernaum, and the smaller cities and towns. The custom-house in which this man Levi held a lucrative position was probably quite near the lake, which was much frequented by our Lord, and thus he may have had opportunities of listening to his teaching. On the other hand, it is possible that the Saviour's summons to him was absolutely unexpected, though it elicited an instant response, for he rose up, left all, and followed Jesus. No doubt he returned later to make up his books, and hand in the balance that may have been in his charge.

Our Lord called him 'Matthew' - which means 'a gift'. He was a great addition to the band of disciples, and the gift of his Gospel to the church has made the whole world his debtor. Matthew conceals, with beautiful modesty, the fact that he prepared a great feast for the Master, which was perhaps partly to signalize his adherence to his new calling, and partly as an opportunity to introduce his new-found friend to the publicans and sinners - i.e. the excommunicated persons of the city (verses 29, 30). That feast may have been the first step to the foundation of the Christian church. Our Lord gladly availed himself of the opportunity to declare his purpose to seek and save the lost, to create a new society on that principle, and to make possible the enclosure of these lost sheep with the flock.

If Zacchaeus happened to be in the party that day, it is likely that for him it was the inauguration of a new life, and as he sat there under the fascination of Christ, he resolved to make reparation to any whom he had cheated and over-charged!

Let us see to it that there is more joy in our religious life. Let us seek the people who think themselves for ever excommunicated from the church. It may be that we shall find Matthew, or Augustine, or John Bunyan among them!

'He went forth, and beheld a publican, named Levi, sitting at the place of toll, and said unto him, Follow me. And he forsook all, and rose up and followed him' (Luke 5:27, 28).

Prayer: O God, wherever thou leadest we would go, for thy ways are perfect wisdom and love. Blend our wills with thine, and then we need fear no evil nor death itself, for all things must work together for our good. Amen.

The Witness of Conscience
April 29

'They shew the work of the law written in their hearts, their con- science bearing witness therewith, and their thoughts one with another accusing or else excusing them' (Romans 2:15 RV).

Conscience holds the mirror to the inner life, and shows us just what we are in the light of God's infinite purity and righteousness. The word is derived from the Latin, *con* with *scio*, I know. Conscience is what a man knows with or against himself.

Sometimes we can meet ourselves with a smile; this is what we term a *good* conscience; at other times we do not like to meet ourselves, but feel ashamed - we cannot deceive ourselves, or hoodwink conscience. We know, and we know that we know, that this is right and that wrong; this is good, and that evil. Conscience is an ill bed-fellow, says the old proverb, and when we are troubled with evil dreams, turning, tossing, starting up in fear, rest becomes impossible. It is very necessary to keep on good terms with your conscience, and we do not wonder that the apostle made it his aim to preserve a conscience void of offence towards God and man (Acts 24:16).

All men have a conscience, else God could not judge them; there would be no standard by which to try or convict, but in most cases conscience is uninstructed. It judges rightly, so far as it knows, but its knowledge is scant, and its power of making accurate distinctions is limited. The Christian conscience is illumined and instructed by the light that falls on it from the face of Christ. See to it that your conscience is constantly corrected by Christ's standard. Never tamper with con- science, nor gag her protestations, nor drown her voice. Never say it does not matter for *once* in a way. Never dare to let her voice wear itself out. To behave thus is to tamper with the most delicate moral machinery in the universe. Let us see that our hearts are sprinkled from an evil conscience in the blood of Jesus, so that we may draw near with a true heart in full assurance of faith (Hebrews 10:19-23).

Prayer: O Lord, give me thy Holy Spirit in greater measure, that his saving presence may cleanse my conscience, and his holy inspiration enlighten my heart. Amen.

Co-operation in Christian Service
April 30

We all want to fill our nets and boats with the fish that we have caught for Christ. How shall we do it? There are certain conditions for successful Christian service which must be observed.

Our nets must be clean. They were 'washing their nets'. It was a good thing that this necessary work had been performed; otherwise they would have been unable to sail at a moment's notice, and to let down their nets at the Master's command (verse 4). 'If a man shall cleanse himself ... he shall be a vessel unto honour, sanctified, and meet for the Master's use'. Let us see to it that we are always ready to respond at Christ's call.

We must be prepared to obey Christ in little things. Our Lord first asked Peter to put out his boat a little from the land. He knew what he was going to do afterwards in making great demands on Peter's obedience and faith; but first, he made this slight request. With alacrity the Master's wishes were complied with, and the floating pulpit, rising and falling with the ripple of the water, was at the Lord's service as he sat down and taught the people. Remember that whenever you lend your empty boat to Jesus, he will pay for it by giving it back to you filled with fish.

Christ's will must be obeyed even against our own judgment. Peter had spent the whole of his life apprenticed to the lake, and knew everything of the art of fishing. When our Lord bade him: 'Launch out into the deep, and let down your nets', it was against all his knowledge and practical experience to let down his nets in the *daytime*, especially as he had toiled all night in vain! Happily for him, he said, 'At *thy* word I will let down the nets'!

We must be willing to share with others. He might have kept the haul for himself, but he longed that the others should share in the Master's bounty, 'and they came and filled both the boats'.

'They beckoned unto their partners in the other boat, that they should come and help them. And they came, and filled both the boats' (Luke 5:7 RV).

Prayer: O God, thou hast committed our work to us, and we would commit our cares to thee. May we feel that we are not our own, and that thou wilt heed our wants while we are intent upon thy will. Amen.

Our experiences are fickle as April weather; now sunshine, now cloud; lights and shadows chasing each other over miles of heathery moor or foam-flecked sea. But our standing in Jesus changes not. It is like himself - the same yesterday, today, and forever.

It did not originate in us, but in his everlasting love, which, foreseeing all that we should be, loved us notwithstanding all. It has not been purchased by us, but by his precious blood, which pleads for us as mightily and successfully when we can hardly claim it, as when faith is most buoyant. It is not maintained by us, but by the Holy Spirit.

If we have fled to Jesus for salvation, sheltering under him, relying on him, and trusting him, though with many misgivings, as well as we may, then we are one with him for ever. We were one with him in the grave; one with him on the Easter morning; one with him when he sat down on the Father's right hand.

We are one with him now as he stands in the light of his Father's smile, as the limbs of the swimmer are one with the head, though it alone is encircled with the warm glory of the sun, while they are hidden beneath the waves. And no doubt or depression can for a single moment affect or alter our acceptance with God through the blood of Jesus, which is an eternal fact.

F B Meyer *Where am I wrong?*

MAY

OUR DAILY WALK OF COMMUNION

They heard the voice of the Lord God walking in
the garden in the cool of the day.
(Genesis 3:8)

The School of Prayer
May 1

'Lord, teach us to pray' (Luke 11:1)

There is no other such Teacher as Christ. He was the Master in the art of prayer, and has taught all the greatest intercessors among the sons of men. His own example has been their incentive. It was because they saw him praying that one of the disciples asked him to teach them how to pray - an example of the power of unconscious influence. If a boy kneels in prayer in the school bedroom, he will be almost sure to start others praying.

Be natural in prayer. Do not repeat prayers the face of which has become worn away by constant usage. Find out approximately what your needs will be, and ask for the needed grace, as a child of a father.

Intercede for others. Do not use exclusively, 'I', 'me', and 'my', but 'we', 'our', and 'us'. Remember how Christ interwove intercession with every petition of the prayer he taught his disciples.

Be sure to receive as well as ask. No beggar is content with asking. He plies his errand until he receives. Alas, that we are so often content to ask with no thought of receiving. Before we rise from our knees, having pleaded for something that is contained in the divine promises, we should dare to believe that we do receive the petitions that we have desired. 'Have faith in God' really means reckon on God's faithfulness to you. Do not look at your faith. He who is ever considering his health will become an invalid; he who always looks down at his faith will cut the very roots from which faith grows, will shut out the beam by which faith lives. Look away to the character of God - the faithful God, who keepeth covenant and mercy for ever.

Prayer: Teach me to pray, O Lord, as thou didst teach thy disciples of old, and winnow my prayers that I may desire and ask only those things that are according to thy will. Amen.

Leave the ultimate answers to your prayer to his infinite wisdom. Not infrequently, to reverse our Lord's words, children ask for stones and not bread; entreat for scorpions and not fish. Under such circumstances it is wise and good of God to say No to our request, and to give us what we would ask if we knew all as he does. When we get to heaven we shall have to thank him as much for the unanswered as for the answered prayers.

Be sure to give the Master time to teach you how to pray. It is necessary to wait for him, when we feel less earnest, as when the fire burns more vehemently. He likes the regular hours for his pupils, and that they should not hurry impetuously away from his gracious words.

The First Lesson
May 2

Heaven is 'the Father's House'. It is our Home. We are strangers and sojourners here, and on our way home. What fascination is in the word! Home will draw the sailor, soldier, explorer, prodigal from the ends of the earth. God has given to most of us the dear memory of what Home is, that we may guess at what awaits us and be smitten with home-sickness. 'Blessed are the home-sick, for they shall reach home!'

But the charm of Heaven will be *the manifested presence of our Father.* All doubts and misunderstandings will be dissipated. We shall know and see, as we are seen and known. In the closing verses of Jude we are told that we shall be set before the presence of his glory, without blemish and in exceeding joy. It is as though our Saviour will introduce us to the manifested presence of the Father.

But we need not wait till then. If we know our Lord, we know the Father. It troubled Christ that his disciples had been so long with him in familiar intercourse and yet had not realised that the beauty and holiness which shone from his nature were beams of the Father's character. To have Jesus is to have the Father. To know Jesus is to know the Father. To pray to him is to pray to God, for he is God manifest in the flesh. He is not simply an incarnation of God, in the sense of the old Greek mythology, adopting a cloak or disguise which was afterwards cast off. God was in Christ, reconciling the world unto himself.

There must be *reverence in our prayer.* God is in heaven and we upon the earth. We must not rush unceremoniously into his presence, as though it were a common and too-familiar room, where ceremony and respect are laid aside. There should be the constant remembrance that in prayer we stand in the presence-chamber of the great Creator, Preserver, and Ruler of the Universe. We wipe our shoes and remove our hats when we enter the home of our friend; let us not forget our manners in the opening sentences of prayer. Angels veil their faces and cry 'Holy!'

But there may be a blessed *faith and trust when we pray.* The Father of Jesus awaits us. He ascended to his Father and our Father. We pray to one who loves us in his Beloved Son with an everlasting love, and holds out the golden sceptre towards us.

'When ye pray, say 'Father' (Luke 11:2).

Prayer: I adore thee, Heavenly Father! There is no limit to thy power, or to thy love. Thou art greatly to be praised! Thou art greatly to be loved! Accept the homage of my soul and life, through Jesus Christ our Lord. Amen.

'*Hallowed be thy Name*' *(Luke 11:2).* God's Name is his Nature - his attributes, the various qualities that go to make him what he is. When we ask for it to be hallowed, we ask that all which obscures it should be swept away as mists before the dawn. We thank God for all that is known of his wonderful Being, for the message of Nature, for revelation given to seers and prophets, for the Word who came from him, and for the Holy Spirit who reveals him. But there are still vast unexplored tracks in God's Being of which we know nothing, and there are myriads that know still less than we do. By their sinful ignorance and superstition, men have misunderstood and misrepresented the character of God; therefore we need to pray that in this world, and in all other worlds, his glorious personality should be understood, appreciated and loved.

When we pray 'Hallowed by thy Name' it is to remind ourselves of the greatness and glory of God our Father. Before you utter petitions for yourself, be still! Compel the intruding crowd of daily needs and desires to remain outside the fence which surrounds the mountain-foot. Go up to meet with God, desiring to look at the needs of the world and of your own little life, as subordinate to your own great desire that God should be loved, honoured and obeyed. Put God's interests above your own. Enthrone him in thought and petition.

In a world that neither knew nor hallowed God's Name, Jesus set himself to reveal and unfold all its wonderful depths. Let us try every day to know more of that Name, and to make it known. It is through ignorance of God that men turn from him. They have distorted views, obtained from the lives and words of professedly religious people which are often a sad travesty and misrepresentation of God. If only men really knew God, surely the love with which he has loved them would enter and fill their hearts.

Prayer: Heavenly Father, unveil to me, I humbly ask, the sweet mysteries and beauty of thy name - Abba, Father. Amen.

It is said that the passion of the French soldiers for Napoleon was so great, that even when mortally wounded they would raise themselves as he came riding past on his charger, and cry, 'Long live the Emperor!' It is when we have become wholly absorbed in bringing glory to God in the highest, that we shall know peace in our hearts, and become the channels of goodwill to men, as men of goodwill, i.e. the doers of God's Will.

God's Government
May 4

In one of those sublime flights with which the Epistles of St Paul abound, he tells us that the time is coming when the Son shall deliver up the Kingdom to God, even the Father, when he shall abolish all rule, and authority, and power. From this we are at liberty to infer that the Kingdom was originally the Father's; that by man's sin and fall it has been alienated from his control. *'Thy Kingdom come' (Luke 11:2).*

The Lord Jesus became incarnate for the purpose of regaining the Kingdom by his agony, blood and tears; though it is not as yet his, it is being acquired. When, therefore, we pray, 'Father, thy Kingdom come', we are asking that the complete victory of Jesus Christ may be hastened; that he may speedily triumph over all obstacles and enemies; that truth may reign in government, art and science; that trade may be free from chicanery and fraud; that tyranny may be extinguished, corruption exposed; that he may send forth his angels to gather out of his Kingdom all things that offend, and them that do iniquity, destroying that last enemy, death, and bringing in the golden age when all men shall know and love the Father, and become his obedient children.

There are many explanations of the Kingdom of Heaven. Perhaps as a rough and ready way of interpreting the phrase, we may say *Divine Kingship*. When we grasp that idea, it becomes the dominant note of life. It is the master-key which opens every lock. Just to believe, deep down in your soul, that the Father of Jesus - our Father - is King. That the God who is moved by the fall of a little bird from its nest, who is described in the parables of the lost sheep and the lost son, is King of the world and all its forces, and of everything in human life. To know and believe this is to get something which is worth everything else.

Prayer: Hasten, O God, the coming of thy Kingdom, and the consummation of thy redeeming work. May the Kingdom of Christ come in us and through us; his voice speaking through our lips; his power working through our touch; his love beating in our heart. Amen.

Will you not, here and now, place yourself under the government of the King? Let him govern your heart, that you may love only within the limits which his pure and Holy Spirit can permit. Let him govern your mind, that no unholy thought be allowed to lodge and strike root within you. Let him govern the books you read, the companionships and friendships you form, the methods of your business, the investment of your money, the way in which you spend your leisure - all must be under the government of his Kingdom, for he will not be King at all unless he is King in all.

'Thy will be done, as in heaven, so on earth' (Matthew 6:10).

Many people shrink from God's will. They think that it always means pain, or sorrow, or bereavement. They always feel melancholy when you speak of doing the will of God. Alas! how the devil has libelled God. The will of God is the will of a Father. It is the Fatherhood of God going out in action. 'It is not the will of your Father that one of these little ones should perish.' 'This is the will of God, even your sanctification.'

If only the will of God were done on earth, as it is done in heaven, there would be peace between the nations, and love and happiness in all our homes. Love would cement the union of all men in a city of blessedness. The fact of the world's present condition is no argument against the beneficence and blessedness of the will of God. It is because men will not do the will of God that things are as they are!

In our own life we shall never be really right or happy until we have got to the point of saying, 'I delight to do thy will, O my God'. We may not begin there. The first step is to choose it, then we shall come to accept it lovingly and thankfully; but, finally, we shall rejoice and delight in it. If you cannot say, 'Thy will be done', say, 'I am willing to be made willing that thy will should be done'. If your will is like a bit of rough and rugged iron, tell God that you are willing for it to be plunged into the furnace of his love, so that all which is unyielding and obdurate may pass away before the ardent heat of the Divine Fire. Depend on it that he will not fail, nor be discouraged with the long process that may be required, and that he will not be rough or violent. He will stay his east wind. He will keep his hand on the pulse, that he may be aware of the least symptom that the ordeal is too strong.

At first there may be a twinge of pain, as when a dislocated limb is pressed back into its proper position, but afterwards there is the blessed restoration of healthy vigour. You will only lose what you would gladly give up if you know as much as God does of what promotes soul-health. 'Whosoever,' said our Lord, 'will do the will of my Father, the same is my brother, and sister, and mother.' 'In his will is our peace.'

Prayer: Most Gracious God, to know and love whose will is righteousness, enlighten our souls with the brightness of thy presence, that we may both know thy Will and be enabled to perform it. Amen.

God's Provision
May 6

If you want daily bread, and would pray for it aright, you must ask as a child; and you must put first, before your own satisfaction, the hallowing of God's Name, and the doing of his will. Implicitly you suggest that if he gives you bread, you will use the strength it gives for his service.

'Give us this day our daily bread' (Matthew 6:11).

Let us ever think of God as the bountiful and generous Giver. Too often he has been described as hard and austere, and as a result, men dread God, and only think of him when they have done wrong. But we should describe him as the All-Giver, who gives all things to all with the most royal generosity. He gives sunbeams and dewdrops, showers and rainbows, grace and glory, his beloved Son and his Spirit, human love and friendship, the daily spreading of our table, the provision of all that we need for life and godliness. Whether we wake or sleep, whether we are evil or good, whether we are pleasing to him or not; to those who forget and blaspheme him equally as to the saints and martyrs of the Church, God gives with both hands, pressed down and running over. We cannot buy, we do not merit, we cannot claim, but we may rely on him to *give*. God is Love; and Love cannot refrain from giving, or it ceases to be Love.

Yet how low God stoops! He is so great, that his greatness is unsearchable. He dwells in the high and lofty place. His sun is ninety-seven million miles away from our earth; he has filled the heavens with countless constellations, for each of which he has a name. He puts the Himalayas into a scale, and the islands are as dust in his balances; but Jesus has taught us to say, 'Our Father, give us bread!' When we get troubled about the immensity of heaven and the distances of the universe, let us come back to the discourse, of which this prayer is part, and which tells us that the great God thinks about the clothing of the lilies, the down on a butterfly's wings, the food of the young lions in the forest, the store of acorns that squirrels accumulate for their provision. It is wonderful to remember that from the first days of man's sojourn on earth, our Father has been laying up stores for us. Though we may be among the youngest children of Time, we come to a table as richly plenished and provided as those who first tasted of his bounty. 'Fear not, it is your Father's good pleasure to *give*.'

Prayer: Heavenly Father, let me not be anxious about tomorrow's provision or path, but trust thee to provide and lead for today. Open thine hand, and satisfy the desire of every living thing. Amen.

'Forgive us our sins, for we ourselves also forgive everyone who fails in his duty to us' (Luke 11:4 Weymouth).

Forgiveness is the exclusive prerogative of Christianity. The schools of ancient morality had four cardinal virtues - justice in human relations; prudence in the direction of affairs; fortitude in bearing trouble or sorrow; temperance or self-restraint. But they knew nothing of mercy or forgiveness, which is not natural to the human heart. Forgiveness is an exotic, which Christ brought with him from Heaven. As long as he abode on earth, he forgave, and he left it as an injunction and example that his people were to forgive even as they had been forgiven.

Our Lord does not mean that God's forgiveness is measured by our own, or that our forgiveness is the cause of God's. Neither of these is the true rendering of this clause; but that God cannot forgive an unforgiving spirit. The only sure index that our contrition and penitence are genuine is that we forgive those who have wronged us. If we do not forgive, it proves that we have never attained that true position of soul before God in which he is able to forgive.

How is it with you? Do you forgive? Or are there men and women that you obstinately refuse to forgive? If there are, it shows that your own soul is not right before God; your love to God is gauged by your love to men; your relationship to God is indicated by your relationship to your fellows. The man who does not love the brother whom he has seen cannot love God whom he has not seen. Discover where you are today. If there is anyone in your life that you refuse to pray for and forgive, know that your heart is wrong with God.

Prayer: Forgive us, we pray thee; put away our sin, as far as the east is from the west. Remember it no more, cast it behind thee as into the depths of the sea. May we be kind one to another, tender-hearted, forgiving one another, even as God in Christ has forgiven us. Amen.

Do the *first* thing, begin to pray for them, and say, 'Forgive us - that one who has hurt me, that man who has wronged me; he needs forgiveness, but I need it equally. We are both in the wrong. I might have made it easier for him to do right than I have done.' *Second*, ask for the opportunity to meet him. *Third*, claim that when you meet, there may be in you the royalty of God's grace, that you may bear yourself with that rare, gracious love which covers the multitude of sins. Be willing that through your lips God's pitying mercy may pass forth in words of human kindness and tenderness.

God's Deliverance
May 8

Our Lord couples his own prayer with ours when he says, pray, 'Lead us not into temptation, but deliver us from evil'. We remember that he was led into the wilderness by the Spirit, that he might be tempted, and that 'in all points' he was tempted like as we are, though in his case there was no sin. It is wonderful to know that by some marvellous oneness of nature the Son of God himself pursued the dreaded track of temptation.

'Lead us not into temptation, but deliver us from evil' (Matthew 6:13).

And while we have this moral nature which links us, upon the one hand, to the eternal Christ, our Captain, who has gone through the same ordeal, we are also linked to every other man, woman and child the world over. For, though we might suppose that there were such diversities of life that some might be secure of an immunity from temptation, yet a closer inspection of our common lot reveals the fact that it is inevitable to us all.

Temptation creeps into the sick-chamber equally as into the heyday of our health. It finds its way into the seclusion of the student even as it dogs the steps of the man of the world doing his business. It comes to the minister, with its tendency to elation or despondency, as well as to the criminal; to the poor as well as the rich. There is no life, however guarded, that is not exposed to the blast and sirocco of temptation. Therefore we utter this prayer as one - '*us*'.

But let us take heart! Remember it is the Father to whom this prayer is addressed. He made us, and knows just what we can stand; he loves us, and his tender succour is always by our side. He draws near, saying, 'I am with you in this dark valley, and am able to make you stand; I would not have brought you here had I not counted the cost. I am able to be a very present help in this time of trouble. I have carried others through this ordeal, and I can carry you; only keep near my side; look away from the tempter to my face; cease to trust yourself and depend absolutely upon me, and I, who brought you to this testing place, will lead you out. Be of good cheer! See, there awaits you the crown which the Lord, the righteous judge, shall give to each soldier who has stood true to him in the hour of trial, and you could not get that if you did not bear this. It is because I want you to win that I am giving you the chance of this hard fight.'

Prayer: Father, be it so; my heart and my flesh fail, but thou art the strength of my heart, and my portion for ever. Forbid that we should be overcome with evil, help us to overcome evil with good. Amen.

'The Kingdom of the world is become the Kingdom of our Lord, and of his Christ; and he shall reign for ever and ever' (Revelation 11:15).

In the midst of this Babel of varying voices there has never been wanting the cry of the Church: *'Thine is the Kingdom!'* The rule of men is Christ's by right, but as Absalom made himself king in opposition to David, so has Satan made himself the prince of this world in opposition to Christ. Our earth is the scene of a great revolt under the leadership of Satan, but Christ is the rightful king of men for all that. His Kingdom is spreading from heart to heart, and ere long the prince of this world shall be cast out, and every knee shall bow and every tongue confess that Christ is Lord. Everyone will then say, *'Thine* is the Kingdom, the power, and the glory'! But it is our privilege to say it *now* - when appearances seem all against it; *now*, when the usurper's power is so strong!

It is not enough, however, to say it in general, we must say it in particular. We must say to Christ our Lord, as the men of Israel said to Gideon, 'Rule thou over us, for thou hast delivered us'.

'Thine is the Power.' The millionaire says, 'Mine is the power of money'; the orator, mine is the power of moving crowds by speech; the author, mine is the power of written words and songs; the scientist claims, mine is the power of extracting the secrets of nature. But after a time wealth vanishes, the tongue is paralysed, the mind decays, and so we learn that we have no inherent power. Visions of what is good, and the desire to do it, come to us, but how to perform, that is the difficulty, and we cry, 'Give me power for service, over myself, power to live righteously, soberly, and godly in this present world'. And in answer there comes this word of the ascended Lord: 'All power is given unto me in heaven and on earth'; and as we catch the words, we answer thus, 'Thine is the power. It is thine that it may be mine!'

'Thine is the glory.' Let us live out the spirit of this prayer. When anyone praises us for some excellence or achievement in life or character, let us never forget to look up to God and say, 'Thine is the glory.' Let us so live that men may be arrested by the radiance of our characters, that they may say, 'How glorious must the Christ be who has made these so fair,' and be constrained to follow him.

Prayer: Help us, O God, to enthrone Christ in our hearts, that having glorified him, we may receive his Spirit as rivers of living water. Amen.

Our Assent
May 10

Amen means, 'So be it - *certainly*'. It is the word constantly translated in the Gospels by 'verily'. It contains the consent of the heart and the response of the life. *Amen* means that you appropriate each word that is spoken, that your heart says 'Yes' to it, and stamps it with the seal of its consent. Let your life say, 'Amen' to God, 'Amen' to Providence, 'Amen' to Redemption, 'Amen' to the Song of Heaven.

'*S a y i n g ,
Amen!' (Rev-
elation 7:12).*

When tried and perplexed with the troubles and problems of life, turn from these - which make the brain dizzy and the heart sick - and consider the Father of our Lord Jesus Christ - 'Our Father' - from whom every ray of love in the universe has emanated; and remember that nothing can be permitted or devised by him which is not consistent with the gentlest and truest dealings that an earthly father could mete out to his child. So shall you be able to say, 'Amen, Lord'.

We must not dwell upon the dark and perplexing questions that seethe and boil around us. We must look up to the blue sky of undimmed sunshine, our Father's heart. He must be Love, beyond our deepest, tenderest, highest conceptions of what love is. In his dealings with us, and with all men, love is the essence and law of his nature. In proportion as you humbly believe in the Father, you will be able to say 'Yes' which is a true rendering of the Greek word in our version, translated 'Even so' (Matthew 11:26).

*Prayer: O
God, there are
many   things
we dread, but
we are en-
closed in thee;
they   cannot
touch us ex-
cept by thy
permission,*

Our Lord was able to say, not only 'Even so, Father'; but, '*I thank thee*' and there shall come a day when the four-and-twenty elders representing the redeemed Church, shall see the judgment of her great opponent, and say, 'Amen, Hallelujah!' (Revelation 19:4). Here we can say 'Amen', and not often 'Hallelujah'; there the two - the assent and the consent; the acquiescence and the acclaim; the submission to the will of God, and the triumphant outburst of praise and adoration. Let us anticipate that age when we shall know as we are known; when we shall be perfectly satisfied, perfectly jubilant, perfectly blessed; when every shadow of misunderstanding and misapprehension shall be dispelled, and we shall join in the Hymn of the Redeemed Church: 'Great and marvellous are thy works, O Lord God, the Almighty; righteous and true are thy ways, thou King of the Ages.'

*and if thou
dost permit
things that
seem evil to
enter our life,
it must be well.
Make us be-
lieve that all
things   are
working to-
gether   for
good. Amen.*

A Psalm of Blessedness - Psalm 1
May 11

'Blessed is the man that walketh not in the counsel of the wicked. But his delight is in the law of the Lord' (Psalm 1:1, 2).

The Blessed, or Happy, man is described *negatively* (verse 1). There is a gradation in the attitude, the sphere of influence, and the condition of his companions. In *attitude*, we may begin by *walking*, advance to *standing*, and end by *sitting*. If we would avoid the sitting, let us guard against walking or standing. In the *sphere of influence*, the beginning of backsliding is when a man listens to counsel; he then drifts into the path trodden by sinners, and finally is hardened enough to sit where scornful talk surrounds him on every hand. The *condition* of evil companions. We should be repelled if we were to be plunged suddenly into contact with the scornful, but our moral interests may not be specially outraged by the counsel of the wicked. Indeed, the advice which wicked men give sometimes resembles closely what our heart suggests and our taste prefers. It is so specious, so apparently sensible and natural, that we are captivated by it. Only gradually do we slide from those who forget God to those who set his law at defiance or openly blaspheme him.

Our motive in going amongst ungodly men must be carefully considered. If it is to help and save them, as our Lord did, no harm will come to us. But if we go into the way of sinners for our own amusement, need we be surprised if the bloom pass off the fruit, and the fine edge from the tool? Let us examine ourselves. Are we startled and shocked now, as we used to be, by an indecent illusion or a blasphemous word? Is there a coarsening process at work? Even where we are not injured by worldliness, we may suffer by contact with the low ideals of our fellow-Christians. Let us watch and pray; let us consider one another and exhort one another day by day, lest any be hardened by the deceitfulness of sin (Hebrews 3:13).

The Blessed, or Happy, man is also described *positively* (verse 2). This delight comes as naturally as appetite for food, when the soul is in a healthy condition. Under the inspiration of that delight, we shall meditate on God's word continually, storing it in the heart, and reciting it when travelling or in darkness.

Remember that the Lord knows the way you take. He is sensitive to every jolt and lurch, to the stony hills and the easy valley, to the foes that lie in wait. In his keeping you will never become as the light chaff, or the perishing way of the wicked written in the dust.

Prayer: We commend ourselves, and those we love, to thee, dear Lord. We put our hand in thine, that thou shalt lead us by the untrodden way. Amen.

A Psalm of Life - Psalm 23
May 12

This is 'the Nightingale' among the Psalmist choristers! The first that we learn in infancy, the last we whisper with dying lips. It implies consecration, for God is *this* only to the soul which is wholly surrendered to him. You cannot have all of God, or God in all, until you are willing to surrender your all. Do you want to put 'My', the pronoun of possession, before the Name of God? Ah, then, you must be willing to answer his voice, and follow where he leads. '*My* sheep hear my voice, and they follow me, but a stranger will they not follow.'

Morning! The Shepherd's leading. When he puts forth his sheep from the fold, in the dewy morning, he goes before them over the grass or up the mountain-track towards the pastures. It would never do for the flock to precede him. Whatever roughness you find on your path, remember that the Shepherd has gone before. 'He *leadeth* me.' Remember also that his name and character are involved in bringing you through 'for his Name's sake'.

Noon: The alleviations of rest. In all lives there are times when he makes us to lie down, or leads us by the waters of rest. Sometimes it is a period of convalescence after an illness. Sometimes a holiday, an interval between the pressure of engagements, a respite when the stress and strain of toil is over - these are our quiet pasture-lands. At other times, in the midst of life's rush and turmoil, our soul is kept at rest in God's peace. The heart rests for part of a second between its beats. 'He *maketh* me to lie down!'

Night: the oil and the cup. The flock has reached the fold where it is to shelter. At the doorway stands the Shepherd, watching each one as it passes. This one has grazed and torn its head in getting through the hedge, and for it there is the anointing oil. Near his hand is the food and water, from which he fills the bowl, to wash the face, or give refreshment; and as it overflows, there is evidently enough and to spare!

Goodness and Mercy follow the flock, as the Shepherd precedes. 'The House of the Lord' is the fold from which we shall go out no more, and the Lamb shall be our Shepherd and abiding joy for ever.

'The Lord is my Shepherd; I shall not want. Surely goodness and mercy shall follow me all the days of my life' (Psalm 23:1, 6).

Prayer: O Lord, support us all the day long of this troublous life until the shadows lengthen and the evening comes, the busy world is hushed and the fever of life over and our work is done; then, Lord, in thy mercy grant us safe lodging, a holy rest and peace at the last, through Jesus Christ our Lord. Amen.

A Psalm of Communion - Psalm 116
May 13

'I will take the cup of Salvation, and call upon the name of the Lord' (Psalm 116:13). 'And he took the cup, and gave thanks, and gave it to them, saying, Drink ye all of it; for this is my blood of the new covenant, which is shed for many unto remission of sins' (Matthew 26:27, 28).

Every Christian disciple should partake of the Lord's Supper regularly. It is a *Sacrament*. In the days of the Roman republic, the youths were brought to the altar and sworn to serve their country to the death. So our first Communion is our oath of allegiance to our King. It is a proclamation, or confession, of our faith. We bear witness to the death of Christ as our hope of forgiveness and salvation. We testify our desire to put his cross and grave between us and the world. It is also a bond of Christian union.

It is a Pledge of the Covenant. The Death of the Cross was God's sign and seal to the new covenant, the provisions of which are recited in Hebrews 8. When we drink the wine it is as though we said, 'Remember thy covenant'. Let me appeal to all, and especially to the young disciple, to draw near and take the bread and wine, and to meditate deeply and reverently on that supreme Gift which demands our self-giving. 'What shall I render unto the Lord? I will take the cup ... I will pay my vows' (Psalm 116:13, 14).

The expression in this Psalm is remarkable: '*I will take the cup of salvation*'. When we enquire *what salvation*, we read: 'Thou hast loosed my bonds' (verse 16), and we are reminded of Revelation 1:5, 'Unto him that loveth us, and loosed us from our sins by his blood'. We are tied and bound by our sins; our sinful habits bind us fast in our thongs. But our Lord looses us by his cross.

Prayer: We pray that we may eat and drink, and do whatsoever we are called to do, in remembrance of Christ, and to show forth his life. May the spirit of worship pervade every act of daily life. Amen.

Notice how triumphantly the Psalmist avows his loyalty to his Heavenly Master. Again, and yet again, he avows: 'O Lord, truly I am thy servant, *I am thy servant.*' And we are the servants or bond-slaves of Jesus. If it be asked what 'the sacrifices of thanksgiving' are, we may reply: First, the sacrifice of ourselves (Romans 12:1). Next, the sacrifice of our praise and gifts (Hebrews 13:15, 16). Not grudgingly or thoughtlessly, but with cheerful eagerness, let us come to the altar of God. Because of all we owe to him, let us never cease to live and serve, to praise and give.

A Song of the Sanctuary - Psalm 84
May 14

Probably we never value the House of God so much as when we are severed from it. The author of this Psalm was evidently in exile. He envied the very birds that nested in the holy places where he had been wont to worship. The pilgrims who were on their way thither, and the door-keepers who stood on the threshold, seemed to his ardent longing in better case than himself. Robinson Crusoe missed the sound of the church bell when no longer able to obey its call. There is a strange fascination in the sound of worship for those who for years have been deprived of its privilege. Let us be thankful for 'the means of grace' and reverently make good use of them whilst they are at our disposal.

'Lord, I love the habitation of thy House, and the place where thy glory dwelleth' (Psalm 26:8).

In order to find God's Tabernacles 'lovely', we must love the Lord of hosts as our King and God. Put God in his right place in your heart and life, and you will love his Palaces. When God is worshipped as King, we shall be reverent, we shall be punctual, we shall come with prepared and expectant heart. Any detraction in the manner of the minister, the singing of the choir, the atmosphere of the place, will not affect the soul which is occupied with God.

It is blessed when the high ways to Zion have a place in a man's heart - when he is set on them, dreams of them, and loves them because of the goal to which they lead. On our earthly pilgrimage we have our valleys of depression and weeping, as well as our transfiguration heights. Thank God that life is not one long dull monotony. Let us not find fault with the road, but make the best of it. Every phase of our experience has its compensations. Look out for them. If you take the valley you will find the water-spring; if you take the hill, you will get the horizon. But be it valley or hill, either brings you to your desired goal.

Prayer: Give us grace, we beseech thee, not to miss, by our apathy or unbelief, aught which thou waitest to bestow. Teach us how to appropriate what thou dost offer, and to receive what thou wouldst impart. Amen.

This psalm makes it clear that God is the Shield of his people. In the night he is our Sun; in the day when the sunbeams strike us like swords, he is our Shield (Psalm 121:5, 6; Revelation 7:16). Whatever your lot God will be its make-weight and equivalent. When the soul has incurred disaster and pursuit, what a comfort it is to hide in God as our Shield. What an iron-plated door is in the rush of fire along the corridor, that God is to the soul that escapes to him. He besets us *behind*, as well as *before*.

A Psalm of Gratitude - Psalm 103
May 15

'Bless the Lord, O my soul; and forget not all his benefits' (Psalm 103).

The Psalmist is fond of addressing the soul, as though to arouse it from lethargy. Within is a whole choice of minstrels, let them all awake! *All* that is within should be attuned to God and his praise. Let us not repine for the past, or strain after the future. We often forget the rare benefits of the present moment, because we suppose that there is something more absolutely satisfying ahead. *Here and now* God is forgiving, healing, redeeming, crowning, satisfying, and executing righteous acts. Live in the present! Live in God, the same yesterday, today, and for ever! It is enough. The past records of God's dealings with his people are an incentive to faith. What he was, he is. He is a fountain brimming to the full with pitying love, which flows over in mercy and forgiveness.

There are four comparisons and contrasts in verses 10-18. 'As the heaven... As the east... As a Father... As for man.' The ancients thought the sky was solid - a kind of blue ceiling. What an immensity of new meaning we can read in the words: 'As the heaven is high above the earth'. There is an infinity of distance above us, but not more infinite than God's mercy. To the Eastern mind, east and west were the points at which the sun appeared to rise on earth's surface, 'pillowing his chin on the orient wave', and drawing the curtains of the night. For us the telescope reveals the almost inconceivable distance of the earth from the sun, but this is the distance to which God has removed our transgressions. A father's pity for his weak and tiny offspring is very touching. The strongest plea with God is that of helpless weakness! The Son of God was made in the likeness of man, and 'he knoweth our frame and remembereth that we are dust'.

Prayer: O Blessed God, ever engaged in giving thy choicest gifts to us thine unworthy children, accept the gratitude for which we have no words. May we rejoice in all the good thou sendest us. Amen.

The last contrast was in our Lord's mind when he pointed to the flowers at his feet (Matthew 6:30). Generations of flowers bloom and die in the broad expanse of nature - so frail, so beautiful, so transient. The generations of mankind are not more permanent. But the mercy of the Lord dates from everlasting and endures for ever.

The Psalmist's voice is heard, 'Bless the Lord, O *my* soul!' We are reminded of the conductor of a vast orchestra and choir, whose trained ear missed the note of the piccolo. So God will miss your voice if you refrain from his praise.

The Psalm of Penitence - Psalm 51
May 16

This Psalm is a temple-staircase, worn by the feet of myriads of penitents. The page is wet with the tears alike of the most saintly and the most sinful. Augustine had them written on the walls of his tiny cell at Hippo, that he might appropriate them constantly. Perhaps they are more precious to us at the end of life than the beginning.

Note the definitions of sin. It is an *erasure* or *blot* on the fair page of life; hence the cry, '*Blot* out my transgressions'. Oh that God would blot out the scribblings and smudges of our later years, and bring back the fresh beauty of our youth! It is a *stain* on the white robe of the soul; hence the petition, 'Wash me thoroughly from mine iniquity'. There is but one way into the Holy City: 'Blessed are they that wash their robes, and make them white in the Blood of the Lamb'. It is *leprosy*; hence the cry, 'Cleanse me from my sin; purge me with hyssop, and I shall be clean.' There was special significance, then, for you and me when Jesus reached forth his hand and touched the leper, saying, 'Be thou clean'.

Note the condition of forgiveness. It is confession. Transgression must be acknowledged. We must realise that sin is not only against man, but God, to whom man belongs, and who is affronted by all sin as committed directly against himself. And our confession must not be superficial, but deep and heart-searching. We must go back to our earliest origins, to our connection with a sinful race, to our inward and hidden parts.

Note the cry for purity and righteousness of life. The clean heart has to be created, for there are no materials within us out of which it can be shaped or moulded. Ephesians 4:24 tells us that full provision has been made for this. We desire a 'right', or steadfast spirit, which shall not deviate to the right or left, but bear straight onward to the goal. The Greek word for *sin* is 'missing the mark'. We long for a spirit that shall not be deflected. We desire a 'free' or willing spirit (RV marg). Ah, what a transformation is here! But it has been effected in myriads (1 Corinthians 6:11).

'I acknowledge my transgressions: and my sin is ever before me. Against thee, thee only, have I sinned, and done that which is evil in thy sight' (Psalm 51:3, 4). All have sinned and come short of the glory of God' (Romans 3:23).

Prayer: Heavenly Father! Forgive us our many sins, ignorances, and failures, and cleanse us from all iniquity for the sake of Jesus Christ, our Lord. May we hate sin as thou dost, and may thy grace sink deeper into our hearts, purifying the springs of thoughts and action. Amen.

The Soul's Thirst for God - Psalm 63
May 17

'My soul thirsteth for thee, my flesh longeth for thee in a dry and weary land, where no water is' *(Psalm 63:1).*

The longing of the soul for God only makes itself felt when all lesser delights and earthly joys are relegated to their right place. If you are not conscious of this soul-thirst it is because your heart is trying to satisfy itself from the world, and is engaged in digging wells that can hold no water. The woman rightly said to Jesus that she came all the way to draw water, because there was no alternative; but as soon as he satisfied her soul-thirst by opening the spring within her, she 'left her water-pot'. Most of us are so occupied with business, pleasure-seeking, money-making, and trifles, that we have no time or care for God.

'My soul shall be satisfied' (verse 5). It takes very little and very much to satisfy the soul. Very *little* of this world. As our Lord said to Martha, only one thing is really needful. Yet very *much*, because anything less than God will not suffice; more, we cannot ask. To desire God is to have him. To thirst for the water of life is to drink of it. Therefore our Lord says, *'Blessed* are they that hunger and thirst after righteousness.' Let us not long for things and people which are not here with us. We may be in poverty and deprivation and loneliness, yet all things and all people are ours at *this moment*, because we have God. Why not, here and now, say, 'I have God, and therefore I have all that is good in every one and everything!' Why should the fish lament, which has the ocean to swim in?

Prayer: O God, some of us are full of infinite desire. Wilt thou open thine hand and satisfy our longings. Be nigh unto us as we call upon thee. Hear our prayer and save us. Amen.

'My soul followeth hard after thee' (verse 8). God sometimes seems to withdraw from the soul, as the mother will release her hold of the baby who is learning to walk, so that it may be encouraged, without knowing it, to follow her as she retreats with outstretched hands. Did not Christ withdraw from the woman, inclining her to follow hard after him (Matthew 15:21-28). So let us 'follow on to know the Lord'.

As we close this portion, let us ask if we can truly repeat the first verse. Can we say of God, 'Thou art *my* God'? He is ours, but we must seek him. We must, so to speak, build the fences of our faith in an ever-enlarging enclosure of God, our Father and Portion. It is not enough for the emigrant to have what he calls a 'claim'. He must open up the resources that lie buried in his piece of land. The diamonds of the Cape were first discovered through a child playing with a white stone, but they have been *sought* ever since.

The Psalm of Inheritance - Psalm 16
May 18

It is a wonderful thing when we can look upon God as being our portion, when we can lay our hand upon all his nature and say there is nothing in God which will not in some way contribute to my strength and joy. It makes one think of the early days of the settlement of emigrants in the Far West of Canada or Australia. The settler and his family would slowly travel forward with their implements and seeds, till they reached the plot of ground allocated by the Government. At first the family would encamp on the edge of it, then they would prospect it, and go to and fro over its acres with a sense that it all belonged to them, though it needed to be brought under cultivation. In the first year, within the fence hastily constructed, the farmer and his sons would begin to cultivate some small portion of their newly-acquired territory. This would yield the first crops; next year they would press the fences farther out, until at the end of a term of years the whole would have been brought under cultivation.

'I am thy portion and thine inheritance among the children of Israel' (Numbers 18:20). 'The Lord is my portion, saith my soul; therefore will I hope in him' (Lamentations 3:24).

So it is with the mighty Nature of God. When first we are converted and led to know him for ourselves, we can claim to apprehend but a small portion of the length and depth and breadth and height of his Love; but as the years go slowly on, amid the circumstances of trouble and temptation and the loss of earthly things, we are led to make more and more of God, until the immensity of our inheritance, which can never be fully explored or utilised, breaks upon our understanding. No wonder that the Psalmist breaks forth into thanksgiving in verses 6, 7 and 9!

The devout soul rejoices in God as his great Inheritance. When he is always present to our mind, when we are constantly making use of him, when we find ourselves naturally turning to him through the hours of the day, then such quiet peace and rest settle down upon us that we cannot be moved by any anxiety of the present or future. Death itself will make no difference, except that the body which has obscured our vision will be left behind, and the emancipated soul will be able more fully to expatiate in its inheritance, which is incorruptible, undefiled, and unfading (1 Peter 1:4, 5).

Prayer: We thank thee, O Lord, that all things are ours in Christ, working for us, co-operating with us, and bearing us onward to that glorious destiny for which thou art preparing us. Amen.

The Silver Lining in the Dark Cloud - Psalms 42, 43
May 19

'Why art thou cast down, O my soul? and why art thou disquieted within me? Hope thou in God, for I shall yet praise him, who is the health of my countenance, and my God' (Psalms 42:5, 11; 43:5).

These two Psalms are evidently one. See how the same refrain rings through them both! They are generally allocated to that sad time in David's history, when the rebellion of his favourite son, Absalom, drove him as an exile beyond the Jordan (2 Samuel 15:14). But amid the great sorrows that rolled over his soul, there was one glad ingredient. Thrice over the Psalmist encourages himself to *Hope*! For many a sorrowful soul, there is always one chord of Hope - God! We may stand amid the wreck of our earthly hopes. Through misconduct or mistake, as the result of folly or sin, we may have reduced ourselves and those dear to us to the last degree of misery; but the soul may always turn from its low estate to God, sure that he will have mercy, will abundantly pardon, and will turn again the adverse pressure of the tide.

See how the broken-hearted may still speak of God! This man had grievously sinned. He seemed to have forfeited all claim on God's recognition and care. He had brought shame and disgrace on the cause of religion. All down the years the story of his wrong-doing would give the enemies of truth abundant reason to blaspheme. And yet see how he dares to speak of God! He describes him as the God of his life, as his Rock, as the Health of his countenance, the God of his strength, and the Gladness of his joy. This is a great lesson! We may change, but God changes never. We may turn our face from him, or allow some evil thing to loom between ourselves and the clear shining of his face. But he shines on, and when we confess our sins, and put them away, we find ourselves afresh in the clear shaft of his illuminating rays. You may have lost all hope in yourself, your friends, your circumstances, but you must never lose your hope in God.

The past, which can only be viewed with repentance, is forgiven; the present, in which God is willing to be All-in-all; the future, when again the soul shall praise him with joyful lips. Hope looks into the future. 'I shall *yet* praise him'.'

Prayer: Our Father, forgive, we pray thee, our murmuring and discontent, our perverseness and waywardness. Teach us to discern the silver edge of the lowering clouds, and to trust thy love, which is leading us safely and by a right way to our home. Amen.

The Psalm of the Doorkeeper - Psalm 84
May 20

This Psalm has been a favourite with God's people in all ages. When Carlyle was leaving, in doubt and despondency, his quiet mountain home at Craigen-puttock for the untried tumult of London, he quoted this Psalm for comfort to his brother and himself, saying: 'I turn my thoughts heaven-wards, for it is in heaven only that I find any basis for our poor pilgrimage on earth. As surely as the blue dome of heaven encircles us all, so does the providence of the Lord of Heaven. "He will withhold no good thing from those that love him." This, as it was the ancient Psalmist's faith, let it likewise be ours. It is the Alpha and the Omega, I reckon, of all the possessions that can belong to man.'

'For a day in thy courts is better than a thousand. I had rather be a doorkeeper in the house of my God, than to dwell in the tents of wickedness' (Psalm 84:10).

In absence and distance, the heart of the true believer turns to God. He believes that he has direct access to him, and that his prayer will be accepted (verse 8). David, as the anointed King, had the right to ask that God, who was his Shield, should look upon his face; but we have even a better plea, for we may ask that God would look upon the face of his own glorious and beloved Son, and accept us in him (verse 9).

Let us imitate the humility of this man, and be willing to take the lowest place (Luke 14:10, 11); but we must be on our guard against being proud of our humility. Some people take the back seats that they may be asked to come to the front. They mistake the Lord's words. It is said that there is always room at the *top*; it is equally true that there is plenty of room at the *bottom*; and if men and women will really gird themselves with a towel and wash the feet of the disciples, if they are prepared in the literal sense to be doorkeepers and to give themselves in service, they will be allowed to do their work with little praise save that of the King himself.

To all such lowly souls God gives grace and glory (verse 11). With both hands he will give and give again. Only we must practise the habit of *taking. Grace* is the bud of which *Glory* is the flower. If God has given the one, he will not withhold the other (Romans 5:1, 2). If anything is withheld from us, we may be sure that it is not absolutely for our good. No *good* thing will the Father withhold; but he will not give us scorpions, however beautiful their appearance; nor stones, though painted to resemble bread.

Prayer: Teach us to abide with thee in our daily call-ing, and to realise that each sphere may be a tem-ple for priestly service. Amen.

The Voice of God in Nature and Revelation - Psalm 19
May 21

'The heavens declare the glory of God; and the firmament sheweth his handiwork' (Psalm 19:1).

Verses 1-6: Those whose hearts are in tune with God can hear voices in nature which are inaudible to the ordinary man. The poet Blake says: 'When the morning sun ascends the eastern sky, you may behold only a light yellow disc, whereas *I* shall see and hear the infinite multitude of the heavenly host, crying, Holy, Holy, Holy!' Yet, though there is no speech nor language, is it not true that 'their words are gone forth to the end of the world'? There is no nation of men that has not heard the voice of Nature speaking of God (Acts 14:16, 17; Romans 1:20, 21).

In verses 7-11 the Psalmist describes the effect of the word of God when the Spirit of Truth works through it and by it on the soul. There are many ways of reading the Bible - as a history, as a revelation of man's gropings after God, as a piece of great literature; but the best way is to ask the Divine Spirit to make it a medium through which he may approach our innermost nature. Listen to God's voice speaking within you. Be still, that you may hear. The Spirit searches into the deep things of God, and reveals them to our spirit (1 Corinthians 2:10). All that God has ever said or been to others, he will say and be to you, if only your heart is lowly and contrite. 'Speak to me, Lord, by Prophet and Psalmist, by lyric and prose, by narrative and appeal. Speak through thy word to restore my soul, to rejoice my heart, and to enlighten mine eyes!' When to the quiet and waiting soul God uses his own word thus, it is more to be desired than fine gold, and is sweeter than the taste of honey from the comb.

Prayer: I pray thee, gracious Lord, that I may not miss any of those lessons which thou art desirous of teaching me by thy Spirit, thy word, and thy providence. Amen.

The effect of God's word, when used by the Holy Spirit, is very remarkable (verses 11-14). It convinces of sin. Just as linen is shown to be discoloured against freshly-fallen snow, so we realise our errors and cry to be cleansed from hidden and secret sins.

David knew little of the glory and wonder of the Cross, where God spared not his own Son, but in him stooped to reconcile man to himself. The starry heavens, telling of the glory of God, and even the Law itself, are not able to tell us what the Cross of Jesus does - of Love that matched itself against hate, and of Grace that would not be turned away by human sin.

The Psalm of Ascension - Psalm 24
May 22

This twenty-fourth Psalm is apparently in two parts, and yet there is one theme - the ascent of the holy soul and the triumphant Saviour into the presence of God. For us, the ascension of our Lord precedes our own; but in the days of the Psalmist that order was reversed.

Our Lord's Ascension. In an outburst of poetry, kindled by the Divine Spirit, the Psalmist anticipates the coming of the King of Glory to the doors of the Eternal City - that ideal City which through the ages has beckoned forward the hearts of saints and patriots, and which in Revelation 21 is seen descending to our earth. It was as though the doors of the Unseen barred his entrance. They had opened to God, but never before to 'God manifest in the flesh'. It was a new thing that he should take our nature with him into the unseen and eternal world.

The soul's ascension (verses 3-6). In Christ we have ascended and are seated at God's right hand. No change in your emotions, not even the being overtaken by a fault can alter that. But we have to make our calling sure. What is ours in the divine purpose must be claimed and appropriated as a living daily experience. There are certain qualities of character which are requisite to those who should be accounted worthy to stand before the Son of Man, not hereafter only, but now and here and always (Luke 21:36).

We must have *clean hands.* The money that we earn must be clean money. If we are writers, artists, mechanics, professional or commercial men or women, we must never produce anything which would defile the imagination or heart. We must have *a pure heart.* In Isaiah 33:14-17, which is a parallel passage, the Holy Spirit is compared to a devouring fire, in the presence of which no evil thing can live. Let us ask him so to possess us, and to cleanse the thoughts of our hearts by his inspiration. We must not *lift up our soul to vanity,* i.e. we must not allow ourselves to be inflated with the applause or rewards of the world. Many sell their souls for these, and only at the end of life awaken to discover how worthless they are. We must *not swear deceitfully,* i.e. we must be absolutely transparent and sincere, for only the true can stand in the presence of the King of Truth.

'But God, being rich in mercy, for his great love wherewith he loved us, even when we were dead through our trespasses, quickened us together with Christ, and raised us up with him, and made us to sit with him in the heavenly places, in Christ Jesus' (Ephesians 2:4-6).

Prayer: May we live as those who have been raised with Christ, and who are seated with him. Amen.

The Sleepless Watcher - Psalm 121
May 23

This psalm has been called the Traveller's Psalm. When the pilgrims started forth from their distant homes to go up to the Temple, not one of them could forecast his experiences before he reached home again. There were perils of rivers, perils of robbers, perils in the wilderness, perils in travel from wild beasts. It was well, therefore, that they should commit themselves and their dear ones to the care of one who neither slumbered nor slept. It is not enough for the body to be kept; we need the soul to be kept from all evil, as we go out into the world with its microbes of temptation, or come back to the luxury and comfort of our dwelling. There is temptation everywhere; not for one moment are we absolutely immune.

There is a difference between slumbering and sleeping. The mother or nurse watching the child may sometimes get a few moments of slumber; it is not very restful, yet there is a brief pause of unconsciousness. But this never comes to God. Not for one moment does he slumber, or cease his watchful care of us. God keeps us by besetting us behind and before, and lays his hand upon us (Psalm 139:5). As a sentry goes to and fro before the palace given to his charge, so God's peace, like a sentinel, keeps watch and ward around the soul. We speak of the castle-keeper, the inner circle of defence; so God's Presence is our Keep. We think also of the safe, around which the fire may play, but cannot touch its contents; so a child of God may walk in the midst of peril and temptation, but God is round about him; he is inside the secret place of the Most High, and no weapons formed against him can reach that inner sanctuary. Let us hand over the keeping of our souls to him as to a faithful Creator (1 Peter 4:19).

The closing words of this Psalm remind us of John 14:1-6. There will be one last going out and coming in, when the house of our life shall be left vacant, and we shall go forth to the Father, to the house of many mansions, to the great company which awaits us on the other side. Then in the transition between this world and the next, and amid all the mysteries that shall crowd upon us, we need fear no evil, for whatever Eternity may bring to us, we shall always be sheltered and kept by Almighty care.

The Secret of the Quiet Heart
May 24

Paradise has vanished from our world, as the picture of a landscape vanishes when swept by storm. And our race stands in much the same plight as did Naomi and Ruth in this old-world story. We have lost our inheritance, and the one barrier which stands between us and despair is the Person and Work of our Lord Jesus Christ. But, thank God, we need have no doubt as to the sequel. For as Boaz claimed back the estate for Ruth, so may we be confident that Jesus Christ will never be at rest till this sin-stained and distracted world is restored to her primitive order and beauty, as when the morning-stars sang for joy.

'Be still, and know that I am God' (Psalm 46:10).
'Sit still, my daughter, for the man will not rest, until he have finished the thing this day' (Ruth 3:18).

Jesus is our near Kinsman by his assumption of our nature. He is the nearest and dearest Friend of our race, who stooped to die for our redemption. And the fact that he carried our nature in himself to heaven, and wears it there, is an indissoluble bond between us. Sit still! do not fret! he will never fail, as he will certainly never forsake!

Let us seek the quiet heart in our prayers. Prayer must arise within us as a fountain from unknown depths. But we must leave it to God to answer in his own wisest way. We are so impatient, and think that God does not answer. A child asked God for fine weather on her birthday, and it rained! Some one said, 'God didn't answer your prayer'. 'Oh yes,' she replied, 'He did, God always answers, but he said No!' God always answers! He never fails! Be still! If we abide in him and he abides in us, we ask what we will, and it is done. As a sound may dislodge an avalanche, so the prayer of faith sets in motion the power of God.

In times of difficulty - be still! Thine enemies are plotting thine overthrow! They laugh at thy strong confidence! But hast thou not heard his voice saying: 'This is the way, walk ye in it'? Then leave him to deal with thy foes from whatever quarter they come. He is thy Rock, and rocks do not shake. He is thy High Tower, and a high tower cannot be flooded. Thou needest mercy, and to him belongeth mercy. Do not run hither and thither in panic! Just quietly wait, hushing thy soul, as he did the fears of his friends on the eve of Gethsemane and Calvary. 'Rest in the Lord, wait patiently for him.' 'Be still, for he will not rest, until he hath finished the thing this day.'

Prayer: If this day I should get lost amid the perplexities of life and the rush of many duties, do thou search me out, gracious Lord, and bring me back into the quiet of thy presence. Amen.

'All the people went their way to eat, and to drink, and to send portions, and to make great mirth, because they had understood the words that were declared unto them. And there was very great gladness. Also day by day, from the first day unto the last day, he read in the book of the law of God. And they kept the feast seven days' (Nehemiah 8:12, 17, 18).

Gladness is health. If you can get a patient to look on the bright side of things, you have done a great deal to bring back the tides of life. Whenever we are optimistic and glad we are looking at things from the divine side, and imbibing some of God's eternal gladness. And cherishing this temperament, we shall know what Nehemiah and Ezra meant when they said, 'The joy of the Lord is your strength' (verse 10).

If you have some secret sorrow, tell it to God, but do not impose it needlessly upon men. Anoint your head and wash your face, that you appear not to men to fast, and he who sees the secret tears will comfort you openly (Matthew 6:17, 18). The pain and sorrow of the world is understandable, even worse than many of us realise, but this is largely due to the intrusion of sin and selfishness which can only be expelled by love. But even this gives opportunity for that unselfish ministry and devotion which are the keys of the blessed life. In so far as we dedicate our lives to help Christ in his redeeming work of delivering souls out of the power of darkness and translating them into the Kingdom of Life and Light, we share in his perennial blessedness.

It must have been a time of unusual joy when the returned exiles reviewed the finished wall which now engirded the city. There was the *consciousness of a finished work*. It is always delightful when we have done to the very best of our ability a piece of work that needed doing. One of the elements of a thoroughly enjoyable holiday is to be able to look back on a piece of good construction, a piece of brick or stone work which will endure in the edifice of our own lives or of other people's.

In addition, there was the *Book of the Law of God*, in which they read from day to day. Let us take the Bible with us on our holidays! We shall find that it will yield new meaning as we study it by lake or mountain, as we ponder it in country lanes, or by the seashore. One like the Son of Man will walk beside us, and apply its teaching till our hearts burn within us, and we are no more sad.

Prayer: We thank thee for eyes that see, and hearts that love, and natures that can enjoy thy good and perfect gifts. O Father, in whom is no variableness, neither shadow of turning. Amen.

God's Workmanship
May 26

The potter's craft is almost the oldest in the world, and its method has hardly differed through the ages. Jeremiah as well as Isaiah refers to it (Jeremiah 18:1-4). While the prophet was standing watching the potter, he saw him take a piece of moistened clay from the lump that lay beside him, and placing it on the wheel, he began to shape it after a design which was in his thought. As it approached completion, the clay collapsed under his hands, some part falling on the ground, and some on the wheel itself. To Jeremiah's surprise, the potter did not sweep the recalcitrant fragments away, but gathered them up, and made them again into another vessel. This is what God does still.

We are the clay, and thou our potter; and we are all the work of thy hand' (Isaiah 64:8).

The Master-workman is our Father. 'But now, O Lord, thou art our Father.' Some who read these words have themselves been parents. They have tasted the ecstasy of parentage, as the child has been laid for the first time in their arms. At that moment a new passion has arisen in the heart, and new resolves have compelled the soul. To shield, defend, educate, help, love, and teach to love - all this is included in that first embrace. The compulsion of the child's helplessness is a supreme motive to father or mother. Prayers are offered that find an echo in the heart of God, from whom they sprang.

Has God put these sentiments in human hearts, and has he not their original and pattern in himself? For a moment do not think of yourself as a child, but of God as your Father. Your spirit has come forth from the Father of Spirits. You were called into existence by his word. You carry in your nature some thought or conception to which he desired to give expression. Is he not conscious, therefore, of responsibility to perfect that which concerns you? Of course you may thwart him, as the clay was marred in the hand of the potter. You may take your journey into a far country and waste the precious formative years in selfish indulgence. But if you will let the Great Father work out his full purpose in your training, your unfolding, and your prayer-life especially, you will find with Isaiah, that eye hath not seen, nor ear heard such an One as our God, who worketh for him that waiteth for him.

Prayer: O God, our Father, may we never doubt thy enduring mercy. May we not be frightened by the noise of the wheels in thy great workshop. Enable us to believe that thou art weaving the fair fabric of our life on the loom of daily circumstance. We beseech thee to perfect that which concerneth us. Amen.

God's Preparations
May 27

'Since the beginning of the world men have not heard, nor perceived by the ear, neither hath the eye seen, O God, beside thee, what he hath prepared for him that waiteth for him' *(Isaiah 64:4).*

This chapter is a casket of precious jewels. Let us look at some of them! What wonder that St Paul loved that fourth verse, which he quotes in 1 Corinthians 2:9! Here we read that God works for those who wait for him; to the apostle these words conveyed the thought that those who wait for him must be those who *love* him, and that God has thought out his prepared plan, so that they have only to believe in him, and go forward, to find that the path has been levelled for them to walk in. Those that love God are not afraid of the mountains that block their way; they know that God will make them flow down, and will reveal a pathway for their steps. The men of this world, from of old, have never heard with the ear, nor perceived with the eye, what our God will do for his own.

Often, as we tread the pathway of service, rejoicing that he loves us, and working such righteousness as we can, we meet God coming toward us, as the father meets his children who have gone out to welcome him on his return from work. Or, in the hour which we dread, the hour of that operation, of that dreaded meeting, the hour of bereavement, as we walk along the path - we shall see a light approaching us, growing ever brighter. It is the herald-ray of God's approach. 'Thou *meetest* them that remember thee in thy ways!'

It is in the midst of such loving-kindness that we become most conscious of sin. All our righteousnesses, which passed muster in the sunlight, in his searching sight seem as filthy rags, and we realise how evanescent are our resolutions. 'We all do fade as a leaf.'

Perhaps we are most ashamed at our failure in the life of prayer. We do not stir up ourselves to take hold of God.

Here we must use special caution in speaking to others of those hidden passages of the soul, in which God our Father is pleased to meet with us and refresh us, lest we lead to take the higher path those who have not trod the lower. Each soul knows its own secret from the Lord, and we must live only as we have received. St Bernard's motto was: 'My secret to myself.'

> *There is a secret place of rest,*
> *God's saints alone may know;*
> *Thou shalt not find it east nor west,*
> *Though seeking to and fro;*
> *A cell where Jesus is the door,*
> *His love the only key;*
> *Who enter will go out no more,*
> *But there with Jesus be.*

Night and Morning!
May 28

The Night of Doubt - the Morning of Faith. It is indeed a memorable moment in the history of the human spirit, when we suddenly wake up to see that the Almighty is the All-Loving Father, that the righteousness of God is no longer a ground of anxiety and fear, but of assured hope; that he has no pleasure in the death of a sinner, but rather that he should turn from his wickedness and live. What a glad hour it was to Thomas when, after a week of the blackness of darkness, he stood face to face with Jesus, and learnt that his heart was beating in sympathy, and that his pierced hands were held out to him. Dare to believe that the Love which died for thee is dealing with all the mysteries, misfits and dark problems of thy life. Weeping may tarry for the night in which you shut yourself in with yourself, but she is only a lodger! Joy will come in the morning, when you open your heart to Christ.

The Night of Perplexity - the Morning of Vision. We cannot explain all the dealings of God with man, still less the mysteries of the Divine Nature. Clouds and darkness are round about him, though judgment and righteousness are the habitation of his Throne. But from time to time we obtain some broken vision of his Purpose and Achievement and Objective. Then the voice of Joy rings through our heart; then our mouths are filled with laughter and our tongues with singing! Men call *us* dreamers, but we count *them* blind. Sooner or later Christ will come! The power of Satan will be broken and his reign ended. The things that prophets and kings foretold, and died without seeing, shall be realised. The children of Light will lift up their heads, because the time of Redemption will have come. Sorrow and sighing will flee away, and in that glad Morning there will be the shout of Joy!

The Night of Bereavement - the Morning of Reunion. Their stay with us was all too short! We had only begun to fathom their sweetness and beauty. We little dreamed that we would only be allowed to sip the cup of bliss that they had brought into our lives. And then they heard a Voice that called, and saw a beckoning Hand, and they arose and went! Ah, that night of Weeping! But the Morning of Joy cometh, when we shall see again their radiant faces welcoming us on the other side. In that fair Morning, Joy will be at the full tide, never to recede.

'Weeping may tarry for the night. But joy cometh in the morning' (Psalm 30:5 RV)

Prayer: Blessed Christ! The storm is high, the night is dark. Come to me, I beseech thee. In thy presence is fulness of Joy. Amen.

The Fortress of the Heart
May 29

Keep thy heart with all diligence' (Proverbs 4:23).

'The peace of God shall keep your hearts' (Philippians 4:7).

In most of the old castles there was an inner keep, which was protected not only by mighty walls and bastions, but by the portcullis at the gate, and sentries at every approach, who challenged every one that passed in and out. So the heart is continually approached by good and evil, by the frivolities and vanities of the world and the insidious suggestions of the flesh. It is like an inn or hostelry, with constant arrivals and departures. Passengers throng in and out, some of them with evil intent, hoping to find conspirators, or to light fires that will spread until the whole being is swept with passion, consuming in an hour the fabric of years to ashes.

We need, therefore, to be constantly on the watch; we must keep our heart above all else that we guard, for out of it are the issues of life (RV marg). Our Lord says that 'out of the heart of man come forth evil thoughts, murders, adulteries, thefts', etc. The devil and the world without would be less to be feared, if there were not such strong tendencies to evil within - many of them inherited from long lines of ancestors, who, alas! pass down to us the worst features of their characters equally with the best.

Keep it Clean. Just as the eye of the body is perpetually washed with tear-water, so let us ask that the precious blood of Christ may cleanse away any speck of impurity. Remember how delicate a thing the heart is, and how susceptible to the dust of an evil thought, which would instantly prevent it becoming the organ of spiritual vision. *Sursum Corda!* Lift up your hearts! We lift them up unto the Lord!

The Sentinel of Peace. Then the Peace of God will become the warden or sentry of the heart, and *it passeth understanding!* We can understand the apparent peace of some men. They have made money, and their gold-bags are piled around them as a fortress; they have rich and influential friends, within whose protection they imagine they will be sheltered and defended; they enjoy good health, and are held in high esteem. We can understand such peace, though it often proves ephemeral! But there is a peace that passes understanding! It is to this that our Lord refers when he says, '*My Peace* I give unto you; not as the world giveth'. 'Let not your *heart* be troubled, neither let it be afraid.'

Prayer: Keep me, Heavenly Father, as the apple of thine eye; defend me by thine almighty power; hide me from this strife of tongues and the fiery darts of the wicked one. May my heart be as the palace which the Stronger than the strong man keeps in perfect peace. Amen.

The Persistence of Life
May 30

What is Death? It is not a condition, but a transition; not an abiding-place, but a passage; not a house, but a doorway. The Scripture refers to it as a *birth* - 'the first-born from the dead'; as an *exodus* - 'after my exodus', says Peter; as *a striking of the tent* - 'I must shortly put off this tabernacle'; as the *weighing of an anchor* - 'the time for me to loose-off from the shore is come'. Each of these metaphors accentuates the fact that Death is but a momentary act. We are absent from the body one moment, present with the Lord the next.

Persistent Personality. In that other field we shall surely recognise each other, and shall be as close akin, yea, closer than we were in long-past happy days, when heart to heart had sweet converse, or cooperated in useful ministry. Abraham will still be Abraham; Isaac, Isaac; and Jacob, Jacob. Not bodiless ghosts, but living personalities etherealised and transfigured. Moses and Elijah were recognised as such by the startled disciples on the Transfiguration mount; and Mary knew the Master in the Garden. What gain would it have been that Jesus promised the dying thief that he should be with him in Paradise, if, when he reached there, he could not recognise the Lord?

Persistent Love. Love will never fail! But how can it exist without an object; and how can it forget! Why did Jesus promise the 'many mansions', unless he meant that there should be homes! He knows that the heart clings, even in the light of Resurrection, to the dear objects of human affection, else he would never have mentioned Peter's name, nor have sent a message to his disciples, nor come a second time for Thomas! And will he ignore those natural cravings for *us*, whom he has loved better than himself? How deep and sweet his assurance: 'If it were not so, I would have told you'! Charles Kingsley asked that on the grave stone, which stood above his wife and himself, should be inscribed the words: 'Amavimus, Amamus Amabimus' - *We loved, we love, we shall continue to love.* And who shall challenge the truth or appositeness of these words?

Persistent Activity. 'His servants shall serve him!' The tasks we bungled here with our apprentice-hands will become possible; and unravelling our tangled skeins, we shall weave such fabrics as our wildest dreams never imagined.

'The God of Abraham, and the God of Isaac, and the God of Jacob. Now he is not the God of the dead, but of the living: for all live unto him' (Luke 20:37, 38).

Prayer: I pray thee, O Lord, to deliver me from the fear of death; and when mine eyes open in the dawn of heaven, may I see thee standing to welcome me, and may I receive thy Well-done! Amen.

God's Unfailing Love
May 31

'Even to your old age I am he; and even to hoar hairs will I carry you; I have made, and I will bear; even I will carry, and will deliver you' (Isaiah 46:4).

'What a marvellous promise is this! In days of foreboding, when we fear what may lie behind the veil of the impenetrable future! Disease? Poverty? Suffering? Bereavement? We cannot tell, but we may turn in confidence to our God. He knows just how much we can bear, for he has made us: 'I have made and I will bear, and will deliver you.'

Even to old age! The hoar-frost may silver the head, the sound of the grinding may be low, the silver cord may be frayed even to the breaking , lovers and friends may have passed on to the other world; like the last apple on the bough, we may be left alone; but in the second childhood as in the first - 'Even to your old age - I will carry you'; 'For himself hath said, I will in no wise fail thee, neither will I in any wise forsake thee. So that with good courage we say, The Lord is my Helper, I will not fear' (Hebrews 13:5).

Prayer: O God, our Father, we are thine. May we never doubt thy enduring mercy. We thank thee! Amen.

JUNE

OUR DAILY WALK OF FAITH

Walk in the steps of that faith of our father
Abraham ... who against all hope believed in hope
(Romans 4:12, 18)

'Have not I commanded thee! Be strong and of a good courage: be not afraid, neither be thou dismayed: for the Lord thy God is with thee whithersoever thou goest' (Joshua 1:9).

It was a host of young men and women that stood on the verge of Jordan waiting the signal to enter the Promised Land. God had said that he would give them every place upon which the sole of their foot should tread (verse 3). What an incentive this was for pressing on! Every time an Israelite put his foot forward on the territory of Canaan, he realised that piece of land would come into the possession of his people.

There is a counterpart of this in our own experience. We must learn to put down our foot upon the *promises* of God's word, and say: 'These are mine by right, and shall be mine in actual enjoyment'. In General Gordon's journal, he tells us that often before he reached some strange and hostile tribe, it seemed as though they had been given to his faith and subdued before he reached them. In combating your spiritual foes, dare to believe that God has given them into your hand, and go forward assured that not one of them shall stand before you. This is a blessed promise: 'There shall not any man be able to stand before thee all the days of thy life: I will be with thee: I will not fail thee, nor forsake thee' (verse 5). It does not matter how fierce the tempter, how often you have failed, how inveterate the bad habits, if you will dare to believe that God is with you, not one of all the band of besetting sins shall be able to stand before you. God cannot fail, and will not forsake; be strong, and go forward!

The one thing that God asks of all of us is that we should obey up to the hilt.

Here are our marching orders, and we must keep them well before us: (1) We must meditate upon the Scripture day and night; it must not depart from our heart or mouth. (2) We must be strong even when obedience seems impossible, and when all influences are brought to bear to weaken our resolution, we must still dare to obey the voice of God. And as we advance we shall find that the dreaded forms of opposition are but shadows, when they are touched with the spear-point of faith, they will divide and we shall pursue our way.

Prayer: Before we enter upon our work and warfare, wilt thou graciously equip us with the armour of light, that we may be able to stand against the wiles of the devil. May we hear thee saying: Fear not, I am with thee, I will help thee. Amen.

Christian Living
June 2

The heart of true religion is to believe that Christ is literally within us. We must not simply look to him as our Mediator, Advocate, and Example, but as being possessed by him. He is our Life, the living Fountain rising up in the well of our personality. The apostle Paul was never weary of re-affirming this great fact of his experience, and it would be well if each of us could say every day, before starting forth on our daily duty: 'Christ is in me; let me make room for him to dwell.'

'I am crucified with Christ; nevertheless I live; yet not I, but Christ liveth in me' (Galatians 2:20).

We must say *No* to self, that the life of Christ may become manifest in and through us, and our standing become a reality in daily experience and conduct. When evil suggestions come to us, we must remember that we have entered a world where such things have no place. We are no longer in the realm of the god of this world, but have passed into the realm of the Risen Christ. Let those who are tempted believe this, and assert it in the face of the tempter, counting upon the Holy Spirit to make their reckoning a living experience.

In Ephesians 6:13-17 is described the armour of the Christian soul; in Colossians 3:12-14 the habit or dress which he wears beneath his coat of mail. We must be careful to be properly dressed each day. If we lose our temper over trifles, or yield to uncharitable speech, it shows that we have omitted to put on the girdle of love; if we yield to pride, avarice, envy and jealousy, we must not simply endeavour to put off these evils, but take from the wardrobe the opposite graces. It is not enough to avoid doing wrong. Our Master demands that we should always do and be what is right. When we fail in some sudden demand, it is because we have omitted to put on some trait of Christ, which was intended to be the complement of our need. Let us therefore day by day say: 'Lord Jesus, wrap thyself around me, that I may go forth, adequately attired to meet life's demands.' *In Christ* for standing; *Christ in us*, for life; *we with him*, for safety.

Prayer: Set my heart on fire with the love of thee; and then to do thy will, and to obey thy commandments, will not be grievous to me. For to him that loveth, nothing is difficult, nothing is impossible; because love is stronger than death. Amen.

'The steps of a good man are ordered by the Lord: and he delighteth in his way. Though he fall, he shall not be utterly cast down; for the Lord upholdeth him with his hand' (Psalm 37:23, 24).

It is a mistake to think of our Lord's sufferings as a fact of history come and gone, an incident of the great past. It is this, but much more. He does not leave us to bear all the burden of life, unaided and alone. *He shares everything with us now* - our pain, our griefs, our weariness. 'In all our affliction, he is afflicted, and the Angel of *his presence* saves us.' As another has put it: 'Not standing over against me, holding back a hand that might help, but side by side; nay, even "closer than breathing". Within the inmost hiding-place of my sufferings, he suffers also, bears my griefs and carries my sorrows, as though they were his own. If only we will avail ourselves of his sympathy and help, they who watch us shall see one like unto the Son of Man walking in the fiery furnace, by our side.'

God is ordering all things in our life to secure the best results here and hereafter. In the darkest sky there are a few inches of blue. Happy is the soul which watches these, and dwells on them, and believes that they will widen until the darkness is past, and all the sky is clear! We often forget that what seems to be a disaster is really the seed of a joyous harvesting. If we had visited this earth of ours in one of the great eras of the past, we should have found it covered by a dense mass of vegetation. But that era was not destined to last. Volcanic action of the fiercest character over-whelmed those mighty trees, and hurled them into the dark caverns and cellars of the yawning gulfs which seamed the planet. You and I, had we been there, might have cried: 'Wherefore this waste?' To our poor and limited vision, it would have seemed a contradiction to the ordered progress of the Creator's plan. Why hurl into the bowels of the earth all this fair growth! But out of that cataclysm, the profuse vegetation, pressed together in the heart of the earth, became coal to give us light and heat.

Once, when staying in the country with a friend, he took me into his garden and showed me the weather-vane over his coach-house, and asked if I could distinguish the sentence woven into its texture. I discovered it to be: 'God is Love'! 'Yes,' he said, 'for I have found that whatever comes to me is from the quarter of the Love of God!'

Prayer: Help me to believe, O Lord, that all things are of thee; and that thou hast a plan for my life, of which each passing incident is a part. Amen.

Co-operating with God
June 4

In this chapter the apostle describes the Church as a garden or vineyard, in which the divine Spirit is ever at work, superintending, directing, inspiring, and calling to co-operate with him all his servants, whether they be Paul, Apollos, or Cephas; or as a vast temple, rising through the ages, requiring labourers to lay the foundations, others to build the walls, and others to put the final touches in the light of an accomplished purpose. In each case, the design, the successive stages of advancing progress, the engagement of the workers, the direction of their labours and their reward is entirely with the Husbandman and the Master-Builder. It is not *our* work, but *his*; we are not responsible for the results, but only to do his will; he repays us by generous rewards, but there our responsibility ends. When the Garden stands in the mature beauty, and yields the prolific fruitage of autumn; when the Building is completed and stands in symmetrical glory amidst the wrecks of time, then those who have co-operated will stand aside, and 'God will be All in all'.

'For we are labourers together with God' (1 Corinthians 3:9).

All through *human industry* there is this co-operation between God and man. *He* stores the cellars of the earth with gold or coal, and it is for man to excavate it; *he* fills the hedgerows and woodlands with wild fruits and flowers, it is for man to cultivate them; *he* fills the earth with iron, copper, and other priceless treasures, it is for man to work them into all manner of useful implements. In every harvestfield, garden, orchard, industry, and employment of natural law for the purpose of civilization, there is this combined effort of God and man. God's energy works according to laws, which man must study as the key to the unlocking of the forces which he uses to flash his messages, guide the aeroplane or motor or speed him across the ocean.

In the Church the same law prevails. God has given the word, but the company of preachers has been needed to proclaim it. The words of inspiration burn with the fire of God, but man is called into to translate them into every language under heaven. The saving power of Christ waits to heal and bless, but he needs the co-operation of the human hand and life as the medium through which his virtue passes. Those whom God calls into fellowship in serving others may count on him for the supply of all their needs (verses 21-23).

Prayer: Heavenly Father, show me how I may work with thee, and in what direction are thy energies going forth that I may walk and work in fellowship with thyself. Amen.

Glorying in Infirmities!
June 5

'My grace is sufficient for thee: for my strength is made perfect in weakness. Most gladly therefore will I rather glory in my infirmities, that the power of Christ may rest upon me' *(2 Corinthians 12:9).*

The apostle seems to have enjoyed wonderful revelations of God. Not once or twice, but often he beheld things that eye hath not seen, and heard words that ear cannot receive, and God felt it was necessary for him to have a make-weight lest he should be exalted beyond measure (verse 7).

What the thorn or stake in the flesh was it is impossible to say with certainty. He may have suffered from some distressing form of ophthalmia. We infer this from the eagerness of the Galatian converts to give him their eyes (Galatians 4:13-17), and from his dependence on an amanuensis. His pain made him very conscious of weakness, and very sensitive of infirmity, and kept him near to the majority of those to whom he ministered, who did not live on the mountain heights, but in the valleys, where demons possess and worry the afflicted. Be willing that your visions of Paradise should be transient, and turn your back on the mountain summit, where the glory shines, as our Lord did, in order to minister to souls in anguish (verse 4: Matthew 17:14-18).

On three separate occasions the apostle besought the Lord for deliverance from his infirmity, and finally received the assurance that though the thorn could not be removed, yet sufficient grace would be given to enable him to do his life-work and he was more than content. On the one hand, there was the buffeting of this messenger of Satan; but on the other, there were the gains of meekness, humility, and of greater grace than would have been possible if he had not needed it so sorely - and he gladly accepted an infirmity for which there were such abundant compensations.

Prayer: Help us, O Lord, to look on the bright side of things; not on the dark cloud, but on thy rainbow of covenant mercy; not on the stormy waters, but on the face of Jesus; not on what thou hast taken, or withheld, but on what thou hast left. Enable us to realise thine all-sufficiency. Amen.

Do not sit down baffled by your difficulties and infirmities, but turn from them to claim Christ's abundant grace and strength, that at the end of life you may have done all that was set you to do, and more, because the greatness of your need made you lean more heavily on his infinite resources, 'He giveth power to the faint; and to them that have no might he increaseth strength.'

How to Meet Discouragements
June 6

Notice the marvellous antithesis of this chapter: light and darkness; life and death; pressure, perplexity, pursuit and persecution; but side by side, victory, elastic hope, and the brightness of Christian faith. The decay of the outward man and the renewal of the inward; the light affliction and the weight of glory; the brief moment of earth's pilgrimage contrasted with the eternity of reality and bliss.

It is very important that we should not miss the mighty blessing which is within the reach of every troubled soul. Of course it is quite possible to sit down before troubles and afflictions, hopeless and despairing, confessing that we are overpowered and defeated; it is also possible to be hard and stoical, bearing adversity because we cannot help or avoid it, but the highest Christian way is to be thankful that the earthen vessel is breaking if only the torch will shine out; to be content that the dying of Jesus should be borne about in our mortal body, if only his life will thereby become manifest.

When through the deep waters I call thee to go,
The rivers of grief shall not thee overflow;
For I will be with thee in trouble to bless;
And sanctify to thee thy deepest distress.

'Our light affliction, which is but for a moment, worketh for us a far more exceeding and eternal weight of glory; while we look not at the things which are seen, but at the things which are not seen' (2 Corinthians 4:17, 18).

Prayer: Fix my heart, O Lord, on thyself, that amid the changes and chances of this mortal life I may be kept steadfast and unmoveable and ever abounding in thy work. Amen.

The Home of God in the Heart of Man
June 7

'Thus saith the high and lofty One that inhabiteth Eternity, whose name is Holy: I dwell in the high and holy place, with him also that is of a contrite spirit' (Isaiah 57:15).

This verse has reference to God's two homes - the *macrocosm* of the great universe and the *microcosm* of the human heart. Our God is so great that the heaven of heavens cannot contain him, but he is so lowly and humble that he will stoop to fill the heart of a child. He bids us learn of him, for he is meek and lowly in heart.

The humble and contrite heart. It seems almost too wonderful to believe that the Eternal One will care to come and live with the child of Time; that the infinite and holy God will descend to the narrow limits of a human heart! (see John 14:23).

Prayer

Spirit of purity and grace,
Our weakness, pitying, see;
O make our hearts thy dwelling-place,
And worthier thee.

Amen.

A Cure for Anxiety
June 8

The Psalm from which our text is taken breathes the spirit of optimism. The Psalmist says: 'Do not fret. Evil is transient, evil-doers shall be cut off, in a little while the wicked shall not be.' You will not remove the evils of the world by all your anxiety, or by wrath. It is not worthwhile to lose your peace of mind. Be quiet in your heart, full of prayer, looking up to God that he would interpose to deliver.

In this Psalm there are excellent preservatives of the inward tranquillity of the soul when face to face with anxiety, or with high-handed wrong.

Trust in the Lord (verse 3). Reckon on him. Expect great things from your Almighty Guide and Friend. He cannot fail you.

Delight in the Lord (verse 4). If your life twines about earthly things, of course you will be at the mercy of externals. Familiarise yourself with God's way of thinking and looking at things. If this is the bent of your life, you will lose your taste for things of the earth, while you will have great desires for the things of eternity, and God will give you perfect satisfaction in these, because he will give you himself! The petitions of the heart (RV margin) are very sacred to God, and he never, never forgets the. 'He *shall* give thee the petitions of thine heart.'

Commit thy way unto the Lord (verse 5). The margin suggests 'Roll thy way upon the Lord'. It is not enough to roll the responsibility of selecting our way on God in the great crises of our life. We must do so in the small decisions of every hour. Our lives are made up of trifles. To neglect these is to leave it to drift at haphazard. We need perpetually to look up to our Heavenly Friend, saying, 'I cannot see over the hedge, I must leave with thee the decision whether I should go this way or that.'

Rest in the Lord (verse 7). 'Be silent to the Lord' (RV margin). There is so much clamour in the world, and often our heart becomes filled with its noise, so much so that we cannot hear his still small voice. But when every sound has died down into silence, we shall hear the voice of God telling us of things which will answer our questionings and still our doubts. Let your requests be made known unto God, and his peace shall sentinel your heart against all intruders.

'Commit thy way unto the Lord; trust also in him; and he shall bring it to pass' (Psalm 37:5).

Prayer: My God and Father, enable me to roll my way upon thee, to trust thee, and to believe that when I stand with thee in the perfect daylight I shall understand what now I take on trust. Amen.

Cheering Promises
June 9

'Whereby are given unto us great and precious promises: that by these ye might be partakers of the divine nature' (2 Peter 1:4).

Precious faith and precious promise are necessarily linked together (verses 1, 4). The promises excite the faith, and faith reckons upon the fulfilment of promise. One is sometimes asked why it is that God's word seems to fail, and that the righteous do appear to be forsaken! But surely the reason is, not that there is any failure on God's side to fulfil his promises, but that the promise is not claimed. It is possible to carry around a pocketful of bank notes and cheques, and to die of starvation because they have not been cashed. When you have found a promise that just fits your need, do not rest content until you have laid it before God, and *claimed* its fulfilment.

Note that everything which is needed for life and godliness is already granted to us in Jesus our Lord (verse 3). We have not to pray to our Father for things which he has not anticipated, but to claim those which he has already given. The one purpose of God's preparation is that we should not only escape the corruption which is in the world, but become 'partakers of his divine nature'. What a marvellous promise is this, which almost passes human thought and comprehension, that we should become animated and filled by the very nature of God!

Note the recurrence of the phrase 'these things' in the following verses. When they abound in us we cannot be idle or unfruitful. The octave of qualities enumerated reminds us of those Chinese boxes, each of which contains a smaller one, until we finally arrive at some precious article enclosed in the innermost. Faith apprehends everything else - manly courage, knowledge, self-control, patience, godliness, kindness, and above all, love. To be deficient in 'these things' is to be *short-sighted* (RV).

Prayer: Grant us, O Lord, we beseech thee, always to seek thy kingdom and righteousness; and of whatsoever thou seest us to stand in need, mercifully grant us an abundant portion; through Jesus Christ our Lord. Amen.

The apostle says that the soul which has incorporated into itself these qualities of character will be welcomed into the Eternal Kingdom. It will enter the Harbour royally, with every sail set and pennant flying, and receive a choral entrance from the eager crowds that await its approach (verse 11). Let us be diligent in our appropriation of God's great and priceless promises, so that we shall never fail.

God's Providential Care
June 10

At the time when our Lord spoke these words, the fields of Palestine were carpeted with wild flowers, and the air was redolent with their fragrance, bespangling the pastures, clustering in the hedgerows, and hiding in the woodland glades. Theirs was as careless a life as that of the birds which were flying overhead. 'They toil not, neither do they spin.' For some plants, like the exotics of the greenhouse and nurseries, there must be extreme care and expense in their cultivation, in the provision of heat and the experienced skill of the horticulturist. But our Lord was not alluding to these, but to the flowers of the grass, which grow amid the wilds of nature, or in the gardens of the poor, and to him these were very beautiful.

'Seek not what ye shall eat, or what ye shall drink, neither be ye of doubtful mind. But rather seek ye the kingdom of God; and all these things shall be added unto you' (Luke 12:29-31).

This prodigious growth teaches us that God loves beautiful things, and expends thought and skill in their production. He might have made the world without a daisy, and human life without the beauty of childhood. But since he clothed with beauty the short-lived flowers of the wilds; the ephemeral insects of a summer day; the shells of the minute creatures that build up the solid fabric of the rocks - surely this prodigality, this lavishness, this prolific superabundance of creativeness, must mean that he can and will withhold no good thing from them that trust him.

Of course we must fulfil our part! We are not to be careless and improvident; we must certainly sow and reap, and toil and spin; but when we have done all, we must rely upon our Heavenly Father whose good pleasure it is to give, believing that it is vain for us to rise up early, and sit up late, and to eat the bread of sorrows, for our God will give us all that we need, even whilst we sleep. He will not allow his trusting children to starve, or to go unsheltered, unclothed, and unshod. 'Fear not, little flock,' says the comforting voice of the Good Shepherd, 'for it is your Father's good pleasure to give you the kingdom.'

Prayer: Gracious Lord, grant to me, thy poor needy creature, sometimes at least to feel, if it be but a small portion of thy hearty affectionate love; that my faith may become more strong, my hope in thy goodness may be increased, and that love, once kindled within me, may never fail. Amen.

'For to me to live is Christ, and to die is gain' (Philippians 1:21).

How close life and death are! In this verse there is only a comma between them, and every one of us stands where that comma stands, between life and death. Life is the vestibule of death, and death is close on the heels of life. The systole and diastole; the throb and beat of the pulse; the swing of the pendulum this way or that!

St Paul is enamoured with the *joys of life*. He was a toiler and a traveller, and lived amid the busy throng that jostled him in the streets. The philosopher, as he passed, carrying his scrolls of learning, said, 'To me to live is *knowledge*'; the soldier, passing, looked with contempt on the man of letters, and said, 'To me to live is *fame*'; the merchant in passing said, with pride, 'To me to live is *riches*'; the toiling masses passed by, saying, 'To us to live is *toil and trouble*'. Amid all these, the apostle strikes in with no bated breath, saying joyously, 'To me to live is neither wealth, nor labour, nor fame, nor glory, but *Christ*'. If you had asked him just what he meant, he would probably have replied, as Tyndale brings out in his translation, that *'Christ was the origin of his life'*.

If we would become partakers of the divine nature, we also must have such a definite experience. We can trace our natural life back to our parents, and our spiritual life must begin in the hour when, in early childhood, or later, we are made partakers of the nature of the risen Saviour (John 1:12, 13; 2 Peter 1:4).

Christ must be the model of our life. Every man works to a model. Consciously or not, we are always imitating somebody, and every true follower of Christ seeks to approximate to the measuring of the stature of our Lord - 'Beholding, we are changed into the same image, from glory to glory.'

Christ must be the aim of life. That his will may be done on earth as in heaven; that others may know and love and serve him as we do; that he may be the crowned King of men - that must be our purpose and aim. External things have no power over the one who can say, 'I live, yet not I, but Christ liveth in me'; then we can triumph over Death itself, and say: 'To die is to gain'.

Prayer: The mountain peaks of the Christ-life that we would live call to us, but they often seem too steep and high for us to reach, but thou knowest and hast an infinite compassion for thy children. Fulfil in us the good pleasure of thy will, and realise in us the ideals thou hast taught us to cherish. Amen.

Decision for Christ
June 12

Notice the threefold repetition of these solemn words: *he cannot be my disciple* (verses 26, 27, 33). There is a sense in which the Way of Salvation is easy. One look of faith in Christ, and we receive eternal life and are assured by him that we can never perish; but that faith must carry in its heart the germ of discipleship - the tenacity, determination, indomitable resolve to learn everything that the Master has to teach. We are not only saved from sin, but we are saved to learn, redeemed to be taught. The education is free, but there are certain things which we must be prepared to forego if we would be entered in his School. The disciple must bring the unbiased and disengaged mind to the grace of God, which comes disciplining us, teaching us to deny ungodly lusts, and to live righteously, soberly and godly in this present world.

'Whosoever doth not bear his cross, and come after me, cannot be my disciple' (Luke 14:27).

What are the things which we must cultivate for discipleship?

A supreme love (verse 26). Our Lord does not ask us really to hate those related to us by natural ties, but to give to himself so much love that compared with all else, it should be as sunlight to starlight; that for love of him we should be willing to act as one who hates all other loves when they conflict with obedience. We are first converted from the natural to the spiritual, and then from the spiritual to the natural again.

The denial of self (verse 27). We are not simply to cut off this or the other indulgence, but to put the Cross of Christ between ourselves and the gratification of our own will. We must be willing to follow the Lamb, though the old Abraham cries out in grievous pain.

Renunciation (verse 33). We must be prepared to count all things but loss for the excellency of the knowledge of Christ Jesus our Lord. As a matter of fact, Jesus gives us back all that is right and beautiful to use for him, but there must be a definite loosing hold on things, and the placing of all in his pierced hands. Abjuring our ownership, we must be willing to act as his almoners and trustees. It is this that gives savour to life, making it sparkle and resist decay.

Prayer: Accept us as we now yield to thee our entire being with all that we possess. It is our one desire to be utterly, only, and always for thee. Amen.

Profit and Loss
June 13

'Lo, we have left all, and have followed thee! Jesus answered, There is no man that hath left house, or brethren, or sisters, or father, or mother, or wife, or children, or lands, for my sake, and the gospel's but he shall receive an hundredfold now in this time ... and in the world to come eternal life' (Mark 10:28-30).

The principles of this world, and those of our Lord are widely different. The world is set on grasping all it can - accumulation, self-aggrandisement, the piling up of fortunes, the gradual or speedy climb up the ladder of fame, the gathering of hosts of friends. Looking after 'number one' is the readiest way of expressing this principle of life! But it is unsatisfactory and disappointing. The soul which is the centre of its own circumference is doomed to realise that there are more forfeits than prizes, more bitterness than success, more dark hours than bright ones.

On the other side, Christ's principle of life is to give, to trust, to bless! His measure must be always pressed down and running over. The cloak must follow the coat; the second mile must be gladly thrown in with the first. To be willing to surrender *all* for the sake of others, is the ordinary claim of the King on those who own him as their Lord.

In every age there have been thousands who have gladly accepted this as their rule of life. Peter and the rest of the apostles were the leaders of a host which no man can number, who have left all to follow Jesus. He had nowhere to lay his head, and they have been homeless, wandering in the world, with no settled abiding-place; he was poor and they have gone amongst their fellows, saying, 'Silver and gold have we none, but such as we have we give.' But how great has been their reward.

Prayer: Thou hast called us to minister and witness, to go amongst men as our Saviour went, bearing in our hands the balm of Gilead. May we not be disobedient to this heavenly vision. Amen.

Before we can understand what Christ is willing to do for us, there must be not only a taking-hold, but a letting-go. We must step out from the boat, and withdraw our hand from it. It is even good, like St Paul, to need all things, since by faith we come to possess all. Read the wonderful series of paradoxes to which he gives utterance in 2 Corinthians 4.

The Lord promises eternal life as the crown of all. When we kneel at the Cross, and see Jesus as our own Saviour, we *have* eternal life, but we cannot realise all it implies until this mortality is swallowed up of life.

The One-Talented Man
June 14

The five-talented men are the geniuses of the world, successful in everything they touch. The two-talented men on the one hand, are not exposed to the temptations of genius, but are not quite at the minimum. But why did the man with the one talent make such ill use of his gift? Surely, this is a true touch of life! One-talented people can do so little, that they do nothing. They are crushed and enfeebled by a sense of their own insignificance and inferiority. Many start life with high and pure aims, but presently they find their opportunities so meagre, their influence so limited, their power so scanty, that after a few struggles they give up in despair.

'He also that had received the one talent came' (Matthew 25:24)

But the world will never be saved and helped unless the one-talented people, who are the great majority, can be aroused to a sense of their responsibility. Five men can put the whole energy of their manhood behind their single talents, whilst the one man with five talents has only the driving power of one. It is probably a greater thing in God's sight to use one talent faithfully than many. No one notices the man with his humble one talent. There is no outburst of praise or cheering. It is a greater test of the quality of the soul to go on doing one small thing well, than to be able to turn with brilliant versatility from one talent to another. The monotony of life presses hard on those who have only one string to their bow, one tune to play, one act to perform in the great factory where labour is carefully subdivided.

But the one thing that our Lord demands of each of us is to be *faithful* - faithful in a very little. He is watching each of us with great eagerness as we live our daily life, because he knows, as we cannot realise, how much our position in the other world depends on our fidelity in this. It is for our sake that he is so anxious that we should make good use of our one talent.

Have you only one talent? Are you doing anything with it? Remember it is the ounce-weight that may turn the scales where hundred-weights are balanced; it is the tiny tug that can move the great liner. Be thou faithful in thy very little, and thou shalt receive the 'Well done' of thy Lord.

Prayer: O Lord, at the end of every day, may we stand before thee to hear thy verdict, and when all the toil and labour of our life is ended, may we hear thee say: 'Well done, good and faithful servant! thou hast been faithful in a few things ... enter thou into the joy of thy Lord'. Amen.

Jesus, the Mediator of a New Covenant
June 15

'He is the mediator of a better covenant, which hath been enacted upon better promises. He is faithful that promised' (Hebrews 8:6; 10:23).

This is called the 'Better Covenant'. There are no *ifs*; no injunctions of '*observe to do*'; no conditions of obedience to be fulfilled. From first to last it consists of the *I wills of the most High.*

I will put my laws into their minds, refers to the intellectual faculty, which thinks, remembers, and reasons.

I will write them upon their hearts, the seat of the emotional life and affections. What a man loves, he is pretty certain to follow and obey. 'A little lower,' said the dying veteran, as they probed for the bullet, 'and you will find the Emperor.' So with the Christian who has been taken into the Covenant with God, the law is inscribed on the deepest affections of his being. He obeys because he loves.

I will be to them a God, and they shall be to me a people. This last clause is even better than the first, because it implies the keeping power of God. If we are to be a people for his peculiar possession, it can only result from the operation of his gracious Spirit, who keeps us, as the sun restrains the planets from becoming wandering stars.

All shall know me. Oh, wonder of wonders. Can it be? To know God! To know him as Abraham did, to whom he told his secrets; as Moses did, who conversed with him face to face; or as the apostle John did when he beheld him in the visions of the Apocalypse. And that this privilege should be within the reach of the *least*!

I will be merciful to their iniquities, and their sins will I remember no more. As a score is forgotten when blotted from a slate, so shall sin be obliterated from the memory of God. It will be forgotten as a debt paid years ago.

Do you ask how God can call this a covenant, in which there is no second covenanting party? The answer is easy: Jesus Christ has stood in our stead, and has not only negotiated this covenant, but has fulfilled in our name, and on our behalf, all the conditions which were necessary and right. He has become our Sponsor and Surety, so God is able to enter into these liberal terms with us if we will identify ourselves with him by a living faith. This is the new and better covenant.

Prayer: Holy Father! I claim from thee the fulfilment of thy Covenant Promise, that thou shouldst write thy law upon my heart, and remember my sins and iniquities no more. May I hear thee say, 'Thy faith hath saved thee; Go, and sin no more'. Amen.

Cast Down? Why?
June 16

The Lament of the soul, its cause! Many have been brought to this condition - Jacob said 'all these things are against me'; Job complained that God had refused to listen to his prayer, and had fenced up his way; Elijah prayed that he might die; John the Baptist had his doubts; even our Lord himself cried, 'My God, why hast thou forsaken me?'

'O my God, my soul is cast down within me' (Psalm 42:6).

It may arise from physical weakness. Our nature is like a finely-attuned harp, and may easily become tangled and discordant. When we are in good health, and the zest of living is strong within us, the soul sings songs without words, and the heart suns itself in the consciously-realised love of God; but when the lamp of life burns low - the joy of the Lord, the sense of his love are apt to decline.

It may arise from temperament. Some seem born in the dark, and carry through life a predisposition to melancholy. Their nature is set to a minor key. They gaze on the lowering clouds, rather than on the patches of blue. Thomas had such a temperament, yet our Lord called him to be an apostle! Rightness of heart generally shows itself in gladness of heart; but there are those who mourn in Zion, and are more prone to tears than smiles! The valley of shadow is part of the highway to the Holy City; and the souls that are called to tread it may yet find the valley of Baca to be a place of springs.

Now as to the cure. Make much of your standing in Christ! Our feelings are as fickle as April sunshine. But our standing in Jesus is unalterable. John Bunyan used to say that he had two sorts of money. That which was deposited in the bank, and that which he had in his pocket. The former was, on the whole, permanent, while the other was always changing. Thus he said it was between him and the Saviour. His feelings, like the loose coins in his pocket, were always changing, but his capital was lodged safely in the strong keeping of Christ.

Prayer: Gracious God, give me to behold the rainbow of hope on the dark storm-clouds that brood over my life: may I rest confidently on that covenant, ordered in all things and sure, which was sealed by the precious blood of Christ. Amen.

Cease introspection and live in the progress of Christ through the world. He is ever going forth to new conquests, and we must not stand as loiterers, feeling our pulse. Why art thou cast down, O my soul? Canst thou not take thy place in his ever victorious army. Miss Feeblemind and Mr Ready-to-halt, in the care of Great-heart, will go over the River singing!

Courage in Life's Storms
June 17

'There stood by me this night an angel of the God whose I am, whom also I serve, saying, "Fear not, Paul; thou must stand before Caesar: and lo, God hath granted thee all them that sail with thee." Wherefore, sirs, be of good cheer: for I believe God, that it shall be even so as it hath been spoken unto me' (Acts 27:23-25).

Said a boy to his mother, 'What is fear like? I have never seen him.' Paul might have said as much, because his life was hid with Christ in God. He had learned to detect the voice of Christ. Some cannot do so, for it needs the practised ear and the obedient will. But all through his Christian career the apostle seems to have derived comfort and strength from special revelations. Through the murky darkness of the storm, Christ's ministering angel sped to his hammock, and standing beside him bade him be of good cheer. And there is no storm that beats on our life which does not bring God's angels also to our help, though we may not see their forms or hear their voice. The one condition of angel-help is that we belong to their Master. We must be able to say, 'Whose I am, and whom I serve.'

The Prayer of Faith. In verse 24 the Revised Version rendering is 'granted'. It signifies that Paul had asked and God had granted his prayer, and given him his request. What a promise this is! It is said of Miss Havergal that she went to stay with a family not one of whom was definitely for Christ. On the first night of her stay she wrote her well-known hymn, 'Take my life, and let it be, consecrated, Lord, to thee.' And during her short sojourn under that roof she won for her Lord the entire household. So we may claim that all who sail with us in the ship of our life shall become God's children.

The Courage of Faith is consistent with Commonsense. Even though Paul had God's assurance, he felt that he must do what he could, as though all depended on his sagacity. Faith ought not to make us act presumptuously or foolishly. Holy calm and stillness rule in the heart of him whose mind is stayed on God.

We are likely to encounter many storms in our life before we anchor in the Fair Haven of Eternity, but in the heart of every cyclone there is a point of rest; and in the fiercest storm that sweeps our world, we may hide in the secret place of the Most High, and sing Psalm 46.

Prayer: By day and by night, in life and in death, may I ever be true to thee, O Lover of my Soul, my ceaseless Friend, my unchangeable Saviour. Into thy hands I commit my spirit! Amen.

God's Salvation and Comfort
June 18

This exquisite Psalm of Hope seems prepared for the day when Jew and Gentile, gathered into one Church, shall stand on the shores of eternity with palms of victory. Here is the Song of Moses and the Lamb!

Salvation was peculiarly associated with the Feast of Tabernacles, which was the type of that consummation of God's purpose, which shall take place when his Tabernacle is with men, and he shall dwell with them (Revelation 21:3). Do not fear - God is with us, as Strength and Song, and Salvation. He shares our wilderness march; we are folded under the shadow of his tent; we are permitted to reckon on him as our Partner and Companion. Notice the emphasis on the word *my*. The weakest saint can claim all needed supplies from God; and he admits the plea, saying, 'Child, thou art ever with me, and all that I have is thine' (Luke 15:31).

Unfailing supplies - 'wells of salvation' (verse 3). On the last day of the Feast of Tabernacles the priests drew water in a golden pitcher from the Pool of Siloam, and poured it forth in the Temple, while the Choir chanted this verse in memory of the rock-water that followed the desert march. Every attribute of God, every means of grace, every helpful and loving ministry, every promise of Scripture, is a well, and faith is our pitcher (John 7:37).

But we must draw. Faith is the bucket, which we let down into the fullness of the divine supply. It is not simply the general belief that God hears and answers prayer, but the specific and particular belief that God has answered or will answer your prayer for some special needed grace, and that it is yours. Believe that ye have received. *Draw* water out of the well!

'*Thou comfortest me*' (verse 1). There is no such Comforter as God. 'As one whom his mother comforteth, so will I comfort you.' He is expressly described as 'the God of all Comfort'. Is it not too much to ask that thou shouldest stoop out of thy high heaven to comfort me, whose heart is heavy with grief and whose eyes are red with weeping? He wipes the tears from all eyes, and staunches the very fountains of grief. 'Weeping may endure for a night, but joy cometh in the morning.' I shall yet praise thee!

'Behold God is my salvation; I will trust and not be afraid: for the Lord Jehovah is my strength and my song' (Isaiah 12:2).

Prayer: Make us to know, O God, the riches of the glory of thine inheritance, and the exceeding greatness of thy power toward them that believe. We would so live that sweet music may come to thee. Amen.

A Shelter from the Tempest
June 19

'And a man shall be as a hiding-place from the wind, and a covert from the tempest ... as the shadow of a great rock in a weary land' (Isaiah 32:2).

We are reminded that this prophecy was uttered in a time of great unrest. The clouds of war were gathering dark on the horizon, and Israel was looking for help from the arm of flesh. In this emergency the voice of the prophet was heard, saying, 'Look not to Egypt, but to God' (31:1). The kingdom depends on the king: 'Behold a king shall reign in righteousness, and princes rule in judgment'. When all politics and commerce, social and domestic life are under the sway and guidance of Jesus Christ, the Kingdom of God will come, and the will of God shall be done on earth, as in heaven.

The Lord Jesus is many-sided enough to meet all the varied needs of his people. Some need a covert from the tempest, others rivers of water to quench their thirst, others the shadow of a great rock in a weary land. But he is all and equal to all. When a man or woman owns the sway of Christ, eyes and ears are cleansed, there is no longer the hesitation of stammering confession, the judgment becomes rectified and the heart opened to a new generosity. First righteousness, then peace - such is heaven's eternal order.

This is a marvellous chapter! Note the words of warning to the women of Jerusalem. After all, the religious and political life of a nation is very much what the women make it, and there can never be a widespread deepening of religious life unless the women, who have such great capacity for God, turn to him in repentance and faith.

Prayer: Bring us, O Lord, through the troubled waters of life into a haven of repose. Hide us secretly in thy pavilion from the strife of tongues and the fiery darts of the wicked one. May we be at peace with thee, with ourselves, and with all. Amen.

Are our conditions similar? Surely they are! For if in the days of Solomon it was true that all things were full of labour and stress, how much more true is it in our time! The tides of human life are high and stormy, and there is no sense of security. We may surely plead that *we* need the quiet resting-places and sure dwellings, in which our souls may shelter! The promise is made to '*my people*' - to those who have heard and obeyed the voice of the Good Shepherd. If you are one of the weakest and lowliest of these, you may draw comfort here (verse 18).

The Rock of Ages
June 20

The love of God, like a cleft rock, is the age-long shelter of his people, and rears itself above the tumultuous waters of time. The lightning that flashed from the thunder-clouds of Calvary has riven it. A cleft was made in it by the spear that pierced the heart of our Lord, and this was followed, as it was withdrawn from the gaping wound, by blood and water. But there sinful souls may hide! God had said to Moses, 'Behold, there is a place by me, and it shall come to pass that I will put thee in a cleft of the rock, and will cover thee with my hand while I pass by, for thou canst not see my face, and live.' So he speaks to us all, and promises that the water and the blood shall be the double cure from the wrath and power of sin.

'Trust ye in the Lord for ever: for in the Lord Jehovah is an everlasting rock' (Isaiah 26:4 RV).

It is free! The sinner need not seek to acquire the shelter of that Rock of Ages by the labour of his hands, or the fulfilling of the demands of the law. It is not required that he should burn with a zeal that knows no respite, or flow with tears that refuse to be staunched. To be helpless and forlorn, to be in peril of condemnation, to be contrite and humble - this is all that is required. To have no Mediator, no Refuge, no Helper beside, and to lift the eyes of faith to the Saviour - that is the sole condition of being lifted by unseen hands into the cleft of that Rock!

It holds all that the soul needs. Is the soul naked? There is dress for it. Is it helpless? There is grace for it. Is it blackened by sin? There is cleansing for it. Is it sick? There is healing for it. Toplady, the Calvinist, and Wesley, the Arminian, agree here: 'Thou, O Christ, art all I want; more than all in thee I find'.

It is for ever. It is the Rock of Ages! Time may beat upon it, but it cannot alter it or impair it. Whilst this fleeting breath is drawn, when eyes close in death, when unknown worlds are entered, when the judgment throne is set, always and for ever the soul may shelter in the cleft Rock of the unchanging Redeemer, and Peace, like a double window, intercepts alarm from the heart which is stayed on God and trusting in him.

Prayer:
Rock of Ages! cleft for me,
Let me hide myself in thee.
Let the water and the blood,
From thy riven side which flowed,
Be of sin the double cure,
Save me from its guilt and power.

Amen.

Prayer that Obtains
June 21

'Ask, and it shall be given you; seek, and ye shall find; knock, and it shall be opened unto you' (Luke 11:9).

There are many conditions of true prayer. For instance, it must be *earnest*. There are times when we know we are on the line of God's purposes, when we may dare to be *importunate*. Prayer must be offered in the *name of Christ*, i.e. it must be in harmony with the nature of Christ, which was devoted to the glory of God and to the blessing of men. That *name* will eliminate the ingredient of selfishness which will mar any prayer by whomsoever offered. Prayer must also be based on some *promise* of God, which is presented to him as a cheque or note is presented to a bank.

All these are but steps to the faith that obtains, for it is, after all, not prayer but *faith* that obtains promises. That is why our Lord lays so much stress on receiving. Much of our prayer fails because we forget that he said, 'Every one that asketh, *receiveth*'; and again, 'All things whatsoever ye pray and ask for, *believe that ye have received them*, and ye shall have them' (Mark 11:24).

So far as one can describe the process, it seems something after this fashion. The soul reverently kneels before God, glorifying and praising him for his greatness and goodness. It is conscious of needing some very special gift which is promised. In the name of Christ it presents the request with the confidence of a child. With earnestness of desire and speech it unfolds the reasons why the gift sought is so necessary. But it does not leave prayer at this point to go away in uncertainty as to what the issue shall be. By an act of the spirit, the suppliant seems to receive definitely the spiritual or even the temporal gift; and realises that it has received, that the special grace has been imparted, to be discovered and used under stress of need; that the temporal gift has also been received, though it may be kept back until the precise moment when it can be delivered, in much the same way as a present may be purchased long before the time of handing it to its destined possessor (1 Samuel 1:15, 18, 27).

This is what Christ meant by 'receiving' and it has a mighty effect upon prayer, because it makes it so much more definite. It leads to praise, because we are able to thank God for his gift. You must *take* as well as pray.

Prayer: We rejoice that our Saviour ever lives to intercede as our High Priest and Mediator. Through the rent veil, let our prayers ascend to thee mingled with the fragrance of his merit in whom thou art ever well pleased. Amen.

Answered Prayer
June 22

Our Lord expected answers to his prayers, and in all his teaching he leads us to feel that we shall be able to obtain, through prayer, what otherwise would not come to our hand. He knew all that was to be known of natural law; but notwithstanding his perfect acquaintance with the mysteries of his Father's government, he said, 'If ye shall ask anything of the Father, he will give it in my name.'

'If ye abide in me, and my words abide in you, ask whatsoever ye will, and it shall be done unto you' (John 15:7).

When we consider the lives of some who have wrought mightily for God, it is clear that they learned a secret which eludes many of us. This is from the biography of Dr Burns Thomson: 'When much together as students,' writes his friend, 'we agreed on special petitions, and the Lord encouraged us by giving us answers, so early and so definite, as could only have come from himself, so that no room was left for the shadow of doubt that God was the Hearer and Answerer of prayer. Once the answer came the same day, and at another time whilst we were yet speaking. My friend often spoke of our agreement, to the glory of him who fulfilled to us his promise; and I refer to it to encourage others.' This is but one leaf out of the great library of prayers, intercessions and supplications, which stand recorded before God.

Prayer which is to prevail must be: *For the glory of the Father.* Whatever petition we offer must be tested by this thought: will it be for the glory of God? It is for this that our Saviour lives and pleads (John 14:13).

It must be in Christ's name, which stands for nature. In other words, when we pray it must not be as our self-nature but as the Christ-nature indicates. It is not enough to mention his name at the end of our prayer: his Spirit must pervade every petition.

We must bear fruit (John 15:16). Answers to prayer largely depend on our ministry to others. If we are living for the accomplishment of God's purpose and the coming of his Kingdom, we may ask whatever is necessary for the achievement of our endeavour.

Prayer: All our desire is known unto thee, therefore perfect what thou hast begun, and what thy Spirit has awakened us to ask in prayer. We seek thy face, show us thy glory. Amen.

We must abide in Christ; then the sap of the Holy Spirit rising from the hidden root will produce desires and petitions like those which Christ ever presents to his Father (John 15: 7).

The Power of Small Things
June 23

'Verily I say unto you, If ye have faith as a grain of mustard seed ... nothing shall be impossible unto you' (Matthew 17:20).

The grain of mustard seed is the smallest of seeds, but Jesus says that it is a fitting emblem of the Kingdom of God, and the unostentatious beginnings of the Christian era. The number and social position of the disciples was insignificant in the extreme. And the first germ of truth sown in the heart of man, woman, or child is sometimes equally insignificant. It may be just a sentence, a text, a passing remark which results in a mighty harvest (Mark 4:30-32).

What is it that enables this tiny seed to make such a prodigious increase? It lies in its receptive power, as it receives into its nature the mighty forces which slumber in the soil, the effect of sunbeams, moisture and air. So long as a little aperture is kept open, there is no limit to the fertility and usefulness of the plant. You may be but a child, and your life seem weak and ineffective, but if you will open your heart to God by faith, he will pour in his mighty fullness, and the tiny seed become a great tree of strength and usefulness, grace and beauty.

Let us not despise the day of small things. Faith may be as a grain of mustard seed, but as it is used it will grow. Your effort to do good may seem so insignificant that it would hardly be missed, if it were discontinued, and yet out of it may emanate some mighty work which will bring help and comfort to thousands. How many orphanages, schools and philanthropic efforts have owed their origin to the most infinitesimal beginnings. One destitute child cared and ministered to for Christ's sake has led to another until finally thousands of little ones have received a good start in life. What could be more insignificant than the beginnings of the gospel message in many a heathen country? Do not be discouraged. Like Gideon, you may be only a cake of barley bread, but by faith you may overturn the tents of Midian. Like the little lad, you may only be able to place five tiny loaves and two small fish in the hands of Jesus, but he will bless them and make them sufficient to feed the multitude. A stone may bring Goliath to the dust; an arrow may pierce through the armour of the mailed warrior. Have faith in God; reckon on God's faithfulness to you.

Prayer: Lord, increase our faith. Give us a child-like faith to receive what thou dost offer, and from this moment may a new sense of the presence and power of God, through the Holy Spirit, come to us. Amen.

The Basis of Peace
June 24

The basis of redemption and peace was laid on Calvary, when our Lord died for the sins of the world. In Leviticus 17:11, we learn that 'the life, or soul, of the flesh is in the blood' (RV marg); from which we infer that the forth-flowing of the blood of Christ was the forth-pouring of his soul as a sacrifice for sin.

It may be asked: Granted that the blood of Christ represents his soul which was poured out for sinful men, how did this marvellous act of self-sacrifice constitute a basis for peace? The full answer to that question is impossible in our present limited knowledge. It is one of the secret things which belong to the Lord our God, hidden from us now, to be revealed when we are full-grown.

But never suppose that the shedding of Christ's blood was necessary to make God love us, to appease his wrath or wring from his unwilling hand an edict of redemption. *'God was in Christ reconciling the world unto himself.'* The Father does not love us because Jesus died, but he went to the Cross because of God's love for us who chose us to be joint heirs with his Son.

But there is one condition to be fulfilled. The access into peace is open only to those who believe. We are justified by faith; we have peace through believing. The apostle says that 'through our Lord Jesus Christ we have *now received* the atonement' (verse 11). The redemption is accomplished; we have but to receive it. The atonement of peace is made, it is only for us to take it. 'For as sin hath reigned unto death, even so might grace reign through righteousness, unto eternal life, by Jesus Christ our Lord.' As we receive eternal life, and the Holy Spirit with open and thankful hearts, relying on the divine assurance by faith, we enter into the great inheritance of Peace, and the gifts of God in Grace and Nature become our own.

'Therefore being justified by faith, we have peace with God through our Lord Jesus Christ' (Romans 5:1). *'Having made peace through the blood of his cross'* (Colossians 1:20).

Prayer: O Most Merciful Lord, grant to me, above all things that can be desired, to rest in thee, and in thee to have my heart at peace. Thou art the true peace of the heart, thou its only rest; out of thee all things are hard and restless. In this very peace that is in thee, the one Eternal God, I will sleep and rest. Amen.

The Receptivity of Faith
June 25

'Let us draw near with a true heart, in full assurance of faith' (Hebrews 10:22). 'That Christ may dwell in your hearts by faith' (Ephesians 3:17).

Faith is our power of appropriation. The pity is that we are so slow to make use of our Lord's resources! He does not force himself upon us. Though he brings with him gold tried in the fire that we may be enriched, and white raiment for our clothing, and eye-salve for our blindness; and though he knows how urgently we need these things, he will not force them on our acceptance. Rather, he stands and knocks, as a travelling merchant knocks at the door, who has wares to dispose of, and we need to open the door and receive the gifts which are offered, without money and without price (Revelation 3:18-20; Isaiah 55:1-2).

Faith is our reception of the spiritual to make good the lack of the physical. It is a drawing on the Eternal for the deficiencies of our earthly pilgrimage. Probably when we look back on our present life, we shall find that our deficiencies were permitted, and even assigned, that we might be driven to avail ourselves of the fullness of the Lord Jesus (John 1:16; Ephesians 3:19). We were allowed to wander in the sultry heat, that we might know him as the shadow of a great Rock in a weary land; we were exposed to wild tempests and storms, that we might make for alcoves and harbours in him that we should otherwise have missed.

It has been truly observed that Job's rebellious moods arose when he thought that God was afar off, but there was a difference when he realised that God was suffering *with* him. Remember that you are not divided from God by a deep chasm. He knows your sorrows. In all your afflictions he is afflicted. We have not a High Priest, who cannot be touched with the feeling of our infirmities. When Jesus saw the sisters weeping, he not only succoured them, but entered into their distress, and wept with them.

Prayer: O Lord, I open my nature, and since my capacity is small, I pray that by love and faith, by patience and suffering, thou wilt enlarge my heart, that it may be filled with all the fullness of God. Amen.

Are you weary with burdens that are crushing you? Is your lot cast with them that hate peace? Is your heart oppressed with loneliness? Take Jesus into account. Don't face your difficulties alone, but meet them in the fellowship of your Saviour. Have faith, i.e. *reckon* on God. Let the Lord Christ *dwell* in your heart, and he will be responsible for all, as you reckon on him for all.

Practical Christianity
June 26

James is described as 'the Lord's brother' in Galatians 1:19. He was surnamed 'the Just', and was much respected beyond the limits of the Christian Church for his saintly life. While St Paul deals specially with doctrine, James is concerned with practice; Paul expounds the wonderful significance of Christ's death and resurrection; James expounds the teaching of our Lord, especially in the Sermon on the Mount. Paul insists on *faith* as the means of justification before God; James lays stress on the *works* to which faith must lead.

'For as the body without the spirit is dead, so faith without works is dead also' (James 2:26).

It seems likely that James had seen Paul's Epistles, for he uses so many of the same phrases and examples, and probably set himself to combat those who abused the teaching of the great apostle. There were plenty in his time who believed *about* Christ, and prided themselves in the orthodoxy and accuracy of their creed; and James maintains that this is not sufficient to save the soul.

As far as orthodoxy goes, no creed can be more absolutely orthodox than that held by evil spirits. Repeatedly, during our Lord's life, they acknowledged that he was the Holy One of God, but their belief had no effect on their character; it only filled them with fear and dread (verse 19).

'Faith without works is dead.' It is good to test ourselves. We must see to it that our heart is pure and our way absolutely transparent. In our dealings with those around us, we must always seek to *realise* our highest conceptions of love and duty. Even when our efforts of goodwill and affection are not reciprocated, we must never lower the high standard of our action, but always keep before us the conception of our Saviour's life in the home at Nazareth. Be merciless to yourself, but always merciful to others, always bearing the burdens of those around you always moderating your pace to the weak and weary, as Greatheart did for the pilgrims. Even Rahab was justified by a faith which wrought itself out in beautiful and unselfish *action* (verse 25; Hebrews 11:31). Remember our Lord's words in Matthew 7:20, 21.

Prayer: Help us, we beseech thee, O Lord, to add to our faith, brotherly kindness, and pardon the unkind word or impatient gesture; the hard and selfish deed, the failure to give kindly help where we had the opportunity. Enable us so to live that we may daily do something to lessen the tide of human sorrow and need, and add to the sum of human happiness. Amen.

The Great Shepherd
June 27

'Now the God of Peace, that brought again from the dead our Lord Jesus, that great Shepherd of the sheep, through the blood of the everlasting covenant, make you perfect in every good work to do his will' (Hebrews 13:20, 21).

It is most comforting that our Heavenly Father is *'the God of Peace'*. He is the God of the gentle zephyr, of the evening glow, of the mother's brooding care; and may be trusted by his gentleness and patience to make us great. Bruised reeds are not trampled beneath his feet, and the smoking flax is fanned into a flame. Do not be afraid of God - he is the God of Peace!

He brought again from the dead our Lord Jesus, that great Shepherd of the sheep. As our Lord descended into the Valley of Death, he breathed his departing spirit into the Father's hands. He knew that the path of life would unfold before him. He knew that the Father's welcome awaited him. And God did not fail him! However low he went, when he descended into Hades, the Everlasting Arms were always beneath him, and him did God raise up, having loosed the pangs of death, because it was not possible that he should be holden of it.

And will God do less for the Flock! There are many of the sheep that have been scattered in the cloudy and dark days. Will every sheep and lamb be recovered, and led to the green pastures and beside the quiet waters of Paradise? Yes, every one! The great Shepherd would not be content if one were missing of those whom the Father has given him (John 10:28, 29). Remember his own parable of the Shepherd who left the ninety and nine to recover the one. If you have come to him by your will and choice, you are included in the Father's gift.

Prayer: We thank thee, O blessed Master, not only that thou hast cleansed us from our sins, but that thou hast entered into, and ratified by thy precious blood, the eternal covenant which has made us thine for ever. Amen.

We are secure in the position which his grace has given us. It is secured not only by the promise of God, but sealed by the Blood of the Cross. That is the meaning of the words: 'The Great Shepherd of the sheep, through the blood of the eternal covenant.' Note that word *eternal*, which carries us back to the timeless past, when this compact was made. We may therefore humbly believe that our names are written in the Book of Life of the Lamb slain from before the foundation of the world (Revelation 13:8; 21:27). But we are saved to save others! It is thus that we make our calling and election sure (2 Peter 1:10).

An Autograph Letter
June 28

The apostle Paul's life was made weary by the incessant opposition of his enemies and critics, who sowed discord in the churches which he had formed in Europe. Amongst others, they visited Corinth and challenged him to produce letters of commendation from the leaders of the Church. With justifiable indignation he cries, 'Why should I carry letters, when my converts, given me by the Lord, are circulating everywhere, with the attesting signature of Christ upon them? Surely they are a sufficient guarantee and proof that I have been commissioned and sent forth by the Lord himself.'

'Ye are manifestly declared to be the epistle of Christ, ministered by us, written not with ink, but with the Spirit of the Living God' (2 Corinthians 3:3).

St Paul gave utterance to a true and striking description of a Christian disciple. *He is an autograph letter*, the Author and Writer is the Lord himself - 'an epistle of Christ'. The ink is 'the Spirit of the Living God'. The pen is the teacher or preacher of the gospel, 'ministered by us'. The material is the heart and life - 'not on tables of stone, but on hearts of flesh'.

We ought to be Christians in large type, so that it would not be necessary to be long in our society, or to regard us through spectacles, in order to detect our true discipleship. The message of our lives should resemble the big advertisements which can be read on the street-hoardings by all who pass by. The merit of good letter-writing is to state what the writer wants to say as clearly and concisely as possible. Sometimes we have to wade through long and weary pages before we can get at the gist of our correspondent's meaning. Let us take care that the message of our lives is clear, concise and unmistakable.

Prayer: Live in us, blessed Lord, by thy Holy Spirit, that our lives may be living epistles of helpfulness and blessedness. May the name of the Lord Jesus be glorified in us. Amen.

We are to be pens in the hand of Christ - our sufficiency is of God, who makes us ministers. Milton's pen had only to yield itself relentlessly to the hand of the daughter or amanuensis, to whom the blind master dictated his immortal words. And the messages which we are to inscribe on the hearts and lives of men do not originate in us, but with Christ. If others are used more than we are, it is because they are more meet for his use (2 Timothy 2:15, 21).

'My soul doth magnify the Lord, and my spirit hath rejoiced in God my Saviour. Blessed be the Lord God of Israel; for he hath visited and redeemed his people' (Luke 1:46, 47, 68).

These two songs have floated down the centuries, stirring human hearts with the ecstasy of their triumph. It is not given to all to be able to express their exultation in words so eloquent and musical, but all may become as saturated with the words of Scripture as Mary was, and all may triumph in Jesus Christ as gladly as did Zacharias, and show forth his praise, as did these two holy souls.

The most wonderful thing for us all is that God looks upon our low estate. The greater his blessing, the more unworthy we feel of it. There is no reason why he has stooped to our lowliness and obscurity except that he would. He does great things for the weakest and merciful things for the unworthiest, for his name's sake - 'Holy is his name'. In other words, there is no accounting for the putting forth of God's power and love, except his own glorious character.

Princes are put down from their thrones, because they have become proud and tyrannical; whilst those of low degree are exalted by God, because in obscurity they have been educated in virtue, which cannot but rise to the level of its specific gravity. The rich are often sent empty away, because they have no taste or desire for true riches which alone can satisfy. Whether the hunger be for love, or for the power to do good, or for the best gifts that the Spirit of God can bestow, whoever fulfils the conditions of humility and faith - these are 'filled with good things'. 'Blessed are they that hunger and thirst after righteousness, *for they shall be filled.*'

Prayer: We thank thee, O God, for life and light and love; for the light of thy mercy shining across our path, revealing to us thy infinite love without beginning or end. May the name of our Lord Jesus be glorified in us. Amen.

The little babe, known afterwards as John the Baptist, was probably lying in his father's arms, when he burst forth into this glorious song. Let us see to it that we use every opportunity of making known God's wondrous salvation, of pointing men to the only source of forgiveness. Nothing so encourages faith as the proclamation of what God is prepared to do for those who trust him, and when it dawns upon men that there are treasures in Christ, which shall enrich their poverty and dissipate their hopelessness, they will yield themselves to be led into the ways of peace even by a little child!

Love Triumphant over Death
June 30

It was not possible, said St Peter, that our Lord should be holden of death (Acts 2:24). It behoved Christ to suffer; but all the bitter waters of suffering could not quench his love. He was the propitiation for the sins of the whole world. Therefore, every man, even those who pierced him, is included in his great love.

'Fear not. I am he that liveth, and was dead; and behold, I am alive for ever-more, Amen; and have the keys of hell and of death' (Revelation 1:18).

Christ died, not only to put away sin by the sacrifice of himself, but to rob death of its terrors, and deprive it of its sting. In death our Lord Jesus destroyed both the Devil and his power; the prince of this world has been judged and cast out of the seat of power (Hebrews 2:14, 15; John 12: 31; 16:11).

Let us not be afraid of the mystery of death. Christ has shown us that it is the gateway into another life. There is the same spirit, but a different environment. It is a condition of existence in which the same voices are heard, the same human fellowship persists. During the forty days in which Jesus tarried on our earth after his Resurrection, he solved many of the problems of life after death, and illuminated its mystery. To die is to be with him, and to be welcomed into the great company of loving spirits (2 Peter 1:11).

Let us not fear the loneliness of death. The soul passing through the dark valley becomes aware of Another by its side - *'Thou art with me'*. Death cannot separate us, even for a moment, from the love of God, which is in Christ Jesus our Lord. Jesus died alone; he felt forsaken; but none of us need pass through that terrible experience; for he has said, 'I will come again, and receive you unto myself.'

We need not fear what comes after death. The curse and penalty of sin have been put away for ever. 'Who is he that condemneth? It is Christ that died, yea, rather, that is risen again.' That which others call death, we dread no more than sleep. Our bodies lie down exhausted with our long working-day, to awake in the fresh energy of the Eternal Morning, while our spirit is presented before the Presence of his Glory, faultless, and with exceeding joy (Jude 24).

Prayer: O God, may we so trust thee this day, that, when the day is done, our trust shall be firmer than ever. Then, when our last day comes, and our work is done, may we trust thee in death and for-ever, in the spirit of Jesus Christ our Lord. Amen.

Where can I find the power of God?

Jesus Christ is the reservoir in which the power of God is stored. 'It pleased the Father that in him should all fulness dwell.' All power is his. He would not receive it from the devil on the mountain of temptation, but he laid claim to it on the mountain of Ascension. Listen to his majestic words, 'All power is given me in heaven and on earth.' In that august moment he united in himself the power, which he had as the Son of Man, with the power he had with the Father before the world was. And now all power resides in him for evermore, not for himself only, but for us.

How may I get this power for myself?

By faith. Each time you are face to face with some difficulty, or temptation, or service, lift up your heart to the living Saviour, draw upon him, let him feel that you are depending on him for the word to say, and the strength to say it. And immediately there will be a welling up of power within your heart, as lakes are filled from hidden springs.

F B Meyer *The Secret of Power*

JULY

OUR DAILY WALK OF SERVICE

Walk worthy of the vocation wherewith ye are
called
(Ephesians 4:1)

The Call to Service
July 1

'Come ye after me, and I will make you to become fishers of men. And straightway they left the nets, and followed him' (Mark 1:17, 18).

As of old, Christ is still passing through the centres of busy, thronging life, calling men from their nets and boats, from the counting-house and the market-place, or from the seclusion of the study, and saying, with his own inimitable and irresistible charm, 'Follow me, and I will make you fishers of men'. It may be that he has already come to you, casting over you the mantle of service, as Elijah over the young ploughman whilst following his team.

You may be startled at the suggestion, but probably all the mighty band of men and women who have responded to his call, were similarly startled when first the summons awoke them to action. Samuel was startled when the divine voice rang out in the night; Gideon was startled, and replied, 'Behold my family is poor, and I am the least in my father's house'; Jeremiah said, when the call came to him, 'Ah, Lord God! Behold I cannot speak, for I am a child.' Moses drew back, and said that he was unequal for the task to which God summoned him.

Christ's call comes specially to the young - to Henry Martyn amid his books, to David Livingstone at his loom, to Carey at his cobbler's bench, to Mary Slessor in the Scottish factory, and to many another. Young people have a marvellous power of acquiring languages and mastering any difficulties of country, race or condition, and what other men and women are doing for fame, position, and wealth, surely we can do for Jesus. We are his blood-bought slaves, and surely he has the right to say to each one of us, Come, Go, Do this, Follow me!

Prayer: Lord, here am I, send me wheresoever thou wilt. Only make me to know thy will beyond possibility of mistake, and work through me to accomplish all thy good pleasure. Amen.

Listen to the appeal of Christ on behalf of the millions of souls for whom he died, and to some of whom he wants to send you. Yield yourself to him, and let him infuse into you his mighty passion for their salvation. Do not look at your circumstances, or count your five loaves and two small fishes, wondering if they will suffice; or at the waves, questioning if they will bear you up. Keep your eyes fixed on him, and your ears open to his voice, and when once you are sure of his leading, go forward in his name. Jordan will divide before you, and the walls of Jericho will fall flat.

The Joy of Service
July 2

On the eve of Gethsemane and the night before his crucifixion 'these things' were said by our Lord: how could he have even a thought of *Joy*? Note how confidently he speaks of it - abiding, remaining, persistent joy! Like a hot geyser-spring, rising from unknown depths on an ice-bound world. How could he think of joy at such a moment? One answer alone seems possible. He knew that by his supreme sacrifice he was creating a well-spring of joy for all future generations. The spring of *his* joy was perennial because of the joy he was about to create for myriads.

'These things have I spoken unto you, that my joy may be in you, and that your joy may be fulfilled' (John 15:11 RV). 'My servants shall sing for joy of heart' (Isaiah 65:14).

This joy was characteristic of his whole ministry. It seems to have been an unfailing fountain. How could it be otherwise when he was always ministering to others, when he was for ever fulfilling his Father's loving will for men? It is in harmony with his oft-repeated 'Be of good courage,' whether he was about to heal pain and disease, or proclaim the forgiveness of sin. The New Testament rings with his call to rejoice, and to rejoice greatly!

Life of Self-giving. Our joy, like Christ's, consists in self-giving. We pass on to others the joy and love with which he fills our hearts, and in doing so, we are made infinitely happy. Let us today fix these thoughts in our mind. God is Love, and that Love cannot be self-contained.

Day by day let us abide in him, with our heart-gate open to the incoming of his love, that he may be able to speak a word to those that are weary, to proclaim liberty to the captives, and the opening of the prison to them that are bound. We are not to create, but to pass on! Not to inaugurate, but to transmit! The love and grace of Christ were always expressed in acts of ministry. He was not content with speaking the word of cheer, but ministered in such a way that joy and gladness were the immediate result. We must not be well-wishers only, but well-doers. If it be only to help to lift a burden, or to guide the perplexed, or to give a caress to some lonely despairing soul. In all such acts of ministry we are giving our Saviour the opportunity of expressing himself through us, and of fulfilling our joy.

Prayer: O Blessed Lord, give me to know the joy that is unspeakable, the love that passeth knowledge, and the peace that passeth understanding. Amen.

'Neglect not the gift that is in thee, which was given thee by prophecy, with the laying on of the hands of the presbytery. Be diligent in these things' (1 Timothy 4:14, 15 RV).

'Stir up the gift of God, which is in thee through the laying on of my hands' (2 Timothy 1:6 RV).

Prayer: Prosper us, O God, we pray thee, in all that we put our hands unto. May our hearts be filled with thy love, our lips with gentle, helpful words, and our hands with kind unselfish deeds. May thy Holy Spirit in all things direct and rule our hearts. Amen.

Most young people are fond of athletics, and the Roman and Greek youth were specially addicted to them. The Divine Spirit does not undervalue any of these means for keeping our physical health vigorous. But if we pay such earnest attention to these things we ought, all the more, to give attention to godliness, which disciplines the soul for Eternal Life. We all know what it is to discover and bring into play certain muscles of the body which we had not previously used. Are we equally keen to discover the hidden properties and resources of the soul and spirit?

Timothy was gifted in various ways, but specially for public ministry and in this Epistle and the next, the apostle bids him stir it up, i.e. stir into *flame* (marg). The fire may be well provided with coal, the heat and light may be present, but the poker needs to be used to let in the air. We may have gifts, but we must carefully practise the duties in which they can be used for the benefit of others. It becomes us all *to give ourselves* to the duties which lie immediately to our hands, not shirking or scamping them. We must not give part of our thought and care to our appointed tasks, but give our *whole* selves. What our hands find to do must be done with our might. Just as men build arches of brick over slight structures of wood, and when these are taken away the substantial material remains, so on the passing duties of an hour we are building up habits and character which will live for ever. *What* we do is comparatively unimportant, but *how* we do what we do is all-important. We must always be on guard, always on the alert, for we have in our hands the interests of others as well as our own (verse 16).

The grace of God can so reveal itself in a young man or girl, that he or she will become an example in speech, conduct, love, faith, and purity (verse 12).

Serving Christ and Serving Men
July 4

Notice that little pronoun *We*! As our Lord stood face to face with the vast crowd of hungry people, he might have said to his disciples, 'What are *you* going to do?' He might have bidden them devise some way of meeting their hunger and weariness. Instead of that, he identified himself with them, saying, How shall *we* do it? Is not that his way still? He knows the needs of the world of men, but he calls us into fellowship with himself with respect to them, saying, This is a matter not for me alone, not for you, but for *us* together, 'I am the Vine, ye are the branches'.

'He saith unto Philip, Whence shall we buy bread, that these may eat?' (John 6:5).

Whilst our Lord talked about *buying* bread, 'He knew what he would do'. Before his eye was the entire plan of the meal, of which he would be the Host, but he spoke of buying, that he might see what they would suggest, whether they would turn to him in simple faith, or begin to meet the need according to their own ideas. They took the latter course. It is almost always the case, that when we are face to face with some emergency, we begin to calculate our ways and means. When we are tested, we take out pencils and paper, and begin to count up our resources as the disciples did when they said: Two hundred pennyworth of bread is not enough, that every one may take a little!

Then it was that Andrew bethought himself of the little lad, whom he had seen in the course of the day. How proud and pleased the boy would be when they told him that Jesus wanted his little store. He gladly gave it up at the call of that Voice which had thrilled him with its accent.

How can we serve Christ, and what have we to give him? Five tiny loaves and two small fishes do not look much in themselves, but he will take the poorest and simplest things, and make wonderful use of them for his glory and the blessing of men. It is wonderful how much Jesus will do with our lives, if we will only put them into his dear hands. If you have no great gift to offer him, you can bring the special power of doing one thing best, which every one possesses, and he will use you to arrange the people in orderly ranks, and to carry round the bread and wine of the gospel message, offering it without money and without price.

Prayer
Take my life, and let it be
Consecrated, Lord, to thee.

Amen.

God's Bountiful Provision
July 5

'They did all eat, and were filled: and they took up of the fragments that remained twelve baskets full' (Matthew 14:20).

When God is Host, there is enough for all! Probably the disciples at first doled out the supplies with great care, but as they discovered that group after group were provided for, their faith increased, and they became lavish in their distribution. Every appetite could enjoy bread and fish, and there was plenty of it. God's supplies are as great as the demand; nay, greater, for he is able to make all grace abound toward each soul of man.

But though there was prolific provision, there was wise administration, and prudent husbanding of what was left. 'Gather up the fragments,' said the Master (John 6:12). It is marvellous to notice in the world of nature, how careful the Creator is that what might seem to be refuse should be wrought into new texture. Even the body, when it has fulfilled its functions, returns to mother earth, so that its particles may pass into the harvests of coming years. There is no waste in God's great world. Let there be no waste in our lives!

There are other lessons to be learned from this wonderful story. *All things are to be done decently and in order.* The multitude was made to sit down in companies of fifty. There was to be no crowding or pushing, the strong must wait for the weak.

Each meal should begin with the giving of thanks. 'Looking up to heaven, he blessed, and brake, and gave to the disciples.' The holy custom of giving thanks appears to be fading away, from even Christian homes, to our great loss, for 'he was made known to them in the breaking of bread' (Luke 24:30, 31).

Prayer: Teach us, O Lord, the art of so living in fellowship with thyself that every act may be a Psalm, every meal a sacrament, every room a sanctuary, every thought a prayer. Amen.

We may expect more than the bare necessities of life at the hands of our gracious God, who 'giveth us richly all things to enjoy'. He gives not bread only, but fish; luxuries, as well as necessaries. How much there is in life which we enjoy, but which is not absolutely necessary - music and art, flowers and fruit, sunrise and sunset, as well as ordinary daylight. 'If ye then, being evil, know how to give good gifts unto your children; how much more shall your Heavenly Father give the Holy Spirit to them that ask him.'

True Beneficence
July 6

We all have a mission in the world, though we may never be called to cross the sea, or to visit distant lands to preach the gospel. Christ's command to each of us, is begun with the person next to you. Do not wait to be neighboured, but neighbour somebody who is in need. The best way to bring in the Kingdom of God is to bring the person whom you can most easily influence to the Saviour. All great work in the world has commenced, not by committees, but by the consecration, self-sacrifice, and devotion of single individuals.

'As we have therefore opportunity, let us do good unto all men' (Galatians 6:10).

The apostle indicates three methods of helping people. *The restoration of the fallen* (verse 1). How often in daily life a Christian man or woman is suddenly overtaken by some temptation, to which they yield, and which leaves a deep stain on their character. Thus was David overtaken and also Peter! What an agony of remorse ensues! The Psalms are full of bitter repentance for such transgression. The sinful soul has to bear a heavy burden indeed; and too often his fellow-Christians pass him by with averted faces or frowns. No one visits him, or cares to be seen in his company, or tries to help him regain his former footing.

'Christ's law' which we are called to fulfil, is to seek out the erring one, to go after that which is lost, to restore the wanderer, to help carry his burden, considering lest we be tempted, and lapse in the same sin.

The care of Pastors and Ministers (verse 6). If all who are being taught in church and Sunday School would set themselves to minister to those that teach them, how many a weary servant of Christ would pluck up new courage and hope. Communicate helpfulness, sympathy, prayer, the grip of the hand, the expression of thankfulness for blessings received.

Prayer: Give us grace to be encouragers of others, never discouragers;

The ministry of all men (verses 9, 10). These opportunities of doing good are always recurring, and at every turn there are those who need a helping hand. 'The poor,' said our Lord, 'ye have always with you.' Let us bear a little of the burden of each, and specially do it for those who belong to the household of faith.

always making life easier, never harder, for those who come within our influence. Amen.

The Development of Christian Character
July 7

'Pure religion and undefiled before our God and Father is this, to visit the fatherless and widows in their affliction, and to keep himself unspotted from the world' (James 1:27 RV).

It is the experiences of life that reveal us to ourselves. They cannot put into us qualities that are not there, but can develop them. The whole of this wonderful chapter is filled with the diverse discipline of life. *Manifold trials* (verse 2) which probably refer to the persecutions and losses of the early Christians. *Temptations* (verse 12) which refer to the solicitations of evil from without and within. The *burning heat* of the fire of prosperity (verse 11). The *good gifts* which are strewn around our pathway by the Father of lights - home, parents, friendship, love!

The greatest training-ground for us all is the word of God (verses 21-25). It is here compared to a mirror which reflects us to ourselves, but alas, too often we go on our way and forget what manner of men we are. The human soul has a wonderful habit of forgetting any statements that seem to reflect on itself, and to contradict its own notions of its pride and respectability. If, however, we avoid this mistake, and set ourselves to doing, and not hearing only, then we shall grow into strong, brave and beautiful souls, and shall be blessed in our *deed*.

Do not stand gazing at the imperfections which the word of God reveals but having learnt where you come short, dare to believe that Jesus Christ is the true counterpart of your need; that he is strong where you are weak, and full where you are empty.

Keep himself unspotted from the world. We love the dimpled innocence and purity of a sweet child. But there is something nobler - the face of a man or woman who has fought and suffered in the great battle against corruption that is in the world through lust. To keep oneself unspotted from the evil of the world, though perpetually accosted and surrounded by it, is a greater thing than to live in a glass-house, where the blight and dust cannot enter. What a training for character is this daily warfare!

To visit those in affliction. We are related to the world of pain and sorrow by the troubles which are constantly overtaking those with whom we come in contact in daily life. Where the conditions of life are hard, we obtain our best perfecting in Christian character.

Prayer: Make our life deeper, stronger, richer, more Christlike, more full of the spirit of heaven, more devoted to thy service and glory. Amen.

Rich Toward God
July 8

Let us never forget this wonderful assertion, that life consists not in what we possess, but in what we *are*; not in goods, but in goodness; not in things, but qualities. 'How much was he worth?' we ask when a man dies, and we expect an answer in the amount that stood to his credit, and on which his estate must pay death duties. Yet surely a man is worth only the love, humility, generosity and sweet reasonableness which characterise him. Take away some people's wealth, and, as in the case of the rich man of whom our Lord speaks in his parable, you have nothing left; but take away all things from St John or St Paul, from St Francis or Augustine, or Wesley, and you have an abundance left which makes them the millionaires of all time! 'Poor, yet making many rich; having nothing, and yet possessing all things.'

'A man's life consisteth not in the abundance of the things which he possesseth' (Luke 12:15). 'I have all, and abound' (Philippians 4:18).

The rich man in the parable made three foolish mistakes. First *he treated his wealth as though it were absolutely his own*. There is no suggestion that he had made it wrongfully. His wealth had evidently accrued as the gift of prolific harvests, and was certainly due to the goodness of the Creator, on whose co-operation the results of husbandry evidently depend. But to lift up grateful eyes in thankful acknowledgment to God seems never to have occurred to him! Are we not all too prone to magnify our own shrewdness and aptitude, and to exclude God when we make up our accounts for the year.

Second, *he thought that the best receptacle for his overplus was in barns*, and forgot that there were multitudes of poor and needy souls around. When we begin to accumulate more than we need for our use, or the provision for our families, we should consider, not further investments, but the pressing need of others.

Third, *he thought that goods could stay the hunger of the soul*. How often has the heart of a man or a woman been surfeited with goods and remained unsatisfied? Let us give, expecting nothing again with full measure, pressed down, and running over; give, not only money, but love and tenderness and human sympathy; give as one who is always receiving from the boundless resources of God.

Prayer: Help us, O God, to set our affections on things above, not on things on earth, for nothing beneath these skies can satisfy the hearts which thou hast made for thyself. Amen.

Life's Balance Sheet
July 9

'What shall it profit a man, if he shall gain the whole world, and lose his own soul?' (Mark 8:36).

Simon Peter had been urging our Lord to spare himself the suffering to which he had referred, but he answered that this could not be for himself, or for any other who would follow in his footsteps. Proceeding from his own deep experience, he went on to show that in the same measure every one must deny his own choice and will and pleasure, in order that he may reach the highest life for himself and others.

It is not necessary for any man to make a cross; it is our part simply to take up that which God has laid down for us. The cross is no exceptional piece of asceticism, but it is the constant refusal to gratify our self-life; the perpetual dying to pride and self-indulgence, in order to follow Christ in his redemptive mission for the salvation of men. And it is in proportion as men live like this that they realise the deepest and truest and highest meaning of life. When we live only to save ourselves, to build warm nests, to avoid every discomfort and annoyance, to make money entirely for our own use and enjoyment, to invent schemes for our own pleasure, we become the most discontented and miserable of mankind. How many there are who have given themselves up to a life of selfishness and pleasure-seeking, only to find their capacity for joy has shrivelled, and their lives plunged into gloom and despair. They have lost their souls!

Prayer: O God, we have been disappointed because the cisterns that we have hewn out for ourselves have not given the water needed to quench our thirst. Fountain of Living Water, of thee may we drink! Bread of Life, of thee may we eat! Light of Life, shine upon our hearts, that we may walk in thy light. Amen.

If a fire is raging, and a millionaire saves his palace from destruction, but in so doing loses his own life, does it pay? And are there not many who are building for themselves palaces of wealth and pleasure, but are losing the power of enjoyment because they are destroying all the finest sensibilities of their nature. Our Lord asks, What does it profit to gain the whole world, and forfeit one's own soul?

But not to adopt the policy of the world is certain to bring upon us dislike and hatred, before which many have been daunted; and yet to refuse Christ's policy of life, and to be ashamed of acknowledging that we are his followers, will mean ultimately our rejection. For how can our Lord use us in any great schemes of the future, if we have failed him in the limited sphere of our human life?

Love's Constraint
July 10

An ambassador may live in a foreign country, but he does not belong to it. He is there to represent his own country, and no opportunity of helping forward her interests is allowed to pass. We have to represent Christ to the world. The word *constrain* suggests a constant pressure, an urge, as when water is forced down a certain channel. St Paul says: 'I act as I do because I am under the spell of a mighty constraint; I can do no other; I am not master of myself. Do not wonder at what may seem to be unusual and extravagant. Attribute my eccentricity to Christ - his love actuates me, and bears me along.'

'For the love of Christ constraineth us ... We are ambassadors for Christ, as though God did beseech you by us' (2 Corinthians 5:14-20).

What is meant by 'the love of Christ'? Is it his to us, or ours to him? It is impossible to divide them thus, for they are one. As the sunlight strikes the moon, and is reflected from her to the earth, so the love we have to Christ, or to man, is the reflection of his love to us. All love in our cold and loveless hearts is the emanation and reflection of the love which began in him, was mediated to us in Calvary, and is reflected from us, as sunlight from a mirror.

The love of Christ does not constrain all Christian people, because they do not understand the profound significance of the Cross; but when the soul once appreciates that, and passes through the gate of death into the life of God, then it begins to feel the constraining love of Christ. The pivot of our life must be the Risen Christ: 'We no longer live unto ourselves, but unto him who rose again'. We sometimes hear people described as eccentric - *out of the centre*. A man is ex-centric to the world when he is concentric with Christ. It is thus that we become a new creation. When by faith we are united to Jesus Christ in his Cross and Grave, the transition is made. We pass over into the Easter life. He has reconciled us unto himself, and has given to us the ministry of reconciliation - therefore we are *ambassadors*. We have to proclaim forgiveness to the sinful, the loosening of their chains to those who sit in prison-houses, and the near approach of salvation to all (Isaiah 52:7-10).

Prayer:
This empty cup for thee to fill;
This trembling heart for thee to still;
This yielded life to do thy will,
O Lord of Love, I bring thee.

Amen.

Seeking Lost Souls
July 11

'Rejoice with me, for I have found my sheep which was lost... Likewise joy shall be in heaven over one sinner that repenteth' (*Luke* 15:6, 7).

Our Lord sought the proximity of sinners, not because there was any affinity between his character and theirs, but because he desired to bring them back from the far country into which they had wandered. The straying sheep heedlessly nibbles at the grass which lies immediately in front, and so crops its way until it has wandered a great distance from the shepherd, and the rest of the flock.

Is this a picture of your life? Have you lived only for personal gratification, drifting in thoughtlessness and unconsciousness of the dangers which threaten to destroy you? Then remember, that though you care not for yourself, your condition is stirring the deepest solicitude in the heart of Christ. Probably you will never find your way back to him, but Christ is on your track, and he will not relinquish his quest until he has come just where you are, and has extricated you from the rocks on which you have fallen, or from the thorns in which you are entangled.

The lost coin bears the image and superscription of the sovereign, once clear-cut by the mint, but it lies unused, tarnished, and perhaps defaced, amidst the dust of the corner, or the chink of the floor. Its owner sweeps, ransacks, and explores every possible hiding-place until it is found. How aptly that lost coin represents the soul of man, made in the image of God, lying amid the dust of sin. The one hope for the sinner is the anxiety in the heart of God who leaves no stone unturned that he may win us back. There is disturbance and removal, and the house of life is upset in every part, for no other reason than that we should be recovered.

Prayer:

Halts by me that footfall:
Is my gloom, after all,
Shade of His hand, outstretched caressingly?
Ah, fondest, blindest, weakest,
I am He Whom thou seekest!
Thou dravest love from thee, who dravest Me.

Alack, thou knowest not
How little worthy of any love thou art!
Whom will thou find to love ignoble thee
Save Me, save only Me?

Rise, clasp My hand, and come. Amen.

Our Bounden Duty and Service
July 12

In Christ's service there are no hours when we cease to be his bond-servants, or pass from under his eye (RV marg). We are always his, always at his disposal, always bound to ask what he would have us do. In this there is no hardship, because he knows our frame, and understands the complex machinery of life needs time to cool and rest and recreate itself. We remember that our Lord bade his disciples leave the crowded lake-side, to come with him apart and rest awhile. He knows that we need rest and change, but he would keep these hours of relaxation under his own command because they are often the most perilous to the soul's health. How often, when we have been engaged in earnest service to others for Christ's sake, we are inclined to say: 'Now we may have a good time for ourselves; we may relax the girdle, we may sit down to meat'. We are inclined to act at such times as if we were off duty, and as though our Lord had no jurisdiction over us.

But it is when we have done our Master's work that he sometimes says to us: 'You have been so taken up with my work that you have neglected *me*. You have thought more of the depth and straightness of the furrow; more of the wool and safety of the flock, than of the one for whom you work. Give me a little of your thought and love! "Make ready wherewith I sup; gird thyself and serve me!" '

Ah! our Lord Jesus wants our love, and he will not be satisfied if we give time, energy, and thought to his service, and forget *him*.

When we have done all that Christ asks of us, we have nothing to be proud of. Our good works do not earn our salvation, nor merit anything at the hand of our Saviour. Our uttermost service is only our bounden duty and privilege. It is a blessed thing, when we are wholly yielded to obey him, for his service is perfect freedom from envy, dissatisfaction with our lot, jealousy of others, and pride. The wonder is that he takes us into partnership with himself (John 13:13-16).

'When ye shall have done all those things which are commanded you, say, We are unprofitable servants: we have done that which was our duty to do' (Luke 17:10).

Prayer: Lord, we go to our daily work; help us to take pleasure therein. Show us clearly what our duty is; help us to be faithful in doing it. Give us strength to do, patience to bear; by our true love to thee, make unlovely things shine in the light of thy great love. Amen.

'I heard the voice of the Lord, saying, Whom shall I send, and who will go for us? Then said I, Here am I; send me' (Isaiah 6:8).

From the midst of heaven there comes to our earth this cry for help - an appeal from the Eternal Trinity: 'Who will go for us!' It reminds us of the last commission of our Lord to his disciples, that they should go into all the world, and preach his gospel to every creature. The Seraphim may minister to those who have become the heirs of salvation, but only those who have been redeemed from among men have the high privilege of being called to the supreme work of redemption.

Notice the preparation for responding to that appeal. *The vision of the Eternal*: 'I saw the Lord sitting upon a throne'. Suddenly the material temple, in which Isaiah was probably worshipping, gave place to the eternal; the altar and the laver to the throne of God; the cloud of incense, to the skirts of glory that filled the air; the choir of Levites, to the bands of the Seraphim that engirdled the sapphire throne. And above all, he beheld the glory of Christ (John 12:41).

This led to *the vision of his own heart*: 'Woe is me, for I am undone'. It is when a man reaches the snowline that he realises the comparative impurity of the whitest white that earth can produce. Probably there was no one in all Jerusalem who lived nearer to God than Isaiah; but when he learned that, in the estimation of the Seraphim, God was thrice holy; when he saw them veil their faces in adoration; when he discovered that the whole universe was filled with God; then he remembered the hidden evil of his own heart, and cried out, 'I am unclean!' Not a moment intervened between his confession and the cleansing of his iniquity, and he was able to say, 'Send me!'

Have you heard that cry for help from the heart of Christ? Are you seeking to enter into his yearning love for the souls of men? He says to each one of us: 'Could ye not watch with me one hour?' Give yourself to him that you may be used in his service: 'Here am I, send me, use me'.

Prayer: Lord, grant us ears to hear, eyes to see, wills to obey, hearts to love; then declare what thou wilt, reveal what thou wilt, command what thou wilt, demand what thou wilt. Amen.

Entering the King's Service
July 14

It is difficult to decide the occasion of this Psalm which was written to celebrate a royal marriage. But there is much which goes far beyond the immediate circumstances out of which it sprang. We recognise its prophetic character, as well as its historic basis, and that it points onward to Christ the King. It is so quoted in Hebrews 1:8, 9, and we may therefore certainly appropriate the Psalm as directly addressed to our Lord, who is our rightful King.

Christ's claim rests on these grounds: *the Righteousness of his Rule*. His sceptre is not a rod of iron, but of 'uprightness'. Our King loves righteousness and hates wickedness. Therefore his throne stands firm, and he claims the allegiance of all pure and upright souls. Would that all rulers and leaders realised that *right makes might*!

The Gladness of his Reign. The righteous heart is the joyful one; and our King teaches us that so far from holiness meaning gloom and depression, it is the root and fountain of true and abiding joy. Jesus was 'the Man of Sorrows, and acquainted with grief,' but underneath was an abiding and eternal joy, like the spring flowers that nestle under the warm coverlet of snow. There is a blessed attractiveness in Christian joy and gladness, which is characteristic of our King, and should mark all his subjects.

The Love of his Heart. The bride is willing to forsake her own people and her father's house, and if we take the Lord Jesus to be our King and Husband, we shall be willing to count all things but loss for love of him. Therefore he said, 'Whosoever he be that forsaketh not all that he has, he cannot be my disciple.'

'*He is thy Lord*.' We are reminded that however tender may be the sense of Christ's love to us, we must reverence him as our King. Reverence is the best foundation for true affection. We shall never fully know his salvation until we recognise and own him as King. 'Thy King cometh unto thee, having salvation.' 'He is exalted as Prince and Saviour.' Lift up your heads, O gates of Mansoul, and the King of Glory shall come in! (Revelation 3:20).

'Hearken, O daughter, and consider, and incline thine ear; forget also thine own people, and thy father's house; So shall the king greatly desire thy beauty; For he is thy Lord; and worship thou him' (Psalm 45:10, 11).

Prayer: In all things attune our hearts to the holiness and harmony of thy Kingdom. Hasten the time when thy Kingdom shall come, and thy will be done on earth as it is in h e a v e n . Amen.

Three Ambitions
July 15

'We make it our aim (we are ambitious) to be well-pleasing unto him' (2 Corinthians 5:9 RV - see marg).

There is scope for ambition within the sphere of the Christian Faith, and to be without it is to miss an influential incentive to high and holy endeavour. Our Lord does not destroy any natural faculty, but directs it to a worthy object. Instead of living for material good, or the applause of the world, we must stir ourselves to seek those things which are the legitimate objects of holy ambition. In two other passages the apostle Paul uses this same word. See 1 Thessalonians 4:11; Romans 15:20 (RV marg).

There is *the ambition of daily toil* - 'Be ambitious to be quiet, to do your own business, to work with your own hands.' In the age in which the apostles lived there was much unrest, and in the case of the Christian Church this was still further increased by the expectation of the approaching end of the world; many were inclined to surrender their ordinary occupations, and give themselves up to restlessness and excitement, all of which was prejudicial to the regular ordering of their homes and individual lives. But the injunction is that we are not to yield to the ferment of restlessness; we are not to be disturbed by the feverishness around us, whether of social upheavals or for pleasure or gain.

Prayer: Give us grace, O Lord, to work while it is day, fulfilling diligently and patiently whatever duty thou appointest us; doing small things in the day of small things, and great labours if thou summon us to any; rising and working, sitting still and suffering, according to thy word. Amen.

The ambition to be well-pleasing to Christ. At his judgment-seat he will weigh up the worth of our individual mortal life, and he is doing so day by day. Not only when we pass the threshold of death, but on this side, our Lord is judging our character and adjudicating our reward. Let us strive to be as well-pleasing to him in this life, as we hope to be in the next.

The ambition of Christian work - 'Being ambitious to preach the gospel.' The great world lies open to us, many parts of it still unevangelised; and all around us in our own country are thousands, among the rich and poor, who have no knowledge of Christ. Let us make it our ambition to bring them to him, always remembering that the things we do for Christ must be that which he works through us in the power of the Holy Spirit (Romans 15:18, 19).

God's Appointment
July 16

God has a plan for each of his children. From the foot of the Cross, where we are cradled in our second birth, to the brink of the river, where we lay down our armour, there is a path which he has prepared for us to walk in. God also prepares us for the path he has chosen. We are his workmanship, created unto the good works which he has before prepared. There is no emergency in the path for which there has not been provision made in our nature. From the earliest inception of his being, God had a plan for Jeremiah's career, for which he prepared him.

'I formed thee... I knew thee... I sanctified thee; I have appointed thee' (Jeremiah 1:5 RV).

Ask what your work in the world is, that for which you were born, to which you were appointed, and on account of which you were conceived in the creative thought of God. That there is a Divine purpose in thy being is indubitable. Seek that you may be permitted to realise it, and never doubt that you have been endowed with all the special aptitudes which that purpose may demand. God has formed you, and stored your mind with all that he knew to be requisite for your life work. It is your part to elaborate and improve to the utmost the one or two talents entrusted to your care.

Do not be jealous or covetous; do not envy another his five talents, but answer the divine intention in your creation, redemption, and call to service. It is enough for thee to be what God made thee to be, and to be always at thy best.

But in cases where the divine purpose is not clearly disclosed, in which life is lived piecemeal, and the bits of marble for the tessellated floor are heaped together with no apparent plan, we must dare to believe that God has an intention for each of us; and that if we are true to our noblest ideals, we shall certainly work out the divine pattern, and be permitted some day to see it in its unveiled symmetry and beauty. We are to go on occupying the position in which we have been placed by the Providence of God, and to hold it for God till he bids us do something else! Such are golden secrets of blessedness and usefulness.

Prayer: O Lord, may thy all-powerful grace make us as perfect as thou hast commanded us to be; through Jesus Christ. Amen.

The Eager Householder
July 17

'For the kingdom of heaven is like unto a man that is an householder, which went out early in the morning to hire labourers into his vineyard' (Matthew 20:1).

Our Lord, beneath the veil of this parable, tells us what God is like. The heart of God our Father yearns over the perishing souls of men. For some reason, at present withheld, he must have the co-operation of men to reach the hearts of men, and therefore at every stage of life he approaches us, saying, 'Go work! During what remains of life's brief day, go work in my vineyard, and whatsoever is right I will give you. I need you to help in the salvation of the myriads of souls, whose redemption I am seeking with blood and tears.'

He comes to you, dear children, in the dawn of your life. The dew is still on the grass, the birds are only just awaking from their dreams, life is yet at the spring, and God's voice comes to you, saying: 'I want you to help me in my great vineyard. The ground needs weeding, the vines require watering and pruning, there is much to do and few to do it, and I have a tiny plot for you to cultivate. Make haste, and come.'

He comes to you, young men and women. Three hours have passed, and as yet you are standing idle, and have not chosen your life-work. Are you going to be a Missionary, or Minister, a Doctor, or School-teacher; does Art, Music or Commerce appeal to you? Whatever sphere you choose, let it be subordinated to the one great purpose of helping God to save the world.

Prayer: O God, we have heard thy call! Wilt thou accept our hands to labour for thee, and our lips to speak for thee. Send us into thy Vineyard, and use us in thy holy service. Amen.

He comes to you who are in the meridian or late afternoon of life. Perhaps you have been fortunate enough to make a competence, and need not toil as formerly. To you the Master comes, saying, 'Go, work in my vineyard. Administer your money, time, influence for me.' Even though it be but an hour before sunset, the same urgent appeal rings out: though you have been unemployed all the days, he seeks your help. Oh, that the urgency of God's compassions may touch and move us! Will you listen to the call of the great Husbandman, and now answer in your heart, 'Here am I, send me'?

From Disciple to Apostle
July 18

At the basis of all things there is a Divine order. We hear it in the noblest music, we find traces of it in the highest art; we are in contact with it in our purest and simplest meditations. Our souls bear witness to its beauty and truth whenever it confronts us. Our Lord Jesus bears a true witness to this in his beatitudes and the enunciation of other principles, which appeal to our conscience as right and good. As we travel in his company along the road, we find he explains mysteries and enigmas in a fashion which appeals to our heart; we know that he speaks true.

'And when it was day, he called unto him his disciples; and of them he chose twelve, whom also he named apostles' (Luke 6:13).

Finally, we come to a point where he passes beyond the road of our knowledge to the upper reaches of the mountains which we have not trodden before. He speaks to us of the nature of God, he assures us of the forgiveness of sin, he draws aside the veil from the unseen and the eternal. He lifts us into a new and blessed vision of the working together of all things according to the eternal purpose. And we who trusted him where our own conscience substantiated his statements, are able to trust God, and follow him when he deals with questions which eye hath not seen, nor the heart of man conceived. Thus we become his disciples, or pupils in his School.

Out of the disciples, our Lord chose some to be apostles. We begin by learning, and after a while, we are sent forth to teach. During the first years we serve our apprenticeship, and afterwards we are permitted to be master hands. The disciple becomes an apostle, and the apostle is chosen not for his own comfort and enjoyment, but that he may be the instrument through which Christ achieves his eternal purpose. Election is not primarily to salvation, but to service. We are not elect that we may be sheltered from destruction, but that we may go forth to *serve men*, to teach them the law and love of God, and to help bring the world into captivity to the obedience of Christ.

Prayer: Most Blessed Lord, we thank thee that we may become thy disciples. Give us teachable hearts and listening ears; may we sit at thy feet and be moulded according to thy mind. Oh, choose us, and send us forth, and trust us with thy sacred ministry, fulfilling in us the good pleasure of thy will. Amen.

Chosen and Placed
July 19

'Ye have not chosen me, but I have chosen you, and ordained you, that ye should go and bring forth fruit' (John 15:16).

We did not choose him - there we have the evil of the human heart, the film of blindness which sin casts on the sight, the deafness with which it dulls the ear. For to have missed Jesus, to pass him by, is as though the pearl-hunter were unable to recognise the pearl of greatest price; or the mother to recognise her own babe; or the seeker after the holy grail to fail to discover its mystic sheen!

'But I chose you.' He chose us probably because we were useless and helpless and he wanted to show what supreme miracles his grace could achieve. The prophet says that the branches of the vine are more useless than any others (Ezekiel 16:1-5). The principle of God's choice is to take what all others reject - the firebrand plucked from the burning, the feebly-smoking tow, the bruised reed; the younger sons, the halt and lame, the last and least; the things that are foolish, despised and weak - these are God's choice, that he may bring to nought things that are, that no flesh may glory in his presence.

There was no error in the foreknowledge which preceded our election. God knew all that we were, all that we should be. He foresaw our downsittings, our hours of depression, our obstinacy, our wanderings into the far country, but he swerved not. Having chosen us, he is going to justify his choice, unless we definitely refuse to let him have his way.

Prayer: O Heavenly Master, enable us by thy grace to fill the opportunity, and do the work that thou hast assigned. May we not murmur or complain because our place is obscure and the time long, but bear much fruit for thy glory. Amen.

'And appointed you.' Our Master has placed us just where we are, that he might have a suitable outlet for his abundant life, which he longs to pour forth upon the world. Do not repine or murmur at your lot in life, but remember that he has appointed and placed you there. As the branch is nailed to the wall that it may cover it with foliage and fruit, so Christ has placed you where you are. That inevitable circumstance is the rough piece of cloth, that sorrow is the nail, that pain the restraint such as he suffered on the Cross.

'That ye should go.' 'Whither, Master?' 'Into all the world, as my disciples! I have chosen you out of it and now I send you back as my representatives, through whom I may pour out my life and love. Go and bear fruit!'

Ministering to Christ
July 20

Is it not wonderful that our Lord should identify himself thus with the hungry and thirsty, the weary and homeless, the outcast and suffering? If any who read these words should be in one of these conditions, be greatly comforted, for Jesus suffered thus in his earthly career, and remembers what it is like. His sympathy and understanding are warm and inexhaustible, and he accepts any kindness as though it were done directly to himself.

'Inasmuch as ye have done it unto one of the least of these my brethren, ye have done it unto me' (Matthew 25:40).

We must be on the outlook for those whom we can help, remembering that the outstretched hand or petition is his. But we must beware, on the other hand, and endeavour to help people wisely. In giving to every beggar that asks alms we may inflict injury on the moral nature by encouraging them to be lazy and careless. We are not to distribute money, food, and clothing alone, but to give *personal ministry* which may cost us more!

Christ speaks of those who give hand-help to others as *righteous*, because it is only as we are really right with God that we are merciful to men. Righteousness and mercifulness are one.

Prayer: O God, we have been too self-centred. We have forgotten that our best and happiest life must be lived in fellowship with the needs, and sorrows, and trials of others. Help us to cheer them with our love, to hearten them with our courage, and to bear their burdens so far as we may. Amen.

The sin of omission! Notice that those who were banished and exiled from the presence of the King were judged because of what *they did not do*. We may be condemned not simply for actual sins committed, but for what we neglect to do. Not to bind up and care for the wounded or ill-treated, but to pass by on the other side; not to have the oil ready for the lamp; not to make use of the talent or gift entrusted; this involves condemnation, and degrades the soul to the level of the devil and his angels.

Let us ask for the grace of the Holy Spirit that we may follow in the steps of our Lord Jesus, who went about doing good, and healing all who were sick and in need. He has made over the great debt we owe to him to the poor and needy, and says that whatever we do to others for his sake, he will accept as payment to himself.

Victorious over Limitations
July 21

'The salutation by the hand of me Paul. Remember my bonds. Grace be with you. Amen.' (Colossians 4:18).

At the close of his dictation, St Paul took the stylus from the hand of his amanuensis, and appended his signature to the letter, which was awaiting that necessary endorsement. As he did so, he contrasted his irregular and clumsy writing with the flowing current-hand of his scribe, and in excuse, said pathetically: 'Remember my bonds!' It was as though he said, 'You cannot expect a man who for three years has had his wrist fettered by an iron chain to write as well as when he was a student at Gamaliel's feet!' He makes reference to the same subject in Galatians 6:11, where he speaks of the 'large letters' which he had written with his own hand; but in this case it was caused by his failing eyesight rather than the iron fetter.

There are other bonds than iron chains which impose on us their constraints and limitations. Many of us, as we review our work at the close of the day, are overwhelmed with the sense of failure. As we kneel before our Lord, we are constrained to say, 'Alas, we have inscribed thy Name on the hearts which lay open to us, as paper the hand, in very clumsy and unworthy style. Forgive us, and remember our bonds.'

Let us accept our limitations as from the will of God. There is no way to peace or power, save in accepting the will of God, making no distinction between what he appoints or permits, but believing that in either we are in contact with the eternal purpose for us. Paul never forgot that he was the prisoner of Jesus Christ. He believed that for every limitation on the earthward side there would be enlargement on the other and spiritual side. Weakness here, added strength there; the being hourly delivered unto the cross, and from the ground the blossoming of endless life.

Let us do all the good we can in spite of fetters. St Paul could not continue his travels over the world, but there were many avenues of service open to him. He could pray, and he did (1:3; 2:1; 4:12). He could influence others (Philippians 1:11-14). He employed his leisure in writing the epistles that have been the perennial solace of sorrowful hearts. There is a door, nearer to you than you think, opening out of your prison, through which God will enable you to render helpful service for him.

Prayer: Our Father, we thank thee that thou canst make no mistakes. We believe that all things are working together for our good, and we trust thy guiding hand. Amen.

Surrender Leading to Song
July 22

The Hebrew Psalmody became famous throughout the world. Even their fierce conquerors recognised the sublime beauty of the Hebrew temple music. By the waters of Babylon they urged them to sing one of the Songs of Zion, not knowing how impossible it was for the captives to sing the Lord's song in a strange land! For sixteen years no song had poured forth from the sacred shrine. Ahaz had shut the doors, dispersed the Levites, and allowed the holy fabric to remain unkempt, unlit, and unused. There were no sacrifices on the Altar, no sweet incense in the Holy Place, no blood on the Mercy-Seat, no Song of the Lord!

'And when the burnt offering began, the song of the Lord began also with the trumpets, and with the instruments ordained by David king of Israel' (2 Chronicles 29:27).

For too many Christians this, alas, is a picture of their life. The soul, intended to be a holy temple for God, shows signs of disorder and neglect. The lights are not lit, the sweet incense of prayer does not ascend, the doors of entrance to fellowship and exit to service are closed. Outwardly the ordinances of the religious life are preserved, but inwardly silence and darkness prevail, into which bat-like thoughts intrude. Thorns have come up in the court of the Holy Place, where the scorpion makes her nest. The song of the Lord has died out of heart and life.

Why should not this miserable condition be ended today? Why should you not be cleansed from the traces of sin and neglect through the Blood of the Cross? Why should you not come back into fellowship with God, who waits to receive and forgive? Surrender yourself to him now. Do not be general, but specific in your consecration. Weld yourself to some life or lives that sorely need help. Give not words only, but deeds and blood. Merge your little life in the life of Christ, as the streamlet in the wide ocean. And as you yield yourself to Christ first, and next to all who need you for his sake, you will find the Song of the Lord breaking forth again in your heart like a spring, which was formerly choked with *débris*.

Prayer: We pray thee, Heavenly Father, to cleanse the thoughts of our hearts, by the inspiration of thy Holy Spirit, that we may perfectly love thee, and worthily magnify thy Holy Name, through Jesus Christ our Lord. Amen.

Confessing Christ before Men
July 23

'*Whosoever therefore shall confess me before men, him will I confess also before my Father which is in heaven*' (*Matthew 10:32*).

Christ's ultimate aim is to secure peace for our sin-stricken race, and the proclamation of the tidings of peace is spreading throughout the world. We must not falter in our testimony, or hide in our heart the truth which has been committed to us, because it may bring us to contumely and suffering. Nothing is so like to promote our own earnestness and devotion as our constant testimony for Christ. The advance of the Kingdom of God is determined much less by remarkable missions and sermons, as by each one saying to his neighbour, 'Know the Lord'.

We should begin with our next of kin. Andrew's testimony and confession brought Peter to Jesus (John 1:40-42). And whatever blessing came to the Church, and to the world through the testimony and confession of Peter must be partly credited to his brother Andrew.

We must confess Christ to our nearest friends. Philip found Nathanael. Our friends expect that we should let them share our inner thoughts and experience. Sometimes we can only give our simple testimony: 'We have found Christ,' but as we bring those whom we love to Christ, we shall ever find him sympathetic, and willing to meet our endeavours with his mighty help and fellowship. How he welcomed Peter, and read the character of Nathanael.

Our personal testimony is invaluable. The woman of Samaria brought the entire city to the feet of Jesus by her confession. Many of the Samaritans believed on him for the saying of the woman, who testified, 'He told me all that ever I did.' That was the beginning of a great revival.

It was Mr Moody's custom to speak each day, personally, to some one about the Lord Jesus. If any shall say that this habit is apt to become mechanical and formal, I can only answer that the days when I have lived like that have been the most radiant of my life. It is not necessary that one should be always interlarding phraseology with references to religion, but there must be no covering of the light within us (Matthew 5:14-16). How great an honour it will be to be confessed by Christ before all worlds, and to be presented by him with exceeding joy before the Father (Jude 24). 'If we suffer, we shall also reign with him; if we deny him, he will also deny us.'

Prayer: May we so represent Christ our Lord in this world that men may love him for what they see of his likeness in us. Amen.

Glorifying God in our Recreations
July 24

The word *Recreation* is preferable to *Pastime*, for as one realises the priceless moments, with all their opportunities, getting fewer, one is averse to hear people talk of 'killing time'. But *recreation* is a good word, and we all need to find some way of re-creating the exhausted grey matter of the brain which is being used up in long application to study or work.

'All things are lawful for me, but all things edify not. Whether therefore ye eat, or drink, or whatsoever ye do, do all to the glory of God' (1 Corinthians 10:23, 31).

We must not be the 'dull boys' of the old adage, but as Christians our faces should shine like the morning sun; we should be quick, bright, intelligent, and in no danger of being reckoned among the 'back numbers', of which the piles are generally shabby and dusty!

All things edify not is one of the first conditions of healthy recreation. There is really no limit but this to the recreations in which a Christian person can indulge. He may play at manly games, row, skate, swim, drive a motor, sail the ocean, or scale the mountain snows! The more the better, so long as they are recreative; and are not the end, but the means to the end of a healthy manhood and womanhood. That is, they must *edify*, build up physique, muscle, brain, to be used afterwards in the main business of life. Nothing is a greater curse than when people neglect their real business in order to get to their sports and games. Then, so far from *edifying*, these in turn begin to pull down and destroy.

Probably the words 'edify not' put in a plea on the behalf of others. We are not to do things which in themselves may be lawful and innocent enough, but which might have a prejudicial effect on those who are watching every movement of our life.

Do all to the glory of God. So many seem afraid of joy! They fear if they are too happy, God will send some trouble as makeweight. How different is the command in Deuteronomy 26:11 and Philippians 4:4. Even when things do not appear to be good, let us dare to be thankful in all things, and give praise for all. All our Father's gifts are good, whatever be the wrappings or packing-cases in which they come to hand.

Prayer: May the Holy Spirit so fill us with Christ our Lord, that there may be no room in our life for anything inconsistent with his perfect purity and love. Amen.

'To every thing there is a season, and a time to every purpose under the heaven' (Ecclesiastes 3:1).

Do not be in too great a hurry. There is time for everything that has to be done. He who gave you your lifework has given you just enough time to do it in. The length of life's candle is measured out according to the length of your required task. You must take necessary time for sleep, for food, for the enjoyment of human love and friendship; and even then there will be time enough left for your necessary duties. More haste, less speed! The feverish hand often gives itself additional toil. 'He that believeth shall not make haste.'

Do not be impatient. He who made you has prepared the successive steps along which you must travel to realise your full human development. God knows what you need and will bring you to its fulfilment, only you must wait his leisure with whom a thousand years are as one day, and one day as a thousand years. He can mature events with marvellous rapidity, and you will find that he will perfect that which concerneth you, so that no good thing will fail. He who feeds the wild things of the prairie and woodland, giving to each its appropriate portion, will not fail any one of us. He will supply us with food convenient for us. The Creator is faithful to the creature.

Do not be cast down. Sorrow and trial are only for a time. They have their seasons and pass. It is not always winter, and God puts bright and beautiful things into our lives which we need not be afraid of enjoying, it being understood that we do not snatch at them, or use them for our personal pleasure alone. Everything is beautiful after its sort and in its season, and every day has some element of goodwill in it, but we sometimes so strain our eyes towards a distant spot on the horizon that we miss the flowers on which we are treading.

God is in all; find him there! 'Every good gift is from the Father of lights.' They were created that they might be received with thanksgiving and the altar sanctifies the gift. It is only when the gifts of God are severed from the giver that they do us harm (verse 13).

God has set Eternity in our heart, and man's infinite capacity cannot be filled or satisfied with the things of time and sense (see verse 11 RV marg).

Prayer: Cause thy grace to abound toward us, that we may have a sufficiency in all things, and abound to every good work. Help us to fulfil all the duties and responsibilities that this day may bring. Amen.

Spiritual Gymnastics
July 26

The relation of the body to religion has always engaged the attention of thoughtful religious men. Human opinion has oscillated between two extremes. On the one hand, some have considered that the body was the seat of sin, and have set themselves to degrade and debase it with every indignity and torture. This conception has influenced devoutly-intentioned people in the East, and also in Western monasticism. But sin must be dealt with in the heart and soul, where it has its inception and spring. It is easy to macerate the body, whilst the pride of self-mortification is undetected. If we deal with bad thought and evil suggestion, we shall not have so much trouble with the body, which is only the dial-plate, registering the workings within.

Exercise thyself unto godliness: for bodily exercise is profitable for a little; but godliness is profitable for all things, having promise of the life which now is, and of that which is to come' (1 Timothy 4:7, 8 RV).

The other extreme was represented in the Greek religion. The temples that stand in ruins, the superb works of art which have survived the wreck of centuries, its poetry and literature, sustain and illustrate the supreme devotion of the Greek mind to beauty.

The Christian position differs from both. To us the body is the temple, the instrument, the weapon of the soul. The Holy Spirit quickens our mortal body by his indwelling, and in the faces and lives of holy men and women we may trace the growing results of the inward power and beauty of pure and undefiled religion.

It is good to care for the body, but only as we should care for a complex and fine piece of machinery which is to serve us. There are gifts in us, which we must not neglect, or it will go hard with us when we meet our Master, who entrusted them to our stewardship. Probably the trials and temptations of life are intended to give us that inward training which shall bring our spiritual muscles into play. In each of us there is much unused force; many moral and spiritual faculties, which would never be used, if it were not for the wrestling which we are compelled to take up with principalities and powers, with difficulty and sorrow. The apostle bids us take heed to ourselves, and to live in the atmosphere of uplifting thought and of self-denying ministry (verses 13-15).

Prayer: Mould us, O God, into forms of beauty and usefulness by the wheel of thy providence, and by the touch of thy hand. Fulfil thine ideal, and conform us to the image of thy Son. Amen.

'If thou bring thy gift to the altar, and there rememberest that thy brother hath ought against thee; Leave there thy gift ... go thy way; first be reconciled to thy brother, and then come and offer thy gift' (Matthew 5:23, 24).

There is a marked difference between memory and recollection. *Memory* resembles a great box or chest into which a man casts his letters, accounts and MSS; *recollection* is the readiness, be it less or more, with which he can lay his hand on what he requires. We know that it is somewhere in our possession, we remember to have seen and turned it over, but search as we may we cannot find or recall it.

But there is a moment of quickened recollection when we stand before God: 'When thou bringest thy gift to the altar and *rememberest*.' As the Divine searchlight plays upon our past life it reveals many things which had passed from our mind. Conscience is a keen quickener of our powers of recollection.

What has your brother against you? This - that you flamed out against him in passion, with bitter, angry words, in hatred and contempt; or *this* - that you have been sullen and sulky, scarcely answering his advances, meeting his salutations with grudging courtesy. Perhaps you have done him a positive wrong, and have taken from him his only covering, or have forborne to help him when he stood in sore need (Exodus 22:26, 27; 23:4-9).

Prayer: Give unto us, O Lord, we beseech thee, broken and contrite hearts. Help us to do all that ought to be done to make amends, and grant unto our brother the willingness to meet us with forgiveness and peace. So shall we have peace with thee, our Elder Brother, against whom we have grievously sinned. Amen.

We are bidden to get right with man, as the first step to acceptance with God - '*first* be reconciled to thy brother'. Humility is necessary in every approach to God, and nothing so humbles our pride as to confess our faults to our brethren. Truth is necessary to all right dealings with God, and nothing will so promote truth in our inward parts as to be transparent and simple in our dealings with our fellows. Sincerity in confession of sin is an essential beginning of peace with God, but how can we be sure that our confession is sincere unless it costs us something more than words. '*First*, be reconciled with thy brother' - not only with the brother of human flesh - but with our great Brother in the Glory (Genesis 1:17-21; Hebrews 2:11). *Then come!* Offer thyself, as thy gift; he will accept thee, and thy gifts.

Lost Opportunities
July 28

The Greeks represented Opportunity as bald, with no lock of hair by which she could be laid hold of as she turned away and fled. Every one has opportunity, but there is often no symptom of its approach, no sign of its departure; when once it is missed, it rarely comes again! It is said that Queen Victoria once gave a comparatively unknown painter the opportunity of a private sitting. She came at the exact time that was arranged, but *he* was five minutes late, and he lost his opportunity!

Esau bartered his birthright! What cared he for the spiritual prerogative of the first-born to act as the priest of the clan, and to stand in the possible lineal descent of the Messiah. He craved what would satisfy and please his senses. But when he had sold his birthright he was held to the transaction. 'He found no place of repentance' does not mean that he wished to and could not, but that the die was cast, the decision was deemed final. It is within the range of every one to do an act, to make a choice, to barter away the spiritual for the material so absolutely, that the decision is held irrevocable. Let us take care lest we be betrayed by passion into an act which may affect our entire destiny.

The outstretched wing of God's love would have sheltered Jerusalem from its impending fate, but she refused him in his servants and his Son, and her day of opportunity passed!

Even so salvation waits for us all, and there is hope and opportunity for us to repent as long as the day of grace is not closed, but let us not forget, as McCheyne said, that *Christ gives last knocks*. The present is your time of hope, of a fresh beginning, of a new opportunity. Open the door of your life to Christ and make him King. He offers you your chance, rise to it; do your very best, find your niche of service in his Kingdom, and set yourself to follow him with all your heart and mind and strength.

'He found no place of repentance, though he sought it carefully with tears' (*Hebrews 12:17*).

'O Jerusalem ... how often would I have gathered thy children together ... and ye would not!' (*Matthew 23:37*).

Prayer: O Lord, let us not serve thee with the spirit of bondage as slaves, but with the cheerfulness and gladness of children, delighting ourselves in thee and rejoicing in thy work. Amen.

'Whosoever shall compel thee to go a mile, go with him twain' (Matthew 5:41).

Our Lord refers here to the usage of the East in the transmission of royal messages, which were carried forward by relays of messengers, much in the fashion of the fiery cross in the Highlands, as described in *The Lady of the Lake*. The messengers were 'press-men'; each town or village was compelled to forward the message to the next, and the first man happened upon was bound to forward the courier with his horses or mules.

In some such way emergencies are continually happening to us all. We arise in the morning not expecting any special demand for help, or any other circumstance to interfere with the regular routine of the day's work, and then suddenly and unexpectedly a demand bursts upon us, and we are obliged to go in a direction which we never contemplated. We are compelled to go one mile! Then the question arises. Now you have done your duty, performed what you were bound to perform, given what any other person would have given, what are you going to do about the next mile? You had no option about the first; about the second you have an opportunity of choice. Your action in the matter which is optional determines whether or not you have entered into the spirit and ministry of Christ.

Let us not be stingy and niggardly in our dealings with men. There are certain things that must be done, but let us go beyond the *must*, and do our duty with a smile, and with generous kindness. It is not enough to pay our servants or employees, let us be thankful for their service; it is not enough to pay our debts, let us give the word also of appreciation; it is not enough to simply do the work for which our employer remunerates us, let us do it with alacrity and eagerness, willing to finish a piece of necessary service even at cost to ourselves. As the followers of Christ, we are to be stars bearing our light on the vault of night; flowers shedding fragrance on the world; fountains rising in the arid wastes; always giving love and helpful ministry to this thankless and needy world, and as we break and distribute our barley loaves and fishes, our hands will become filled again, and with the measure we mete it, it shall be measured unto us again (Luke 6:38).

Prayer: O God, may we be more gracious to those around us. May we fill up the measure of our possibilities, and so be perfect, as thou, our Father, art perfect in love. Amen.

Fret Not
July 30

It is a mistake to be always turning back to recover the past. The law for Christian living is not backward, but forward; not for experiences that lie behind, but for doing the will of God, which is always ahead and beckoning us to follow. Leave the things that are behind, and reach forward to those that are before, for on each new height to which we attain, there are the appropriate joys that befit the new experience. Don't fret because life's joys are fled. There are more in front. Look up, press forward, the best is yet to be!

Fret not because your ideals appear to mock you. Every ideal which we cherish is the herald and precursor of a reality which, in a better form than ever we dreamed, shall one day come to our possession. The ancient alchemists spent their lives in the pursuit of the Philosopher's Stone, which they thought would turn every substance it touched into gold. They never discovered it, but they laid the foundations of modern chemistry, which has been more fruitful in its blessing to our race than the famous magic stone would have been. Who shall say that those old explorers were deceived? Was not God leading them on, by a way that they knew not, to better things than they dreamed?

Fret not because the future seems dark. After all, the troubles we anticipate may never really befall. It is a long lane without a turning, and the dreariest day has some glint of light. In any case, worrying will not help matters; it can alter neither the future nor the past, though it will materially affect our power in dealing with troubles. It will not rob tomorrow of its difficulties, but it will rob your brain of its clear-sightedness, and your heart of its courage. Let us turn to God with faith and prayer, looking out for the one or two patches of blue which are in every sky. And if you cannot discover any where you are, dare to anticipate the time when God shall make all things work together for good to them that love him.

'Rest in the Lord, and wait patiently for him; Fret not thyself because of him who prospereth in his way, because of the man who bringeth wicked devices to pass' (Psalm 37:7).

Prayer: Heavenly Father, we have been careful and troubled about many things. Forgive us, and breathe into our hearts a great faith in thee, that doubts and fears may not be able to break in on our peace. Fence us around today as with a wall of fire; let us hear thy voice saying: Fear not, I am with thee. Amen.

'All things whatsoever ye pray and ask for, believe that ye have received them, and ye shall have them' (Mark 11:24 RV).

It is not enough to pray and ask; we must *believe that we have received.* We can only do this when we know that we have asked according to God's will (1 John 5:14, 15). This can be determined by referring to his word, which teems with great and precious promises, like so many banknotes or cheques waiting to be cashed.

Prayer: We thank thee, O God, for the daily gifts of thy Providence, but above all for the gift of thyself in Jesus our Lord, in whom all good and perfect gifts are contained. Amen.

In prayer, it is well to be deliberate, to consider what we are about to ask, to discover some promise under which we can make our request; and then, having asked, to wait while the soul, so to speak, takes or appropriates what it needs. It may be that the time is not ripe for it to be actually bestowed, but the request is granted, and the coveted gift is already set aside in God's storehouse, labelled with the name of the petitioner, just as we sometimes get our Christmas presents ready and put them aside, and at the right moment they shall be dispatched.

AUGUST

OUR DAILY WALK OF WISDOM

Walk circumspectly, not as fools, but as wise
(Ephesians 5:15)

The Wise Use of Time
August 1

'Look therefore carefully how ye walk, not as unwise, but as wise redeeming the time, because the days are evil' (Ephesians 5:15, 16 RV).

God desires to give each life its full development. Of course, there are exceptions; for instance, in some cases the lessons and discipline of life are crowded into a very brief space of time, and the soul is summoned to the Presence-chamber of eternity. But, on the whole, each human life is intended to touch all the notes of life's organ. There is an appointed time when it shall be born or die, shall weep or laugh, shall get or lose, shall have halcyon peace or stormcast skies. These times have been fixed for you in God's plan; do not try and anticipate them, or force the pace, but wait thou the Lord's leisure. In due time all will work out for thy good and for his glory. Say to him: 'All my times are in thy hand.'

Times and seasons succeed one another very quickly. Milton, in his glorious sonnet on the *Flight of Time*, bids her call on the leaden-stepping hours, referring to the swing of the pendulum; and, indeed, as we look back on our past life it will seem as though each experience was only for a moment, and then had vanished, never to return. We are reminded of the cobbler, who, as he sat in his kitchen, thought that the pendulum of his clock, when it swung to the left, said, *For ever*, and to the right, *Where*? For ever - where? For ever - where? He got up and stopped it, but found that, although he had stopped the questioner, he had not answered the question. Nor could he find rest until, on his knees, he had been able to face the question of the Eternal and reply to it.

We must be on the alert to meet the demand of every hour. 'Mine hour is not yet come,' said our Lord. He waited patiently until he heard the hours strike in heaven, and then drawing the strength appropriate to its demand, he went forth to meet it. Each time and season is kept by the Father in his own hand. He opens and none shuts; he shuts and none opens. But in that same hand are the needed supplies of wisdom, grace, and power. As the time, so the strength. No time of sighing, trial, temptation, or bereavement is without its special and adapted supplies. Take what is needed from his hand, and go forth to play the part for which the hour calls.

Prayer: Oh, that thou wouldst bless us indeed and enlarge our coasts of useful service. Let thine hand be with us, and keep us from all evil that would grieve thee. Amen.

The Wise Use of Influence
August 2

Influence may be defined as the flowing in of our soul to enthuse and help, or to debase others. The law of action and recreation, of attraction and repulsion is always at work, in virtue of which it may be truly said that no one liveth or dieth to himself. The position of each atom of sand upon the seashore affects the position of all others, and the quality of our personal character is more pervasive than a good or ill odour. What we are affects others much more deeply than what we say. Probably waves of spiritual influence are continually going forth from our inmost nature, and it is the impact of these upon those around us which makes it easier or harder for them to realise their highest ideals.

'Ye are the light of the world ... Let your light so shine before men, that they may see your good works, and glorify your Father which is in heaven' (Matthew 5:14, 16).

The first circle which we can touch and influence is that of our friends. Our counsel may be sweetness or bitterness, but whatever we do or say, we must see that we are absolutely true and faithful (Proverbs 27:6,9). Sincerity means to be without the wax which the cabinet-maker may put into the cracks of the wood to make it appear sound. It is the true and pure soul that most readily and forcibly helps another. Do not be selfish in your friendship, but always give out as *much* and *more* than you expect to receive. Love is a tender plant, and needs culture. We must not suppose that it is able to thrive without light and truth.

The second circle of influence is that of our associates. The great world of men may not appreciate our reproduction of the Beatitudes of the Kingdom, but still reproach, persecute, and say all manner of evil falsely; nevertheless, we must continue to bless the world by the silent and gracious influence of holy living. Reviled, we must bless; persecuted, we must endure; defamed, we must entreat. We must be as salt to our persecutors and as light to our defamers. It is wonderful how love and consistent, patient, prayerful influence finally prevails.

Prayer: Grant, we beseech thee, O God, that our behaviour may be as becometh the gospel of Christ. May the savour of Christ be in our influence, his light in our face, his love in our hearts. Amen.

We are to be as *salt*; i.e. our consistent holy living will act as antiseptic to arrest evil. We are to be the *light of the world*. Inconsistency and cowardice are like bushels which are put over the lamp. Let us put all these hindrances away, that the light which is within us may shine out on the dark world.

The Wise Use of Money
August 3

'*Every man ac-cording as he purposeth in his heart, so let him give; not grudg-ingly, or of ne-cessity: for God loveth a cheerful giver. And God is able to make all grace abound toward you; that ye, always having all sufficiency in all things, may abound to every good work' (2 Corinthians 9:7, 8).*

We must not look on money as our own, for on every coin you may discern the letters: D G - *By the Grace of God.* Therefore money is God's gift to us. 'Both riches and honour come of thee.' David was right when he said, after his people and he had made a noble gift to God's work: 'Of thine own have we given thee.'

But you say: 'I earn my money by the sweat of my brow.' Granted; but 'thou shalt remember the Lord thy God; for it is *he* that giveth thee power to get wealth.' It is God who enables us to keep our situations; who delivers us from paralysing disease, maintains the balance of reason, and renews our daily strength. Is it not our constant profession that we have devoted to Christ all that we are and have, and surely this consecration, if it means any-thing, means that concerning all that belongs to us we would say to our Lord: 'What wouldst *thou* have me to do?'

It is our duty to provide for our own (1 Timothy 5:8). It is also right to hold a certain amount as capital, for the increase of business and the employment of labour. When a man uses his capital rightly, taking no more than a legitimate profit for his time, experience, and responsibil-ity, and allowing his employees to share with him in the overplus, he is doing more real good in the world than if he gave away his property by distributing a pound each to a vast number of beggars. We are to be stewards of the Lord Jesus. This is his own comparison (Matthew 25:14).

In order to guard against the love of money, we should be careful to give a stated proportion to the cause of Christ. It may seem needless to insert this caution for those who should use *all* for Christ. But our hearts are so fickle that we sometimes imagine that we are giving away a larger share of our income than is the case, unless we are accurate in adjusting the balance between Christ and ourselves. It is not possible for one to assign for another the proper proportion, but whatever we fix, it should be rigorously deducted when we receive our income or wages. In the first place, *give your own selves* to Christ, and then all else will fall into line (2 Corinthians 8:5).

Prayer: Help me, dear Lord, to walk in the foot-steps of thy holy life. Teach me how to gain by giving, and to find by losing, according to thy word. Amen.

Understanding God's Lovingkindness
August 4

There are many ways of understanding the lovingkindness or mercy of the Lord.

We may know it as a matter of doctrine. The best way of increasing our knowledge of God's infinite nature, is by the reverent study of his word. It is a flimsy religion which discounts doctrine. What the bones are to the body, doctrine is to our moral and spiritual life. What law is to the material universe, doctrine is to the spiritual. The doctrines of grace are the jewelled foundations of a holy life. Seek the ministry that builds on them; read the books that acknowledge them!

We may know it by meditation. Would that we yielded more silent hearts to the Holy Spirit, that he might fix our vagrant thoughts on the love of Christ that passeth knowledge! The love that loved us in Eternity, that has never let us go in Time, and that has shown its uttermost intensity by the wounds of Calvary!

We may also know it sympathetically. Kepler, the great astronomer, exclaimed one day: 'I have been thinking over again the earliest thoughts of God;' and surely every time we sacrifice ourselves for others, or carry another's cross, in the glow of a warm heart, we are feeling a tiny pulsation of his love.

Do we sufficiently praise God for his lovingkindness and truth? We are keen to pray, to cry out for help, but do we stop to enumerate the mercies and to render praise for them? 'Oh that men would praise the Lord for his goodness and for his wonderful works to the children of men!' (verses 8, 15, 21, 31). How often I have awoke tired and out-of-heart, the harp on the willows, the soul like a lark beaten down by an east wind; and when the usual Bible-study has failed to grip, or prayer has seemed cold and mechanical, the disconsolate heart has started to praise, to give thanks for mercies received, and to adore the majesty and glory of God. As one has thus continued, the soul has thawed, the spirit has found wings, the horizon has cleared, and the angel-song has broken in with its Hallelujah! We are thus transported into the Divine Presence-Chamber; we have obtained joy and gladness, our night is gone, and 'sorrow and sighing have fled away'.

'Whoso is wise and will observe these things, even they shall understand the lovingkindness of the Lord' (Psalm 107:43).

Prayer: Father, thou hast loved us; thou dost love us; thou wilt love us for evermore. Thy love passes knowledge. It is like a warm, sunlit ocean enwrapping the tiny islet of my life. I bathe in it, but can never reach its limits. I thank thee for its depths and lengths. Amen.

'Teach us to number our days, that we may apply our hearts unto wisdom. O satisfy us early with thy mercy; that we may rejoice and be glad all our days' (Psalm 90:12, 14).

This psalm was evidently composed towards the end of the wilderness wanderings, and records some of the sadness which must have oppressed the heart of Moses, as he saw the companions of his earlier life being buried amid the sand-dunes.

He compares the centuries to the memory of yesterday, which fades so quickly from our mind; to a watch spent by the camp fires; to the short rush of the mountain flood; to the dream which flashes for a moment before the mental eye; to the short-lived grass, which flourishes in the morning and is cut down at night. Each emblem full of significant beauty, and evidently culled from the incidents of the long march through these vast solitudes. It was as though the heart of this mighty servant of God turned from the fleeting ages and the decay of human life, to God, whose Being is timeless, unchangeable and eternal. Here is transition and change; there is the Rock of Ages, with its everlasting stability and glory.

Let us number our days against the eternal ages of God's Being; against the age of the mountain and the universe; against the rise and fall of great nations. It is when we realise how short life is that we set ourselves in good earnest to redeem the time, to buy up each golden opportunity.

The heart of wisdom will show itself in giving God a just proportion of our time. Every day it is wise to set apart time for the reading of his word, for prayer and holy fellowship; in every week it is wise to reserve a seventh part for his holy service. We may learn deep lessons from the amount of time that the Hebrews gave to their religious institutions. 'Prayer and provender hinder no man' says the old proverb. It is specially wise to make God to be our Guide, that he may show us how to use this precious thing called life. Apart from him all our desire to use our time aright will be in vain, but when the soul walks in fellowship with God every action tells, every day adds something to the growing power and influence of existence. Nothing is little, nothing trivial, nothing unworthy, if your soul holds fellowship with God. Then will come satisfaction and gladness, and the work of our life will be established by the divine hand.

Prayer: O faithful Lord, teach us to trust thee for life and death, and to take thee for our All in All. Amen.

The Coming Kingdom
August 6

The basis of this magnificent Psalm is the Reign of Christ. No king of David's line realised its sublime ideal, but the mind of the singer is borne forward to the reign of the Messiah, to whom it is applied in the New Testament (Acts 13:33; Hebrews 1:5).

There are four strophes of three verses each.

In 1-3 the nations are depicted as assembling and planning revolt. A widespread conspiracy has arisen against the authority of Jehovah, exercised through the Messiah.

In 4-6, by a bold metaphor, the absurdity of man's rebellion is made clear; but the laughter of the Most High is not inconsistent with the tears and sorrow of Jesus, as he beheld Jerusalem and wept over it. The strenuous resistance by man can never alter the Divine purpose. The hammer cannot break the anvil!

In 7-9, the Anointed King discloses his relationship to the Almighty, and claims universal dominion. The Divine Sonship was an eternal fact, but it was openly certified by the Resurrection (Romans 1:3, 4). As he left our earth to ascend to his throne, our Saviour claimed that all power was given to him in heaven and on earth. His rule is founded, not only on the glory of his essential Deity, but on his suffering and sacrifice. 'He became obedient to death, even the death of the Cross ... therefore God also hath highly exalted him.'

In verses 10-12, the Psalmist urges the rebellious to accept the findings of common sense. It is madness to dream of thwarting God's purpose. Kiss the hand of Jesus outstretched to you in love and forgiveness, and take shelter in him from the wrath to come on the disobedient (Revelation 6:16, 17).

'Yet I have set my King upon my holy hill of Zion. Happy are all they that take refuge in him' (Psalm 2:6, 12 RV marg).

Prayer: Behold, thou commandest that I should love thee with all my heart and soul, with all my mind and strength: Grant thou me what thou commandest, and command what thou wilt. Amen.

The Bible as a Dictaphone
August 7

'When thou saidst, Seek ye my face; my heart said unto thee, Thy face, Lord, will I seek' (Psalm 27:8).

The Bible reminds us of a dictaphone. God has spoken into it, and as we read its pages, they transfer his living words to us. There are many things in the Bible, which, at first, we may not be able to understand, because, as the heaven is higher than the earth, so are God's thoughts higher than ours. Mr Spurgeon used to say that when he ate fish, he did not attempt to swallow the bones, but put them aside on his plate! So when there is something beyond your understanding, put it aside, and go on to enjoy that which is easy of spiritual mastication and digestion.

The Bible contains ten thousand promises. It is God's book of signed cheques. When you have found a promise which meets your need, do not ask God to keep his promise, as though he were unwilling to do so, and needed to be pressed and importuned. Present it humbly in the name of the Lord Jesus! Be sure that, so far as you know, you are fulfilling any conditions that may be attached; then look up into the face of your Heavenly Father, and tell him that you are reckoning on him to do as he has said. It is for him to choose the time and manner of his answer; but wait quietly, be patient, and you will find that not a moment too soon, and not a moment too late, God's response will be given. 'My soul, wait thou only upon God, for my expectation is from him' (Psalm 62:5); 'Blessed is she that believed: for there shall be a performance of those things that were told from the Lord' (Luke 1:45).

Whether for the body, the soul, or spirit, there is no guide like Holy Scripture, but never read it without first looking up to its Author and Inspirer, asking that he will illuminate the page and make you wise unto salvation. 'Speak, Lord, for thy servant heareth.'

Prayer: Thy word is a lamp unto my feet and a light unto my path. I am thy servant; give me understanding, that I may know thy testimonies. Amen.

Life is Worth While
August 8

Nothing is more disastrous than aimless drift! God endows each soul for a distinct purpose. Probably in every life there is a lucid moment, when we take our bearings, and there flashes before us a glimpse of the life-work for which we were sent forth. We stand on the mount of vision, like Moses, and see the pattern of the tabernacle, which we are presently to erect. God has a purpose for the soul, as well as for the body, all the members of which were fashioned, when as yet there was none of them (Psalm 139:16). Is it conceivable that he should spend thought and care on the body, and have no purpose for the soul? But if that be so, he will reveal his will; he will gradually unfold our life-purpose step by step. Let us go steadily forward reckoning on our Almighty Friend to supply the needed grace, wisdom, and strength.

When the captain of a cricket team leaves the pavilion for the wicket, the crowds watching his every movement, he is probably saying to himself: 'I am going to score my hundred, to say the least!' As he faces the man yonder, who may be one of the swiftest and cleverest bowlers in the county, it is as though he says, 'You may do your best, but I am going to win out!' It is in such a spirit that each of us should step out to face life: 'I am going to win through, by God's grace.'

Never forget that God is working with you. 'The Lord will perfect that which concerneth me.' He will not desert the work of his own hands! In my long life of eighty-one years, I have experienced more fluctuations and difficulties than fall to many, but I unhesitatingly assert that where God gives the plan he stands Surety for the result! Dare to trust him and keep in step with him as he leads you onward.

'Whatsoever ye do in word or deed, do all in the name of the Lord Jesus' (Colossians 3:17).

Prayer: O God, the God of all Goodness and all Grace, who art worthy of a greater love than we can either give or understand; fill my heart with such love towards thee as may cast out all sloth and fear, that nothing may seem too hard for me to do or to suffer in obedience to thee. Amen.

'The Lord had said unto Abram, Get thee out of thy country, and from thy father's house, unto a land that I will show thee... And I will bless thee, and make thy name great' (Genesis 12:1-2).

The clue to the beginning of this chapter is given in various parts of the Bible. From Acts 7:2-5, we learn that the call to Abram to go forth, which originally came in Ur of the Chaldees, was repeated in Haran, after his father's death. Probably Terah delayed his son's obedience. Let us help our children to realise God's call, even though we be left lonely on the other side of the river.

In Hebrews 11:8, we realise that this Pilgrim of the Eternal stepped out on the wide expanse of the desert, only learning his course day by day; he was like a Columbus, sailing month after month through unknown seas, never knowing at what moment the dim outline of the shore might appear.

In Romans 4 we are told that these promises were vouchsafed to him while still a Gentile. Thirty years passed before he became the founder of the Hebrew nation. The apostle therefore argues that these promises are guaranteed to *all* his children, not only to those under the Law, but also to us who have his faith (verse 16). Turn back, my reader, to that ancient page, and realise that it includes thee in its amplitude of blessing! Galatians 3:8, 9, 14, assures us that all these blessings are included in the one gift of the Holy Spirit. The blessing of Abraham is for all of us who are in Christ Jesus, as we walk in the steps of this great Pilgrimage.

Prayer: O God, may the great cloud of witnesses, who have trodden the Pilgrim Way before us, be to us an example of a godly life, so that we may run with patience the race that is set before us, looking unto Jesus. Amen.

A vast gulf of Time lies between us and the far-away days of Abraham's life; but recent discoveries have shown that Ur of the Chaldees enjoyed a high state of civilisation a thousand years before his exodus. His experiences and ours meet across the gulf of ages!

The Supreme Choice
August 10

The soul that has taken God as its portion can afford to be generous! As the older man, Abraham might well have claimed the priority of choice, leaving the rest to Lot; but he was quite content to waive his rights, since his Almighty Friend had fixed the place which he was destined to receive for his inheritance. Let Lot choose as he might, he could not obtain an inch of the land which God had included in his Divine purpose for his faithful and obedient servant. 'Wait on the Lord, and keep his way, and he shall exalt thee to inherit the land.'

It was, therefore, in quiet confidence that the Patriarch stood beside his kinsman and watched him, as he lifted up his eyes to take and claim the fullest advantage of his uncle's unexpected offer. When Lot chose for himself the Plain of Sodom, which was well watered everywhere and lovely as Paradise itself, Abraham acquiesced in the choice with unperturbed equanimity. Looking into the face of God he said in effect: '*Thou* art the portion of mine inheritance; *thou* maintainest my lot; the lines are fallen to me in pleasant places; yea, I have a goodly heritage.'

Then - the separation having taken place - God called his servant back to the hill-top, and gave him *all* the land in a covenant for ever, and bade him pass whither he wished over the soil, for it was all his own (verses 14-17).

Let God choose for you! Especially, at the beginning of life, as you stand on its threshold and view the land, dare to follow the promptings of his inner voice. His call still comes ringing down the ages: 'Follow me.' 'Lo, I am with you all the days!'

'And Lot lifted up his eyes, and beheld all the plain of Jordan, that it was well watered everywhere ... as the garden of the Lord. Then Lot chose him all the plain of Jordan ... and they separated themselves the one from the other' (Genesis 13:10, 11).

Prayer: O God, I believe that thou knowest just what is best for me. I can ask nothing better than this, to be thy care, not my own. Through thy grace, I will follow thee whithersoever thou goest. Amen.

God in the Heavens (verses 1-6). The Psalmist knew little or nothing of modern astronomical discovery, but his words can still be applied to the glorious march of suns and mighty planets toward their distant goal. Voices still speak to us from the vault of heaven, though no sound breaks on our listening ears.

The sun was not a god, but a creation. He can only pursue his destined path and retire at night to the tent of darkness. This is evidently metaphor, but is not the orb of natural day a true emblem of the Sun of Righteousness, the Bridegroom of human souls, who once tabernacled amongst men? Let us warm our cold hearts in the heat of his life-giving rays.

God in the Scriptures (verses 7-11). In the first division of the Psalm he is known as *El*; here as *Jehovah*. Nature may reveal his strength, but the Bible tells of his redeeming love. Notice that each sentence contains a name for Scripture, an attribute and one of its effects. *Perfect* - no flaw; *sure*, reliable; *right*, a straight road; *pure*, as sunlight; *clean*, making impurity loathsome; *true*, as a reflection of God; *righteous*, revealing his demands, and the way in which we may become righteous. Ponder its effects! The Old Testament, as David knew it, was only a fragment of Divine revelation. What would he have said of our Bible! Alas, for those who instead of enjoying its fragrance are content with merely dissecting it.

God in the heart (verses 12-14). He reads its innermost secrets, and his Blessed Spirit longs to cleanse us from secret faults, and to hold us back from presumptuous sin.

Prayer: Let the words of my mouth, and the meditation of my heart, be acceptable in thy sight, O Lord, my Strength and my Redeemer. Amen.

God's Even-handed Goodness
August 12

Yes, God is good! Our eye may be evil; the thick atmosphere of this earth-sphere makes our vision oblique, but our warped judgment avails nothing against the verdict of the Universe. So good is God that he will give full wages to those who would have been glad to fill their lives with helpful service, if only they had had the opportunity. All day long they may have waited for their chance, but the sun slowly crept from horizon to horizon, and no opportunity was offered to them. Or, if finally their chance came, it lasted but for one brief hour! Nevertheless, their reward will be counted not only for the service of the hour, but for what they would have done if they had been called in the early dawn.

'Go ye also into the vineyard, and whatsoever is right, that shall ye receive.' 'Is thine eye evil, because I am good?' (Matthew 20:7, 15).

This is not after the manner of men, but it is God's way of dealing with men. He gives of 'his own' to those labourers who have been faithful to their opportunity, whether the hours were longer or shorter. 'His own!' His own Love! His own Joy! His completed Satisfaction!

But all who are admitted to that inner circle must be prepared to drink of his cup, and to be baptised with his baptism (verse 23). Those who shall sit on the right and left of his throne in glory are the ones who have stooped lowest in bond-slave service. The followers of Jesus are not to be ministered to, but must be willing to follow their Lord even to the giving up of their lives. They must resemble their Master who, when he was on his way to redeem mankind, was willing to stand still and relieve the misery of two blind beggars (verse 34).

Prayer: Oh Son of God, pour thy gentleness into our hearts, thy compassionate touch into our fingers, thy tender sensitiveness to human need and sorrow into our cold and callous human senses. Amen.

The Day of Reckoning
August 13

'After a long time, the lord of those servants cometh, and reckoneth with them' (Matthew 25:19).

The three parables recorded in this chapter are of vast importance. Each contains a striking contrast, and in each there is the possibility of supreme joy or the inevitable sentence of deprivation and rejection. In each there is instruction and encouragement on the one side, and on the other we are solemnly warned.

In the parable of the Virgins, we learn the necessity of having adequate reserves; of possessing more than the lamp of profession, however chaste and rare; and of procuring without money or price the oil of the gracious indwelling and inspiration of the Holy Spirit. That religion is entirely valueless which is not due to his kindling and maintenance.

In the parable of the Talents, we learn that the gravest peril in Christian experience attaches not to the highly, or even the moderately-gifted people, but to the poorest and humblest one-talented folk! Because they can do so little they often do nothing. The one talent, which is death to hide, is lodged with them as utterly useless. But with God the smallest things count! He does not crush the bruised reed nor quench the smoking flax. He chooses the foolish things of this world to confound the wise, and the weak things of the world to confound the things which are mighty.

Prayer: Let me not be put to shame, O my Lord, but make me to love and fear thee with all my heart. Help me to be faithful in the very little things, and to hear thy well-done at the last. Amen.

In the Judgment of the Nations, we learn that the ultimate test of Christianity is not in profession or doctrine, but our care for those with whom our Lord has always identified himself - the outcast and helpless, the sick and sorrowful, the stranger and prisoner. Love to God has for its reverse Love to man. Even now the nations are standing before his judgment-bar, and some are being cast on the rubbish heap before our eyes.

The Keys of the Kingdom
August 14

Although these words were spoken to the apostle Peter, there is a profound sense in which every true disciple of Christ can exercise the power of locking and unlocking the door of Faith, Hope or Love to another soul. You may be aware of some one who is carrying a heavy burden, is oppressed with some over-mastering dread, or is fighting some besetting sin. You try to gain that person's confidence, endeavour to find some way of escape, promise some much-needed assistance, speak words of cheer and encouragement, and in this way unlock the door of the dark cell in which he has been incarcerated. The manifestation of your ready sympathy and help have emancipated him. Is not this a true use of the power of the keys of the Kingdom?

'I will give unto thee the keys of the kingdom of heaven: and whatsoever thou shalt bind on earth, shall be bound in heaven; and whatsoever thou shalt loose on earth, shall be loosed in heaven' (Matthew 16:19).

Or it may be some one who is suspected of evil things which are untrue. You listen carefully to the story, and endeavour to put the matter right; you take steps to bring out the purity and sincerity of motives before those who have misunderstood and misjudged.

Perhaps it is a boy or girl whose life is clouded by some entanglement from which it seems impossible to get free. By your friendly counsel and experience you are enabled to unlock the prison door and emancipate this young soul.

Look out for these opportunities of Christian service, for the life which is hidden with Christ in constant fellowship has an extraordinary power in setting free lives which are bound in fetters of iron. Above all, we can point the fettered soul to Christ our Lord.

Prayer:
He breaks the power of cancelled sin,
He sets the prisoner free;
His Blood can make the foulest clean,
His Blood avails for me.
Amen.

'And Jesus said, Are ye also yet without understanding?' (Matthew 15:16).

In this chapter, our Lord teaches that true Religion is certainly not a matter of eating and drinking or outward ceremonial. It is the intention of the soul, the continual drawing from Christ the life-power needed for our work and ministry to others. It may be illustrated by the experience of the diver, who explores the ocean-bed, but draws upon the breeze that sweeps the ocean-surface.

Our Lord did not underestimate the outward observance of the forms of religion; he set us a definite example by his attendance at the Synagogue and the Temple services, by nights spent in prayer, by constant reference to Holy Scripture - but these were only the outward and natural expression of his unbroken fellowship with his Father. Human love does not consist merely in outward expression, but in the hidden purpose of the heart, and yet, if there be no outward expression the spring will dry up!

Perhaps the two greatest definitions of pure religion are these - the first from the Old Testament: 'Do justly, love mercy, walk humbly with thy God.' And the second from the New Testament: 'Pure religion and undefiled before God and the Father is this: To visit the fatherless and widows in their affliction, and to keep himself unspotted from the world.' But to fulfil each of these we need the aid of the Holy Spirit.

Prayer: Give unto me, gracious Lord, the pilgrim spirit that I may be in the world and not of it. Give me thy grace to abstain from fleshly lusts, which war against the soul. May I ever walk worthy of the heavenly calling. Amen.

To be truly religious is within the reach and scope of us all; but we must avail ourselves of what Jesus Christ has done to bring us to God. In him there is absolute forgiveness for all the past, and infinite help and grace for the future. He is willing to be our Surety, Friend, and Helper. Through him we may become partakers of the Divine Nature, and escape the corruption which is in the world through lust.

The Soul's Venture
August 16

It is very helpful to ponder these words, for it gives the assurance that not only will God take care of cattle, and birds, and every living thing, as we learn from Deuteronomy 25:4; Psalm 104:11-22; Jonah 4:11; Matthew 6:26; but that he will much more think of and care for us, his children! Like Noah and his family, you may be shut away from all human help. It may be as impossible for you, as it was for him, to extricate yourself. You may have the responsibility of providing for those in need. Your supplies may be continually decreasing before your eyes, but God remembers you amid the waste of waters, and beneath those dark cloud-covered skies. As a mother cannot forget her sucking child, so God cannot forget you.

'And God remembered Noah, and every living thing, and all the cattle that were with him in the ark' (Genesis 8:1).

The ark grounded on the lower slopes of Ararat on the seventeenth day of the seventh month, and the waters decreased so rapidly, that, as Noah had reaped the harvest before the Flood came, he left the ark in time to sow for the succeeding year. Dare to trust the times and seasons of your life to your Heavenly Father's care. He only waits to be trusted, and then life becomes woven into a beautiful mosaic of his loving forethought and care.

Be sure to guard against raven-like thoughts, which are restless and evil-feeding; seek to cultivate meek, gentle, pure and dove-like thoughts that cull the olive-leaves of promise from the word of God. Presently he who said, 'Come in' will say 'Go forth!' Then build your altar of self-sacrifice and self-giving.

Prayer: Heavenly Father, strengthen me that I may look, not on the dark cloud, but for thy rainbow; not on what thou hast taken or withheld, but on what thou hast left; not on the stormy waters, but on the face of Jesus. Amen.

The Providence of the Trifle
August 17

'O Lord, the God of my Master Abraham, send me, I pray thee, good speed this day ... thereby shall I know that thou hast shewed kindness to my master' (Genesis 24:12-14).

From this beautiful incident we can learn much of God's guidance of the soul. Evidently Eliezer, the faithful servant, had absorbed something of his master's faith and method; so that, as we read this artless narrative, we can realise some of the principles on which the entire camp was conducted. Four times he speaks of 'the God of *my* master Abraham'. When he had been taken into Abraham's confidence, he entered into the plan with as much zeal and interest as if it were his own private concern. Would that we were equally intent on our Heavenly Master's business, and that those who are our dependants and associates were equally impressed by the reverence and prayerfulness of our lives!

Each step was taken in fellowship with God; but that did not prevent him from exercising his own careful management of the successive steps for ascertaining the disposition of this young girl who was so suddenly summoned from the obscurity of Haran to become a link in the Messianic chain. Eliezer's faith in the Providence of a trifle is most interesting and instructive. He held his peace as the girl drew the water; then, in the assurance of faith that his prayer for guidance had been answered, without further hesitation he placed the bracelets on her arms. Be on the outlook to see God's hand in everything!

Prayer: Send me, O Lord, I humbly ask, good speed this day. May I know when to speak and when to be silent; when to act or refrain from action. In all details of daily life may I faithfully serve thee, my Master and Friend. Amen.

Count up the number of times in which this worthy man contrives to bring in the two words, 'My master!' We may learn from him how to speak of our Saviour, wherever we get the opportunity - '*Rabboni*, which being interpreted, is, My Master!'

When asking for good speed to be sent to himself, he alleged as his plea that it would be showing kindness to his master Abraham. So when we ask great things from God, we can plead in the Name of Jesus and be sure that he will show kindness to us for his sake (John 15:16). This old-world story is a beautiful lesson for those who call Jesus Master and Lord.

Religion and Ridicule
August 18

The building of the ruined walls of Jerusalem, as the record shows, was undertaken in troublous times. Some of the petty rulers in the neighbourhood, exulted in the low estate of the city, because it left room for the exercise of their authority, and they viewed these renewed activities with chagrin. They plotted for the overthrow of the work, and had to be met by incessant watchfulness.

If you are endeavouring to do God's work in the world, to clear away the rubbish of sin, to rebuild the walls that are broken down, and to seek the welfare of God's people, do not be surprised if your steps are beset with scorn and ridicule, by the secret or open malice of Sanballat and Tobiah. For some it is easier to face bitter opposition than to bear mockery and ridicule. If only these scornful and carping tongues were silenced, we could make more headway, but such persecution drives us back on God, makes him a living fact in life, and opens the door to the manifestation of the saving health of his right hand (4:4, 9, 20). How good it is, at such times, to cease from man, and to remember the Lord who is the great and terrible one (1:5; Isaiah 51:12, 13). Be quite sure that you are on his plan, doing his work in his way; then go forward in his Name, and he will make all the mountains a way.

The lesson for us all is the threefold aspect of the Christian life.

There is our *up-look* into God's face - 'I prayed to the God of Heaven.' We must never forget to pray, for more things are wrought by prayer than we realise.

Second, there is our *out-look* against our foes and the foes of God - 'we made our prayer unto our God, and set a watch against them day and night.' We must watch as well as pray.

Lastly, there is our *down-look* towards the work entrusted to us, at which we must labour with unslacking devotion, in fellowship with our Lord (1 Corinthians 3:9). Let each inquire: 'Am I inside the city amongst its builders, or outside amongst its detractors and foes?'

'When Sanballat ... and Tobiah ... and Geshem ... heard it, they laughed us to scorn and despised us, and said what is this thing that ye do? Then answered I them, The God of Heaven, he will prosper us; therefore we his servants will arise and build. So built we the wall; for the people had a mind to work' (Nehemiah 2:19, 20; 4:6).

Prayer: O God, teach us day by day what thou wouldst have us to do, and give us grace and power to fulfil the same. May we never from love of ease, decline the path which thou pointest out, nor, for fear of shame, turn away from it. Amen.

The Value of Friendship
August 19

'Two are better than one ... for if they fall, the one will lift up his fellow' (Ecclesiastes 4:9, 10).

We cannot have many inner friends, but sad is the life that has not its other self. The friendship of David and Jonathan, of Damon and Pythias, has passed into the current talk of the world. It is especially good for the Christian disciple to travel to heaven with a comrade, Hopeful with Christian, and Mercy with Christiana.

A friend is invaluable if we stumble or fall on the path of life. 'Woe to him that is alone when he falleth.' 'Brethren,' says the apostle, 'if a man be overtaken in a fault, ye which are spiritual, restore such an one in the spirit of meekness, considering thyself lest thou also be tempted.' Let us watch for each other's souls; if any is falling away from the truth, or into some insidious trap, let us lift him up. Let us exercise the brotherly solicitude that Barnabas did for Paul.

Friendship ought to make our spirits glow. 'How can one be warm alone?' Of course, in a spiritual sense there are divine sources of caloric. The love of Christ kindleth to vehement heat. But it is certainly easier to keep up the temperature when we have a kindred heart beside us. Perhaps this was one reason why our Lord sent forth his disciples by two and two (Mark 6:7).

Prayer: We pray for our companions in life's pilgrimage. Help us to hearten them with our courage, cheer them with our love, and bear their burdens so far as we may. For ourselves may we find in Jesus the Friend that sticketh closer than a brother. Amen.

Without companionship, material things cannot satisfy. The ties of nature, friendship, and religious communion give a zest to a poor man's life, which the miser with all his wealth forfeits. It is all-important, not only in ordinary life, but pre-eminently in the pilgrimage of the spirit, to have fellowship with some kindred soul.

In temptation a true friend makes us more able to withstand the devil. It is a real help in the hour of trial to have a friend who will appropriate the words of our Lord, saying: 'I have prayed for thee, that thy faith fail not.' There is no fellowship like that of Jesus, our Faithful Friend, who lifts us when we fall, chafes us when chilled with cold, and succours us against the Tempter. Does he not make the *third* in the threefold cord - 'Where two or three are gathered together in my Name, there am I in the midst of them' (Matthew 18:20).

Digging Wells
August 20

Isaac seems to be rather a disappointing character, and we sometimes wonder that he should be classed with Abraham, the father of all who believe; and Jacob, who prevailed with the Angel and became a Prince! He was passive, quiet, given to thoughtful meditation (Genesis 24:63). God's purpose includes all sorts and types of men, and Isaac dug wells of which men have drunk for thousands of years.

He was constantly pursued by enmity, jealousy, and strife, as the names of his wells attest. But each time he consistently retired from the conflict, and yielded his well to dig another. Finally, his enemies had to confess that he was mightier than they (verse 16). Best of all, God appeared to him 'the same night', and promised that he would be with him and bless him.

Let us learn to sublimate our resistance to evil, and lift it from the physical to the moral and spiritual level. 'He that is slow to anger is better than the mighty' (Proverbs 16:32). Go on digging wells - the wells of Family Prayer, of love for the Bible, of holy exercises and habits! You will find spring water (verse 19). That is God's side of your life. You are called to dig wells, but God's Holy Spirit will rise up in your soul, and in the souls of others, like the geyser-springs in Arctic regions (John 4:14). Let us present to him ourselves - our souls and bodies, to be the wells and channels, along and through which his eternal Godhead and Power, arising from the fathomless depths of his own nature, may reach this thirsty and parched world!

God is Love; Love is Self-Giving; but God depends on the co-operation of us, the well-diggers, to make outlets for the outflow of his Love and Goodness.

'He removed from thence, and digged another well ... and he called the name of it Rehoboth; and he said, For now the Lord hath made room for us, and we shall be fruitful in the land' (Genesis 26:22).

Prayer: Most Merciful Father, give us grace that we may never be drawn to do anything that may dishonour thy Name; but may persevere in all good purposes, and in thy holy service, unto our lives' end. Amen.

The Clue to Life's Maze
August 21

'There was a man whose name was Job; and that man was perfect and upright, and one that feared God, and eschewed evil ... Satan said, Doth Job fear God for nought?' (Job 1:1, 9).

This marvellous poem, one of the profoundest studies in the Bible deals with the great problem of evil. At some time or other in our lives, we come back to study it, as a clue to life's maze, the expression of our heart's out-cry, and the solution of life's mystery in the will and love of God.

From first to last, the supreme questions in this wonderful piece of literature are: 'Can God make man love him for himself alone and apart from his gifts?' and 'Why is evil permitted, and what part does it play in the nurture of the soul of man?' These questions are always with us. In fact, the Book of Job may be said to be a compendium of the existence and history of our race.

The first chapter teems with helpful lessons. The anxiety of parents for their children should expend itself in ceaseless intercession on their behalf. The great Adversary of souls is always on the watch, considering our conduct so as to accuse us before God, not only for overt sins, but for unworthy motives. We cannot forget our Lord's words to Peter: 'Satan asked to have you ... but I made supplication for thee, that thy faith fail not' (Luke 22:31 RV). Christ never underestimated the power of Satan, the 'prince of this world', but he is our great Intercessor (Hebrews 4:14-16; 7:25).

In circumstances of prosperity and happiness, we must never forget that it is God who plants a hedge about us, blesses our work and increases our substance. It is good to realise that whatever be the malignity of our foes, there is always the Divine restraint, and we are not tempted beyond what we are able to bear. It is not enough to endure our griefs sullenly or stoically. It should be our aim not only to hold fast to our integrity, but to trust God. There is a clue to the mystery of human life, which comes to the man who differentiates between the Real and the Unreal; the Seen and the Unseen.

Prayer: My flesh and my heart faileth; but God is the strength of my heart, and my portion for ever. Amen.

God's Delays are not Denials
August 22

There are many illustrations of this Divine method in the word of God. The Angel at the Jabbok-ford waited till Jacob could wrestle no more, being completely exhausted by his struggles; and then, as his helpless antagonist clung to him for support, he whispered in his ear his mystic name and blessed him there.

Our Lord waited till the Syrophenician woman fell helpless at his feet, with the cry: 'Lord, help me!' that he might grant to her the boon she craved for her child. From his throne in Heaven he pursued the same method, waiting to be gracious till the apostles and others in the upper room had reached such a condition of helplessness that he could give them their Pentecost; waiting till the little group of disciples had exhausted every other expedient, that he might release to them Peter from his prison; waiting till Paul had renounced all creative energy, that he might take him strong in his almighty power, while he whispered: 'My grace is sufficient for thee; My strength is made perfect in weakness.'

Too often we have misinterpreted God's dealings with us. When he has tarried beyond the Jordan, in spite of our entreaties that he should hasten to save Lazarus, we have concluded that he was strangely neglectful. But, in fact, he was waiting, at no small cost to his heart, till we had come to the end of ourselves, and the way was clear for him to work a more astounding miracle than we had dared to hope.

God's delays are not denials; they are not neglectful nor unkind. He is waiting with watchful eye and intent for the precise moment to strike, when he can give a blessing which will be without alloy and will flood all after life with blessings so royal, so plenteous, so divine, that eternity will be too short to utter all our praise.

'Therefore will the Lord wait, that he may be gracious unto you, and therefore will he be exalted, that he may have mercy upon you; for the Lord is a God of judgment; blessed are all they that wait for him' (Isaiah 30:18).

Prayer: We ask from the treasures of thy grace for a more childlike trust, a more faithful spirit, a more loyal will. May our obedience open to us all spiritual knowledge. Amen.

The Equilibrium of Life
August 23

In every life there should be the worship of the Temple and the service of the Home. Do we realise that God is directing and locating our life-plan? The Home is his arrangement for us equally with the Temple, and the daily meal may be an ordinance as the Lord's Supper. Do you take your food 'with gladness and singleness of heart' or do you grumble over your meals? Do you perform common tasks gladly and gratefully? This is only possible when we come to understand that the greatness of life consists, not so much in doing so-called great things, but in doing small things greatly! 'Whatsoever thy hand findeth to do, *do it with thy might.*'

We have been compared to the weavers of the Gobelin tapestry, who may have to work a number of apparently drab and sombre, uninteresting and common things into the pattern on the wrong side of the woof. It is only when the texture is completed that they can see and admire the design that is worthy of the palace of the king! So it is with your life and mine. 'We work, we suffer and see neither the end nor the fruit. But God sees it, and when he releases us from our task, he will disclose to our wondering gaze what he, the great Artist, has woven out of those toils that now seem so sterile.'

There was great joy in the lives of these early Christians. They parted with their worldly possessions, but they were filled with gladness, and probably this gave them favour with the people. There was true helpfulness among them. Each went shares with the rest. The *give* and *take* of life is so important. We are all glad enough to take what we can get, but how about to *give*! We like to be waited on, but how about the serving? Yet true gladness and happiness depends, not on being ministered to, but in ministry. When we have learnt the secret of praising God in and for everything; when we refuse to shut ourselves up in our own griefs, but compel our dull spirits to enter into the joys of those around, then we shall have no difficulty in living joyfully and gladly.

Prayer: O Lord, renew our spirits and draw our hearts unto thyself, that our work may not be to us a burden, but a delight; and give us such a mighty love to thee as may sweeten all our obedience. Amen.

God's Response to our Cry
August 24

This is one of the most exquisite chapters in Isaiah's prophecy. Notice its profound teaching. God permitted the Assyrian to come because of the deep lessons it would teach the king and people that certain abuses must be checked. The siege would surely come, and they would know something of the bread of adversity and the water of affliction, but the Almighty would be near, speaking to his people not only by their sorrows, but by his servants, and by the still small voice of the Holy Spirit. Thus we have an example of the persuasive providence of God. His grace surrounds and keeps his people, but if we wilfully sin, we break the cordon of his protection. When we repent and turn back again to cry to him, the gentle hand of the Lord will bind up our wounds and soothe our spirits; songs break forth in the night, and our heart is filled with gladness.

'He will be very gracious unto thee at the voice of thy cry; when he shall hear it, he will answer thee' (Isaiah 30:19).

The latter part of this chapter (verses 27-33) describes the coming of Sennacherib's troops. They are terrible, and yet there was a sense in which they were called into existence with God: 'Behold the Name of the Lord cometh from afar'. The advance is compared to a terrific thunderstorm, and then to the rush of a mountain torrent. In verse 28 the final check is given, as when a wild animal is lassoed and brought to its knees. Presently the animal would vanish silently, and once more the stricken land would be ploughed up for sowing the seed, streams would flow as before, and joyful harvests reaped.

How tender and gracious are these words to those in pain and distress. Be of good cheer, God has not forgotten to be gracious to you! Take to heart these sweet promises, and ask that the counterpart of these blessings may be granted in your experience.

Prayer: Our Father, we realise that thou dost need to discipline us when we cease from walking in thy faith and fear! Make us more sensitive and responsive to the voice of the Holy Spirit, saying: this is the way, walk ye in it; that with gladness of heart we may once more return to thee. Amen.

God our Defence and Deliverer
August 25

We have in this chapter, three beautiful synonyms for God.

He is Wise (verses 1-3). The politicians of that time were boasting of their wisdom in having secured the Egyptian alliance, but their cleverness and strategy were not destined to be of any help to them. Why did they not consult the Holy One of Israel, and seek the help of the Almighty? Was his wisdom only in heavenly and religious matters? Had he not the power to infuse men like Isaiah with a wisdom for earthly and human politics? Surely the boast of wisdom was mockery in the leaders of the people, at that dread hour of Jerusalem's history, when they turned away from the Light and Glory of the Shekinah to seek human counsellors and worldly stratagems. Not only in religious matters, but in the daily ordering of our human life, 'if any man lack wisdom, let him ask of God, who giveth to all liberally and upbraideth not; and it shall be given him. But let him ask in faith, nothing doubting'! (James 1:5).

He is as a Lion (verse 4). The lion is more than a match for the groups of shepherds who endeavour to stand against him with their crooks. He is not afraid of their shouting and views them with contempt. Does not this mean that the mighty presence and power of God would shelter the soul that trusts him? All the nations might assail the city in vain whilst the Lion of the Tribe of Judah stood as sentry! If you are fearful of heart, and dread the attack of man, flee to God for refuge and defence (Psalm 46:1).

He is as a mother-bird and her nest (verse 5). How wonderful these words are! How near God comes to each one of us! We are reminded of our Saviour who longed to gather Jerusalem under his wings! Amid all the fret and worry and anxiety of your life, dare to believe in a Love that will not let you go!

Prayer: O God our Father, how can we thank thee for thy holy word, and the many methods by which thou wouldst gain our confidence and love! Give us grace to return unto our rest beneath the shadow of thy wings! Amen.

Walking with Jesus
August 26

The daily walk of the Christian soul is so absolutely important because it is our witness to the world. Our character, as exemplified in our behaviour, is the world's only Bible and sermon (2 Corinthians 3:2, 3). Let us learn to walk so as to please God, and to bless mankind. To walk is at first a matter of considering every little step, but afterwards it becomes the habit of the soul (Colossians 1:10).

'As ye have therefore received Christ Jesus the Lord, so walk ye in him' (Colossians 2:6).

We received Jesus into our hearts by faith. He entered through the open door and became our Lord and Master. In the same manner we must live always and everywhere, receiving from him, by faith, grace upon grace, and allowing what he works in to work out in all manner of godliness, tenderness, and Christlikeness. This practice of looking to Jesus for grace in every circumstance of life tends to become more and more habitual - and this is what the apostle means when he says, 'Rooted and built up in him, and stablished in the faith.'

But such a walk is only possible when we have learned to 'crucify the flesh with the affections and lusts' (Galatians 5:24). The flesh is the assertion of our self-life, whether in lesser or grosser forms, but whenever self intrudes it exercises a baleful influence on our behaviour and conversation. Just as the iron of the steamer will deflect the needle of the compass, so the intrusion of our self-life will act as a drag upon our character and walk.

How can we crucify the flesh? Only by allowing the Holy Spirit to have supreme control. He makes the Cross every day dearer and more effective. He will conquer evil habits in us and for us, while we stand by as more than conquerors through his grace. If we will be led by him, there will not only be deliverance from the self-life, but he will produce in us the fruit of holy living which will please God and refresh men.

Prayer: Let thy Holy Spirit be continually with us, and may we feel the powerful effects of thy divine grace constantly directing and supporting our steps. Amen.

'Serve the Lord with gladness: Come before his presence with singing' (Psalm 100:2).

'Let us offer the sacrifice of praise to God continually, the fruit of lips which make confession to his name' (Hebrews 13:15 RV).

The hundredth Psalm is rightly entitled, 'A Psalm of Thanksgiving' (RV). The Psalmist calls for a 'joyful noise', i.e. an audible expression of worship. Do not be content with a thankful heart, but express it! It is good to let God have 'the fruit of our lips'. As a bird will awaken the whole choir of a woodland glade, so the soul really aglow with loving adoration will spread its own contagion of song. How often Christian people hinder the progress of Christianity by their dullness, gloominess, and depression. His service is perfect freedom, and if we delight ourselves in the Lord, we should serve him with *gladness*!

It is very important to maintain the habit of regular church-going because of its opportunity for worship. Let us 'enter into his gates with thanksgiving, and into his courts with praise'! By meditation and prayer let us ask that we may be accounted worthy to stand in his Presence and offer praise and adoration to the Most High God, mingled with the fragrance of our Saviour's name (Revelation 8:3, 4).

'The Lord is good!' There are many mysteries, and much pain and sorrow in the world. We must dare to believe and affirm the goodness of God beneath all the distressing elements of modern life. With his goodness are combined his mercy and his truth. Let men do their worst, 'His truth endureth to all generations.' It is an impregnable Rock, on which the waves of sin can make no sensible impression. What comfort there is in knowing that equally his mercy is everlasting. We need so much patience, forbearance and longsuffering, that if God's mercy were anything less we should despair, but it is extended to every generation till Time shall be no more!

Prayer: Bless the Lord, O my soul, And forget not all his benefits. Amen.

Proposals and Disposals
August 28

Men are often more eager to get God's help in termporalities than in spiritualities. The man in the crowd, who appealed to Christ, was more anxious that he should interpose on his behalf in a family dispute than to give him the life of the ages. But our Lord refused to be Judge and Arbitrator. His ministry went deeper to the springs of action, and he knew that in each brother there was the root of covetousness, which led the one to wrong the other. He struck at the sin which lay at the root of all such disputes about property.

'Take heed, and beware of covetousness: for a man's life consisteth not in the abundance of the things which he possesseth' (Luke 12:15).

Our Lord insisted that life does not consist in the abundance of things of which we may happen to be possessed. We say: 'So and so is worth a million pounds!' Heaven estimates a man's worth by the courage, faith, purity, self-control, and love to God and man, which have grown up in the soul by the careful discipline of the years! Acceptance and rank in the Kingdom of God depends on character not on possessions.

How often man proposes and God disposes! We say, 'We shall yet live for *many years*, and enjoy the fruit of our labours'; but God says: '*Tonight*!' Listen to the apostle James, speaking to those who said, 'Today or tomorrow we will go to this city or that, and spend a year there, and carry on a successful business! All the while you do not even know what will happen tomorrow. For your life is but a mist, which appears on the hillside, but vanishes at the touch of dawn. Surely, we ought to say: If it is the Lord's will, we shall live, and do this or that' (James 4:13-17).

Prayer: Lord, I know not what is before me, but thou knowest. Choose thou my portion for me. Lead me by thine own hand; and keep me close to thee, day by day, and night by night. Amen.

Many talk of *seeing life* who see only its most sordid and ugly side. If a man really wishes to see life, and know happy days, the secret is given in 1 Peter 3:10-19. This is the message of the gospel, 'That God has given us the life of the ages, and that this life is in Christ Jesus. *He who has the Son has the Life*' (John 3:36; 1 John 5:12).

Our Duty towards our Neighbour
August 29

'Thou shalt love thy neighbour as thyself' (Matthew 22:39; Leviticus 19:9-18).

Our neighbour is the next person who needs our help - man, woman, or child. It is enough that your help is needed, and that you are near! As we read this paragraph from the old Jewish law we see who are our neighbours, and what we are to do for them.

We must give them the chance to live (verses 9, 10). We have no right to waste anything that may be of service to others, or to use for ourselves all our possessions. There must always be a margin left which we can give to those who are in need. Well would it be if each reader of these lines would set apart a certain proportion of produce and increase, as well as money, for the cause of Christ and his poor.

We must not withhold payments which are due (verse 13). How many tradesmen and others have been ruined by the long delays of customers in settling their accounts. If only all Christian people would insist on paying cash, especially to small shopkeepers, what a blessed revolution would ensue. It is neither honest nor just to withhold payment from those to whom it is due.

We must be very gentle and considerate to those who suffer from any infirmity (verse 4). God's Love is always endeavouring to make up in some way to those who are handicapped. The blind Milton sings of Paradise, and Helen Keller has been enabled to triumph over insuperable obstacles. We are to become ears to the deaf, and eyes to the blind.

We must not hesitate to rebuke sin (verse 17). This needs deep humility, tact, the removal of the beam from one's own eye, the love of Christ for souls; but how much might be done if we would stay the little rift within the lute!

Prayer: O Lord, soften our hard and steely hearts, warm our icy and frozen hearts, that we may wish well to one another, and may be the true disciples of Jesus Christ. Amen.

We must not bear a grudge (verse 18). Ah, this is hard! To feel hurt, to take offence, to be cold and stiff, to stand at a distance - how many of us fail here! But we must act and speak to others in the power of God's Love, as we would do if there were no grudge within.

The lawyer asked Christ: 'Who is my neighbour?' suggesting that some one should neighbour *him*. Our Lord reversed his inquiry, saying in effect: 'Whom will *you* neighbour?' If you go through life seeking people to neighbour you, life will be full of disappointment; but blessed is he who seeks to neighbour others; he shall not lack those who, in the hour of trial, will neighbour him.

Victory over Death
August 30

In this marvellous chapter, Isaiah sings a Song of Hope, as he sees the return of the Hebrew people from captivity, and the overthrow of their foes. The apostle Paul takes up this thought in 1 Corinthians 15. He shows that death is the penalty of sin, and it is by the demands of the law that sin is stirred to activity. But Christ has satisfied and met the claims of the law, and gives power by which we are enabled to obey it; therefore the strength of sin is broken, and the sting of death is gone.

The Christian need not dread to die. For him there is no uncertainty about the future. There is no fear of what may come after death, for the condemnation of the law has been met and borne. We may apostrophise death in these exultant words. The viper has been deprived of its fangs! The prison-house cannot hold its inmates! Bunyan describes Satan as exhorting Captain Sepulchre to be sure to hold Christ, but the injunction was useless. No bars or bolts, no seal or sentry would suffice.

Notice that we are to *put on* incorruption and immortality (verses 53, 54). It is as though the new body will be put on over the old, and as this takes place, all the elements of the old body will be swallowed up and absorbed. When the Holy Spirit completes his work in our souls, there will be no trace of the old rags left in the shining robes in which we shall be arrayed, as we go forth to meet the welcome of our Lord. Death to those who believe in Christ is now only a Home-going; the falling asleep to open the eyes in the City of God; the loosening of the anchor, to float down stream in the full tide. 'There shall be no more death, neither sorrow, nor crying, neither shall there be any more pain.'

'He will swallow up death in victory; and the Lord God will wipe away tears from off all faces' (Isaiah 25:8).

'O Death, where is thy sting? O Grave, where is thy victory? (1 Corinthians 15:55).

'God shall wipe away all tears from their eyes' (Revelation 7:17).

Prayer: O God, whensoever thy ways in nature or in the soul are hard to be understood, then may our quiet confidence, our patient trust, our loving faith in thee be great, and as children knowing that they are loved, cared for, guarded, kept, may we with a quiet mind at all times put our trust in the unseen God. So may we face life without fear, and death without fainting. Amen.

The Growth of the Soul
August 31

'My soul followeth hard after thee: thy right hand upholdeth me' (Psalm 63:8).

There are three notes in this Psalm which betoken the stages of the soul's growth: 'My soul *thirsteth* for thee;' 'my soul shall be *satisfied*;' 'my soul *followeth* hard after thee.' We may be passing through a wilderness of spiritual drought, the dark night of the soul, the seasons of dryness and depression which are apt to befall. In some cases, as when Elijah asked to die, or when John sent his despairing question to Christ from his prison, it is the result of physical or mental overstrain. But at such times, let us never hesitate still to speak of God as '*my* God'. Nothing can sever you from his everlasting Love. You may not have the glad consciousness of it, but you must never surrender your belief in it. Go on blessing him, as long as you live, and lift up your hands in prayer.

Prayer: Living or dying, Lord, I would be thine. Draw me day by day nearer to thyself, until I be wholly filled with thy love, and fitted to behold thee face to face. Amen.

But we can never be satisfied with what we have attained. God is ever moving forward! Let us follow hard after him.

SEPTEMBER

OUR DAILY WALK OF WATCHFULNESS

Blessed is the man that heareth me, watching
daily at my gates, waiting at the posts of my doors
(Proverbs 8:34)

Blessed are those servants whom the Lord
when he cometh shall find watching
(Luke 12:37)

'Keep thy heart above all that thou guardest: For out of it are the issues of life' (Proverbs 4:23 RV marg).

Said Peter to our Lord, 'Spare thyself this death of which thou speakest - this bitter suffering and anguish shall never be thine.' These words are continually spoken still, and many are the voices that bid us spare ourselves - the voices of our friends who love us; the voices of prudence and worldly wisdom; the voices of our own wayward hearts.

Do not spare your judgment of yourself. Never permit yourself to do things which you would be the first to condemn in others. Never suppose that there are reasons for you to do a wrong, which, under no circumstances, would you tolerate in your neighbour.

Do not spare yourself in confessing your sins and mistakes. Confession is one of the tests of nobility. Not a few are willing to confess to God, who never attempt to confess to men. It is a serious question whether that sorrow for sin is genuine and deep enough which does not lead the offender to ask his fellow-man for pardon, even as he asks his God. Nothing could be clearer than Christ's words, that whenever we remember that our brother has aught against us, we are to leave our gift at the altar, and go first to seek reconciliation with him, before we offer our sacrifice to God.

The supreme test of goodness is not in the greater but in the smaller incidents of our character and practice; not what we are when standing in the searchlight of public scrutiny, but when we reach the firelight flicker of our homes; not what we are when some clarion-call rings through the air, summoning us to fight for life and liberty, but our attitude when we are called to sentry-duty in the grey morning, when the watch-fire is burning low. It is impossible to be our best at the supreme moment if character is corroded and eaten into by daily inconsistency, unfaithfulness, and besetting sin.

You cannot really help people without expending yourself. The only work that tells must cost you something. Gold, silver, and precious stones can never be built into the new Jerusalem unless you are willing to part with them from the stores of your own life.

Prayer: Most loving Father, may love fill and rule my heart. For then there will spring up and be cherished between thee and me a likeness of character, and union of will, so that I may choose and refuse what thou dost. Amen.

Watching for Souls
September 2

The ministry of warning should be a recognised part of the work of the Church and of each individual member. The foghorn warns the ship from the deadly rocks; the red light warns the train of imminent danger; in the days of the plague people were warned from infected areas; how much more should we, who know the wrath of God which abides on those who refuse Christ, raise our voice in warning. We should do it deliberately, earnestly, patiently, and in reliance upon the Spirit of God to make our words, however much they may be resented, the means of arresting the wicked from the error of his ways, and those who are taking their first steps in forbidden paths from pursuing them (Ezekiel 33:7-9).

How wonderful it is that God does not commission angels to carry his warnings and appeals; instead of this, the work that angels might love to do is entrusted to men. It is at our peril that we neglect our opportunities in this direction. If the signalman is placed at a point where many lines of rail cross or diverge, and he sleeps at his post, or neglects his duty, he may be tried for manslaughter; and if we know of people in the immediate circle of our influence who are in danger of ruining their physical, moral and spiritual wellbeing, we are bound to raise a warning voice. If we saw, upon the upper reaches of a river, a boat full of people hastening towards the rapids unheeding the danger, surely we might be guilty of being an accessory in their destruction, if we failed to do something to warn them of their peril.

Accompanying our words of warning, there should be the clear reiteration of the *Love of God*. He does not desire the death of a sinner, but rather that he should turn from his wickedness and live. It is not enough to try and prevent men from taking the wrong path, we must urge and allure them to take the pleasant ways of righteousness and peace. All are included in the love of God. Even sin cannot turn away his love, which is like that described in the parable of the Prodigal Son, or 1 Corinthians 13.

'Christ in you, the hope of glory; whom we preach, warning every man, and teaching every man in all wisdom' (Colossians 1:27, 28). '...Watch and remember ... I ceased not to warn every one night and day with tears' (Acts 20:31).

Prayer: O God, we have left undone many things that we ought to have done. Hands have been reached out for help which we have not given; hearts have turned to us for sympathy which we have not blessed. Forgive us, we pray thee, and at whatever cost may we follow Christ in his redemptive purpose. Amen.

The Folly of being Unprepared
September 3

'While they went to buy, the Bridegroom came; and they that were ready went in with him to the marriage: and the door was shut' (Matthew 25:10).

The foolish virgins made five great mistakes.

They made no provision for the continuance of their light. It is not enough merely to have the lamp; it must be lit and maintained, because there is something for the fire to feed on. How many there are who are on fire and in earnest during the first stage of their religious life, but they have made no provision. They have lamps, but have neglected to take oil. The oil stands for fellowship with the Lord Jesus, for the grace of the Holy Spirit, for the daily study of the Bible, for the kindling communion of worship with fellow-Christians.

They slept. There was a difference between the sleep of the foolish and that of the wise. There are two kinds of sleep. The one arises from a sense of security and trust. Every preparation has been made; all has been done that could be done, and we resign ourselves deliberately to the care of God. So Peter slept in the prison, before the angel came to deliver him. But there is another kind of sleep. The sleep of the sentry, when the foe is stealing up the pass; of the pilot, when the ship is making for the serried teeth of the rocks; of the nurse, when the patient's life is quivering in the balance. These foolish ones had no right to sleep, when they were so utterly unready to meet the Bridegroom. We must not take things for granted, or say 'Peace, peace, when there is no peace!'

The thought they could procure oil from the wise. But the appeal was in vain. Each must bear his own burden of responsibility in the sight of God. We may 'buy without money and without price', but each must appropriate the living grace and power of Jesus for himself.

They thought they could get in: 'Lord, Lord, open to us!' But the door was irrevocably closed! 'How shall we escape, if we neglect so great salvation?'

They thought that the Bridegroom would recognise them. But he said: 'I know you not.' Let each ask himself: 'Does Jesus know me? Will he recognise me at last?' The only way to be sure, is to kneel at the foot of his cross until he seals us with the Holy Spirit, and says, 'Fear not, for I have redeemed thee; I have called thee by thy name, thou art mine.'

Prayer: O Lord, we pray that our lives may be lamps to which thou shalt supply oil. Help us to be burning and shining-lights for this dark world. Amen.

Wheat and Tares
September 4

How clearly our Lord taught the personality of Satan! In his explanation of this parable, he said distinctly, 'The enemy that sowed them is the devil'! He knew that in every heart - in the Church as well as in the world - the great enemy of God's Kingdom, and of human happiness, is always at work, sowing tares. The seed may be very small, but in a single night irreparable injury may be wrought.

'But while he slept, his enemy came and sowed tares among the wheat, and went his way' (Matthew 13:25).

Notice that we become as the seed we receive - those who receive the wheat-seed become wheat; those who receive the tare-seed become tares. 'As a man thinketh in his heart, so is he.' How careful we should be over the books we read, the companionship and friendship that we form, the recreations that we take part in. Such are some of the processes by which our characters are being made. If we are thoughtless and careless, we expose ourselves to the reception of tare-seed, which germinates into weeds and rubbish. Of course, if our necessary duties take us into scenes where evil is rife, we may claim the keeping power of Christ, and hide ourselves in him. As the doctor or nurse will saturate themselves with disinfectant when called to a house where plague or fever is incurred, so the Holy Spirit in whom we may bathe our souls, will be as the antiseptic, and deliver us from the microbes of temptation (Galatians 5:16, 17).

There is not much difference, it is said, between wheat and tares, in the earlier stages of growth; it is only when the harvest comes that the distinction is clearly defined. So in the Church and the world, there are many counterfeits, people who seem to be good and true, but they are not what they seem, and in the day of reckoning they will be rooted up and cast forth as rubbish. The two classes that will be rejected at last are 'All that cause stumbling, and them that do iniquity' (verse 41 RV). It may be that you are not amongst those that do iniquity, in any of its glaring forms, but are you causing others to stumble by your inconsistent behaviour or worldliness? Let each of us carefully examine ourselves, and open our hearts to receive from the hand of the Lord Jesus the incorruptible seed which he waits to implant by his word.

Prayer: Give us a pure judgment and a true understanding of thy word, O Lord, that we may not be deceived and carried away by any error; but grant that we may grow in grace and in the knowledge of our Lord and Saviour Jesus Christ. Amen.

'That ye may be blameless and harmless, children of God without blemish in the midst of a crooked and perverse generation, among whom ye are seen as lights in the world, holding forth the word of life' (Philippians 2:15, 16 RV).

The spirit of man, says the wise man, is the candle of the Lord (Proverbs 20:27). By nature we are like so many unlit lamps and candles. As the wick is adapted for the flame, but stands dark and cold until it is ignited, so we are unable to shed forth any light until our nature is kindled from the eternal nature of him who 'is light, and in whom is no darkness at all'. Has the candle of your life been lit by contact with Christ, the Sun of Righteousness?

Our Lord says: 'Let your light shine before men.' He shows how absurd it is to light a lamp, and then obscure its rays by placing it under a bushel. The purpose of ignition is frustrated if the light is covered. Ah! how many of us place bushels on the light of our testimony for God - the bushel of uncharitable speech! Of ill-temper! Of a discontented and querulous spirit! These as well as more conspicuous failings will prevent us from shining forth as light in a dark world. It is not for us to ignite the flame or supply the oil. All we have to do is to keep our lamps clean and bright, to guard against anything that may obstruct the out-shining of the Love and Life of God through the soul. If we are careful to see that anything which might hinder the effect of our testimony and mar our influence is put away, Christ will see to it that our light shall effect the full measure of his purpose.

In contrast to the bushel is the stand or candlestick. The Master of the House may place you in a very small dark corner, and on a very humble stand, but some day, as he passes by, you shall light his footsteps as he goes forth to seek and save that which is lost. What is your stand? - your place in society, your position in the home, your situation in some business house, factory or school - wherever it be, it doesn't matter, so long as your light is shining forth, steady and clear, warning and directing men and women in the path of life.

Prayer: O Christ, may the fire of thy divine love burn up our bushels; help us to shine forth as lights in this dark world. Amen.

The Cure for Short Sight
September 6

The Christian graces which we have to supply present themselves to the apostle's mind as the golden links of a chain or necklace, which begins with faith, and ends with love, so that faith and love clasp in the centre (verses 5-7).

The idea of lavish expenditure is here associated with the word translated *supply* (verses 5, 11). Among the ancient customs of Greece, was the expression of goodwill to society on the part of leading citizens by the provision of public entertainments, in honour of benefactors, or generals returning victorious from war. Rich men craved permission to bear the cost, as in modern days men will endow hospitals and libraries.

So the apostle says, See to it that you spare no cost in the glorious provision of 'these things'; spare neither thought nor pains, if only these Christian graces are in you and abound. Then, for you also, there will be a profuse expenditure of heavenly welcome. You will not enter the Heavenly City unnoticed and alone. A choral and processional greeting will be yours. You will not enter the port like some water-logged vessel, but with colours flying and all sails set! (verse 11)

Notice the order of these graces. Each is in the other like those Chinese boxes, each of which contains a number of smaller ones which fit inside. Opening the one marked *Faith, manly courage* should be discovered; opening courage, *knowledge* should present itself; from knowledge, we should come on *self-control*; within self-control should be *patience*; inside patience we have towards men should be *godliness* towards God; then we find *brotherly love*; and finally we come on *love*!

The apostle says that those who lack 'these things' are short-sighted - they see only the things of this world, not the real things of eternity. The tenth verse warns us that the careful culture of these things in the heart will prevent stumbling in the outward life (Jude 20-24). So many people wait to *feel good* before they act goodness. The divine method is to step out on the path of obedience to Christ, believing that he will supply the needed grace.

'If these things are yours and abound, they make you to be not idle or unfruitful unto the knowledge of our Lord Jesus Christ. For he that lacketh these things is blind, seeing only what is near' (2 Peter 1:8, 9 RV).

Prayer: Accept, O most Merciful Father, of this renewed dedication which we make of ourselves, our bodies, souls, and spirits unto thee. Grant that we may be like Jesus, pure and undefiled, meek and gentle, peaceable, patient, contented and thankful. Amen.

Stand at the Bow!
September 7

'Forgetting the things which are behind, and stretching forward to the things which are before, I press on toward the goal' (Philippians 3:13, 14 RV).

Always stand at the bow! Leave the stern with its backward look and make for the bow. To spend time in sad review of past sins and failures is not to put them to the best account. Confess them, and believe that for Christ's dear sake they are absolutely forgiven! Failure often provides the material for success, and our dead selves may become the stepping-stones to better things. Did not our Lord say to his disciples, 'Sleep on now and take your rest' - the past is irreparable - but immediately added: 'Arise, let us be going!' - the future is available. Therefore, leave the stern with its backward look, and make for the bow.

True, the sky before us may be dark with storm-clouds. The weather-prophets say that the world is shedding its old sanctions without replacing them with better ones; that seven civilisations have already passed, and we are to see the death of the eighth. Be it so, but they forget that God holds the stormy waters in the hollow of his hand; that Jesus walked the threatening billows to succour his friends. They forget that when the earth was without form and void, the Spirit of God brooded in the chaos and darkness, creating the heavens and earth. They cannot detect the voice of the Creator saying, 'Behold, I make all things new!' Out of chaos is born the cosmos. Each age ends in travail, out of which a new age is born.

Look out to the vast circle of the horizon, and prepare for the new lands to be explored, the wonderful discoveries that await us, the great missions hidden in the future which are waiting to be fulfilled. Never doubt that the clouds will break. Never dream that wrong will triumph. Never count yourself God-forsaken or forgotten. The Master may seem to be asleep on his pillow, oblivious and uncaring, but his hand is on the helm. He guides your course. He rules the waves and they obey him.

Prayer:
He maketh the storm a calm, so that the waves thereof are still.
Then are they glad because they be quiet;
So he bringeth them in the haven of their desire.
Oh that men would praise the Lord for his goodness!
Amen.

The Devotional Use of Scripture
September 8

In each verse of Psalm 119, the Psalmist mentions the Scriptures, with one exception, and the constant quotation of the Old Testament by our Lord and his apostles yields abundant evidence of loving and reverent fellowship with the holy men of past ages, who wrote and spoke as moved by the Holy Spirit. It is specially remarkable that the Lord Jesus in his Temptation, in all his teaching, and in the agony of the Cross bore constant witness to the unique authority of the word of God spoken through the Old Testament saints.

'Thy word is a lamp unto my feet, and a light unto my path' (P s a l m 119:105).

We may know God, says the Psalmist, through a threefold revelation. Though they have no audible voice or language, the heavens declare the glory of God, and the firmament of space, studded with myriads of stars, shows his handiwork. Though speechless, their words witness for him to the uttermost parts of the earth.

The closing stanza of this great Psalm unfolds God's handiwork in the construction and direction of our moral nature. Between these golden clasps the Psalmist extols the Scriptures under ten striking similitudes, and that disposition must be indeed extraordinary that does not come within the scope of one of them. The soul that needs restoring; the simple who would become wise; the sad heart who would rejoice; the eyes that would be enlightened; the soul that longs for the gold of truth; the desire for sincerity and reality; the search for understanding and righteousness - all such needs and many more are met from a devout reading of Holy Scripture.

Prayer: Teach us, O blessed Spirit of Inspiration, so to read, mark, learn and inwardly digest thy words, that we may be t h o r o u g h l y furnished unto all good works, and be enabled to lead others into a true understanding of and love for its hidden treasures. Amen.

All great ministries which have remained fresh and fragrant through long courses of years have proved the wealth of inexhaustible teaching and inspiration which lies hidden in the Bible. Let us each one resolve to soak ourselves in the Scripture before turning to prayer, as water poured in to moisten the sucker will help to draw water up.

'Blessed is the man that walketh not in the counsel of the ungodly ... but his delight is in the law of the Lord' (Psalm 1: 1, 2).

The theme of this first Psalm is the *blessedness* of keeping 'the law', which is the transcript of the mind and will of God. David was never weary in its praise - 'How I love thy law; it is my meditation all the day!'

What we all need today is a passionate love for the will and commands of God. Docility to learn, and faith to fulfil are the two qualities by which our heart may be kept pure and childlike, and through which we shall come to understand the Bible, nature, and human life. Well may the Psalter, which enshrines obedience to God's law, begin with *Blessed* and end with *Hallelujah*!

Here are, first the negations of the loyal and true soul. If we refuse to walk in the counsel of the wicked, we shall never *sit* in the seat of the scornful. But these negatives are chiefly valuable as contributing to the positive, as the wall protects the plant that grows behind it. Our religious life must be fed from hidden springs, as the rootlets of the tree creep under the soil to drink of the stream (verse 3). Such a life becomes fruitful and beautiful. It is also prosperous, because it abides in the will of God. It cannot be really injured by evil, and in the deepest sense it realises the purpose for which God commissioned it.

Any life which refuses reverence and obedience to God's will must resemble the rootless, fruitless, and lifeless chaff, which is scattered by the winnowing wind.

Which type does your life resemble? Are you the deeply-rooted tree, yielding beauty and fruit and shelter to many, or is your life being frittered away like the worthless chaff?

Prayer: Open to me, I pray thee, O Spirit of Truth, the treasures of thy word, that my soul may be continually enriched, and that I may abound in every good word and work, to thy honour and glory. Amen.

The Attraction of Christ's Humanity
September 10

A sentence which was once uttered in a Roman theatre, *'Great multitudes* and welcomed with thunderous plaudits, was abundantly *followed him'* true of the Son of Man - 'I am a man, and nothing that *(Matthew 19:2).* touches humanity is foreign to me.' This was true during *'All men seek for* his earthly life, and it is true always, and of this we have *thee!' (Mark 1:37).* ample illustration in the Gospel story.

Our Lord blesses man and wife as they live in holy wedlock; he takes their children in his arms; inspires young men and women with the loftiest ideals; warns men against the evil use of wealth and power; promises to those who are willing to pass through this life, denying themselves the joys of home life, parents, and children for his sake, that they shall be infinitely compensated.

There is no phase of human life which Jesus is not willing to share, and through all relationships and circumstances he waits to breathe the fragrance of perfect love. Is not that a boon which we all need, but which so many miss? Why do so many marriages turn out ill? Is it not often because each seeks rather to get than to give, to be ministered to rather than to minister? If each were inspired by a love that made the other the centre of thought and care and tenderness, the wedding bells would ring on through all the passing years.

Christ's love is so attractive that when he is rightly presented boys and girls will turn to him as flowers turn to the sun. Alas! that by our evil example and failure we so often forbid them. How poor is our appreciation and response to his love! We are willing to keep the commandments of a moral and respectable life because it suits and pleases us, but when it comes to following him and renouncing wealth, position, and self-pleasing for his dear sake, we turn back! We admire his ideals and teaching, but so often go sorrowfully away because we really love ourselves more than we love him!

Prayer
Higher than the highest heavens,
Deeper than the deepest sea.
Grant me now my soul's petition,
None of self, and all of thee.

Amen.

The Dividing Line
September 11

'Lord, when saw we thee an hungred, or athirst, or a stranger, or naked, or sick, or in prison, and did not minister unto thee?' (Matthew 25:44).

We can no longer serve our Lord as they did in the days of his flesh, when they ministered to him of their substance. But he has left behind his representatives, and whatever we do for them he takes as to himself. Therefore we are debtors to all men; to every unit of the human family we must pay back a proportion of our infinite debt to the Son of Man (Romans 1:14).

The dividing line hereafter will not be a *Credal* one - not 'How much do you believe?' Nor even a *Devotional* one - 'How much did you pray?' But a *Practical* one - 'What did you do?' The apostle James shows that our faith is evidenced by our works (James 2:14-20). It is not enough to say 'Lord, Lord!' We must show the same spirit as our Master in love for our fellows, or we shall be rejected at the last.

The Lord's brethren are spread widely through the world. Whenever we meet the hungry and thirsty, the stranger and the homeless, the sick or imprisoned soul, we encounter one whom he calls 'Brother' or 'Sister', and to help any such is to send a thrill of joy through the soul of our Redeemer. We must have the quick eyes of love to penetrate the many disguises that our Lord assumes. It is said that when St Francis was riding across a plain, he saw a leper standing by the roadside, asking for alms. Dismounting, he not only gave to him, but kissed him on the cheek. As he was riding away, he looked back, and saw Christ himself standing where the beggar had been, and he knew that he had been permitted to kiss his Lord.

Notice that the saints do not generally realise that they have done anything *directly for Christ*: 'Lord, when saw we *thee*?' The beauty of goodness is its modesty and unobtrusiveness, as the charm of childhood is its unconsciousness. Notice, also, that in Christ's eyes, it is a crime *not to do*. Moses says that it is wrong to do wrong; Jesus that it is wrong not to do right. Some were cast away, as men reject weeds, not because they had violated the Ten Commandments, but because they failed to fulfil the Law of Love.

Let us consecrate ourselves to the service of men, women and children for the sake of him who loved us and gave himself for us.

Prayer: Help us, dear Lord, to minister to the needs of others, to care for the poor and needy, the destitute and outcast, to show our love to thee by our sympathy and help to the least of thy brethren. Amen.

Secret Idols
September 12

How many there are who know in their hearts what their duty is, but fail to do it because they are hiding some forbidden thing; they refuse to launch on the current sweeping past them, because they are secretly anchored to a sandbank; they go from one teacher to another, with an appearance of earnest inquiry after eternal life, which never comes to anything, because they are unwilling to renounce their secret idol.

In the case of this young man, it was the love of money. 'He had great possessions.' There is no harm in money. It is one of God's gifts to men, but it is hard to own it without coming to look upon it as *one's own*, instead of realising that we are stewards only. It was for this reason that our Lord proposed this supreme test. St Francis of Assisi thought that these words applied universally, and founded the Order of the Franciscans, pledged to poverty. But it seems more in harmony with the spirit of the gospel to believe that it was a special test put to this seeker after truth, to reveal him to himself.

The law of love is not negative only but positive. The most essential condition for each of us is to be willing, like another young man who was living at that time, 'to count all things but loss, in order to win Christ and to be found in him' (Philippians 3:8). If you would follow Christ and are prepared for love's sake to surrender all, you will probably be entrusted with manifold more, because Christ knows that he can make you his almoner with no fear of gold dust adhering to your palm in its transmission.

Let us guard against the idol of money or possessions. Riches which open most doors, will not furnish a pass-key to Heaven. Let us see to it that we always act as stewards of God's property, but this is not possible unless we are living perpetually in fellowship with our Master, who though he was rich, yet for our sakes became poor, that we through his poverty might be made rich, and who says to us also, 'Come, take up the cross, and follow me'.

'Jesus beholding him loved him, and said, One thing thou lackest... sell whatever thou hast, and give to the poor ... Come, take up thy cross, and follow me. And he was sad, and went away grieved: for he had great possessions' *(Mark 10:21, 22).*

Prayer
The dearest idol I have known,
Whate'er that idol be,
Help me to tear it from thy throne,
And worship only thee.   Amen.

Fishers of Men
September 13

'Jesus saw two brethren, casting a net into the sea; for they were fishers. And he saith unto them, Follow me, and I will make you fishers of men' (Matthew 4:18, 19).

It is thus that Christ adapts himself to the understanding and the heart. He caught these fishermen with bait suited to them. Notice the undoubting certainty of his promise to make these two brothers fishers of men, casting their dragnet not into the waters of the sea of Galilee, but into the great ocean of humanity. How impossible it would have been to convince Peter then that within four years he would make the great haul of three thousand souls (Acts 2:41). Ah, we never know what awaits us when we leave all to follow in obedience to the Master's call!

'*Follow Me!*' Our Lord is always making this challenge (John 21:19, 22). It means bearing the cross, but we must be willing to follow Christ until, like him, we fall into the ground and die - die to our own ambitions, our love of power and influence, our own strength and gifts, that we may make way for God to work through us. We must learn not to obtrude ourselves, but to lie hidden. The first, the second, and the third condition of successful fishing is to be hidden from sight. The best line and bait for catching men are those where the human element is out of sight, and our one aim is to serve Christ's purpose and to glorify him.

There must be a leaving of our nets and boats, and even those who are nearest and dearest (verses 20, 23). It must have been something of a wrench for these brothers to leave their nets and fishing to follow Christ. But the attraction of his personality prevailed. There is no difficulty in persuading men to surrender the lower and inferior article, if you can unfold to them the immense value of the Pearl of great price. Then they will gladly sell all that they have to buy it.

Prayer
Jesus call us: by thy mercies,
Saviour, make us hear thy call.
Give our hearts to thine obedience,
Serve and love thee best of all.
Amen.

Love's Compulsion
September 14

We can never estimate the yearning love of God for the souls of men. He sees us absorbed with farming and industry; business and pleasure; with our homes and family life, and knows that these will all pass away, as a dream before the first touch of eternity. With intense passion he desires that we shall be really satisfied with abiding joys.

'Go out into the highways and hedges, and compel them to come in, that my house may be filled' (Luke 14:23).

The Feast that he spreads is abundant and ready (Isaiah 25:7; 55:1, 2). A banquet is a happy-making time. As the guests sit together, there is the brilliant flow of conversation, the sparkle of laughter, the enjoyment of the good things provided, the interchange of friendship and fellowship. Everything that a feast stands for God is waiting to give us. 'He gives us richly all things to enjoy.' How strange it is that men, mocked by the Evil One, are cajoled into forfeiting their places at the banqueting table, which God has spread for them!

The Jewish people were first bidden, but they were too much occupied with material things to respond to the gracious invitation. The excuses offered were shallow and stupid; the real reason lies much deeper, in the disinclination of the soul to arouse itself to lay hold of the life which is life indeed! But God's purpose of love cannot be defeated (Luke 13:28-30; Acts 13:45-48).

Prayer: Blessed Lord, have mercy upon those who reject the invitation of thy love! Take from us all ignorance, hardness of heart, and contempt of thy word; and so fetch us home, dear Lord, to thy flock, that we may be saved, and become one flock under the Great Shepherd of souls. Amen.

'*Go out into the highways and hedges.*' Here is our work as his servants! The high-roads, along which the streams of commerce and pleasure, weddings and funerals, statesmen and businessmen, young men and women, housewives and children - are constantly passing! The hedgerows are the quiet sequestered lanes of the countryside, now covered with spring flowers, and again with autumn tints. The up-to-date motor car, or the slow-jogging country wagon are symbols of different modes of life, but the souls that use them alike need the message of Good News. Let us go forth and constrain them to come in that our Master's House may be filled!

Where there's a Will there's a Way!
September 15

'And when they could not find by what way they might bring him in because of the multitude, they went upon the housetop, and let him down through the tiling, with his couch, into the midst before Jesus' (Luke 5:19).

What a lovely human story this is! The crowds that gathered around our Lord, as he taught them, were so great that they filled not only the house where he was staying, with the Pharisees and learned men sitting by, but overflowed into a vast multitude in the forecourt. The Master may have stood on the balcony of a double-storied house, so as to be able to reach the crowds within and without.

As he was teaching, presently four men approached, carrying on a hammock slung between them a paralysed man. We are not told in so many words that they were young men, but their earnestness and ingenuity incline one to this idea. Perhaps they had been school-chums together, and as they grew up they may have entered upon evil ways - 'sown their wild oats' together, and one of their number may have been suffering from the consequences, for our Lord very distinctly set the pardon of his *sins* before the healing of his body. His four companions had probably heard Christ preach and had become his followers, for it was *seeing their faith* that he performed this miracle of salvation and healing. They agreed that by hook or by crook they would bring their friend into Christ's gracious presence. Unable to make their way through the throng, they were not daunted, but climbed up on to the roof, and the record says, 'let him down through the tiling'. Lowered by strong hands, with its four ropes, the hammock swung to the feet of the Master, and the expectant imploring eyes of this poor fellow could not make a more eloquent appeal for help than did the evident faith of his bearers.

Prayer: Enlarge our souls with a divine love, that we may hope all things, endure all things, and become messengers of thy healing mercy to the grievances and infirmities of men. Amen.

The words with which our Lord saluted him were very tender and gracious: 'Man, thy sins are forgiven thee!' One of the sure means of physical health is to be assured of spiritual cleansing and forgiveness (James 5:14-16). Would that we were all equally anxious to bring our friends to Christ. If four would agree about a fifth, and never rest until he or she was brought to Jesus, what a revival would break out (John 4:28-30).

Looking Backward
September 16

The keynote of this chapter is '*Remember*!' Faith begins without certain evidence of an external and positive kind, but as life advances, one day after another adds the weight of its indisputable testimony. If we step out on the supposition that there is an eternal and spiritual world enwrapping us on all sides, we shall come to so clear and distinct and assurance of it, that it would be easier to doubt our existence. It is a good thing to *look back* and see the *way*; it is as certain as possible that the thread of Divine purpose is stringing together the many-coloured links of our life.

'Thou shalt remember all the way which the Lord thy God hath led thee these forty years' (Deuteronomy 8:2).

Notice the alliteration of verses 15, 16: 'Who *led* thee'; 'Who *fed* thee.' Where God leads, he feeds! Look back on the past, and see that just as sure as the guidance of God, has been his care. There is no lack to those who allow him to lead them in his own paths.

Look back on the past! - *Its sins and backslidings* - leave them behind for ever, and rise to newness of life. *Its discipline* - intended to chasten and strengthen us. *Its trials* - meant to reveal God's power to deliver in the hour of trouble that we may glorify him. The terrible wilderness of *loneliness*, the fiery serpents of *temptation*, the *manna* which has never failed to fall, the *water* which the Rock has ever yielded.

Verses 17 and 18 teach us the lesson of *humility*. If, for some reason, you have been put into a position of wealth, honour, or influence, do not be proud, or think that your talents or abilities are to receive the praise. Thank God, and remember that it is he who gives the power to get wealth or honour, and he does it with a very definite purpose! Will you not pledge yourself to serve and worship him? As you climb the crest of the hill, and begin to descend into the plain, not knowing what lies before, veiled in the mist, far not, tighten your girdle, put your hand in his, and walk with him to be his instrument to bless the world of men.

Prayer
Lord God of Hosts, be with us yet;
Lest we forget - lest we forget!

Amen.

The Royal Triumph
September 17

'Behold thy King cometh unto thee, meek, and sitting upon an ass. And the multitudes cried, saying, Hosanna to the Son of David! Blessed is he that cometh in the name of the Lord: Hosanna in the highest!' (Matthew 21:5, 9).

The King of Glory approached the Holy City, seated not on the richly-draped war-horse, or followed by a glittering band of soldiers, but riding on a lowly ass, and attended by a vast crowd of rustic pilgrims! He was welcomed, not by the Governor Pilate, or Caiaphas the High Priest, but by the children, the poorer folk, the blind and the lame whom he had healed. His lodging-place was the bare ground on the Mount of Olives, and on one occasion, at least, he was hungry enough to seek fruit from the fig-tree!

Yet there was a mystic power about him before which the rabble, that filled the courts of the Temple with noise and filth, were driven forth, and which the chief priests and scribes had to acknowledge when they challenged him as to his authority (verse 23). His authority was that of Truth and Purity and God. It was a stray beam of his intrinsic Majesty. One who knew him intimately said, 'We beheld his glory, as of the Only-Begotten of the Father, full of grace and truth' (John 1:14).

Soul of man, to thee, also, thy King cometh! Let the gates of thy heart lift up their portals and admit him! At first you may dread the revolution which his coming suggests, but be quick to give to Emmanuel, the Prince, all the keys of Mansoul. Enthrone him in thine heart! He is the King and Heir, and he will make thee a joint-heir with himself. Let the kingdom of your life become the kingdom of God and of his Christ. Let every thought be brought into subjection to him. But if, on the other hand, you are content to build the house of life apart from him, be very sure that you are rejecting the one Chief Cornerstone, which can alone give the necessary stability and beauty to its structure. To forfeit that will involve the absolute destruction of the edifice on which your whole life-energy may have been expended (Matthew 7:27; 1 Corinthians 3:10-15).

Prayer

But chiefest in our cleansed breast,
Eternal, bid thy Spirit rest;
And make our secret soul to be
A temple pure and worthy thee.
Hosanna in the highest!

Amen.

The Practice of God's Presence
September 18

The story of the monk who constantly used this phrase is well known to most people. It was in the sixteenth century, one winter's day, as Brother Lawrence was walking in the forest, he found himself standing beneath a tree stripped of its foliage. The thought suddenly flashed on him that before very long that same tree would be covered with the leaves and glory of spring. 'Then God must be here,' said he to himself, and his whole being became awed and filled with the thought of God. That impression remained with him for the rest of his life, and he said that he was more deeply impressed with the actual sense of God's presence in the kitchen, when he was preparing the food for his brother monks, than when he was kneeling before the Sacrament.

'Whither shall I go from thy Spirit? or whither shall I flee from thy presence? If I take the wings of the morning, and dwell in the uttermost parts of the sea; Even there shall thy hand lead me, and thy right hand shall hold me' (Psalm 139: 7, 9, 10).

It is a blessed experience when the soul lives in this awareness of God; when we live, and move, and have our being in him; whether we take the wings of the morning, and go with the sun in its passage to the western sea, or descend into the valley of the shadow of death. Let us read this Psalm again, remembering that our Lord said, 'Lo, I am with you all the days, even to the end of the age.'

The habit of practising God's presence is specially acquired when we accustom ourselves to draw on the divine resources. We can recall two outstanding illustrations - one given by Abraham's faithful servant, and the other by Nehemiah. In the one case, the traveller lifted up his heart to God for direction as to the choice of a wife for his master's son; and the other tells us that between the king's question as to the reason for his sadness, and his reply, he flashed a cry to God for a suitable answer, and it was given him. Why do not we, in every moment of uncertainty and perplexity, when the tempter draws near, instantly claim the equivalent of God's gracious help?

Prayer: Gracious Spirit, wilt thou so enable us by thy grace, that we may live in the fear of God all the day long; may the difficulties and temptations of our daily experience have the effect of leading us to take each step in the consciousness of the presence of God. Amen.

Earth Crammed with Heaven
September 19

'Holy, holy, holy is the Lord of hosts; the whole earth is full of his glory' (Isaiah 6:3).

The prosperity of King Uzziah's reign seems to have weakened the national character; a deep-seated degeneracy was eating out its vitals. The unbroken summer of fifty years of prosperity and wealth had induced a moral decay which filled the heart of the prophet with dismay. It was in this depressed frame of mind that Isaiah entered the Temple, where the ceremonial of the priests and Levites, the offering of the sacrifice, the antiphonal chanting of the choirs, appear to have further moved his spirit.

The Vision (verses 1-4). The limitation of the earthly fabric faded from his sight, and he became aware of the worship of the Seraphim, their faces veiled before the divine Majesty, their persons clothed with humility, and their remaining wings prepared for immediate obedience. They sang antiphonally, inciting each other to lowlier reverence and more ecstatic praise.

What a lesson is present to ourselves! What a contrast is here to our lethargic worship and often tardy obedience! This great God is our Father through our Lord Jesus Christ but do we blend sufficient reverence with our childlike trust? Are we not too often glib in our prayers? Do we realise the need of pure hearts and clean hands as we kneel before him?

Prayer: Great and Holy God, cleanse us in heart and speech and action, with the blood shed on Calvary and the fire of thy Spirit, that we may be fitted for thy holy service. Cleanse, Call and Commission us! Amen.

The Call (verses 7-8). The humble confession of sin must be ours also. The Seraphim knew that there was only one answer. The altar coals had absorbed the blood of the sacrifice and were now glowing with white heat. They would serve for cleansing and inspiration, and when this was completed, there was nothing left to delay the call to service.

The Commission (verses 9-13). The prophet was not to be disappointed. He was to persist in his message, even though there were only gleams of light through the darkness.

Our Sheet Anchor!
September 20

Our destiny is the highest possible - 'We shall be like him.' For this we were created, redeemed, and sanctified, that we should be conformed to the image of God's Son, that he might be the First Born among many brethren (Romans 8:29).

The apostle says that those who have this *hope* will purify themselves. A young friend of mine once asked me if I would try to see her lover, as my train stopped at a wayside station in a far-distant western State. It was a dark night when we arrived, and a hurried conversation took place on the steps of the great Pullman car. I found that amid the many temptations of a rancher's life, this young fellow was holding on to purity and truth. He said that he had very infrequent opportunities of attending any religious services, but that the letters which came from the old country had been his sheet anchor. I understood what he meant. He realised the strong drift of circumstances, but to be loved by a sweet pure girl who made him the object of her incessant prayer, and to receive her inspiring letters, kept him from yielding to the evil which enveloped him as an atmosphere; the thought that before long he might claim her as his bride helped to purify and steady his life. So the expectation of being with, and like, Christ, should be to us as a sheet-anchor, who bear his name.

To see Christ face to face, to be with him in unbroken fellowship, and to be like him - this is the threefold destiny of every Christian soul. But how little can we imagine our future life! We strive to penetrate the dense veil of mist in vain - what the resurrection body will be like; what the converse with holy beings will amount to; what ministry may be assigned to us - we know not what we shall be, but '*we know that we shall be like him*' - and it is enough! All that we have ever dreamed and hoped for will find its flower and fruitage in that glad summer time.

'That we be no more children, tossed to and fro, and carried about with every wind of doctrine; but speaking the truth in love, may grow up into him in all things' (Ephesians 4:14, 15)

'Every man that hath this hope in him purifieth himself, even as he is pure' (1 John 3:3).

Prayer: O God, it is my earnest desire that I may not only live, but grow; grow in grace, and in the knowledge of my Lord and Saviour Jesus Christ. May I grow in patience and fortitude of soul, in humility and zeal, in spirituality and a heavenly disposition of mind. Amen.

'Is anything too hard for the Lord?' (Genesis 18:14). 'Ah Lord God! behold, thou hast made the heaven and the earth by thy great power and stretched out arm, and there is nothing too hard for thee' (Jeremiah 32:17).

There is no doubt as to the identification of these three guests that suddenly appeared before the tent-door of Abraham. We are expressly told that 'Jehovah appeared unto him'. It was thus that our Lord anticipated his incarnation. He came *incognito* and 'his delights were with the sons of men' (Proverbs 8:31). During his earthly life, he loved the homes of men, lodged with Peter and Zacchaeus, and in the dear home where Mary loved and Martha served. After his resurrection he tarried with two of them in the village inn. So he will come to thy heart and mine. Though he is the High and Lofty One, who inhabits Eternity, yet he will plead for admission to sup with us and we with him (Revelation 3:20). But he often comes disguised as a wayfaring man, hungry and athirst. Let us 'run to meet him', remembering Matthew 25:40.

Prayer: Now unto him that is able to do exceeding abundantly above all that we ask or think, according to the power that worketh in us. Unto him be glory in the church by Christ Jesus, throughout all ages, World without end. Amen.

God is no man's debtor; he always pays for his lodging, hence his promise to Sarah! She laughed with incredulity, but is anything too hard for the Lord? That is one of God's unanswered questions. It has accosted the human conscience all down the ages. Let us look away from the difficulties imposed by nature, to him who holds the oceans in the hollow of his Almighty hand. Then we can stand with him on the mountainside, and plead for Sodom; then God himself will draw us on to ask for more and yet more, till, when our faith gives out, he will do something far in advance of all that we asked or thought.

The Grace of Christian Speech
September 22

The ideal of Christian speech is given in the apostle's words to the Colossians. Our speech should be always gracious; and grace stands for mercifulness, charity, the willingness to put the best constructions upon the words and actions of another. It is a great help in dealing with envy, jealousy or unkind feeling to compel our lips to speak as Christ would have them. If you are jealous of another, the temptation is to say unkind or depreciating things, but if we live in the power of the Holy Spirit, he will enable us to check such words and replace them by those that suggest kindly consideration on the part of ourselves and others. Endeavour to say all the good that can be said, and none of the evil. It is remarkable that when we make the effort to speak kindly on behalf of those against whom we feel exasperated, the whole inward temper changes and takes on the tone of our voice.

'He that will love life, and see good days, let him refrain his tongue from evil, and his lips that they speak no guile' (1 Peter 3:10). 'Let your speech be alway with grace, seasoned with salt' (Colossians 4:6).

There should be salt in our speech - purity, antiseptic, and sparkling like the Book of Proverbs. A playful wit, a bright repartee, are not inconsistent with the apostle's standard, but whenever we mix in conversation with people, they should be aware of an element in us which makes it impossible for them to indulge in ill-natured gossip or coarse jokes.

We must continue in prayer that God would open to us doors of utterance, so that we may speak of the hidden beauty and glory of our Saviour. Sometimes, also, when we are hard-pressed to know how to answer difficult questions, it is given to us in that same hour how we ought to speak, and we find that the Holy Spirit has found an utterance by our lips (Luke 12:12; 1 Peter 3:15).

It is recorded of our Lord that during his trial, he spoke not a word to Pilate or Herod, but as soon as he reached the Cross, he poured out his heart as their Intercessor, saying: 'Father, forgive them: for they know not what they do!' Speak more to God than to men who may be reviling and threatening you. It is blessed to realise that he is able to guard the door of our lips, for probably there is no part of our nature that stands more in need of his keeping power.

Prayer: Live in us, Blessed Lord, by thy Holy Spirit, that our lives may be gospels of helpfulness and blessedness. May all foolish talking and covetousness, bitterness, wrath, and anger be put away from us, with all malice. Amen.

The Holiday Spirit
September 23

'Come ye your-
selves apart, and
rest awhile: for
there were many
coming and go-
ing, and they
had no leisure
so much as to
eat' (Mark 6:31).

There is something in our blood which cries out at certain times for rest and change. We may love our home, our work, and chance of doing our share in the toil of this work-a-day world, but when the summer comes we long to escape from the crowded city, the arduous toil, and pine for respite and rest. The love of Nature is a sacred heritage from the love of God, and it is his voice that calls to us: 'Come, my children, be glad with me, breathe the scented air which I have flavoured in its passage through clover-fields, gorse, and heather; rejoice in the woods and flowers, golden sunsets and purple mountains; the glory of the ocean and the sea-shore'.

But we must be unselfish, if we would really enjoy our holiday. It is difficult to resist the temptation to obtain the best possible return for our money, and a little over, even at the expense of others. Always think of someone else - the short Zacchaeus who cannot see over your shoulder! The child who loves to look out of the carriage window; the invalid who cannot stand the draught! The tired mother with the restless children. Look out for daily opportunities for showing the gentleness, sweetness, and unselfishness of the Lord Jesus.

Prayer: What
shall I render
unto the Lord
for all his ben-
efits to me? I will
praise, and bless,
and give thee
thanks, all the
days of my life.
Thou art wor-
thy, O Lord, to
receive glory,
and honour, and
power. Amen.

Make time to be alone sometimes. It is a mistake always to be in the presence of another. The soul must be still and quiet. There are accents in the voice of God so deep and still, that the breathing of a companion may make them inaudible. But it is delightful to have a choice friend and companion with whom you can hold sweet fellowship, and 'there is a Friend that sticketh closer than a brother'. He will draw near and walk with you, and as he talks with you by the way, your hearts will burn within you.

Remember those who are in poverty, in sickness, and in need, and amidst your own gladness and joy, send a portion unto them for whom nothing is prepared (Nehemiah 8:10, 12).

Bread Winning!
September 24

The question which Satan put to our Lord, has to be settled in every life. Where does bread and bread-getting come in? Is it to be our first consideration or the last? According to Satan's way of looking at life, the bread question is paramount; according to Christ, secondary. Have you ever seriously considered which policy is yours, and what you would do if you had to choose in any supreme crisis? This temptation which came to our Lord occurs to us all; sooner or later, whether on the lone mountainside, or in the crowded thoroughfares of life, the Devil comes to us with the suggestion that we must live, and in the last resort we must make or get our bread, leaving considerations of purity, truth, honour of God and Eternity to come in second best!

At every important turning-point in the history of the inner life these two methods are suggested: Satan says: 'Make these stones into bread;' Christ says: 'Man shall not live by bread alone, but by the word of God.' We must choose between God and mammon. We are liable to attacks of hunger in various parts of our nature - for food, Satan bids us snatch it; for love, we are tempted to gratify it apart from God; for knowledge, we are apt to seek it in ways that are not illumined by the light of eternal truth.

God, who gave us these strong appetites and desires, knows that we need food. The body is more than meat, and if he gave the one, he is responsible for meeting the other. The blessed angels of his help are even now on their way to you, and have been commissioned to bring with them supplies for every need in your life. Do not take your life out of God's hands and act at the dictate of passion! Throw all the responsibility on him; they cannot be ashamed that wait for him. Remember the angel that prepared the meal for Elijah in the desert, and the breakfast that our Lord himself prepared for his tired and hungry friends. If you will dare to trust and wait for him even though there be but a step between you and death, he will supply all your need, according to his riches in glory. 'Trust in the Lord and do good; so shalt thou dwell in the land, and verily thou shalt be fed.'

'He answered: It is written, Man shall not live by bread alone.' Seek ye first the kingdom of God and his righteousness; and all these things shall be added unto you' (Matthew 4:4; 6:33).

Prayer: Give us grace to seek first thy kingdom and its righteousness, in the sure and certain faith that all else shall be added unto us. Amen.

The File Leader
September 25

'Behold, I have given him for a Witness to the people; a Leader and Commander to the people' (Isaiah 55:4).

Four times in the New Testament our Lord is called Leader or Prince. Originally the word means the First of a file of men, and therefore their Captain or Commanding Officer (see Acts 3:15; 5:31; Hebrews 2:10; 12:2).

Christ leads from death into Life. Probably Joshua was the first to pass over the dried bed of the Jordan, as the priests stood by bearing the Ark of the Covenant; but this at least is true, that our Saviour has preceded us through the waters of death, and will hold them back until each of the ransomed has passed 'clean over' (Joshua 3:17).

Christ leads his followers into victory. When our Lord was exalted to the right hand of power, he opened up a path to be trodden throughout the ages by a company which no man can number. As he overcame, we may overcome; as he reigns over all principality and power, so we believe that he will bruise Satan under our feet, and make us more than conquerors.

Prayer: O Lord, whose way is perfect, help us always to trust in thy goodness: that walking with thee and following thee in all simplicity, we may possess quiet and contented minds; and may cast all our care on thee, for thou carest for us. Amen.

Christ leads those who suffer to perfection. Though he was the Son of God, he learned obedience by the things that he suffered, and transformed suffering, showing that it was an elembic, a purifying furnace, a means of discipline, strength and ennoblement. If we are thrust into the fiery furnace we shall find the Son of God walking at our side, and shall emerge without our bonds, and with no smell of fire upon us. Jesus is the Leader of a long procession of martyrs and sufferers. He leads through no darker rooms than he went through before; he knows exactly how much we can bear, and will not test us beyond our strength. He is with us 'all the days' and will help us to learn obedience, faith and hope, as we follow in his footsteps.

Beautiful Garments
September 26

Put on strength. We have not to purchase it, or generate it by prayers and resolutions, but simply to *put it on*. As we awake in the early morning hour, and have to pass out into the arena of life, which has so often witnessed failure and defeat, let us put on the strength and might of the living Christ. He waits to strengthen us with all power, according to the riches of his glory. Do not simply pray to be kept and helped, but put on the whole armour of God. 'The Lord is the strength of my life, of whom shall I be afraid?'

Put on beautiful garments. The emblem of the life of the Christian soul is that of the bridegroom or the bride decked with jewels; or a garden filled with beautiful flowers (Isaiah 61:10, 11). We are not only to do right things, but we must do them beautifully; not only to speak the truth, but to speak it in love; not only to give to those who need our help, but to do it graciously and joyously. We must cultivate the bloom of the soul, which is made up of compassion, kindness, humility, meekness, generosity. The beauty of the Lord our God must be upon us.

We cannot weave these beautiful robes, or fashion them out of our own nature, but they are all prepared for us in Christ, who is 'made unto us Wisdom, and Righteousness, Sanctification, and Redemption'. Let us wake up out of sleep, put off the works of darkness, and put on the Lord Jesus Christ, who is the armour of Light.

'Awake, awake; put on thy strength; put on thy beautiful garments' *(Isaiah 52:1).* *'It is high time to awake out of sleep; let us cast off the works of darkness; let us put on the armour of light' (Romans 13:11, 12).*

Prayer: Lord of Power and Love! I come, trusting in thine almighty strength, and thine infinite goodness, to beg from thee what is wanting in myself; even that grace which shall help me such to be, and such to do, as thou wouldst have me. I will trust thee, in whom is everlasting strength. Be thou my helper, to carry me on beyond my own strength, and to make all that I think, and speak, and do, acceptable in thy sight, through Jesus Christ. Amen.

Modern Miracles
September 27

'Many re-sorted unto him, and said, John did no mira-cle; but all things John spake of this man were true. And many believed on him there' (John 10:41, 42).

The people were inclined to disparage the life of John the Baptist because he performed no miracle. But surely his whole life was a miracle; from first to last it vibrated with Divine power. This is still the mistake of men. They allege that the age of miracles has passed. If they admit that such prodigies may possibly have happened once, they insist that the world has outgrown them, and that in its maturity mankind has put them away as childish things!

No miracles! But last summer God made the handfuls of grain, which the farmers cast on the fields, sufficient to feed all the populations of the world as easily as he made five barley loaves suffice for more than five thousand persons! No miracles! But last autumn he changed the dews of night and the showers of morning into the fruits that rejoice the heart of man, as once in Cana he turned the water drawn from the stone jars into the blushing wine! No miracles! But next spring, from tiny seeds and dead-looking bulbs, he will clothe the world with beauty and colour and perfume.

Many who will read these lines seem powerless to work miracles. For them the monotony of the commonplace, the grey sky of uneventful routine seems the predestined lot. But let all such take heart! The real greatness of life is within their reach, if they will only claim it by the grace of God. Do not try to do a great thing, or you may waste all your life waiting for the opportunity which may never come. But since little things are always claiming your attention, do them as they come from a great motive, for the glory of God and to do good to men. No such action, however trivial, goes without the swift recognition and the ultimate recompense of Christ. All life is so interesting, but we need eyes to see and hearts to understand! Dare to be yourself - a simple, humble, sincere follower of Jesus, and it may be said also of you: 'He or she did no miracle, but by life and word spoke true things about Jesus Christ, which we have tested for ourselves. Indeed they led us to believe in Christ for ourselves.'

Prayer

Teach me, my God and King,
In all things thee to see,
And what I do in anything,
To do it as for thee.
A servant with this clause
Makes drudgery divine!
Who sweeps a room as for thy laws,
Makes that and th'action fine.   Amen.

Obedience
September 28

The light of Christ is always distinguishable because it means the deepest impression of what is right, the clearest conviction of the will of God. Everywhere men are asking how they may come to know Christ, and there is but one answer: believe that he loves you, that he died on the Cross to save you, that he is prompting you by his Spirit to follow every perception and longing for a better and holier life.

'I am come a light into the world, that whosoever believeth on me should not abide in darkness' (John 12:46).

How different is this teaching from that of the world around! There we are bidden to know before we dare entrust our lives to any leader, whatever be his fair speeches and promises; but Christ bids us obey the first glimmer of light breaking on us, and he undertakes that if we do, we shall not walk in darkness. Disobedience, like scales, veils Christ from us; whilst obedience leads us into his very presence. The judgment always becomes just, and the vision clear, when we deny ourselves to follow whatsoever things are lovely, true, pure, just, and of good report.

It may be that as you read these lines there is some duty you shirk, some cross you refuse to lift, some act from which you flinch. Though you may not have directly associated it with Christ, yet you cannot doubt that it is his will for you and that in the doing he will be pleased. It is useless to try to know him until that nearest act of obedience is wrought. Men can never know what the mighty forces of Nature will do for them until they set themselves to obey, in the minutest detail, its laws. And it is so in relation to Christ and the laws of the spiritual realm. That was a true word which the mother of our Lord spoke to the servants at Cana, when she said: *'Whatsoever he saith unto you, do it!'* She had probably learnt that lesson in those long, quiet, blessed years at Nazareth. She knew that there was no such way of understanding him, as by rendering him literal obedience, and she passed on the results of her experience to us all.

Prayer: My son, forsake thyself, and thou shalt find God! Lord, how often shall I resign myself, and wherein shall I forsake myself? Always, yea, every hour, as well in small things as in great. Amen.

'Walk while ye have the light,' so you will know the Light, and become light in the Lord.

'For all our days are passed away in thy wrath: we spend our years as a tale that is told' (Psalm 90:9).

This Psalm is almost without parallel for sublimity, a worthy monument of the inspired genius of Moses, 'the man of God'. It reflects the wanderings and experiences of the wilderness march; the watch in the night against the intrusion of the Bedouin thief, or the prowl of the wild beast; the rush of the flood, caused by torrential rain, but disappearing as quickly as on the sandy soil; the morning grass, scorched by the sirocco; the tales borne by the camp spies so soon ended; the disappointment of the springs of Marah; the inevitable leaving of Elim! The long weary days of marching, the mother and babe, the aged and little children, the weakling on the desert trail; the constant pitching and removal of tents - all these emblems of transitories, depicting the hard experiences of life's toil and trial. Secret sins and iniquities; the averted face of God because of transgression; the death of the old at eighty, and of the young child cut down as a frail flower. Yes! But in spite of all this, God as the dwelling-place and home of the individual soul, as of the succeeding generation.

Prayer: How shall we thank thee sufficiently, dear Lord, that thou hast demolished death, and brought life and immortality to light. Give us grace to follow thee all the days of our life, and when the call comes to us to pass over may the waters of the River be at the lowest ebb. Amen.

Shall we not make the concluding petitions of this Psalm our own? For we, too, are pilgrims over the desert-waste to the eternal Home. We need to be more careful of our days, watching their decreasing number, with careful anxiety to make the most of those that are left. We need to be satisfied and replenished each morning with God's mercy, that we may have perennial springs of rejoicing and gladness. We long to help in the overthrowing of the power of evil, and as we grow older, we pray that the beauty of the Lord our God may be upon us, and may we feel that he has given permanence to the work of our hands.

The Talisman of Victory
September 30

Can anything separate me from the love of Christ? was the only question that St Paul felt worth consideration. In this paragraph he takes the extreme conditions of being and carefully investigates them, knowing that they include all between. First, he interrogates *Existence* - 'death and life'; next, *Created Intelligences* - 'Angels, principalities, and powers'; next, the *Extremes of Time* - 'things present, things to come'; next, of *Space* - 'height and depth'; lastly, the *Created Universe* - 'any other creature'. Each of these extremes is passed in review. He is like a man proving every link of the chain in which he is going to swing out over the abyss. Carefully and fervently he has tested all, and is satisfied that none of them can cut him off from the love of God.

'In all these things we are more than conquerors, through him that loved us' (Romans 8:37).

We strangely misjudge and mistrust the love of God our Father, and think that our distresses and sufferings, our sins and failures, may make him love us less. But in the home, it is not the troop of sturdy children that engross the mother's care so much as the puny feeble life, that lies in the cot, unable to help itself and reciprocate her love. And in the world, death and pain, disease and sorrow, sin and failure, so far from separating us from God's love, bind us closer.

Oh blessed love! that comes down to us from the heart of Jesus, the essence of the eternal love of God - nothing can ever staunch, exhaust, intercept it. It is not our love to him, but his to us, and since nothing can separate us from the love of God, he will go on loving us for ever, and pouring into us the entire fullness of his life and glory. Whatever our difficulties, whatever our weakness and infirmity, we shall be kept steadfast, unmovable, always abounding in the work of the Lord; gaining by our losses, succeeding by our failures, triumphing in our defeats, and ever more than conquerors through him that loved us.

Prayer

Yea thro' life, thro' sorrow and thro' sinning
He shall suffice me, for he hath sufficed:
Christ is the end, for Christ was the beginning,
Christ is the beginning, for the end is Christ.

Amen.

We need to look at our positions from the standpoint of eternity, and probably we shall be startled at the small differences between the lots of men. The one thing for us all is to abide in our calling with God, to count ourselves as his fellow-workers, to do what we can in his grace and for his glory: never excusing ourselves; never condoning failure and misdoing; never content unless, by the help of the Blessed Spirit, we have wrought out his promptings and suggestions to the best of our power, whether in the gold of the extraordinary, or the bronze of the cheaper and more ordinary achievement.

Of course there is no saving merit in what we do. Salvation is only by simple trust in our Saviour, Jesus. But when we are saved, it gives new zest to life, to do all for him, as Lord and Master; and to know that he is well-pleased in the right doing of the most trivial duties of the home or daily business (1 Peter 2:20).

May each reader learn this happy art, and go through life offering all to God, as the white-stoled priests in the Temple of old, for indeed all believers have been made priests to God; every sphere may be a holy temple; and every act done in the name of Jesus, may be a spiritual sacrifice, acceptable to God, through Jesus Christ.

F B Meyer *The Trivial Round, The Common Task*

OCTOBER

OUR DAILY WALK OF LOVE

Walk in love, as Christ also hath loved us
(Ephesians 5:2)

The Dimensions of God's Love
October 1

'That Christ may dwell in your hearts by faith; that ye, being rooted and grounded in love, may be able to comprehend with all saints what is the breadth, and length, and depth, and height; and to know the love of Christ, which passeth knowledge' (Ephesians 3:17-19).

The dimensions of the love of Christ! It is *broad* as humanity, 'for God so loved the world'; the *length* - God's love had no date of origin, and shall have none of conclusion. God *is* love, it continueth ever, indissoluble, unchangeable, a perpetual present tense. Its *height* - as the Flood out-topped the highest mountains, so that love covers our highest sins. It is as high as the heaven above the earth. Its *depth* - Christ our Lord descended into the lowest before he rose to the highest. He has touched the bottomless pit of our sin and misery, sorrow and need. However low your fall, or lowly your lot, the everlasting arms of his love are always underneath.

The apostle talks by hyperbole, when he prays that we may attain to a knowledge of the knowledge-surpassing love of Christ. We cannot gauge Christ's love, but we can enjoy it. Probably the only way to know the love of Christ is to begin to show it. The emotionalist, who is easily affected by appeal to the senses, does not know it; the theorist or rhapsodist does not know it, but the soul that endeavours to *show* the love of Christ, knows it. As Christ's love through you broadens, lengthens, deepens, heightens, you will know the love of Christ, not intellectually, but experimentally (1 John 4:11, 12, 20, 21).

Prayer: We thank thee, O God, for the infinite love which thou hast given us in Jesus Christ. We have no measure for its heights and depths, its breadths and lengths. Teach us with all saints to know more because we love more. Amen.

But you say, 'there are people in my life whom I cannot love.' Granted, but you must distinguish between love and the emotion and feeling of love. You may not be able to feel love at the outset, but you can be willing to be the channel of Christ's love. I cannot love, but Christ is in me, and he can. Is it too much to ask that all this should be realised in ourselves and in others? No, because God is already at work within us by his Holy Spirit, and he is able to do infinitely beyond all our highest requests or thoughts. Ask your furthest, think your highest, and the divine love is always infinitely in advance.

The Knowledge of God's Love
October 2

God is Love. Jesus Christ first brought to men the conception that man loves God only because God has first loved him. In vain we search for such an idea in the philosophies of Greece and Rome. The men who fixed this thought in the literature of mankind were followers of Jesus Christ. Might and majesty were the dominating ideas of BC, but since AD, we think of love enthroned in the divine nature.

'We have known and believed the love that God hath to us. We love him, because he first loved us' (1 John 4:16, 19).

His love passeth knowledge. We may apply to it the masterly arraignment of Psalm 139. It winnows our rays. It besets us behind and before. It lays on us its gentle restraining hand. It is high, we cannot attain to it. If we ascend into heaven, it is there; if we make our bed in the grave, it is there to lift us to his heart; if we take the wings of the morning, it shines as sunrise; if we pass into the darkness, it makes the midnight shine as the day. It covered us in our birth, it will tend us in old age. How precious it is, and how multitudinous in its expression, no mortal lips can tell.

Even our sin will not lessen that love. That Peter sinned deeply, who can doubt, but did it put a screen between him and Christ? Nay, for when Christ arose, he sent specially for him. In the garden he restored him, and at the lakeside he taught him that his love would be as acceptable as ever (Mark 16:7; John 21:15).

His love will not spare. Jesus looked on the young man and loved him! But he read him through and through, and mercifully gave the unwelcome verdict: 'Go, sell all that thou hast ... and follow me.' He went away sad, and Christ went away sad! But he loves us too well to spare us! God's love is consistent with stern dealings at those things which may cause us to fail of the best.

Prayer: May I not be satisfied with talking or musing on thy love, O God. Grant me the grace of manifesting it, not only in great crisis, but amid petty annoyances and the daily fret of life. Amen.

We believe in God's love when it seems not so. 'We have known,' says the apostle, that 'God is love', unutterable and changeless! But there are times when we have to *believe* in it, i.e. in the perplexity of life's problems. We are often facing incidents and providences that strike us as inconsistent with God's love. Then we must believe that the same love is there. God *is* love, and nothing can reach us save through his love.

'For God so loved the world, that he gave his only begotten Son, that whosoever believeth on him should not perish, but have eternal life' (John 3:16).

As children we read *Alice in Wonderland*, but at the end of life we shall find ourselves in Wonderland! Perhaps there is a deeper truth than we know in the description of old age as a second childhood, because the child-spirit ever lives in a Paradise of mystery, questioning and wonder!

There are causes for wonder in the small compass of this verse! The first is that *God loved and loves the world*. We are not surprised to learn that he *made* the world, because - except where men have spoilt it - it is so beautiful. Or that he has *a name* for it, because he calleth them all by name, as he bringeth out their hosts by number. So small is our world amid the myriad constellations, but nevertheless it is belted, environed, encompassed by the love of God!

The second wonder is *that the Only Begotten Son came to dwell with us*. Is it not wonderful that the Son of God should have passed by all other worlds, and come to *this*? That this earth was trodden by his blessed feet; that he has incorporated its transfigured dust into the texture of his divine nature - this is all so wonderful, that we are disposed to believe that our world must be the pivot of the universe - its nursery, college, and training ground.

Prayer: The world is dear unto thee, O Heavenly Father; thou didst send thine only Son to save it, and thy Spirit to comfort and renew. May he brood over the chaos of this distracted world, and may order and peace and love reign among men. Amen.

The third wonder is *that Eternal Life is within the reach of whosoever*. The Authorised Version gives the word *everlasting*, but the Revised Version translates it as *eternal*. God gives us not quantity but *quality* of life. Time is a method of thought necessitated by our human limitations, and therefore some day will come to its end. Eternal life is an ever-present *NOW* - of love and life and light, enjoyed in fellowship with God. And this is for *Whosoever*! Each of us may insert his or her name in the blank, and say, 'that I may have eternal life'. It is *so* wonderful, that the thought could not have been invented or suggested by the wit of man. It bears the imprint and seal of God himself, who made us in his image, and after his likeness, that we might become the partakers of the divine nature, having escaped the corruption that is in the world through lust (Genesis 1:26; 2 Peter 1:4).

Love and Liberty
October 4

The key to this wonderful chapter, so full of sound judgment and sanctified common sense, is the reiterated reference which the apostle makes to the Lord, which occurs some ten times in fourteen verses. The fact of Jesus being Lord both of the living and of those who have died, and are living on the other side of death, is the solution of the difficulty as to what the Christian should do or leave undone. Let each of us stand before the judgment seat of Christ, or at least before the reflection of that tribunal which is mirrored in the tranquil expanse of conscience, and we shall have an unerring guide for conduct.

The question agitated in Rome was as to the observance of the seventh or first day of the week as the Christian Sabbath; and, what principle should direct the use of food - that of Leviticus, or of common use. The apostle insists that these are not questions which affect either our personal salvation or our acceptance with God. In his opinion they are matters for each individual Christian to settle and decide for himself. There are certain factions clear as light, or black as night, about which there can be no controversy; but there are other questions for the solution of which each must apply one or other of these general principles for guidance through the maze.

What would Jesus Christ, my Lord and Master, wish me to do? I am his servant, and he will let me know his will by the teaching of his Spirit in my heart. Whether I act or forbear, it must be done unto him; and in my liberty or abstinence, I must give him thanks.

What is best for others? I have an influence over some; perhaps more look to me for guidance than I know. I must be on my guard not to put a stumbling block in another's way. Though certain things are innocent to me, yet, if they will destroy, directly or indirectly, one for whom Christ died, it will be better for me to abstain from them.

What is best for myself? I ask God not to lead me into temptation, but I must not put myself into it. I must put aside all *weights* as well as sins, that I may follow Christ as he goes forth to the conquest of evil.

'None of us liveth to himself, and no man dieth to himself. For whether we live, we live unto the Lord; and whether we die, we die unto the Lord: whether we live, therefore, or die, we are in the Lord's' (Romans 14:7, 8).

Prayer: O Lord and Master, may we be faithful to thee in the little things, always following the inner light, till it lead us into the perfect day. Amen.

Loved and Loosed
October 5

'Unto him that loveth us, and loosed us from our sins by his blood; and he made us to be a kingdom, to be priests unto his God and Father; to him be the glory and the dominion for ever and ever. Amen.' (Revelation 1:5, 6 RV).

Whatever else the Blood of Christ may mean, it certainly means that Christ has viewed our sin as of tremendous gravity. With him it is no slight malady to be cured by a regimen of diet and exercise. It is deep-seated, radical, perilous, endangering the fabric of our soul's health and the scope of its outlook on the future.

No religion that ignores this elemental fact in human consciousness is destined to permanence. To say with Buddha - sin can be wiped out with good deeds; or with Mahomet - God is good, and will not be hard on you - is not enough. The religious creed that deals most radically and drastically with sin is the one which will ever appeal most strongly to the human heart, and it is because Jesus Christ has not treated sin lightly, but has loosed men from it by his blood, that he is enthroned for ever.

Prayer: Most holy and adorable Lord, who hast loosed me from my sins, I thankfully accept the redemption which thou hast purchased, and the glad freedom from the guilt and power of sin. Enable me henceforth to walk in newness of life. And to thee, my Lord and King, shall be glory and dominion for ever and ever. Amen.

It is thus that he speaks to every sin-burdened soul, profoundly conscious of its heavy binding links, sighing for the liberty of the sons of God. This forgiveness and loosing is for thee. What Christ was as Alpha, he is as Omega. He is the same today as in the yesterday of the past. All that he did for those first believers in himself, he waits to do for us, if only with humble penitence and faith we will claim it at his hands. He loveth us! He purchaseth us for himself, not with corruptible things as silver and gold, and tells us that we are loosed from its bondage. He has made us free, and we need not again yield to the evil things of which we are ashamed, any more than the woman whom he healed needed to continue to be bent double (Luke 13:11-13 RV). Let us lift up ourselves, and go forth to glorify God in an upright walk and conversation; *to reign in this life* through the one man, Christ Jesus (Romans 5:17).

God's Restoring Love
October 6

The causes of backsliding are many. We have pretended to be living a more devoted life than was actually the case; we neglected to watch unto prayer; we allowed secret sin to eat out the heart of our piety, as the white ant works destruction in the East; or we yielded to temptation, and then sought to justify ourselves against the remonstrances of conscience; or we yielded to the fear of man, and drifted with the multitude to do evil; or we become prosperous, and trusted only in our wealth; or poor, and succumbed to covetousness and the bitterness of despair.

'Take with you words, and turn to the Lord; I will heal their backsliding, I will love them freely' (Hosea 14:2, 4).

'Simon ... lovest thou me? He saith unto him, Yea, Lord, thou knowest that I love thee' (John 21:16).

The world despises the fallen, and does not believe in the possibility of entire restoration. It is always suspicious of those who have fallen from their high estate - the prisoner in the cell, who was once an honoured financier; the beautiful woman who has come under the degrading influence of drink or drugs; the minister or doctor who has incurred shame and disgrace - all such find it hard to be reinstated. But God stoops over the outcast with infinite compassion and love, and promises forgiveness and restoration to all who will return to him.

It was thus that our Lord dealt with Peter. He knew that in spite of his grievous fall, there was a strong undercurrent of devoted love, and he did not hesitate to entrust to him the care of his sheep and lambs.

In a certain museum there is a lovely marble statue which was found broken into hundreds of pieces. The fragments were carefully collected, and with infinite patience fitted together. Finally a seemingly impossible task was accomplished, and the statute stands in all its original completeness and beauty. So the Lord Jesus will take the broken pieces of any life that will come to him, and with his skilful and tender touch will remake it into something useful and beautiful in his service. This is the meaning of Redemption.

The one thing that Christ asks of any of us is that we should follow him. Whether we can walk, or need to be carried; whether life is young within us, or waning, let us follow him, love him, obey him, and he will turn back our backslidings, and never mention them again.

Prayer: O Lord, we would be thine; let us never fall away from thee. Amen.

'And the Lord direct your hearts into the love of God, and into the patience of Christ' (2 Thessalonians 3:5 RV).

The beloved disciple greets his companions as sharing 'in tribulation, and in the kingdom and patience of Jesus Christ' (Revelation 1:9). It is a noble combination; as though the royalty of Christian character were in proportion to the share we have in the quiet waiting of our Lord. He waited patiently from all eternity, until the fullness of the times had come, and the hour of his Incarnation struck; he waited patiently for thirty years in Nazareth, whilst preparing for his life-work. When he returned in triumph to the Father, he sat down at his right hand until his enemies were made his footstool. Throughout the ages he quietly waits, in sure expectation of the destined end, when all rule and authority and power shall be put down. All the anguish of the world lies on his heart; every question as to the righteousness and equity of God is felt by him. He bears all with unfaltering patience, because he sees the end, and knows that at the last God will be All in All. It is into this love and patience that we are to be led.

Prayer: Most Blessed Lord, guide our wandering feet, we beseech thee, into the love of God and into thine own infinite patience. Forgive us that we have so often been impulsive and headstrong, that we have murmured against thy apparent slowness in answering our prayers. Hush our unquiet hearts with thine own peace. Amen.

Into the Love of God. Every time we dare to affirm that, notwithstanding appearances, God is love; every time that we evince that love to others, even though our own heart is breaking; every time we say No to self and Yes to God, we make further progress into his love. Dare to believe in the love of God, even when the darkness seems to veil it. Dare to believe that it is over all, and through all, and in all.

Into the patience of Christ. Let us exercise Christ's patience until the sorrows and trials of life have achieved their destined purpose. There is a sufficient explanation for the present condition of the world, if we knew it. Therefore, judge nothing before the time, but be of good cheer, and stablish your hearts, for your God will come and not keep silence. In the meanwhile, let us keep the word of his patience, and manifest that patience and faith of the saints.

Practising Christianity
October 8

It is a great comfort to find that *love* is not regarded by the apostle as though it were merely an emotional or sentimental matter, for every reference points to *action*! The love of God was manifested in the laying down of his life, and we are to be willing to follow in his steps (verse 16). The injunction is that we should love in our *deeds*. We are not to shut up our hearts in compassion, but to help our brother in need. If we begin with *doing* kind and loving actions, we shall end by *feeling* the same. Often when people come to me, saying that love has completely died out of their life towards some other person, I have bidden them go back again, and act with love, making the other one the centre and object of helpful ministry; the invariable result is the refreshing and rekindling of the hot geyser-springs of affection.

Do not wait to feel love, but begin at once to show it, because it is right, and your duty, and as you step out in simple faith you will find that God will make this grace to abound towards you that you may also abound in this good work. Love of such kind is self-giving and it is the gift of the Spirit of God. This exotic bloom cannot flourish on our wintry soil; the heart of man cannot furnish it. There may be a few wild growths, but they bear small comparison to its beautiful flower and fruit. Love is of God. It proceeds from his nature, and is shed abroad in our hearts by the Holy Spirit which is given unto us. 'The fruit of the Spirit is love', and as we are united with Christ by faith, the love of God will be shed abroad in our hearts by the Holy Spirit, and we shall be able to love with God's love.

We know that we have been born from above as soon as we find ourselves willing to put the interests of another before our own, not because we have a natural affection or affinity for him, but because he and we belong to God. If there is hatred or dislike in our hearts towards any, let us beware! We must uproot it by generous action, or it will bring darkness into our own lives (1 John 2:9-11).

'We know that we have passed from death unto life, because we love the brethren. He that loveth not his brother abideth in death' (1 John 3:14).

Prayer: Enable us, O God of patience, to bear one another's burdens, and to forbear one another in love. Oh, teach and help us all to live in peace and to love in truth. Subdue all bitter resentments in our minds, and let the law of kindness be in our tongues. Amen.

My Brother!
October 9

'The Lord said unto Cain, Where is Abel thy brother? And he said: I know not: Am I my brother's keeper?' (Genesis 4:9). 'He that hateth his brother is in darkness, and walketh in darkness' (1 John 2:11).

Man's fall, whatever else it may have been, resulted in a complete change of the centre of his being. He was made in the likeness of God, and God's nature is absolutely selfless. God's will and purpose was the one rule of man's existence until the moment came when our first parents substituted the gratification of self for the will and law of God. From that hour the self-life became the dominant principle of mankind, and the world is what it is because the essence of life is the service of self.

We do not know what really caused the difference in the disposition of Cain and Abel. There are hints and suggestions, but the fundamental reason why these two brothers differed so is veiled in mystery, though the like of it still shows itself in our homes. St John gives us the clue in his first Epistle, where he says that Cain slew his brother, because his own works were evil, and his brother's righteous.

God remonstrated with Cain and warned him that sin was lying at the door of his heart, waiting to enter. He exhorted him to watch and not allow it to intrude. When the dreadful deed was done, Cain found that all nature was in arms against him, and he became an outcast. The blood of Abel cried against Cain, for all sin cries to God, and he is the Avenger and Vindicator of wronged ones who in simplicity and faith have cast themselves upon him. Thank God, also, there is a cry louder than that of Abel's, which pleads not for judgment but for mercy (Hebrews 12:24).

Prayer: Our Father! Help us to consider the interests of others, and to act generously towards them, because we are thy children, and thy infinite resources are at our commands. Amen.

This world is full of envy, jealousy, strife, and murder, because men keep themselves instead of keeping their brothers; because our own instead of another's welfare revolves round the pivot of '*I*'. The first Epistle of St John is the antipode of this story in Genesis, and contains its corrective, for it is when we love God first and best that we love our brother, and as we open our whole soul to the tidal wave of God's love, we are lifted above the jagged rocks of the self-life into the broad full ocean of life which is life indeed (1 John 3:14, 17).

Forgiveness
October 10

The religious teachers of Christ's day taught that *four* times was the extreme limit of forgiveness. Peter exceeded this in his estimate, but how far even he fell short of the divine ideal. Seven was to the Jews the number of perfection, so that no expression could more forcibly convey the impression of ever-renewed, eternal, repetition than '*seventy times seven*'! What comfort there is for each one of us here! For if God expects man to forgive his brother thus, how may we not count on his forgiveness!

This parable shows the great wrong we do to ourselves as well as to our brother, when we fail to forgive. Here was a man who had been forgiven the enormous debt of two millions sterling, but was not softened and chastened by its remission, for he went immediately from his Master's presence to lay violent hands on an unfortunate fellow-servant, who owed him less than a five-pound note. He is deaf to the reasons which had filled his own mouth previously, and oblivious of everything except that this debt should be paid instantly.

Are we not all tempted to abuse the forgiving love of God, and to be censorious, vindictive, implacable, and unforgiving? If you want to be the reverse of this, consider how much you have been forgiven! Sit down and count up your enormous debt to God, and how freely he has forgiven you. Only the forgiving are forgiven - 'If ye forgive not men their trespasses, neither will your Father forgive your trespasses.' If we are unrelenting, slow to recognise merit, quick to observe faults, cherishing ill-will and resentment for injuries inflicted, perhaps years ago; and if we cling to and nourish this spirit, we may be sure that we have never been forgiven.

How are we to attain the state of mind which forgives so often, and can win the most wayward? The parable teaches us that we must receive God's pardon in a right spirit, that we must remember our own failures and sins, and that we must ever be willing to cast the mantle of forgiving love over the sins and failures of those around us.

'Lord, how oft shall my brother sin against me, and I forgive him? until seven times?' (Matthew 18:21).

Prayer: O Lord, may we hear thee say to us: Thy sins which are many are all forgiven, go in peace; and may we, in our turn, forgive as we have been forgiven, and may the sun not go down on our wrath. Amen.

Our Possessions
October 11

'Take heed, and keep yourselves from all covetousness; for a man's life consisteth not in the abundance of things which he possesseth' *(Luke 12:15).* *'Little children, guard yourselves from idols' (1 John 5:21 RV).*

The petition addressed to Christ, in this paragraph from which our text is selected, has been constantly made to him in subsequent ages. Men are always demanding that he should divide the inheritance more equally. But our Lord did not come to adjust human relationships by the exercise of his autocratic will. He deals rather with the over-reaching and grasping avarice which leads the rich to withhold, and the discontent which compels the poor to murmur. He saw in the demand of the suppliant a tendency to the same covetousness which prompted the other brother to withhold the portion of the inheritance, which was not justly his.

Our Lord announced the far-reaching truth that life does not consist in what we possess, but in what we are. We are rich, not in proportion to the amount standing to our credit in the bank, or to the acreage of our inheritance, but to the purity, strength, and generosity of our nature. When we lay up treasure for ourselves, we become paupers in God's universe. The only way of dealing with covetousness, which makes an idol of money or possessions, is to regard our property only as gifts entrusted to us for the benefit of others. Let us mortify the spirit of greed, which is so strong within us all, by sowing the acreage of our life as indicated in 2 Corinthians 9.

Prayer: O Lord, the Portion of our Inheritance, give us grace, we pray thee, never to aim at or desire anything out of thee. What we can enjoy in thee, give us according to thy will; what we cannot, deny us. Amen.

Sensual appetite is an idol with many (Philippians 3:19). Eating and drinking, feasting and pleasure-seeking are idols before which many prostrate themselves. And there are other idols than these, for whenever any earthly object engrosses our soul, and intercepts the love and faith that should pass from us to God, it is an idol which must be overthrown. Whenever we can look up from anything that we possess into the face of God, and thank him as its Giver, we may use and enjoy that without fear. We are not likely to make an idol of that which we receive direct from the hand of our Heavenly Father, whose good pleasure it is to give good gifts to his children (1 Timothy 4:4, 5).

God's Largesse and Bounty
October 12

This is always the cry of unbelief, *Can God*? whilst the triumphant assertion of faith is: *God can*. What a difference is wrought by the collocation of words! Can God furnish a table in the wilderness? God can spread a table, even in the wilderness, and in the presence of our enemies our cup can overflow. Can he give bread also? He can satisfy the desire of every living thing, by the opening of his hand. Canst thou do anything for us, our child is grievously possessed of the devil? If thou canst believe, all things are possible to him that believeth.

The wanderings of the Israelites for forty years were due to the fact that they looked at their difficulties and questioned if God could overcome them. Amongst the people, only Caleb and Joshua looked away from the Canaanites and their fortified cities to him who had brought them where they were, and was pledged to extricate them. Some people speak of Giants with a capital G, and forget to magnify the power of God. What wonder that they account themselves as grasshoppers, and lose heart! Let us not forget that we are sons and daughters of God, 'heirs of God, and joint-heirs with Christ'. (Compare Numbers 13:33 and Romans 8:17.)

Look back on the past; see what God has done for you; remember he is pledged to finish what he has begun. If he gave water, he can certainly give bread.

'They did eat, and were well filled.' When we are poor and needy, we are inclined to humble prayer. But if suddenly our lot is changed, and there is abundance instead of poverty, how often there is a change in our demeanour. We are apt to become self-indulgent, and forgetful of the needs of the world. Instead of remembering that we are still God's pensioners, we magnify ourselves as though we were exclusive owners. Probably this is why God keeps some of us in poverty, for no greater temptation could befall us than to find ourselves with riches. In this way he answers our daily prayer, 'Lead us not into temptation!'

'Can God furnish a table in the wilderness? Behold, he smote the rock, that the waters gushed out, and the streams overflowed; Can he give bread also? They did eat, and were well filled' (Psalm 78:19, 20, 29).

Prayer: We thank thee, our heavenly Father, for the new mercies of each returning day, for all that thou hast given to us, and not less for that which thou dost withhold. May we be receptive of all things that pertain to life and godliness. Amen.

The Blessing of Thankfulness
October 13

'Giving thanks always for all things unto God and the Father in the name of our Lord Jesus Christ' (Ephesians 5:20).
'Let us offer the sacrifice of praise to God continually' (Hebrews 13:15).

Some people seem born with a sullen and feverish temper, and it is very difficult for them to brighten into smiles and songs. But whatever our natural disposition may be, if we belong to Christ it is our bounden duty to cultivate a thankful heart. A melancholy person has a bad effect upon others. It is miserable to have to work with or under a confirmed pessimist. Nothing is right, nothing pleases, there is no word of praise or encouragement. Once, when I was at Aden, I watched a gang of Lascars trans-shipping the mails. It was a pleasure to see them, one after another, carrying the bags cheerily because their leader kept them all the time singing as they did their work. If, instead of finding fault with our employees or servants we would look out for things for which we could commend and thank them, we should probably find a miraculous change in their attitude.

The advantage of joy and gladness is that it is a source of strength to the individual soul, and to all others who come within its range, and commends our Christianity! Sidney Smith says: 'I once gave a lady two and twenty recipes against melancholy; one was a bright fire; another, to remember all the pleasant things said to her; another, to keep a box of sugar-plums on the chimney-piece and a kettle simmering on the hob. I thought this mere trifling at the moment, but have in after life discovered how true it is that these little pleasures often banish melancholy better than more exalted objects.'

We may interpret the advice of this humorist and essayist by turning into joyous praise all the incidents of our daily life, arising with gratitude and thankfulness from every good and perfect gift to the Father of our Lord Jesus Christ. The world is sad and has to pay her jesters and entertainers; it is a mystery to her that the face of the Christian should be bright and smiling, although the fig-tree does not blossom, and there is no fruit in the vine. Let us count up our treasures and blessings, and we shall find that even in the saddest and loneliest life there is something to turn our sorrow into singing (2 Corinthians 6:10).

Prayer: Help us, O Lord, to rejoice always; to pray without ceasing, and in everything to give thanks. Amen.

Burden-Bearing
October 14

In these words the apostle is evidently thinking more especially of the trespasses and sins into which men and women fall. We are not to rejoice over their failure, nor talk about it to others, but to consider ourselves, remembering our own liability to fall in the event of temptation. We are to be tender, gentle, and compassionate, helping to bear the burden of temptation, remorse, and shame. There is great comfort for us all in these words, for surely, if our Lord expects us to forgive and restore our brother, we may count on him to do as much for us!

'Bear ye one another's burdens, and so fulfil the law of Christ' (Galatians 6:2).

But sin is not the only burden we are to bear with our brethren. The young man or girl who fails to make good; the business man who meets with sudden reverse; those who suffer bitter disappointment; when faces are averted, and tongues are busily engaged in criticism - let us seek out the one who has consciously disappointed everybody, and help by our strong and tender sympathy. It is like the coming of the good Ananias into Saul's darkness, with the greeting: 'Brother Saul!'

We may help to bear the burden of bereavement - when the husband is suddenly stricken down, or the mother is taken away and there is no one to care for the children, then we may show our practical sympathy and helpfulness. All through his life on earth our Lord sought to carry the burdens of the people, and we are to follow in his steps. Sympathy means *suffering with*; and as we endeavour to enter into the griefs and sorrows of those around us, in proportion to the burden of grief that we carry do we succeed in lightening another's load. You cannot bear a burden without feeling its pressure; and in bearing the burdens of others, we must be prepared to suffer with them.

This was the law of Christ, the principle of his life, and the precept which he enjoined on his followers to fulfil. Let us remember, also, that in carrying the burdens of others, we often lose our own.

Prayer

For friends above; for friends still left below;
For the rare links invisible between.
For sweet hearts tuned to noblest charity;
For great hearts toiling in the outer dark;
For friendly hands stretched out in time of need,
For every gracious thought and word and deed;
We thank thee Lord! Amen.

What it Means to be a Christian
October 15

'Whosoever he be of you that forsaketh not all that he hath, he cannot be my disciple' (Luke 14:33).

Three times over in this chapter, our Lord says these solemn words: 'he cannot be my disciple'. There are three conditions of discipleship. First, we must be prepared to put first things first; second, we must be willing to suffer daily crucifixion; third, we must be detached from all things, because attached to Christ. The conditions seem severe, but they must be fulfilled, if we would enter Christ's School.

Disciple stands for learner. Our Lord is prepared to teach us the mysteries of the Kingdom of God; but it is useless to enter his class unless we have resolved to do as he says. *Put first things first*. When our Lord uses the word *hate*, he clearly means that the love we are to have for him is to be so much greater, that comparatively our natural affection will be as if it were hate. No one could have loved his mother more than our Lord did. In his dying agony his special thought and care was for her, but on three different occasions he put her aside. We are sometimes called to put aside those who are nearest and dearest, if their demands conflict with the claims of Christ.

The daily cross. In each of us there is the self-principle, and for each of us there is a perpetual necessity to deny self. Some talk about bearing the cross in a glib fashion, but its true meaning is shame, suffering, and sorrow, which no one realises but God, and which perhaps strikes deeper down into the roots of our being as we grow older. There is an opportunity in your life, in respect to some person or circumstance, for an ever-deepening appreciation of union with Christ in his death, and for which you must be daily prepared to surrender your own way and will.

Renunciation. It may be necessary to surrender all we have for Christ, or it may be that he will ask us to hold all as a steward or trustee for himself and others. No one can lay down the rule for another. The main point to decide is this: 'Am I willing to do what Christ wants me to do; to yield my will for him to mould it, and my life for him to work through it?' If so, all else will adjust itself.

Prayer: O Lord, save me in spite of myself. May I be thine; wholly thine, and at all costs, thine. In humiliation, in poverty, in self-abnegation, thine. Thine in the way thou knowest to be most fitting, in order that thou mightest be now and ever mine. Amen.

The Joy of the Lord
October 16

Joy and gladness is a very necessary element in human wellbeing. We cannot live our best life if sorrow and depression holds undisputed sway. There are three sources of joy mentioned in this chapter.

The people understood the divine word and profited by it. Their eagerness to hear, as Ezra opened the Sacred Book, was remarkable (verses 3, 5, 12, 18). Let us also delight in God through his word. Let us not read the Bible as a task, but dwell upon it, until its beauties become woven into our thoughts and lives. It is thus that life becomes purified and enriched. We shall no longer desire base or corrupting things, but God will give us the desires of our heart, and we shall be satisfied, if we delight ourselves in him.

They communicated good things to those for whom nothing was prepared (verses 10, 12). There is no cure for sorrow and heartbreak like healing broken hearts. There is no such comfort for ourselves as that which we administer to others. Nehemiah could not have given better advice than when he bade his people share their joys and sweets with those whose lives were bare of comfort and luxuries.

Of course Christianity has within it other sources of joy. Our Saviour gives us his joy, because he reveals the Father to us, makes us to rest in him, and gives a worthy object for our lives; he makes work light because he has appointed it, sorrow supportable because he shares it, and death desirable because he has opened the door of the Father's Home. In his joy we may participate (John 15:11; 16:22, 24).

Their obedience. As soon as they understood the words they heard, they began to put them into practice. No wonder there was joy, for in the keeping of God's commandments there is great reward. It was during the Feast of Tabernacles that our Lord spoke of the Holy Spirit entering the heart to remove its thirst, and to pour forth as rivers to a dying world (John 7:37-39). We cannot do much apart from the indwelling of the Holy Spirit. Only through him can we be right with God; only through him can we be really glad; only through him can we pass on joy and comfort to others.

'This day is holy unto our Lord; neither be ye sorry; for the joy of the Lord is your strength' (Nehemiah 8:10).

Prayer: We thank thee, O God, that we may have fellowship with our Lord in his redemptive purpose. May the gifts which he has received even for the rebellious fill our hearts and lives with joy and gladness. Amen.

Making a Covenant with God
October 17

'We make a sure covenant, and write it' (Nehemiah 9:38).
'He is the Mediator of a better covenant' (Hebrews 8:6).

It is good for a soul to make a covenant with God. On his twenty-third birthday Milton wrote these memorable words:

> 'Yet be it less or more, or soon or slow,
> It shall be still in strictest measure even
> To that same lot, however mean or high,
> Toward which Time leads me and the will of Heaven.
> All is, if I have grace to use it so,
> As ever in my great Taskmaster's eye.'

This was his covenant with God; and through all the years, now in his prime under Cromwell, and again in his lovely old age under Charles II, he never swerved from the path he had selected.

Who can forget those magnificent lines of Wordsworth, which tell how he was returning from a village merrymaking, which had lasted through the night, and lo, the glory of a summer dawn was breaking over the hills! He describes its beauty, and adds:

> 'Vows were made for me,
> That I should be, else sinning greatly,
> A dedicated spirit.'

There are certain principles outlined in these chapters in Nehemiah, which may well be included in our covenant with God: (1) Never to allow anything in private or business life which is not in keeping with the high ideals of the Bible. (2) To set aside a certain proportion of our income and time for the maintenance of the work and house of God. (3) To observe the Rest-Day.

Prayer: We present to thee, O God, ourselves to be a living sacrifice, holy and acceptable, our reasonable service. Fulfil through us the good pleasure of thy goodness and the work of faith with power. Amen.

But a covenant is between two. No resolution of ours is strong enough to keep us true. The most fervent protestations and vows may fail us in the day of trial, and our covenants are permanent only so far as God is party to them. But if Jesus is our Co-Signatory, there will be a safeguard and certainty which all the powers of evil will not be able to overthrow.

Livingstone's covenant with God was that he might heal the open plague-spot of the Arab slave trade. A covenant like this, in some cases, has been signed with blood. This was D L Moody's prayer, as a young man: 'Great God, let the world learn, through my life, what thou canst do by a man wholly devoted to thee!'

Prevailing Power
October 18

The prayer which prevails is that which is indited by the Holy Spirit. He is the medium of communication between heaven and earth, and reveals to us the thoughts and desires of God, so that we do not ask amiss. Just as the ether will connect up one continent with another, so long as the transmitter and receiver are in accord, so the Holy Spirit is the Medium between ourselves and the glorified Redeemer. Prayer is in the heart of our Lord. It is perhaps better to say that it originates there, is transmitted to us, and sent back from us to him. We know that by our thought-waves we can help our friends in distant places, so it is surely possible for our thought-waves to reach the Lord Jesus. Oh, that we may be ever in such sympathy and accord with him that there may be no loss of his thoughts towards us.

'And when they had prayed, the place was shaken where they were assembled together; and they were all filled with the Holy Ghost, and they spake the word of God with boldness' (Acts 4:31).

There are four kinds of prayer.

The Prayer of Communion and Fellowship. It is like a father asking his little boy why he keeps coming into his study, and discovers that the child has no special reason, but only wants to be with him. So we should not be satisfied with the knowledge of God our Father which ordinary men possess, but have such aptitudes and yearnings which can only be satisfied by fellowship, communion, and adoring love.

The Prayer of Request. Perhaps we make more of this at the beginning of life than after. As life goes on we are content to leave ourselves in the wise and tender hands of our Heavenly Father, and it is enough that he cares. We learn to be thankful that some prayers have not been answered, and to realise that God is doing for us ever so much better than we ask or think.

The Prayer of Intercession. This is nearest to the mind of Christ. He wears our names on his heart, and ever lives to intercede.

The Prayer of Conflict. At times we are called to enter into the Garden, and to bear with him some of the burden of his conflict for souls against the principalities and powers of evil. At such times there is urgent need to watch and pray!

Prayer: Warm my cold heart, Lord, I beseech thee. Take away all that hinders me from giving myself to thee. Give me grace to obey thee in all things, and ever to follow thy gracious leading. Amen.

'When he came to himself, he said ... I will arise and go to my father, and will say unto him, Father, I have sinned...' (Luke 15:17-19).

We need not travel far to reach the far country - the *thought* of sin, the wings of passionate evil desire, the lightning flash of a look, may land us as far from God as the east is from the west. The essence of the far country is *selfishness*. Notice the stress of the prodigal's emphasis upon himself - 'give *me* the portion of the goods that falleth to me.' It is not wrong to make use of and enjoy all the good and perfect gifts with which God strews our life, so long as they are held in thankful recognition of and fellowship with himself. But when we depart from God, there is *waste*, for we lack the one object which gathers up all our activities for a worthy focus; *riot*, because in the absence of God there is no sufficient corrective or antidote for strong and masterful passion; *want*, because the soul was made for God, and can never be satisfied till it rests in him.

How foolish it is for a man to disjoin himself from God, and to join himself to a citizen in the land of forgetfulness! The citizens of this world have nothing to give to the starving soul of man, save to send it forth to feed the swine, which stand for the lower desires of our nature. This is the alternative which too many wiseacres suggest: 'See life, take your fill of pleasure; fill the passing hours with revelry, amusement, dissipation.' But the hunger of the soul cannot be appeased thus. Though husks are good for swine, they will not suffice for the sons of men. Like the wise man of old, we cry: 'He hath put eternity in my heart - vanity of vanities, all is vanity!' We cannot rest in that which contents others. From the putrid swine-troughs we long for the food which the servants enjoy in our Father's home; from the stagnant pools we thirst for the crystal water.

Prayer: Thou knowest, O Lord, what most I require; help me, and out of the treasury of thy goodness, succour thou my needy soul. Amen.

It is under such circumstances that we come back to ourselves - that we come back to our Father. Let us believe in the love of God our Father, which yearns after us in our absence from him, which sees us while we are yet a great way off, and will run to welcome us, as we return, with forgiveness and restoration.

Victory Out of Defeat
October 20

The valley of Achor is the emblem of defeat, failure and the fainting heart. Down its long pass the terrified fugitives had fled, bearing to Joshua the story of defeat (Joshua 7). Is there a single life without its valley of Achor? Is there one of us who has not gone up against a foe, which in the distance appeared quite insignificant, but it has proved to be more than a match for all the resolutions with which we had braced ourselves to meet it. Can good come out of such evil, and sweetness from such bitter despair?

'I will give her vineyards from thence, and the valley of Achor for a door of hope: and she shall sing there, as in the days of her youth' (Hosea 2:15).

The tragic story told in the seventh chapter of Joshua tells how that defeat wrought good. The disaster led to the searching out of the sin of Achan, and the cutting away of gangrene, which, otherwise, would have eaten out the heart of Israel. It led to humiliation, self-examination, prayer and faith, and finally to victory. May we not say as much of our defeats? Certainly, it would have been better had they not cast their shadow on our past; but they have not been without their lessons of priceless value. Each valley of Achor has had its door of Hope. Sin has reigned unto death, but the grace of God has reigned unto eternal life. Through our sins we have learned, as never before, to appreciate God's forgiveness; through our failures we have been taught our own weakness, and led to magnify the grace which is made perfect in weakness.

Prayer: Heavenly Father, we thank thee for opening doors of Hope in the valley of Achor, for giving us beauty for ashes, and the oil of joy for mourning. Put a new song into our mouths today, and let us taste afresh the glad sense of thy pardoning love. Amen.

Out of such experiences comes the song - 'She shall sing as in the days of her youth.' You say that the spring and gladness of life are gone for ever. You insist that you must go mourning all your days, and that life will only bring added grief. But God says that you *shall* sing! Though the summer is gone, there will be a second - an Indian summer, even mellower than the first. God wants to give you a new revelation of his love, to draw you into his tenderest friendship and fellowship, to lift you into the life of victory and satisfaction. And when all these things come to pass, and they may begin today as you return to him, you will find that he has put a new song into your mouth, even praise unto our God.

A New Creation
October 21

'Wherefore if any man is in Christ, there is a new creation: the old things are passed away; behold, they are become new' (2 Corinthians 5:17 RV marg).

True Christianity is very different from much that we see around us, and which is known as such, and is summed up in orthodoxy of creed, in religious service, in gifts and deeds which cost little or nothing. If Christianity is anything, it is self-giving even to death. If Christianity means anything we must renounce self as the centre of our life, and be willing to sacrifice ourselves for others. Nothing will save the world, which is cursed with the spirit of selfishness, but the repetition and filling-up as far as possible of Christ's sacrifice by those who profess to be his servants and followers. Selfishness is destructive, but the love that gives itself even to blood and tears is constructive.

But we must be sure that the supreme thought of every word and act must be Christ who died and rose again (verses 14, 15). Let us not live only for humanity, but for the Son of Man, and as we live for him the bitter will be sweet and the rough smooth, and we shall find ourselves living for the whole race of men for whom he died.

When this becomes the law of life, we are necessarily a new creation; we live under a new heaven, and walk over a new earth. There is a new aspect upon the most familiar objects of our environment. It is not that they have altered, but that we are changed from self to the spiritual; from the old life of sin to the new life of which the centre is the glorified Saviour. In his book *Grace Abounding*, Bunyan gives expression to this thought of the wonderful change that passes over the face of creation, and the aspect of human life, so soon as the heart is full of the love of God.

Let us notice the emphasis of verse 18. God was *in* Christ when he bore the burden of the world's sin upon the Cross and that we have been brought to know and love him as of his grace. It is God also who has given us the right to carry the message of mercy and forgiveness to all within our reach. 'He hath given to *us*', that is, to you and me, 'the ministry of reconciliation'. It is for us to go forth into the world, our hearts filled with Christ's love, telling men and women that this is a redeemed world, and that God is waiting for them to accept his love and mercy. This is the message of Christianity.

Prayer: O Lord, forgive what I have been; sanctify what I am; and order what I shall be. Amen.

The Promise of the Holy Spirit
October 22

In his sermon, on the Day of Pentecost, the apostle Peter quoted the latter part of this prediction by the prophet Joel (2:28). Not much is known of this prophet, who probably lived in Judah during the reign of Uzziah. But evidently his anticipation of the outpouring of the divine Spirit had its fulfilment in those memorable scenes in which the Christian Church was born.

'And it shall come to pass in the last days, saith God, I will pour out of my Spirit upon all flesh: and your sons and your daughters shall prophesy, and your young men shall see visions, and your old men shall dream dreams' (Acts 2:17).

Before the Day of Pentecost, the Holy Spirit had descended only upon the elect souls of the Hebrew race - upon Abraham and Moses, upon Samuel and Elijah, upon Isaiah and others of the prophets. This supreme gift of God was reserved in those days for the spiritual aristocracy of Israel, for the men who were called to eminent office and responsibility, as kings, prophets, or leaders. But Joel said that the time would come when the Holy Spirit who had been reserved for the few, was to be poured out upon the many - the young men and maidens would prophesy; even the slaves and the most despised classes of the community would partake of the divine experience.

Whatever Pentecost means - it is open to the reception and enjoyment of us *all*, 'Every one of you,' said St Peter, 'shall receive the gift of the Holy Ghost.' *To you is the promise*, and to your children, and to all that are afar off, even as many as the Lord our God shall call (Acts 2:38, 39). Let us take this to heart.

Some years ago, electricity was the perquisite of the few, but now the poorest girl or lad may utilise it and be carried along in the electric car; and it is the boast of our scientists and inventors that they are able to bring the benefits of their discoveries within the reach of the most needy amongst us. And Pentecost resembles this, in that the forces and gifts of the Eternal Spirit are now within the grasp of the feeblest hand which is stretched out to appropriate them. But there must be first the putting away of evil, the emptying of our hearts, the hunger and thirst of the soul for righteousness, before God can give us our share in the Gift which was made once for all to the Church, but must be claimed by each successive believer.

Prayer: Let thy Holy Spirit dwell in me continually, and make me thy temple and sanctuary. Amen.

The Roll of Faith
October 23

'Time will fail me if I tell of Gideon, Barak, Samson, Jephthah ... who through faith subdued kingdoms, wrought righteousness, obtained promises' (Hebrews 11:32, 33 RV).

Faith is the link between our souls and God. It is the capacity of entering into fellowship with the Eternal Love and Power, so that we are able to do all things with the sense that it is not we who do them, but God in us and with us. Faith is the open door and window towards God. In faith our heart goes out towards God in clinging dependence, and God comes in to strengthen us with his divine fullness.

In human life, when we trust a man, we draw from him all that he is able to supply; in the divine life, faith draws upon the resources of God, so that they flow freely into our nature, and the results of our life-work are immensely increased. Faith is possible amid a great deal of ignorance. It is clear that Gideon, Barak, Samson, and Jephthah were ignorant of the truth which the gospel has revealed, and yet we learn that their work was largely due to their faith. Dispensations come and go; the revelation of God grows from less to more; but the attitude of faith is always the same - in the simple woman that touched the hem of Christ's garment, as in St John the beloved disciple, who had years of training in Christ's School.

Faith achieves very different results. In some, it produces the heroic strength that turns the battle from the gate; in some, the passive suffering that endures the long ordeal of pain. Here, it turns the edge of the sword; there, shuts the mouths of lions. We know how electric force may be applied to all the various machinery of human life. In one place used for the beaming light, in another to drive the motor car, or to flash the message of music and speech from one continent to another. So Faith is able to appropriate God's might for any purpose that lies within the compass of the life-task, whether active or passive. (See verses 32-34, 35-39.)

God bears a *witness* to all who trust him. He never fails us in the hour of need. His response is the echo of our appeal. As soon as the uplifted arm of the tramcar touches the overhead wire, there is the spark, and the immediate entrance of electric power. So God answers faith.

Prayer: O God, we are full of need, but we have learnt that thou givest power to the faint and to those that have no right. Change our weakness into thy strength; our ignorance into thy wisdom; our changefulness into thine everlasting constancy. Amen.

Christt the Good Shepherd
October 24

Good does not mean merely benevolent and kind, but genuine and true. It is contrasted with the *robber* and the *hireling*. Up to a certain point the latter may do his work creditably. He will not desert the flock for trifling considerations; he will earn his pay! But when it comes to the supreme test of sacrificing his life, the hireling breaks down and leaves his flock to the peril of the wild beast. There are such shepherds who have taken up the pastoral office as a livelihood.

'I am the Good Shepherd, and know my sheep, and am known of mine' (John 10:14).

How different is our Lord - the Good Shepherd - who gave his life for the sheep. Why did he love us so? It will always be a mystery! He seeks those who belong to his fold, but have wandered off into the dark paths of sin. Jesus goes after the one which is lost *until he finds it*! That is the way of the Chief Shepherd.

The Revised Version rendering brings out the intimate knowledge of Christ of his flock: 'I know mine own, and mine own know me; even as the Father knows me, and I know the Father.' None knoweth the Father save the Son, and none the Son save the Father. But in this same intimacy and certainty the Lord Jesus knows each of us. He knows our down-sitting and our uprising; our motives, sometimes misunderstood; the anxieties which overcast our joys; our fears and hopes. He assuages, as no stranger can, our heart's bitterness. It is good to be known thus, for we need enter into no laboured explanation of ourselves.

Prayer: O Lamb of God! Who art in the midst of the Throne, but wilt be our Good Shepherd and tread the rough pathway of this world with each trembling heart. May we be abundantly satisfied with thy provision and follow in thy footsteps. Amen.

Christ seeks those who do not belong to a fold (verse 16). Probably there will always be many folds, for by the constitution of their minds men are ever disposed to view Truth from different angles. Some do not see this, and hold that if we do not believe just as they do, we have no right to assume that we belong to the flock. They forget that there may be many folds, yet *one flock* (RV). Whatever may be your special fold, the one great question to answer is: Do you hear and obey the Shepherd's voice? If so, you certainly belong to the one flock, and no one shall snatch you out of the Shepherd's hand (verses 27, 28 RV).

'Holy Father, keep through thine own name those whom thou hast given me, that they may be one, as we are' (John 17:11).

This marvellous seventeenth chapter of St John's Gospel has been called the Incense Altar of the New Testament. It is full of the sweet fragrance of our Lord's intercession for his own. Let us linger over it for a little, that its wondrous depths may unfold before our eyes. It is a window into his inner consciousness, from which we may read some of the thoughts that habitually filled his soul.

Christ's self-obliteration. The motives that animated our Lord's earthly ministry were all for the Father's glory. He anticipated, in fact, those great words of the apostle: 'Of him, and through him, and to him, are all things: to whom be glory for ever' (Romans 11:36). In this we have an example, that we should follow his steps. *We* also must find our fresh springs in him, as he found them in God; we also must be willing to forsake and surrender all things to him, holding them as his stewards; we also must appropriate moment by moment, his unsearchable wealth. If any glory should ever fall to our lot, we must lay it at his feet, and share it with those entrusted to our charge.

Christ's self-assertion. Though our Lord obliterated his own interests, there were many things which were inalienable and of which he could not dispossess himself. He knew that he had ever been one with God, and ever would be, that the love which had existed between the Father and himself was to be shared by a multitude that no one could number. It is ours to know that we are loved with an unchanging love, that in Christ we are enriched into the measure of God's unchangeable fullness. Oh, why do we not more deeply share the self-obliteration of Christ for others, that we may stand with him on these glorious heights, beyond the reach of doubt and fear?

Christ's self-realisation. Listen to his joyous words: 'I am glorified in them.' 'I in them, thou in me, that they may be made perfect in one.' It is only as he sees his joy glowing in myriads of redeemed souls, and finds his love reproduced in their lives, that he is fulfilled and satisfied.

Prayer: We thank thee, our heavenly Father, for the gift of Jesus our Lord to be our Saviour and Friend. Draw us into closer union with him, that we may know thee better through him, and be conformed to thine image. Amen.

The Blameless Life
October 26

He will do it. There is a tone of confidence in these words which bespeaks the unwavering faith of the apostle in the faithfulness and power of God to do for these early Christian folk what indeed is needed by all of us; first, to be sanctified wholly, and secondly, to be preserved without blame until the coming of our Lord Jesus Christ.

'I pray God your whole spirit and soul and body be preserved blameless unto the coming of our Lord Jesus Christ. Faithful is he that calleth you, who also will do it' (1 Thessalonians 5:23, 24).

We can hardly realise how much this meant for men and women reared amid the excesses and evils of those days, when religion was another name for unbridled indulgence. Blamelessness of life, the stainless habit of the soul, self-restraint - these were the attributes of the few whose natures seemed cast in a special mould. And yet how strong the assertion of the apostle that, in the face of the insurmountable difficulties, the God of Peace would do even as much for them.

We must distinguish between *blamelessness* and *faultlessness*. The latter can only be ours when we have passed into the presence of his glory, and are presented faultless before him with exceeding joy (Jude 24). The former, however, is within the reach of each of us, because God has said that he will do it. The Agent of the blameless life is God himself. None beside could accomplish so marvellous a result, and he does it by condescending to indwell the soul. As his glory filled Solomon's Temple, so he waits to infill the spirit, soul, and body of those who trust him.

Prayer: Almighty God, who lovest us, and to whom are known our yearnings for this blessed life; work thou within us, quietly, gently, mightily, ridding us of the love of sin, and producing within us that blamelessness of soul which in thy sight is of priceless value. Amen.

He will do it as the *God of Peace*. The mightiest forces are the stillest. Who ever heard the day break, or detected the footfall of Spring? Who thinks of listening for the throb of gravitation, or the thud of the forces that redden the grape, golden the corn, and cover the peaches with bloom? So God works in the hearts of those who belong to him. When we think we are making no progress, he is most at work. The presence of ozone in the air can only be detected by a faint colour on a piece of litmus paper, and God's work in the soul is only apparent as the bloom of perfect love is shown in the life.

'The wilderness and the solitary place shall be glad for them; and the desert shall rejoice, and blossom as the rose' (Isaiah 35:1).

There are three things that make Springtide in the soul. *The sense of God's Presence.* We know that he is near, though the woods are bare, the frost holds the earth in its iron grip, and the wind gathers together the dead leaves; but we feel him nearer when every hedgerow is clothed with flowers, every bush burns with fire, every tree claps its leafy hands, and every avenue is filled with sweet choristers. *The optimism of an illimitable hope.* Spring is the minstrel of Hope. She takes her lyre and sings of the fair Summer, which is on her way. Life pours through a myriad channels, and shows itself stronger than death for Spring is victorious over Winter, as good shall prove to be over evil. *The exuberance of Love.* Spring is the time of love. The whole creation is attracted by a natural affinity, and love rules in forest and field.

These three elements met in the heart of the returning exiles, and made the world seem young and fair again. The heart views the outer world in lines borrowed from itself. When life is young and gay, all the echoes ring with joy notes; but when the joy of life is fled, what mockery comes back on us from even the tenderest outward scenes!

For us, the lesson is clear. Cherish the sense of the Presence of God; cultivate an illimitable Hope; be conscious of a Love flowing towards you and from you. Dwell on the loving-kindness and tender mercy that have preceded and followed you all the days of your life, and for you, too, the wilderness and solitary place will be glad. After all, life is not altogether what circumstances make it.

Prayer: Lord Jesus, bring us back from our captivity. Fill our hearts with the sense of thy presence, that they may be transformed and renewed, and filled with the spirit of Heaven. Amen.

They may be everything that heart can wish, and yet the Frost-King may reign within and cast its icy mantle over all; whereas there are men and women who have everything adverse in their circumstances, but because they have Spring in their hearts, they find flowers and songs everywhere.

The thirsty land shall become springs of water. You know what thirst means - for human affection, for appreciation, for a word of cheer, for success! Ah, that thirsty land! But when your heart is full of God you will find it musical with streams, and in the places where dragons lay there will be a greenery of rushes.

Gird and Serve
October 28

There are two aspects of rural industry - agricultural, ploughing; pastoral, keeping the sheep. Between them they also cover our service to men for Christ's sake. Some of us are engaged in *ploughing*. In the short wintry days, when the last leaves are falling from the trees, and the skies are covered by dense and dripping clouds, we go forth with our plough, or bearing precious seed. In loneliness, depression, and fear, we tread athwart the furrows, and return crying: 'Who hath believed our report, and to whom is the arm of the Lord revealed?' Or we are called to *keep the flock*, seeking the straying, defending the attacked, tenderly nursing the sick and weak. In either of these avocations we often become weary, and in that condition 'come in from the field'.

'Make ready wherewith I may sup, and gird thyself, and serve me ... and afterward thou shalt eat and drink' (Luke 17:8).

When the spell of hard work is finished, how apt are we to relax! Surely, we think, we may give ourselves to the indulgence of natural and innocent appetite! But that is exactly what our Master does not intend, because he knows the subtle temptation of hours of ease. When we return from our labour, he does not say, 'Go and sit down to meat,' but he meets us on threshold, saying, 'Make ready and serve *me*, till I have eaten and drunken, and *afterward* thou shalt eat and drink.'

From this parable we are surely to infer that our Lord says in effect: 'You have been working for *me*, but I have missed you. You have been so engaged in guiding the plough through the heavy clay, or watching against the lion and bear, that you have forgotten me, and have allowed the hours to pass without speaking to me a single word, or listening for my voice.'

When Christ's work is done, let us turn to our Lord himself, and minister to him; prepare for him a feast of faith and love and joy; of heart-melody and voice-music. After this we may eat and drink. He will even gird himself, and come forth to serve us (John 13:4-14).

Prayer: We desire, dear Lord, that thou shouldest be more to us than thy work. It is not enough for us to plough thy fields or keep thy sheep, we want to serve thee most of all. Help us to keep thee in view all day, and whatsoever our hands find to do, may we do it in love to thyself. Amen.

Kept for Jesus Christ
October 29

'Judas, a bond-servant of Jesus Christ, and bro-ther of James, to them that are called, beloved in God the Fa-ther, and kept for Jesus Christ' (Jude 1 RV marg).

The word *keep* rings like a refrain throughout this letter. It suggests a power which originates in the divine will and operates through the Holy Spirit's energy within us. Behind our willing and working, our choosing and elect-ing; behind all the influences that are brought to bear upon us, there is a gracious and divine movement, in virtue of which we are being *kept for Jesus Christ*. Our spirit is being kept for his Spirit to tenant it; our soul is being kept that his mind may energise it; our heart is being kept as the bowl of a fountain that his love may flow in and out; our imagination and fancy are being kept, that he may utilise them as he did Bunyan and Rutherford; our body is being kept that he may have the use of its members- a vessel meet for the Master's use! Let us realise how much Christ needs each one of us, and how much we shall miss if we neutralise the very purpose for which we were born and sent into the world.

Do not presume on the divine keeping power, for there is always the dread possibility of neutralising it. Keep yourselves therefore in the love of God! Have you the light? Follow the gleam! Are you in mid-current? Do not get turned off into a back eddy! Are you being used by God? Keep under your body and bring it into subjection, lest after having preached to others you may yourself be rejected.

There is one who is able to keep us from stumbling, not only from within, by a garrison, but from without, by sentries which keep watch and ward. We are greater than worlds or suns, greater than time or space, greater than the universe in which we are found, as the child is greater than the royal palace, because the Lord hath need of us. We are *kept for Jesus Christ*; let us not be unmindful or ungrateful, for, throughout the ages, this prayer never ceases to rise from the heart of our Redeemer: 'I pray, not that thou shouldst take them out of the world, but that thou shouldst keep them from evil.'

Prayer: We thank thee, Heavenly Fa-ther, that thou hast called us into the fellow-ship of thy Son. Keep us by thy mighty power through faith unto thy salva-tion and service. Amen.

The Timeless Cross
October 30

What is the meaning of that great word *eternal*? Too often it is employed as though it were synonymous with *everlasting*. But the two words stand for two very different things. *Everlasting* conveys the idea of the duration of time; whereas *eternal* stands for the quality and character of the existence referred to, which is absolutely timeless. The *eternal* is that which is not measured by duration, which has no succession of years, which cannot be described as past or future. It is the dateless present, and can only be used, therefore, of God, the I AM, because he lives in the *eternal now*. He never *was* and never *will be* anything that he is not at this present moment, and only that which partakes of his Being can be termed eternal.

'How much more shall the Blood of Christ who through the Eternal Spirit offered himself without spot to God, purge your conscience from dead works to serve the living God?' (Hebrews 9:14).

When, therefore, we are told that our Lord offered himself to God through the Eternal Spirit, we must believe that in the Cross there was this element of *timelessness*. Our Lord was the Lamb slain from before the foundation of the world (Revelation 13:8). The Cross of Christ has been contemporaneous with all the generations of mankind, and it is this attribute of timelessness which gives the Cross its perennial power. There is a sense in which Christ is always being wounded by our transgressions, bruised by our iniquities, chastised for our peace, and bearing the stripes that procure our healing.

The Cross of Christ stands with open arms to welcome every sinful soul. The nails are not rusted or blunted by the years that have passed since they were driven into the flesh of Christ our Lord. And as we humble ourselves, and submit our proud and selfish soul-life to be nailed with him to the Cross, in the power of the Eternal Spirit, out of suffering comes life to those to whom we minister, as we serve the living God, and we can say with the apostle: 'Death worketh in us, but life in you' (2 Corinthians 4:10-12).

Prayer: We bless thee, Lord Jesus, that thou didst not withhold thyself from the Cross. Enable us by the Eternal Spirit to surrender our life to Calvary, that thy risen life may become manifest in our mortal flesh. Amen.

Giving God Pleasure
October 31

'The Lord taketh pleasure in them that fear him' (Psalm 147:11).

God takes pleasure in our faith. 'Without faith it is impossible to please him'; but surely the alternative is true, that our faith is precious in his sight, though it be only as the touch of the hem of his garment.

God works in us to will and to do of his good pleasure. The apostle says that we ought to walk so as to please God. How can we walk thus? It is not within our power. But how blessed to know that if only we will work out what he works in, and abandon ourselves to him, he will perfect us in every good work to do his will (Hebrews 13:21).

There are many ways in which we may please God. Generosity is a sacrifice well-pleasing and acceptable unto God; obedience is well-pleasing unto the Lord; a holy and humble walk with God, like Enoch's, will elicit this testimony, that it has pleased God. Let us not disappoint him, but 'walk worthy of the Lord unto all pleasing'.

Prayer: O God, we pray that thou wouldst make us what thou wouldst have us become, that we may perfectly please thee, and worthily magnify thy holy name. Amen.

NOVEMBER

OUR DAILY WALK IN THE HOLY SPIRIT

If we live in the Spirit, let us also walk in the
Spirit
(Galatians 5:28)

Walking in the Spirit
November 1

'Walk in the Spirit, and ye shall not fulfil the lust of the flesh' (Galatians 5:16).

When we walk in the Spirit we shall be led by him. In the early stages of life we are apt to be headstrong and impulsive, as Moses when he felled the Egyptian. But as we grow in Christian experience, we wait for the leadings of the Spirit, moving us by his suggestion, impressing on us his will, working within us what afterwards we work out in character and deed. We do not go in front, but follow behind. We are led by the Spirit.

The man or woman who walks in the Spirit has no desire to fulfil the lust of the flesh. The desire for the gratification of natural appetite may be latent in the soul, and may flash through the thoughts, but he does not fulfil it. The desire cannot be prevented, but its fulfilment can certainly be withheld.

When we walk in the Spirit he produces in us the fruit of a holy character. The contrast between the *works* of the fleshly - i.e. the selfish life - and the *fruit* of the Spirit, which is the natural product of his influence, is very marked. In *works* there is effort, the clatter of machinery, the deafening noise of the factory. But *fruit* is found in the calm, still, regular process of Nature, which is ever producing in her secret laboratory the kindly fruits of the earth. How quiet it all is! There is no voice nor language. It is almost impossible to realise what is being effected by a long summer day of sunshine. The growing of autumn arrives with noiseless footsteps. So it is with the soul that daily walks in the Spirit. There are probably no startling experiences, no marked transitions, nothing special to record in the diary, but every year those who live in close proximity witness a ripening wealth of fruit in the manifestation of love, joy, peace, long suffering, gentleness, goodness, faith, meekness, self-control.

Prayer: Gracious Lord! May thy Holy Spirit keep me ever walking in the light of thy countenance. May he fill my heart with the sense of thy nearness and loving fellowship. Order my steps in thy way, and walk with me, that I may do the thing that pleaseth thee. Amen.

The Message of Pentecost
November 2

It is good to know that there is just as much of the Holy Spirit's presence today, wherever two or three are gathered in Christ's Name, as there was in the upper room at Jerusalem. The difference is that we have not the same receptive attitude. We cannot say of God, who is infinite, that there is more of him in this place than in that, or at one moment more than another. He is always equally everywhere. But where hearts are prepared, as were those of the disciples, can there be other than Pentecost! We may have the counterpart of all these wonderful experiences that came to them. The Spirit of God may inspire us, the fire of Divine love may kindle in *our* hearts, and we may obtain a new and marvellous power in speaking to men of the wonderful works of God.

'And they were all filled with the Holy Spirit. Be filled with the Spirit' (Acts 2:4; Ephesians 5:18).

They were all filled with the Spirit, and this is the command laid on us also. Let us ask whether this is our abiding experience, which is not intended for apostles and prophets only, but for the mother with her children, the businessman in his store, the young men and women in office or shop.

The result of this baptism of spiritual power was very remarkable. Thousands were converted and baptised, and they continued *steadfastly*. Such converts are a gain to any church, and it becomes invested with a divine attractiveness and adhesiveness.

The teaching of doctrine, breaking of bread, and fellowship in prayer were the beginning of our Church-ordinances. When young converts are given to any Church, provision should be made for services in which they may take part. The principle of having all things in common seems to have been abandoned by mutual consent. It seemed necessary at the outset that the converts might be trained in Christian living, but it was evidently liable to abuse, and might have allured into the ranks of the Church lazy and undesirable impostors. It is probably a much wiser principle to administer our property for God than to give it away. (See Matthew 25:20, 21; Luke 12:42-44).

Notice their exuberant joy (verses 46, 47). It is characteristic of the presence of the Holy Spirit in the life, and the result is love, joy, peace, etc., which is wonderfully attractive.

Prayer: We ask of thee, Heavenly Father, and claim of thee by faith, this best of all good gifts, thy Holy Spirit, that he may abide with us for ever, and that the fruits of the Spirit may abound in us. Amen.

The Indwelling Spirit
November 3

'I will pray the Father, and he shall give you another Comforter, that he may abide with you for ever' (John 14:16).

The gift of the Holy Spirit was due to the intercession of our Lord, and St Peter refers to it when he says: 'Having received of the Father the promise of the Holy Spirit' (Acts 2:33). In 1 John 2:1 (RV marg) the word *Comforter* is translated *Advocate* - 'One who makes us strong by his presence, as Helper, Guide and Instructor.' Think what this means, to have always beside us, not a vague influence, but a divine Person, who waits to be our strength in weakness, our peace in trouble, our wisdom in perplexity, our conqueror in temptations, our consoler in sorrow. The Lord meant that the Holy Spirit should be to us all that he himself had been. This is the meaning of *Another*. There are two Advocates, or Paracletes. When the one ascended to the glory, the other descended into the hearts of his disciples. 'He abideth with you, and shall be in you.'

'I will not leave you comfortless: *I will come to you.*' Christ had been speaking of sending Another; now he says, I am coming myself, so that we learn that he is so indissolubly one with the Holy Spirit, whom he sends, that the coming of the Spirit is his own coming. Do not look for the Spirit apart from Jesus. As the sun comes in the light, so does Jesus come in the Spirit. When we are filled with the Spirit, we shall not think of him, but of Jesus to whom he bears witness, and when our hearts are taken up with the Lord, we may know that we have received him, who is the Gift of gifts.

Prayer: Thou hast not left us comfortless, O God. May life be renewed in its springs, by the gracious operation of thy Holy Spirit dwelling within us, and leading us from grace to grace. Amen.

Open your whole nature to the entrance of the Holy Spirit. Unlock every door, uncurtain every window, that entering he may fill you with the glorious indwelling of the Father and the Son. 'I will prepare a mansion,' Jesus said; and, 'We will make the holy soul *Our Mansion.*'

'*He shall teach you all things.*' His lesson-book is the life and words of our blessed Lord. We may think that we are fully informed of all that he has said, but as we study the Bible, the Holy Spirit brings us back to them again and again, always revealing new light, and undreamt of depths. Never let a day pass without reading some of the words of Jesus under the guidance of the Holy Spirit.

The Leading of the Spirit
November 4

Teach me to do thy will, i.e. throw the responsibility of your life back on God. The one important thing for you to be absolutely sure about is that you desire, at all costs, to do God's will. If you do not so *desire*, at least you must be willing, and believe that he undertakes it. His people shall be made willing in the day of his power. When this point is settled, then God by his Holy Spirit will sooner or later teach you what he wants to be done, and enable you to do it. Like Samuel, if you say: Speak, Lord, for thy servant heareth, you will hear the voice behind you saying, This is the way, walk in it; this must be said, say it; this needs to be done, do it; and as you endeavour to obey the gentle promptings of the Spirit, you will discover that adequate strength and grace are being poured into your soul.

'Teach me to do thy will; for thou art my God: thy Spirit is good; lead me into the land of uprightness' (Psalm 143:10).

Thy Spirit is good. There is our only hope. If it were not for the infinite goodness, the patient gentleness, the loving forbearance of the Holy Spirit, we could have no chance, for nothing but infinite Goodness could bear with our frailties and backslidings, our lapses into coldness and indifference, our perverseness and obstinacy. But because God's Spirit is good, we may reckon on him pervading us with his holy influence till our evil nature is overcome by his goodness, and we also in our measure become good. It is said of Barnabas that he was a 'good man', because he was full of the Holy Ghost and of faith.

Lead me. The Psalmist's prayer is - Teach me, lead me, quicken me. Let us make this prayer our own. What better guarantee of being led aright than for us to yield ourselves to our gentle gracious Guide. We are like little children that require to be led, as the mother or nurse takes the child by the hand and leads him to the school-house, and fetches him again. Some of us are blind, and need a kindly hand to guide us as we grope in the dark. Let us walk in the Spirit, be led by the Spirit, and be very sensitive to the Spirit. Then we shall instinctively know God's will, and do it.

Prayer
I need a hand to lead me through the darkness,
For I am weak and helpless as a child;
And if alone I have to take my journey,
My feet will stumble on the mountains wild.

Amen.

Witness-Bearing for Christ
November 5

'Ye shall receive power, when the Holy Ghost is come upon you: and ye shall be my witnesses both in Jerusalem, and in all Judaea and Samaria, and unto the uttermost part of the earth' (Acts 1:8).

All machinery needs driving-power. A motor-car may be bright and new, the wheels tyred with rubber, and it may contain the latest contrivances for speed and comfort, but it will not move until the driving-power is applied. So it is with the gospel message. Christ died and rose again, and the work of redemption was finished. His disciples were appointed to carry the tidings of salvation to the world of men, but they could do nothing until they received the power of the Holy Spirit. It is a serious question for each of us - Have I received the Holy Spirit, to be in me the source of power? (Acts 19:2.) If not, is it to be wondered at that we are weak, and our testimony for Christ faltering?

Notice the circles of our life: witnesses in Jerusalem - our home; in Judaea - the society in which we mingle and work; in Samaria - the city or town or village in which we live; the uttermost part of the earth, which represents the claim of the heathen world upon us all. For each of these we have some responsibility. Let us begin at Jerusalem, in our home, and God will lead us on step by step to the great world beyond. Alas, there are many who are eager enough for the 'uttermost parts' while they neglect Jerusalem, and ignore the claims of Judaea!

God wants *witnesses*. A witness is not expected to reason or argue, but simply to state what he saw or heard, and to give facts. We are required to tell people what we have found Jesus to be to ourselves - to say what we have known and tasted and handled of the Word of Life (1 John 1:1-3). Our witness-box may be the shop in which we are employed, or the position in life where we are daily called to rub shoulders with those who know not Christ. Men cannot see him, unless they see him in us. As the moon reflects the sun during the dark hours of the night, so the Church of Christ bears witness to her unseen Lord. In every emergency, let us lift our hearts to Christ, and ask that his Holy Spirit may enable us to be true witnesses for his glory.

Prayer
*My gracious Master and my God,
Assist me to proclaim
And spread through all the earth abroad
The honours of thy Name.*

Amen.

The Fruit of the Spirit - Love!
November 6

Let us lay the emphasis on the word *fruit*, as contrasted with the *works* of the law. In work there is effort, strain, the sweat of the brow, and straining of the muscles; but fruit comes easily and naturally by the overflow of the sap rising from the root to bough and bud. So our Christian life should be the exuberance of the heart in which Christ dwells. The apostle Paul prayed that Christ might dwell in the hearts of his converts, that they might be rooted and grounded in love. It is only when the Holy Spirit fills us to the overflow that we shall abound in love to all men.

'But now abideth Faith, Hope, Love, these three, and the greatest of these is Love' (1 Corinthians 13:13).

We must distinguish between *love* and the *emotion of love*. The former is always possible, though not always and immediately the latter. Our Lord, repeating the ancient words of the Pentateuch, taught us that we may love God with our mind and strength, as well as with our hearts. We all know that the mind and strength are governed not by our emotions, but by our wills. We can love, therefore, by determining to put our thought and energies at the service of another for the sake of God; and we shall find our emotions kindle into a sacred glow of conscious affection.

In the chapter from which our text is taken, St Paul distinguishes between the Gifts of the Church and Love. After passing them in review he comes to the conclusion that all of them, without Love as their heart and inspiration, are worth nothing.

The greatest word in the world is the unfathomable phrase, 'God is Love'. You can no more define the essence of love than you can define the essence of God, but you can describe its effects and fruits. I give Dr Weymouth's translation: 'Love is patient and kind, knows neither envy nor jealousy; is not forward and self-assertive, nor boastful and conceited. She does not behave unbecomingly, nor seek to aggrandize herself, nor blaze out in passionate anger, nor brood over wrongs. She finds no pleasure in injustice done to others, but joyfully sides with the truth. She knows how to be silent; she is full of trust, full of hope, full of patient endurance.'

We ought to take each of these clauses, and ponder whether our lives are realising these high ideals. God send us a baptism of such love!

Prayer: O Lord, my love is like some feebly glimmering spark; I would that it were as a hot flame. Kindle it by the breath of thy Holy Spirit, till thy love constraineth me. Amen.

The Fruit of the Spirit - Joy
November 7

'These things have I spoken unto you, that my joy may be in you, and your joy may be fulfilled' (John 15:11).

Joy is a spontaneous thing. The joy of a little child, like the carol of the lark, arises naturally and easily when certain conditions are fulfilled, so if we would experience the joy of Christ we must realise the conditions he lays down. If we are grafted into the true Vine, there is nothing to check the inflow of his love to us, if we do as he tells us, and forbear doing what he forbids - then Joy will come to us as a flood.

Abide in me - it is inferred, of course, that we are *in* Christ. It was not always so. Once we were outside, separate from Christ, 'aliens from the commonwealth of Israel, strangers from the covenants of promise, having no hope, and without God in the world'. We were shoots in the wild vine, partaking of its nature, involved in its curse, threatened by the axe which lay at its roots. But all this is altered now. The Father, who is the Husbandman, of his abundant grace and mercy, has taken us out of the wild vine, and grafted us into the true, and we have become one with Christ. When, therefore, we are told to abide or remain, it is only necessary that we should stay where he placed us. You are in a lift until you step out of it; you are on a certain road until you take a turning to the right or left, although you may be too engrossed in converse with a friend to think of the road; so amid the pressure of duties and care, you remain in Christ unless you consciously, by sin or unbelief, thrust yourself away from the light of his face into the darkness. When, therefore, the temptation arises to leave the words of Christ for the maxims of the world, resist it and you will still remain in him. Whenever you are tempted to leave the narrow way of his commandments to follow the desires of your own heart, reckon yourself dead to them, and you will remain; whenever you are tempted to forsake Christ's love for jealousy, envy, hatred, resist these impulses and say, 'I elect to remain in the love of God'.

Thus abiding in him you will learn to know his mind, and will naturally ask those things which his love is only too willing to grant. *'Ye shall ask what ye will.'* We must remove any hindrances from the indwelling of Christ, then his love will break out into song, and we shall share in his joy. It will remain in us, and our capacity for joy will be fulfilled.

Prayer: O thou who art the True Vine, I desire to abide in thee, that I may bear abundant fruit for thy glory, and my life be full of thy joy. Amen.

The Fruit of the Spirit - Peace
November 8

Being justified by faith in his blood we have peace! What peace can there be so long as our guilty conscience dreads each footstep, lest it be for its arrest. Though some rich evil-doer is surrounded by the trappings of wealth and state, what is their value, when at any moment he fears that the story of his crime may get out. The first condition of peace is to see your sin borne by Christ in his own body on the Cross.

'Peace I leave with you; my peace I give unto you: not as the world giveth, give I unto you. Let not your heart be troubled, neither let it be fearful' (John 14:27).

The second condition is to keep his words, his commandments. See in every pressing duty your Master's call. Do everything in his name and for his glory. This is the way that Jesus lived. He came down, not to do his own will, but the Father's; and in every incident, as it offered, he felt that God's bell was ringing to some new opportunity of service. Sometimes you must just bear his will, at others you must fulfil it. Say to him each day: 'I delight to do thy will, O my God.' The rule of duty is changed into the service of love, that counts no sacrifice too great, no alabaster box too costly.

Peace for the troubled heart! Jesus is not unmindful of your human affections and anxieties. Does he expect you to be absorbed with his interests, and will he not look after yours? He knows where your loved ones are, their names, their needs, their sorrows. He will do exceeding abundantly for them. Did not David have the lame Mephibosheth to his table, because he was Jonathan's son; did not the Lord heal Peter's wife's mother out of love for Peter? Hand over to Christ all that makes you anxious, both for yourself and others. Transmit and commit! Hand over, and then hands off! Let the peace of Christ keep heart and mind as a sentry, and rule within as the sole judge and arbiter of thought and action. If any thought would intrude, which break in upon our peace, let it be arrested on the threshold; if any passion would arise that threatens the harmony of our inner household, let the solution be the Peace of Christ. 'My peace,' he said, i.e., the peace that kept and ruled him. He calls us to share it, not hereafter only, but here and now. It is his legacy guaranteed to us, by his blood, and by the gift of the Holy Spirit.

Prayer: O Lord, may I not be satisfied with refraining from sin; but as I abide in thee, may I bear the fruits of the Spirit, which are love, joy, and peace, to thy honour and glory. Amen.

The Fruit of the Spirit - Longsuffering
November 9

'If a man suffer as a Christian, let him not be ashamed; but let him glorify God in this name. Inasmuch as ye are partakers of Christ's sufferings, Rejoice!' (I Peter 4:13, 16).

The long-suffering silence of our Lord was the marvel of his foes. 'As a lamb that is led to the slaughter and as a sheep that before her shearers is dumb', he opened not his mouth. Before the high priests, he held his peace. To Pilate he gave no answer. Amid the challenge and reproach of the Cross, he answered nothing, save in benediction and prayer. 'When he was reviled he did not answer with reviling; when he suffered, he uttered no threats, but left his wrongs in the hands of the righteous Judge.'

Surely this has been his habit through the centuries. In every child suffering through drunken parents, in every martyr burnt at the stake, in every innocent sufferer before high-handed oppression, he has been led as a lamb to the slaughter, but how silent he is! Man may murder his servants and blaspheme his name, but he says never a word! This is the purport of one of those strange announcements which make the Book of Revelation so remarkable. 'When he had opened the seventh seal, there was silence in heaven about the space of half-an-hour.' The songs of heaven are hushed; the multitude which cannot be numbered listens to the groans and appeals of their unhelped brethren; the angels stay their anthems, and seem intent on the tragedies about to be described (Revelation 8:1). But there does not appear to be any help.

But remember that silence does not imply indifference. At the very time that our Lord was silent before his judges, he was bearing the sin of the world. When the silence is proclaimed in Heaven, we find that the prayers of the saints are being presented on the throne - prayers of intercession, mingled with much incense of Christ's merit.

It is in this spirit that we are to suffer. We are to conceal our anguish as stoics. No suffering rightly borne is in vain, but in some little way, which you may not understand, you are helping Christ in his redemptive work. Be calm, and quiet, and glad! Pray for those who despitefully use you, and ask that your sufferings, rightly borne, may lead to their conversion, as Stephen's did in the case of Saul.

Prayer: Heavenly Father, of thine infinite mercy, give me such assurance of thy protection amid the troubles and tumults of this mortal life, that I may be preserved in quietness of spirit and in inward peace. Amen.

The Fruit of the Spirit - Gentleness
November 10

It is not easy to cultivate this fruit of the Spirit because it has many counterfeits. Some people are naturally easy-going, devoid of energy and ambition, at heart cowardly, or in spirit mean. Many of us are characterised by a moral weakness and decrepitude that make it easy for us to yield rather than contest in the physical or intellectual arena.

'The Lord's servant must not strive, but be gentle towards all ... forbearing' (2 Timothy 2:24).

But in gentleness there must be the consciousness of a considerable reserve of force. The gentleness of God is combined with omnipotence. The movements of creation, in which there is neither voice nor language, prove the infinite forces which are at work. When a boy is trying to lift or carry a heavy beam, as likely as not there will be a great crash when he reaches the end of his task, and puts it on the ground. His strength is so nearly exhausted that he is only too glad to get rid of his burden, anyhow, and at any cost. But if a strong man shoulders the same burden, and carries it for the same distance, he puts it down *gently*, because he has not taxed his strength and has plenty left.

It is the prerogative of great strength to be gentle. Always remember that you are linked with the Infinite God, and that all things are possible to you. There must also be infinite pity. We must be tolerant and pitiful to those who abuse us, or have been embittered by disappointment, or have been ill-used. It must be our aim to make allowances for such, and always to be sweetly reasonable towards any brusqueness, rudeness and bad manners of their behaviour. Let us be willing to admit that much is due to congenital moroseness. Therefore, we bear gently with the erring, and with those who are out of the way, because we also are encompassed with infirmity.

It is necessary also that there should be a deep humility. Thomas a Kempis says: 'If thou wilt be borne with, bear also with another. Endeavour to be patient in bearing with the defects and infirmities of others, what sort soever they be: for that thyself also hast many failings which must be borne by others.' Our resentment against others should be always tempered by our remembrance of our own sins. So shall we be God's own gentlefolk.

Prayer: O God, our behaviour has not manifested all the fruits of the Spirit, or been full of the graciousness and gentleness of Christ. Forgive us, and enable us so to live that his beauty may be on our faces, the tone of his voice in our speech, the gentleness of his tread in our steps, and unselfishness of his deeds in our hands. Amen.

The Fruit of the Spirit - Goodness
November 11

'He was a good man, and full of the Holy Ghost, and of faith' (Acts 11:24).

Goodness is the radiance or out-shining of a pure and happy Christian soul. It is quick to see and magnify whatever is good in others, as Barnabas was. It is incapable of jealousy or envy, else he would never have gone to Tarsus to seek Saul. The goodness of this man was evinced in his generous donation of the proceeds of his patrimony, and in the ministry of consolation which he exercised among the disciples.

Such goodness is not natural to us. It is the fruit of our union with the true Vine, whose sap may be compared to the Holy Spirit. Before we can be the good man, for whom some would even dare to die, we must become grafted into Christ, that his goodness may make its way through our sour dispositions.

The most difficult thing of all is to continue to manifest this goodness when our lives are united, as Abigail's was, to that of a churl (1 Samuel 25:3). She was a beautiful woman, of good understanding, and full of tact. Her speech, which arrested David when about to avenge himself on Nabal, is a model of good sense. He heartily thanked her for it, as having saved him from a hasty deed, which would have filled his after-life with regret. Nabal was a churl, evil in his doings, and as his servants said,

Prayer: Teach us to exert a wholesome gracious influence on those with whom we come in contact, diffusing in every look and gesture the sweet savour of Christ, and shedding in every act the genial light caught from his face. May the world be really better because we are living in it today. Amen.

'such a son of Belial, that none could speak to him' - a man who did not know what it was to be merry. Nabal was his name and his nature! What a constant pain it must have been to this noble woman to be united to such a churl! That is a test of real goodness; it is a triumph of God's grace.

Guard against stinginess and niggardliness. Give liberally and generously to every good cause. Be very careful of going back on your first intentions, which in the matter of giving are probably more trustworthy than the proverbial afterthoughts. Be always careful to dwell on and extol whatever you find admirable and noble in the character of others.

It was said of Charles Kingsley: 'No fatigue was too great to make him forget the courtesy of less wearied moments, no business too engrossing to deprive him of his readiness to show kindness and sympathy. To school himself to this code of unfaltering high and noble living was truly one of the great works of his life.'

The Fruit of the Spirit - Faith
November 12

Faith is an attribute of the heart, rather than of the head. It is largely intuitive in its first promptings. It is impossible to argue men into faith. Do not think, discuss, or reason too much about *faith*, or you will miss it. It is like *love* in this, that when you turn the dissecting knife on it for the purpose of analysis, its spirit and life vanish, leaving only the faded relics of what was once a thing of beauty and a joy for ever. If, however, turning from *faith* to any object which is worthy of it, you concentrate heart and mind there, almost unconsciously *faith* will have arisen and thriven to maturity.

'Let us hold fast the profession of our faith without wavering; for he is faithful that promised' (Hebrews 10:23).

Faith has two kinds of objective - first a person, and secondly a statement. When we are drawn powerfully towards a person, so as to feel able to entrust our soul, our destiny, our most precious possessions to his care, with an inward feeling of tranquillity and certainty that all is safe with him, and that he will do better for us than we could do for ourselves - that is faith.

We may be attracted by a statement, which appeals to our moral sense; it is consistent with the decisions of our conscience, or perhaps, as the utterance of one in whom we repose utter confidence, it commends itself to us for his sake. We accept that statement; we rest on it. We believe that what it attests as fact either did happen or will happen. We are as sure of it as though we have been able to attest to it by our senses of sight, hearing, or touch. *That also is faith.* 'Faith is a well-grounded assurance of that for which we hope, and a conviction of the reality of the unseen' (Hebrews 11:1 Weymouth).

We must indicate a difference between this faith and 'the faith once delivered to the saints'. The former is the heart that accepts and the hand that reaches out to obtain; the latter is the body of *Truth* to be accepted.

Out of faith comes faithfulness. Faith is your trust in another; faithfulness is your worthiness to be trusted. A faithful soul, one that can be absolutely relied upon, is of great price. Nothing so quickens our faith as to meditate on God's absolute trustworthiness. 'Blessed is the man that trusteth in him.'

Prayer: Give us faith in thy love that never wearies or faints. Whatever else we doubt, may we never question the perfectness of thy loving-kindness. Fulfil in us the good pleasure of thy will, and the work of faith with power. Amen.

The Fruit of the Spirit - Meekness
November 13

The meek man, according to Luther, is the sweet-tempered man. Meekness and lowliness are the two aspects of the same disposition, the one toward man, the other toward God. 'Blessed are the meek,' said our Lord, 'for they shall inherit the earth.' It is profoundly true, because to the meek and chastened, the sweet and tender spirit, there is an unfolding of the hidden beauty of the world which is withheld from the arrogant and proud. Here is a millionaire who has just purchased a beautiful and valuable picture, which he exhibits to all his friends, taking great care to tell them the price he has paid. To him it is written all over the canvas, 'This picture cost me ten thousand pounds!' Does he really possess or inherit its beauty? In his employ is a girl with culture and keen artistic sense. Whenever she gets the chance she enters the room in order to absorb the inspiration of the picture into her soul. Does not she really own it? So it is that the meek inherit all that is good and beautiful. All is theirs, since they are God's.

One of the most exquisite gems in the Psalter is that beginning, 'Lord, my heart is not haughty, nor mine eyes lofty' (Psalm 131). The writer describes himself as a weaned child, which at first works itself into a passion because of the change in its diet; but afterwards becomes soothed and quieted. This is the symbol of the meek and quiet spirit, which in the sight of God is of great price.

To acquire this meekness of spirit, ask the Holy Spirit that he would keep your proud and vainglorious nature nailed to the cross. Next, we must believe that the meek and lowly Jesus is in our hearts, and we must ask him to live, think, and speak through us. Lastly, look to the Holy Spirit for his sacred fire to burn out all that is covetous, envious, proud, angry and malicious within our hearts, for these are the five elements of hell. Let us always take the low seat, confessing that we are not worthy to loose the shoe-latchet of our brethren.

The Fruit of the Spirit - Self-Control
November 14

In his early life Paul must have been keen on sport! He uses the phrases for the gymnast, the boxer, and the racer. He had probably stood, many times, watching the great games, which were held in various parts of the Greek-speaking world. He knew the long and arduous training through which competitors had to pass.

'Every man that striveth for the mastery is temperate in all things. Now they do it to obtain a corruptible crown; but we an incorruptible' (1 Corinthians 9:25).

Paul was running a race for an imperishable wreath. He had no doubt as to his goal, and therefore did not run uncertainly. He went straight as an arrow to its mark, and his mark was to win souls for Christ. To gain some, to save some, was his passion (verse 22). He needed to discipline himself, putting aside much that was innocent in itself, and which others could enjoy without reproach (Romans 14:13-21). The apostle was also engaged in a boxing-match, his own body being the antagonist. He knew that spiritual power existed for his appropriation in Christ, but to have it he must be a spiritual man, and to be that necessitated the subdual of his fleshly appetites.

We must exercise 'self-reverence, self-knowledge, self-control'. It is best to hand over the whole of our nature to the Master, and ask him to direct, control, suggest each day whatever we think, or do, or say. It is infinitely happier to be Christ-controlled than self-controlled. Happy are they who from the earliest are able to subordinate the delights of sense, however innocent, to some high quest of the spirit. The soldier has to forfeit many things which are legitimate for the civilian, because he must be able to march rapidly from place to place. He has to forego the use of many comforts, but he is compensated if his name is placed on the honours list. The husbandman has to submit to hardships of weather, and to encounter difficulties and discomforts which do not occur in the lives of others; but there is no other way if he is to procure the fruits of his toil. These deny themselves for lower considerations, but we have an infinitely higher object in view; but by so much the more should we lay aside every weight. Never forget Jesus Christ risen from the dead, your great Exemplar and Life-giver - the source of all spiritual power.

Prayer: Heavenly Father, engraft thy Son, Jesus Christ my Lord, inwardly in my heart, that I may bring forth the fruit of holy living, to the honour and praise of thy Name. Amen.

Jesus, the Life-Giving Spirit
November 15

'The first Adam became a living soul; the last Adam became a Life-Giving Spirit' (1 Corinthians 15:45).

Are you, my friend, in the first Adam or the second? It is a vital question, and it would well repay you to put aside all else in order to give a considered answer to this question. You ask for the fundamental difference between the first Adam and the second. The apostle states it clearly in this chapter from which our text is taken. The contrast between the two is the *soul*-life of the first and the *Spirit*-life of the second. This is the distinction which Jesus made at the beginning of his ministry, and it pervades the New Testament. The sphere of Christianity is the realm of the spirit. Its object is to lift man from the soul-level to the spirit-level.

The soul is the centre of our personality. It is *you*, or *I*, or any other *person*! From it we look on two worlds. To the material world we are related by the organs of touch, sight, smell, taste and hearing. To the eternal world we are related by the organs of the spirit. We have the option of descending by the spiral staircase *downward* to materialism, or of ascending *upward* to fellowship with God. Alas, that too often we descend to the lure of the savoury pottage, instead of climbing the ladder which reaches to Heaven.

It is clear that we must die to the self-life, to the promptings, suggestions and solicitations of the *ego*, which is entrenched in the soul. Self is the root of our alienation from the Life of God. All the evils of fallen angels and man have their birth in the pride of self. On the other hand, all the blessedness of the heavenly life is within our reach, when the self-life is nailed to the Cross of Jesus.

Prayer: Behold, O Lord, I am thy servant, prepared for all things; for I desire not to live unto myself, but unto thee; and Oh, that I could do it worthily and perfectly! Amen.

How is this self-life to be brought to death? Only by our identification with the Cross on which Jesus died. We were nailed there in the purpose of God, and we must accept that position and extract its help by a living faith. It was by the Eternal Spirit that Jesus offered himself unto God, and it is by that same Spirit that we, too, may say: 'I have been crucified with Christ; nevertheless I live, yet not I, but Christ liveth in me.' There must be an exchange of lives, from the self-life to the life of the Crucified and Ascended Saviour, communicated by the Holy Spirit.

Daily Renewal
November 16

This seventh chapter of Romans reflects, as in a mirror, the inward conflict of the Christian soul, who has not yet learned to appropriate the full power of the Holy Spirit. It will be noticed that the personal pronoun 'I' occurs frequently, while there is no word of the Holy Spirit who lusts or strives against the flesh. It is the endeavour of a man to keep pure and holy in the energy of his own resolutions, and by the putting forth of his own power and will. But as Satan cannot cast out Satan, so the will of man is unable to exorcise its own evil.

'For the good that I would I do not; but the evil which I would not, that I do. Who shall deliver me ...? I thank God through Jesus Christ our Lord' *(Romans 7:19-25).*

We turn, thankfully, therefore to the eighth chapter, which is as full of the power of the Holy Spirit to overcome evil, as the seventh is full of human endeavour. It is only when we learn to hand over our inner self to the Spirit of God that we can become more than conquerors through him that loved us. As long as the conflict is in our own strength, there is nothing for it but to experience the up and down, fickle and faulty life, which the apostle describes so graphically.

How is it that the soul of man is so full of evil, and that it is unable to deliver itself by its resolutions which lack the necessary dynamic force, we cannot tell. But we find this 'law of sin and death warring in our members and bringing us into captivity'. It is a wretched experience, indeed, when we find the current running so swiftly against us, and carrying us down in spite of our strenuous desire to stem and conquer it. Who has not, again and again, experienced failure after the most earnest desire to do right? The bitterness of our origin overcomes the better choice, of which in our noblest moments we are conscious.

Prayer: O God, may we live very near to thee to-day, not in the energy of our own resolution, but by the anointing and indwelling of the Holy Spirit, who shall teach us to abide in Christ.

It is a great comfort to know that the Spirit of God is prepared to renew our inward man day by day (2 Corinthians 4:16), and to make us free from the law of sin and death. It is the daily renewal that we need. Day by day, and hour by hour, it is necessary to seek by faith a fresh infusion of the power of the Holy Spirit, that we may be overcomers.

If our wayward hearts tend to stray, recall us before we have gone too far. Amen.

The Secret of the Inner Way
November 17

'Walk in the way of good men, and keep the paths of the righteous' (Proverbs 2:20).

This chapter abounds in references to the *Way* and *Path*. *Walk* occurs three times, *paths* seven, and *ways* five. Here we read of the way or path by which good and righteous men have preceded us. The old Christian mystics were fond of talking of the inward way and its various stages. They said that God was alone the centre and satisfaction of the human soul, that we must advance along the pathway traversed by holy souls before us until we have realised the motto of Monica: 'Life in God and union there.'

True knowledge of God and union with him are only to be attained by those who will not shrink before the perils and steepness of the strait gate and narrow way. It is not necessary to leave the body to reach the inner secret of God. The path may be trodden on this side of the grave. Stony and steep it may be, but when it climbs the crest, and the whole glory of the heavens is in view, the soul is satisfied. In the attainment of true wisdom God is willing, yea, eager to give, but we must be sincere and earnest in our desire to obtain (verses 1-9). Notice the many words that are employed to stir up our search. Receive! Hide! Incline the ear and apply the heart! The treasures of God,

Prayer: Make us more conscious, O Lord, we beseech thee, of the indwelling of thy Holy Spirit: may he witness within us that in spite of our sin we are still thy children: may he enable us to mortify the deeds of the body, and to reckon ourselves dead to the solicitations of the flesh. Amen.

like those of the mine, do not lie on the surface, but no labour is more profitable. Our Heavenly Father not only gives good things to them that ask him, but he becomes our Shield and Buckler, our Protector and Guide (verses 7, 8).

These are the stages of the inner Way, which the saints have trodden before us: *Detachment* from the ambitions, passions and sins of nature; *Attachment*, i.e. the attitude of fellowship with Christ; *Illumination*, which reveals to the soul its unworthiness; *Union with God*. This is the experience of few, but they who have described it remind us that eye hath not seen, nor ear heard, what God's Spirit reveals to those who love and wait for him. But you must be prepared to sacrifice all. He who seeks diamonds, or gold, will face hardships and relinquish much that other men hold dear, that he may prosecute his quest. Not otherwise must it be with those who would understand the fear of the Lord and find the knowledge of God.

Abounding in this Grace also
November 18

If St Paul were living today he would surely be in great request to preach the special sermons for the gathering of funds to maintain religious and charitable work. Judging by this chapter, he must have been inimitable in extracting gifts for all purposes from God's people. He stirs the Corinthians up by reminding them of the liberality of the churches in Macedonia, notwithstanding their deep poverty. He reminds them that as they abound in so many gifts and graces, they must see to it that they are not lacking 'in this grace also' (verse 7). He quotes the example of our blessed Lord, and reminds them that they owe everything to his condescension. He suggests that the one thing God wants is willingness to give, and that he accepts the desire of the poor man to give all with as much delight as the vast possessions of the millionaire (Mark 12:41-44).

'If there be a willing mind, it is accepted according to that a man hath, and not according to that he hath not' *(2 Corinthians 8:12).*

What a wonderful text is the ninth verse! George Herbert, in one of his poems, depicts our Lord stripping himself as he descended from the Throne to the manger-bed of Bethlehem. He put off his tiara, and its jewels became the milky way; he laid aside his sceptre, and it became the lightning flash; he put off his girdle, and it became the rainbow; he doffed the robes of his royalty, and they became the sunset clouds! But how wonderful it is to think that the Lord of Glory became so poor that he had nowhere to lay his head, that he was often without food and always dependent upon charity.

But because he was poor, we are made rich; because he was homeless he has opened to us the 'many mansions'; because he was stripped of all we may wear the white robes, and sit with him in heavenly places. He calls to each one of us to minister to himself in caring for the least of his brethren. We can only really help people when we impoverish ourselves, but in the end we are not losers. God will be in no man's debt. What we keep we lose; what we give is like scattered seed that comes back in bountiful harvests. Lay your heart against the heart of Christ, until you become filled with his love and spirit, and are content to call nothing your own. Be the steward of everything you possess for his glory and the help of others.

Prayer: O God, we have nothing worth our giving, or thy receiving; our best was given to us by thee. Graciously accept us and all that we have. Whatever thou hast given, enable us to count it a stewardship for others. Amen.

'He that taketh not his cross, and followeth after me, is not worthy of me' (Matthew 10:38).

How wonderful it is that in the thirty-seventh verse of this chapter, our Lord faces the whole race of men, and claims their supreme love, asking that they should love him more than their dearest from whom they have derived, or to whom they have given life. He does not attempt to justify his demand, and the only consideration that makes his claim reasonable is that he is the Son of God, who died for us on the cross, and that each one of us has a separate place in his divine-human love. What a rebuke lies in the words: 'is not worthy of me'. Surely in this sense there is no one of us worthy of our divine Lord.

Christ asks for the surrender not of the heart only, but of the life. Self-denial for his sake is the badge of the disciple. It is a strange procession of cross-bearers, following the Crucified. Each man has his own special form of self-denial, which is required of him, and it must be undertaken willingly.

Prayer: Be the corrective, the complement, of every trouble and need through which we may be called to pass; if we suffer for Christ, may we not threaten; if we are spoken against, may we answer with blessing; if we are tried by the fiery trial, may we rejoice; if we are lonely and desolate, may the Holy Spirit make Jesus real to us. Amen.

Of course, it must be understood that the confession to which Christ summons us does not consist in a single utterance of the lips; it is the constant acknowledgment of him by voice and life, maintained to the end, and the context makes it clear that this will have to be maintained in the face of opposition, and that often in its bitterest form - the opposition of the home. Many of us would find it easier to face outward persecution and the tyrant's frown, than to stand against the light banter, the sneers and suspicions, the cruel words of those who live within the home. In every age there have been those who have had to stand absolutely alone for Christ, not hating their dear ones but being hated by them because of their allegiance to Christ, and destined to find the most dutiful love and care repaid by stony indifference or active persecution. Nothing is harder to bear, and there is no other course for us but to silence the enemy and the avenger by patient continuance in well-doing, always believing that God is faithful, and that he will not allow us to be tempted above that we are able to bear.

Stilling Life's Storms
November 20

This Psalm contains five wonderful pictures of life. First, we see the travellers who have lost their way (verses 4-9); next, prisoners and captives who sit in darkness (verses 10-16), then we see a sick-room (verses 17-22); next, a terrific storm at sea (verses 23-32); and finally, the lovely picture of a desert land being turned into a fertile landscape (verses 33-38). The refrain, calling upon men to praise the Lord for his goodness, is repeated four times, and the Psalm closes with the fervent thought that all who are wise will give heed to the various dealings of God, as shown in these acts of his loving-kindness.

'He maketh the storm a calm, so that the waters thereof are still. Then they are glad because they be quiet; so he bringeth them unto their desired haven' (Psalm 107:29, 30).

In all lives there are periods of tumult and storm. We are whirled about by angry billows, and it seems as though we shall never reach the harbour of peace and rest. Some give themselves up to such experiences as a fate which they cannot avoid, or attempt to drown their fears and dull their senses to suffering and danger. But faith cleaves its way through the murky mists and driving cloud-wrack, and establishes a sure connection with the throne of the Eternal Father. This is what the New Testament calls the anchorage of the soul, and however severe the storm that sweeps over the earth, the soul that shelters there is safe. 'Then they cried unto the Lord in their trouble, and he delivered them out of their distresses.'

At this moment you may be passing through a storm of outward trouble. Wave after wave beats upon you, as one calamity is followed by another, until it seems as though the little barque of your life must be overwhelmed. Look up to God and cry to him. He sees you, and will not allow you to be engulfed.

Or you may be experiencing inward sorrow. Your affections have been misplaced; the one you love has deceived and failed you, and the sky is now dark and stormy. The one resort of the soul when it is hard driven, is to look up to him who holds the winds in his fist, the waters in the hollow of his hand, and who cannot forget or forsake those who cry to him.

Prayer: O God, we will praise thy Name for thy goodness to us, and for thy wonderful works to the children of men. May thy gentle voice hush our fears, and still life's storms into a great calm. Amen.

'But Mary stood without at the tomb weeping... Jesus saith unto her, Mary. She turned herself, and saith unto him, Rabboni, which is to say, Master' (John 20:11, 16).

When the disciples had returned to their home, Mary stood at the door of the sepulchre, weeping. Then she took one more look at the place where he had lain. Thus still we look down into the grave of ordinances, of past emotions, of old and sacred memories, seeking for the Redeemer. The angel-guards sought in vain to comfort her; but what could they do for her, who longed to hear his voice only?

The sense of a Presence behind - or perhaps, as St Chrysostom finely suggests, because of an expression of love and awe that passed over the angels' faces - led her to turn herself, and she saw one standing there whom she supposed to be the gardener. Then he called her by the old familiar name, with the same intonation of voice, and she knew that it was her Lord. The knowledge that he was there, to whom she owed all, thrilled her and she answered in the country tongue they both knew so well, 'Rabboni!'

Does not this suggest that in the new life, which lies beyond, we shall hear again the voices speak with which we have been familiar? 'As we have borne the image of the earthly, we shall also bear the image of the heavenly, and shall have fellowship again with those whom we have lost awhile.'

'Rabboni' is 'my Master'. *We must take the Risen Lord not only as our Saviour, but our Master.* Too many look to him only for what he shall do for them in the way of salvation and deliverance from sin, but we shall never realise the fullness of either until we fall at his feet and own him Master and Lord.

It must be a personal act - 'My Master'. It is not enough that he should be Lord of others, or of his Church. He must be *thine*. Give *your all* for *his all*. Begin to live as if there were none but he and you in this world. He is ever appealing to us: 'Son! Daughter! Give me thine heart, thy love.'

When he is Master, we obey his bidding. It is useless to call him 'Lord, Lord', and not do the things which he says. Ours must be the alert ear, the swift foot. 'Go, tell!' So he speaks still.

Prayer: Open our eyes to see the Face of Christ looking down upon us amid household duty or daily business. Give us a quick ear for thy voice, and may we go on doing good, as thou shalt give us opportunity. Amen.

The God of Patience and Comfort
November 22

We all need Patience and Comfort, especially in times of stress and difficulty. Patience under long-drawn-out trial; Comfort, when the heart is at breaking-point; and God is the source of each! The God of Patience! 'I waited patiently for the Lord, and he inclined unto me and heard my cry.' The God of Comfort! 'As one whom his mother comforteth, so will I comfort you.' Let us hush all other voices of consolation, that we may listen to the still small voice of the Comforter, who proceeds from the Father and the Son.

'Now the God of patience and of comfort grant you to be of the same mind one with another according to Jesus Christ' (Romans 15:5).

But notice that he speaks through the patience and comfort of Holy Scripture. 'Whatsoever things were written aforetime were written for our learning, that through patience and comfort of the Scriptures we might have hope.' What the Bible has been to the martyrs, to the sufferers on the rack, and to the harried Covenanters of the Scottish moors; to the myriads of unknown souls who have been persecuted, to lonely exiles and bereaved hearts, can never be told.

If we were condemned to banishment, and could take only one Book of the Bible with us to Patmos, or to prison, we should find it extremely difficult which to choose. Some would select the Psalter, some the Fourth Gospel, some would probably decide on that wonderful anonymous writing, the Epistle to the Hebrews. And in each they would have matter enough to explore for a lifetime. Always his Spirit will be teaching and enabling us. Always his Shepherd rod and staff will lead us to living fountains of water. He is always realising more deeply in us the Divine ideal, and increasing our capacity for God.

Prayer: Comforter of the comfortless, bind my soul with thine in intercession! Wherever there are broken hearts, bind them: captives, release them. Bless especially my loved ones. Visit us with thy salvation, and suit thy gifts to our several needs. Amen.

Is not this comforting! The minister, to whom you owe your conversion, or who has helped your Christian growth, may die or be removed; the friend on whom you depended for help and guidance may have to leave you, but our Saviour will continue his care of us, his nurture of our growth, his unfailing intercession, when the sun has ceased to shine, and the universe is wrapped up as a worn-out garment. His ministry is unchangeable. The God of Patience and Comfort will never fail us!

The God of Hope
November 23

We all need to abound in Hope. Hope is the artist of the soul. Faith fills us with joy and peace, which brim over in Hope. When Faith brings from God's word the materials of anticipation and expectation, Hope transfers the fair colours to her palette, and with a few deft dashes of her brush delineates the soul's immortal and unfading hope. Faith thus excites Hope to her fairest work, until presently the walls of our soul become radiant with frescoes. Our faith rests on God's word, and hope rests on faith, and such hope cannot be ashamed. It is the anchor of the soul, which enters that which is within the veil, and links us to the shores of eternity (Hebrews 6:18, 19).

Faith rests on the promises of God. She does not calculate on feeling, is indifferent to emotion, but with both hands clings to some word of promise, and looking into God's face, says: 'Thou canst not be unfaithful.' When God has promised aught to thee, it is as certain as if thou hadst it in hand. Faith not only takes the word of God, and rests her weight on it, but often when hard-pressed goes beyond the Bible back to God himself, and argues that God is faithful and cannot deny himself. Because God is God, he must ever act worthily of himself.

It was thus that Moses argued when he was with him in the Holy Mount - to do thus, would not be worthy of thyself! (Numbers 14:13-20). We may be assailed with a hundred questions of doubt in the day, but must no more notice them than a barking cur. A businessman once said that when he is convinced of the rightness of a certain course, he is sometimes assailed by doubts which arise like the cloud-mist of the valley, or the marsh gas from the swamp; but when thus tempted, he turns to the promises of God, often reading three or four chapters of the Old Testament. This brings him in touch with the eternal world, filling him with joy and peace and abounding hope in believing, through the power of the Holy Ghost. They shall not be ashamed that hope in him!

Prayer: Make me, O Lord, to know the Hope of thy calling, the riches of the glory of thine inheritance in the saints, and the exceeding greatness of thy power toward them that believe. Above all, grant me the spirit of wisdom and revelation in the knowledge of thyself. Amen.

The God of Peace
November 24

We all need Peace! There are sources of Peace which are common to all men. The peace of a happy home; of an increasing business and enlarging influence; of the respect and love of our fellows. As a man is conscious of these, he is inclined to say with Job, 'I shall die in my nest.' We can all understand a peace like that; but there is a 'peace that passeth understanding'. It is too deep for words. It is like the pillowed depths of the ocean, which are undisturbed by the passing storm. Here is a sufferer, almost always in acute pain, and needing constant attention, and yet so happy. Joy and Peace, like guardian angels, sit by that bedside; and Hope, not blindfolded, touches all the strings of the lyre, and sheds sunshine - how do you account for it? Let the sceptic and the scoffer answer! Here is a peace that passes understanding which comes from the God of Peace.

For the Christian soul there is a silver lining in every cloud; a blue patch in the darkest sky; a turn in the longest lane; a mountain view which shall compensate the steepest ascent. Wait on the Lord, and keep his way, and he shall exalt thee to inherit the land. The thing impossible shall be; because all things are possible to God.

The peace of God is the peace of the Divine Nature - the very tranquillity which prevails in the heart of the God of Peace. It was of this that Jesus spoke when he said, 'My peace I give unto you;' for his own being was filled and blessed with it during his earthly career. 'The Lord of Peace himself give you peace always.'

There are three things against which we must ever be on our guard lest they rob us of our peace. First, unconfessed sin; second, worry; third, the permission of an unrebuked selfish principle. The apostle says, 'Let the Peace of God rule in your hearts.' The Greek word means *arbitrate*. Let God's Peace act as umpire.

We shall not escape life's discipline. We may expect to abound here, and to be abased there. But amid all, God's Peace, like a white-winged sentinel angel, shall come down to garrison our heart with its affections, and our mind with its thoughts.

'Now the God of Peace be with you all' (Romans 15:33). 'Having made peace through the blood of his Cross' (Colossians 1:20).

Prayer: I humbly ask, O God, that thy Peace may be the garrison of my heart and mind; that it may ever rule within me, asserting itself over the tumultuous passions that arise within. And out of this Peace may I arise to serve thee. Amen.

How the Song of the Lord began
November 25

Hezekiah, at the age of twenty-five, came to the throne, and set himself to reverse his father's evil policy. The doors of the Temple were reopened, and under his direction the Levites were commissioned to cleanse the desecrated courts of the rubbish and filth that had been allowed to accumulate. After eight days of strenuous labour, they were able to report that their work was successfully accomplished; that the altar of burnt offering, and the table of shewbread were ready for the renewal of their wonted service. It was good news, and in the early morning of a memorable day, the king, accompanied by his princes and officers of state, took part in a solemn service of re-dedication. Amid the tense expectancy of the vast congregation which had assembled, Hezekiah commanded that the burnt sacrifice should be offered; and 'when the burnt offering began, the song of the Lord began also.'

These ancient sacrifices have passed for ever. 'Sacrifice and offering thou dost not desire; mine ears hast thou pierced (nailing me to thy cross); burnt-offering and sin-offering hast thou not required. Then said I, Lo, I come, I delight to do thy will, O my God!' To yield up one's life to the Saviour, to surrender our lives for others for his sake, to maintain the steadfast resolve of self-sacrifice - *this* surely fulfils the conception of the burnt offering, which the king ordered that morning as the symbol of national devotion to the will of God. Can we wonder that the Song of the Lord began also? Does not that same Song arise in every heart when the sacrifice of love and obedience begins?

It is the self-contained life that has made itself snug within its four walls, sound-proof, sorrow-proof, as it thinks, and love-proof, which is song-less and pitiable.

Our Lord said, 'Whosoever shall lose his life for my sake shall find it.' That finding is the correlative and source of the 'Song of the Lord'. Unite thyself with Jesus on the cross, and one day thou wilt find thyself sharing with him the New Song of accomplished Redemption!

Prayer: Give us loving and thankful hearts. May thy mercies bind us like cords to the horns of the altar. Let our whole nature be consecrated for thine indwelling, and as the burnt offering begins, may the Song of the Lord begin also in our hearts. Amen.

The Grace of Gratitude
November 26

God's benefits are here compared to a cup or chalice brimming with salvation. It seems natural to speak of man's lot, either of sorrow or joy, as the cup of which he drinks. The cup or lot of our life brims with instances of God's saving help - 'my cup runneth over', and we ask, how may we thank him enough? What shall we render unto him, for all his gracious help?

'What shall I render unto the Lord for all his benefits toward me?' (Psalm 116:12).

There are many answers, and the first is, that we will *Take*. In other words, as one has truly said, *Taking* from God is the best giving to God, for God loves to *give*. St James says: 'He is the giving God, who gives not only liberally, but with no thought of personal advantage, and for the mere joy of giving.' What, then, will gratify him more than to be trusted, to find recipients for his gifts, to know that we are prepared to be his poor debtors, owing him ten thousand talents, with nothing to pay, but still receiving and receiving from his great heart of Love. Nothing hurts God more than that we should not take what he offers - 'God so loved that he *gave*', and when we refuse to appropriate his greatest gift, we inflict the deepest indignity and dishonour of which we are capable.

Then, *we must call upon his name* (verses 13, 17). Take the name of the Lord as a test. Friendships, plans, profits, amusements, studies - all these cups should be tested by this one mighty Talisman.

We must be sure to pay our vows (verses 14, 18; Ecclesiastes 5:4, 5). We make vows in our trouble, which we sometimes forget when it is past. Surely, it is the height of ingratitude not to redeem our promissory notes. All devoted things, which are laid on God's altar, are absolutely his, and the giver forfeits all rights to their disposal.

Our gratitude demands the gift of ourselves (verse 16). When Robinson Crusoe freed the poor captive, the man knelt before his deliverer, and put his foot upon his neck, in token of his desire to be his slave; and the love of Christ, who loosed us from our bonds, constrains us to live not to ourselves but unto him (Revelation 1:5 RV). Loosed from the cords of sin, we become bound to the service of love.

Prayer: Father, we would thank thee for all the benefits that we have received from thy goodness. The best thanksgiving we can offer to thee is to live according to thy holy will; grant us every day to offer it more perfectly, and to grow in the knowledge of thy will and the love thereof. Amen.

The Garden of our Soul
November 27

'A pleasant vine-yard, sing ye of it. I the Lord do keep it; I will water it every moment: lest any hurt it, I will keep it night and day' (Isaiah 27:2, 3 see RV marg).

The vineyard and its divine keeper. God's redeemed children are here compared to a vineyard. We remember also our Lord's references to the vineyard in Matthew 21:33-41 and John 15. God our Father is the husbandman or keeper, watching, watering, and guarding always. There is no anger in his heart against *us*, but against our sins, and he is ever battling with these, as the gardener digs up the weeds and burns them in the bonfire.

God's moment-by-moment care of us is our one hope. The dry winds of this world are always parching the tender verdure of our inner life making the soil hard and impenetrable. We shrivel and wither beneath the sun of prosperity, but God is ever seeking to water us with his grace.

Sometimes it is by the mist - 'There went up a mist from the earth, and watered the whole face of the ground' (Genesis 2:6). Thus it was in Eden, and so it is in our experience. The mystery of life, its uncertainty, our sense of impotence and ignorance, the withdrawal of our beloved ones within the envelopment of the unseen, the strange sense of incomprehensible enigma - these are some of the mists that help to soften our character.

Sometimes by the dew - 'I will be as the dew unto Israel'. On clear nights the air deposits its moisture in dewdrops. How beautiful it is in the spring morning! In the tropics it is profuse, so that Gideon was able to wring a bowlful of water from the fleece which he had spread out! Yet how gently it distils - not a flower stalk, however fragile, is broken. So the gracious influences of the Holy Spirit gather on our souls and refresh us. We know not whence or how, but are sweeter, gentler, tenderer for his beneficent care. The sun does not scorch us, the heat does not exhaust.

Prayer: Forbid, O Heavenly Father, that we should lose the freshness, fertility and beauty which thou canst maintain in hearts which are open to thee. May we be like a watered garden. Amen.

Let us enter into a holy fellowship with God in his antagonism to whatever is unworthy and evil in our lives, taking hold of his strength, and being at peace with him. Then shall we be blossom and bud, and become his pleasant vineyard; and fill the world with refreshing fruit. 'Thou shalt be like a watered garden.' 'By their fruits ye shall know them.'

Spiritual Food
November 28

It is the artifice of many advertisers of the present day to secure customers for patent foods by associating the figure of some person in perfect health and strength with the article of diet they desire to recommend. It is certain that spiritual health and power can only be produced when the spirit is dieted on the word of God.

From his earliest boyhood, the young Timothy had been instructed in the Holy Scriptures. When the apostle first met him there was a rich subsoil of knowledge of the Old Testament, in which the seed of the gospel message readily germinated. Perhaps the reason for the instability of some of our young people is that Eunice and Lois in our Christian homes fail to do for the children what mothers and grandmothers did for previous generations.

It is not necessary to discuss all that is involved in Inspiration, as the apostle uses that term nor is it necessary to be profoundly familiar with books of theology before we are able to pronounce on it. Inspiration is a quality which is apprehended by the spiritual taste, just as the tongue can detect sweetness or briny saltness of flavour. The Bible is the word of God, and the whole of it is profitable for one of the four uses mentioned in verse 16.

We should read the Bible daily, and it is helpful to use the references and discover the parallel passages. It is good sometimes to kneel down and turn what we read into prayer. We must get beyond the outside husk to the inner kernel, as we 'read, mark, learn and inwardly digest'. Ask the Spirit of God to give you some message directly for yourself.

There are some kinds of food which are destitute of the properties that sustain life. But Christ is all we want, and every faculty of our nature can be satisfied in him. He is the Living Bread, on whom we must feed if we would have eternal life. It is not the Bible only, but the Christ of whom it speaks who is the true spiritual food of the soul. 'He that cometh to me shall never hunger; and he that believeth on me shall never thirst.'

'All Scripture is given by inspiration of God, and is profitable. ... that the man of God may be perfect, thoroughly furnished unto all good works' (2 Timothy 3:16, 17). 'I am the living bread which came down from heaven: if any man eat of this bread, he shall live for ever' (John 6:51).

Prayer: O Lord, open thou mine eyes, that I may behold wondrous things out of thy law. Thy word is a lamp unto my feet, and a light unto my path. Amen.

The Message of the Seraphim
November 29

'Then flew one of the Seraphim unto me, having a live coal in his hand... and said, Lo, this hath touched thy lips; and thine iniquity is taken away, and thy sin purged' (Isaiah 6:6, 7).

Each Seraph had six wings. 'With twain he covered his face.' Here was *Reverence*, which is one of the noblest traits in character, whether angelic or human. The statesman who beneath human movements sets himself to understand the divine purpose. The artist, whether in music, poetry or painting, who discovers a Presence which fills him with elevated and pure ideals. The scientist who compares himself to a child gathering pebbles on the shores of a boundless ocean. These resemble the Seraphim with their veiled faces.

'With twain they covered their feet' - *Self-effacement and Humility*. If we begin to think and talk of ourselves, we prove that we are second-rate. We may be attractive and useful, but we have not attained the first and best. The angels forget themselves in their absorbing love for God. When shall we forget ourselves in his constraining love, so as not to live to ourselves, but to him who died for us and rose again!

'With twain they did fly' - *Obedient Service*. The third part of our energy should be spent thus. Two-thirds of communion and worship must work themselves out in service, else we become dreamy mystics. Such life becomes contagious - 'One cried to another.' There is always a cry going forth from the eager soul which is right with God, and this awakens response in others and stirs them to service. One bird in the woodlands singing at dawn will wake the whole forest-glade to music. The Seraphim declared that the whole earth was full of God's glory!

Prayer: Give us, O Lord, more than an angel's love, for thou hast redeemed us. Give us the swiftness of an angel's obedience; may we do thy commandments, and hearken to the voice of thy word. Cleanse us from all iniquity and purge us from sin, and use us in thy service. Amen.

The prophet saw his need of cleansing: 'Woe is me! I am a man of unclean lips.' We do not need to agonise with God for cleansing, but to open our hearts in confession. Immediately one of the Seraphim will fly to meet our need. Nay, the Lord himself - Lo, this live coal, saturated with blood and steeped in flame, which combines Calvary and Pentecost, hath cleansed our iniquity and purged our sin! Then we shall cry: 'Here am I; send me.' Redeemed, forgiven, and cleansed sinners make the best evangelists!

Our Heritage and our Goal
November 30

We are far from being perfect. When in our deepest moments, we ascend into the Holiest, on the wings of faith and prayer, we pass through a vast host of sympathetic spirits, all of whom are devoted to the same Lord and Master, and are joining in the same act of worship. Many of them have known and helped us in our earthly life, and they have been sent forth to minister to us, and to help us on our way. 'Ye are come to the spirits of just men made perfect.'

'Ye are come unto the City of the living God... to God the Judge of all, and to the spirits of just men made perfect, and to Jesus the Mediator of the New Covenant' (Hebrews 12:22-24).

We are also come unto God, the Judge of all. When Moses stood before God on the Mount, he said: 'I exceedingly fear and quake.' But we may come with boldness to the footstool of the Eternal Throne, though our God is a consuming fire, for in Christ Jesus we stand accepted. He is the Mediator of the New Covenant, and his blood speaks better things than that of Abel. That blood cried against Cain. But the blood of Jesus cries on our behalf; it has opened the way into the Holiest; has cleansed us from our sins; has ratified the New Covenant, and is the pledge of our redemption.

Therefore, although we realise our sinfulness and imperfection, let us arise into the unseen, and join with the one Church of the Redeemed in heaven and on earth. We are come to it in the purpose of God, and by the all-sufficing work of Christ our Lord, but let us see to it that we come also in our spiritual realisation, communion, and fellowship.

Prayer: Accept our thanks, O God, for this foretaste of the bliss of Paradise. To thee we would pour forth our tribute of adoring love, and join with angels and the spirits of the Redeemed in worship. Unto him that sitteth upon the Throne, and unto the Lamb, be blessing and honour, glory and dominion, for ever. Amen.

We are members of the Church Universal, citizens of the Heavenly City. Heirs of that precious Redemption, which has severed us from things that are seen, and made us part of that blessed throng that no man can number - 'the general Assembly and Church of the First-born, which are written in heaven.' Neither life, nor death, nor rite, nor church-order, can divide those who are for ever one with each other because they are one with Christ. Nothing but sin and obtuseness of soul can exclude us from living fellowship with saints of all communions and sects, denominations and ages.

Also published by Christian Focus Publications

For your Daily Readings next year use

Twelve Baskets Full

Twelve actively involved Christians each
contributed one month of readings.

DECEMBER

OUR DAILY WALK IN THE LIGHT

Walk in the Light, as he is in the light
(1 John 1:7)

Walking in the Light
December 1

'God said, Let there be Light and there was Light' (Genesis 1:3).

'Ye were sometimes darkness, but now are ye light in the Lord: Walk as children of Light' (Ephesians 5:8).

St Paul makes use of this passage in Genesis, when he says, that 'God who commanded the light to shine out of darkness, hath shined in our hearts, to give the light of the knowledge of the glory of God in the face of Jesus Christ'. He seems to go back in his experience to that remarkable vision on the road to Damascus, when the light shone, and he saw the face of the Lord Jesus. It was as though he had passed through the experience of chaos, while kicking against the goad of conviction, and at that moment, which he could never forget, God said: 'Let there be light.' Looking up, he saw the light of the glory of God reflected in that dear Face that looked down on him with ineffable love. It was life out of death; light replaced darkness, and peace chased away the last vestige of storm.

This is ever the result and climax of the work in our hearts wrought by the Holy Spirit. He leads us out of darkness; he takes of the things of Christ and shows them unto us. His one aim is to glorify our Saviour, and to make him the Alpha and Omega of our faith, as we walk in the light.

When I was in Tasmania, I was shown a great mountain range on which was a vast lake, fifty-two miles in circumference. The overflow yielded a perennial waterfall of a thousand feet, the force of which was translated into electricity which made light and power cheap for great factories and for domestic needs. It seemed to me, as I thought about it, that the great sheet of water resembled the love of God, in its longing to help mankind; that the descending waterfall might be taken to illustrate the Incarnation of our Saviour, who was the Sent-One of the Eternal Trinity; and that the electric current, invisible but mighty, was typical of the Holy Spirit, who brings to our hearts the light and power of the divine nature. The lesson is obvious, that as the manufacturer or the scientist invents machinery to meet the conditions on which alone the electric current can do its work, so must we learn to adapt ourselves to receive and transmit the power and light of God, which comes to us through our union with Jesus.

Prayer: May the Holy Spirit keep us ever walking in the light of thy countenance. May he fill our hearts with the sense of thy nearness and loving fellowship. Order our steps in thy way, and then walk with us, for is thee is no darkness at all. Amen.

Jesus, the Light of the World
December 2

The star Sirius is so far away from our little earth, that its light travelling at the rate of 186,000 miles per second, has to travel for eight long years before it can reach our eyes; and yet it is so bright that, when its ray shines down the telescope, the eye of the astronomer is dazzled as though by the sun. But if the light of a single created world is thus in the physical sphere, what shall we say of him of whom we are told 'God is Light, and in him is no darkness at all'? Yet we may live and work in that searchlight, and have fellowship with him!

Present-tense cleansing. Years ago in my congregation there was a sweep who was a friend of mine. On Sundays he sang in our choir, and his face shone with the love of God. But if I happened to call at his home close on his return from work, his face was begrimed as to be almost unrecognizable! Yet even then there was one part as clear and bright as on the Sunday! The pupils of his eyes set in pearly white! It seemed as though these were impervious to the soiling touch of the smoke-dust. And why! Because Nature, which is the glove on the hand of God, has provided eyelids, eye lashes, and above all, *tear-water*, so that whatever be our environment, the eye is kept washed and clean. Is not this an illustration of what the apostle meant by the 'blood of Jesus Christ cleansing from all sin'? It is the same truth as our Lord taught, when, having washed the disciples' feet, he said that he who had bathed in the morning needed only to wash his feet.

The ultimate purpose of the soul, therefore, should be to walk in the Light as he is in the Light. God covers himself with light as with a garment. It is an emblem of purity and love and joy. And our life is meant to be like that, even when we are compelled to spend the hours of the day in the company of those who know not God, and perhaps blaspheme his Name. That Light may shine in heart and face, and fall on those around. That fellowship and communion with him may be unbroken! The song of the Lord may rise in our hearts without a jarring note! It seems incredible and impossible, especially when one is conscious of so much sin and failure! Nay, it is not impossible, if once we have learnt the secret of this present tense - 'the blood of Jesus Christ *cleanseth* from all sin'.

'I am the Light of the world: he that followeth me shall not walk in darkness, but shall have the light of life' (John 8:12).

Prayer: Fill me with thy light and joy, O Lord, that I may have wherewith to give to my home and friends, and to the dark world around me. Keep me from hiding my light under the bushel of my own anxieties. Amen.

'The spirit of man is the candle of the Lord' (Proverbs 20:27). 'For thou wilt light my candle' (Psalm 18:28).

The Tabernacle constructed by Moses, and Solomon's Temple were each modelled on the divine pattern, and consisted of three parts - the outer Court, with its altar and laver, facing the world of human life; the Holy of Holies, facing the unseen and divine; between them, the Holy place, with its candlestick, altar, and table. Transfer that picture to your own nature. The body is the outer court, and through it we touch the world around us; the spirit is our most holy place, and through it we enter into fellowship with God; the soul lies between the two, the seat of our personality, including conscience, will, intellect, and emotion.

Our text tells us that 'the spirit of man is the *candle* of the Lord'. The candle is for illumination, but there are many unlit candles! Has the divine Spirit kindled your spirit, and is the flame burning clear? The windows of your spirit command a view of the Delectable Mountains and the City of God, but have the blinds been drawn up all round, so that the sunshine may shed its radiance into the common places of daily living. In other words, Is your religious life in living touch with the person of Jesus Christ?

In its ultimate essence, Christ is the All and In-All of our holy religion. Not creed, nor ceremonials, nor the life of active philanthropy, but his personal life and presence in the heart are the supreme goal of the New Testament. What the Father was to him, he desires to be to us.

Prayer: O Holy Spirit, Love of God, infuse thy grace, and descend plentifully into my heart; enlighten the dark corners of this neglected dwelling, and scatter there thy cheerful beams; dwell in the soul that longs to be thy temple. Amen.

Remember he said: 'As the living Father hath sent me, and I live by the Father, so he that eateth (receiveth) me, he also shall live because of me', but this indwelling can only be experienced when we have learnt to find all our fresh springs of life, love, and inspiration from him with whom our life is hid in God.

When we sit before the Lord in meditation, or kneel in our accustomed place, we shall know that the Lord, whom we seek, has suddenly come to his Temple, and the glory of the Lord will illuminate the house of our life, and shed its radiance on the world around. Our life will still retain its characteristic nature, but it will be infilled by the 'second man, the Lord from Heaven'.

The Solar Look
December 4

Writing of Emerson, Margaret Fuller says in her diary: 'Emerson has been here this morning with a sunbeam in his face.' It is recorded of Daniel Rowlands, the famous Welsh preacher - to hear whom on the Sunday morning people would travel through the entire Saturday night - that when he was preaching there was a *solar look* on his face. Like Moses, he wist not that his face shone. Is not this what our Lord meant when he bade his disciples anoint their heads and wash their faces that they might not appear to men to fast! We have no right to go through the world looking dour and dark, as though our religion had a depressing and saddening effect on its professors. 'Light is sown for the righteous and gladness for the upright in heart.'

'Light is sown for the righteous, And gladness for the upright in heart' (Psalm 97:11).

Of course, there are the darker aspects of human life, and hours when we must endure chastening. Each heart has its own bitterness, every home its skeleton, every year its autumn. What family is without the empty chair, and its memory of a voice that is still? But these moods should be reserved for God alone. In the quiet hours of thought and prayer, we may talk to him who seeth in secret, of our sins and sorrows, the cares that oppress and the forebodings that molest. But when once we have rolled our burden on God, we must leave it there, and go forth, like Hannah, 'whose countenance was no more sad' (1 Samuel 1:18).

But Light must be *sown*! No farmer calculates on a harvest for which he has not prepared the soil. Those who refuse the terms of peace, offered us in Jesus Christ, purchased by his blood, and sealed by his resurrection, cannot know the uprising of that fountain of joy and gladness which casts a radiance on the face, and a beauty on every act. It is only when we receive the At-one-ment, that we can rejoice in God. It is only when we are justified by faith, that we can have the peace which passeth understanding. It is only when we walk in the light, as he is in the light, that we have fellowship one with another, and his Light will begin to glimmer on our faces and transfigure our lives. 'The redeemed of the Lord shall come with singing unto Zion. They shall obtain and joy; sorrow and sighing shall flee away.'

Prayer: Thou hast given me gladness, Lord; help me to make others glad, and pass on to them the comfort wherewith thou hast comforted me. At whatever cost, may I have fellowship with thee in thy redemptive purpose and ministry. Amen.

'The people that walked in darkness have seen a great light: they that dwelt in the land of deep darkness, upon them hath the light shined' (Isaiah 9:2 RV marg).

As every one is affected by the first man, Adam, so every one has a direct claim upon Jesus Christ, the second Man, whose Death and Resurrection and Ascension affect us all. He is the Light who has shined in our hearts, to give the light of the knowledge of the glory of God in the face of Jesus Christ. Because Christ lay upon Mary's breast, and was cradled in her arms, we have been delivered from darkness, and it is possible for us to climb, by the staircase of his Cross, over angels, principalities and powers, to be seated with him on his Throne of Glory.

'Unto *us* a Child is born!' *He is Wonderful*, because in him the most marvellous extremes meet. He is the Babe just born, but he is the Ancient of Days who fills space. He grows in knowledge, but in him are stored the riches of eternal wisdom. He hangs in mortal agony upon the Cross, but he gives life to uncounted myriads. He is laid in a borrowed tomb, but he lives for evermore, and death has no power over him!

Prayer: We thank thee, O God, for the Son of thy Love; for all that he has done for us, and will do; for all that he has been to us, and will be. We know that he holds us in his strong hand, that he loves us with a love that cannot let us go, that we are one with him in a union which nothing can break. Amen.

He is Counsellor. Tell him thy heart's problems. Ask his counsel, and he will not mislead thee. *He is the Prince of Peace*, and 'of the increase of his government' - over new regions of the inner life, over new departments of the soul, over new openings - out of your existence, the increase deepening, heightening, widening - of the increase of his government as the years pass, there shall be no end, because the soul of man is infinite, and it will take eternity to bring out all the meaning of the Empire of Christ over our nature.

What is your reply to the claim of Christ? I urge you today to humbly put the government of everything that concerns your life upon the shoulders of Christ, and then you will find that joy and peace will increase. Such joy as thou hast never known! Such peace as has never before uttered its benison upon thy heart (verse 3).

Man's Way! God's Direction
December 6

The ways of a man - we justify them to ourselves, and think that they are necessarily right, but we are liable to be self-deceived. We must employ our sanctified commonsense, or, to adopt the phrase of our text, our heart must seriously and thoughtfully devise our way. First pray for direction; then weigh the *pros* and *cons*; then view the matter from the standpoint of trusted friends; see that your eye is single to do only the will of God; be sure that no selfish or evil consideration is allowed to bias or divert you: then make your decision, asking God to block you in whatever would be hurtful, foolish, or perilous. You will not make a mistake if you sincerely and prayerfully adopt these rules. If your eye is single (i.e. *straight*), your whole body will be full of light.

'A man's heart deviseth his way; but the Lord directeth his steps' *(Proverbs 16:9).*

There is every reason why we should employ the faculties of judgment and choice. When Samuel sent the young Saul away, he said, 'Thou shalt do as occasion shall serve thee;' we are also told of Peter, that when the angel left him, he considered the matter, and came to Mary's house.

But God's purpose is behind all human decisions. There must be room for man to devise his steps, else we should become automatons. But all our volitions and choices must be ultimately subjected to the Rule and Will of the Most High. Let us commit our works and ways to God. We must roll our burden and ourselves on our faithful Creator. Of what use is it to worry over past mistakes? We cannot undo them, but we can ask God to bring good out of evil. He will put right the mistakes, and compensate for the failures. Let the Father's hand direct your steps. If with all your devising and planning, you cannot settle the matter, throw the whole responsibility back on him, and ask him to undertake it.

Let us seek so to live that our ways may please the Lord (verse 7). 'We beseech you,' said St Paul, 'that as ye received of us how ye ought to walk and please God, even so ye do walk.' We need to wait on God that he may show us the right way, and there is a sure sign - *Via Crucis, via lucis.* Jesus said, 'I am the Way: Follow Me!'

Prayer: Lead us, O God, by paths we have not known. Make the darkness light before us, the crooked place straight, and the rough places plain. Let thine Angel lead us forth into the liberty of the sons of God. Amen.

The Quest for the Eternal
December 7

This Psalm has a special fascination for those who can no longer gather with the assemblies of God's people. David was in flight from Absalom, wandering in the wilderness. The land around is waterless and weary, and his enemies are on his track. But all this seems secondary to his longing for God. Weary and thirsty though he is, his most agonising desire is for God, the living God, as he had seen and known him in the tent, which he had reared on Zion for his worship. The barren wilderness, seemed to reflect the craving of his soul for God.

In many hearts and lives his mood is reflected today. Our soul thirsts and pines for the vision of the power and glory of God, for the communion of saints. Perhaps David lays greater emphasis on the Sanctuary than we do on our places of worship. We must remember that the Glory of the Shekinah shone between the Cherubim in that hallowed Shrine.

In verses 5 to 7, the longing soul seems satisfied. As we long for God, we find him. As we seek, we possess (Isaiah 41:17, 18). As we remember him, we break into song. The fact is that our yearnings after God are the response of our hearts to the beat of his heart and to the knock of his hand. Prayer is the response of our nature to the circulation of his lifeblood within us. When we seek his face, it is in answer to his own summons. 'When thou saidst, Seek ye my face; my heart said unto thee, Thy face, Lord, will I seek.' As one has stated it: 'Our desires and aspirations are responses to the outflowings of the Holy Spirit in silent or expressed communion.'

The climax of the Psalm is reached in verse 8. Notice the three-fold steps: my soul thirsts; my soul is satisfied; my soul followeth hard after thee. Remember him upon thy bed. Meditate on him through the night-watches! Hide thyself under the shadow of his wings! Keep step with his purposes! Follow close behind him! Whosoever follows hard on God's track, trusting in him, rejoicing in his companionship, reaching out toward him, will feel his own outstretched hand enclosed in a strong and tender grasp, steadying against weariness and failure, and making his own footsteps a way for our feet.

Prayer: Bestow upon me also, O Lord my God, understanding to know thee, diligence to seek thee, wisdom to find thee, and a faithfulness that may finally embrace thee. Amen.

The Mirror of Truth
December 8

There is an old fable of a palace, in which one room was remarkable above all others because it was lined with glass of a special quality. Whenever a person entered whose life was inconsistent with truth, a mist blurred the surface of the mirrors so that he was unable to see himself clearly. It was when the apostle Paul compared his own self-centred goodness with the love and purity of Christ, he lost all hope of justifying himself, and confessed that the things which he had counted gain were only loss.

'If any be a hearer of the word, and not a doer, he is like unto a man beholding his natural face in a mirror: for he goeth away, and straightway forgetteth what manner of man he was' (James 1:23, 24).

Truth and Love are indissolubly connected. Love is of God, and so is Truth. If you have the one, the other must follow. If the soul, looking into the mirror of God's word, perceiving that there is a blur, and sets itself to remove all that has caused it; and if it continues in this attitude, not being a hearer who forgets, but a doer that works, he shall be *'blessed in his doing'*.

The blessedness of doing and becoming. It is only as we do, that we become. Even to behold Christ will not make us Christlike in character, unless we translate into *action* what we have discovered in him. The impressions made on the hearer through the ear are very vagrant, like the breeze on the water. We look at ourselves in the mirror held up before us, and straightway go off and forget what manner of persons we were. It is only as we cease to be hearers who forget, and become doers that work, that we can make any progress in the Christian life and walk.

Listen attentively to the Word of Truth, written or spoken. Be quick to notice the smallest symptom of inconsistency between your life and the perfect beauty of Jesus, and set yourself immediately to correct it. Be merciful to the failings of everyone else, but be merciless to your own. Let no fault remain uncorrected, and no call to duty unanswered. For you to live, let it be Christ. Your blessedness and happiness will come in choosing the Christ-life, in doing, and continuing to do, what he would have you do.

Prayer: Help us to cast out all those things which are contrary to thy peace, or that are not according to thy will, so that ours may be the quiet life of trust, and faith, and obedience, longing for thy truth, and walking in the light thereof. Amen.

Christ's Revelation of God
December 9

'Lord, shew us the Father, and it sufficeth us... Jesus saith... he that hath seen me hath seen the Father' (John 14:8, 9).

Philip's inquiry bore witness to the growth of a human soul. Only three short years before Christ had found him. At that time he was probably much as the young men of his standing and age, not specially remarkable, save for an interest in the earnestness about the advent of the Messiah. His views, however, were limited and narrow; he looked for Christ's advent as the time for the re-establishment of the Kingdom of David, and deliverance from the hated Roman yoke. But three years of fellowship with the Master had made a wonderful difference. He is not now content with beholding the Messiah - he is eager to know the Father: 'Show us the Father, and it sufficeth us.'

But surely this request was based on a mistake. He wanted to see the Father. But how can you make Wisdom, or Love, or Purity visible, save in a human life? Philip was so absorbed in his quest for the transcendent, that he missed the revelation of the Father which for three years had been passing before his eyes. 'Have I been so long time with you, and yet hast thou not known me, Philip?'

Our Lord revealed the Father in his works (verses 10, 11). The story of his miracles are leaves from God's diary. The right way to read them is not to say: This is what Christ did; but, Thus God is ever doing - always healing the sick, giving sight to the blind, restoring the leper, and raising the dead.

He reveals the Father in answering our prayers (verse 13). He is ever anxious to answer our petitions, that he may reveal the nature and glory of God our Father.

Christ reveals the Father by communicating the Holy Spirit, who comes to abide in us. No miracle could tell us so much of God as the Spirit does when he communicates the divine nature. When our Lord says that he will manifest himself to the soul that obeys him, and that the Father will come in to make his abiding-place with us, he not only shows, but he gives to us the Father (verses 21, 23). The life and ministry of our Lord during his earthly life, and throughout the ages, unfolds to us the Father, in the sweetness, tenderness and strength of that glorious Being, whose Love pervades the universe.

Prayer: We bless thee, O Lord Jesus Christ, that thou hast revealed to us the Father, and hast brought us nigh unto God. Make us pure in heart, not only in our walk, but in our inward temper, that we may never lose sight of God by reason of the obscurity of our own nature. Amen.

The Broad and the Narrow Way
December 10

At the beginning of life, each soul stands before these two paths. In each of us the love of life is strong, and in each is the desire to get as much as possible out of the years which may be given. Amiel expresses this strong passion for life when he says: 'A passionate wish to live, to feel, to express, stirred the depth of my heart. I was overpowered by a host of aspirations. In such a mood one would fain devour the whole world, experience everything, see everything, learn everything, tame everything, and conquer everything.'

'Wide is the gate, and broad is the way, that leadeth to destruction ... Narrow is the way which leadeth unto life' (Matthew 7:13, 14).

In our early years each of us wakes up to the throb of strong natural impulses, and we are tempted to argue, if God has given me these strong desires, why should they not be gratified? Why should I not throw the reins on the necks of these fiery steeds, and let them bear me whither they may? To do this, is to go through the wide gate, and to take the broad road. It is the way of society, of the majority - the 'many' go in there. It is pre-eminently the way of the world, and no one who goes by this way, allowing his course to be dictated by strong natural impulses, need fear that he will be counted strange or eccentric.

It must be admitted that, in its first stages, the broad way is generally easy and rather delightful. The boat launched on the flowing stream sweeps merrily and pleasantly along the gradient of the road slopes so as to make walking easy, the sun shines, and the path is filled with bright flowers. But to a life given up to self-indulgence, there is only one end - destruction.

There is a more excellent way, but it is too narrow to admit the trailing garments of passionate desire, too narrow for pride, self-indulgence, greed, and avarice - it is the Way of the Cross, but it leads to Life! We all want to see life - and the remarkable thing is that those who expect to get most out of it by self-indulgence miss everything; whilst those who seem to curtail their lives by following Christ, win everything. Few find and enter this path, is the lament of our Lord. Let us put our hand in his, that he may lead us into the path of life, 'that shineth more and more unto the perfect day'.

Prayer: Dear Lord, as Enoch walked with thee of old, so would we walk each day, choosing the narrow path; order our steps in thy way, and graciously walk with us. Amen.

'Who is on the Lord's side!' (Exodus 32:26) 'How long halt ye between two opinions! If the Lord be God, follow him; but if Baal, follow him. And the people answered him not a word' (1 Kings 18:21).

Moses and Elijah uttered practically the same call, which is always being spoken to each fresh generation. As soon as we can think for ourselves, we are accosted by the challenge of the divine voice: Art thou for me or against me? Which side dost thou take? From the lips of our blessed Lord comes the additional challenge, which compels us to face the alternative as one that may not be trifled with or put aside: 'He that is not *with me is against me.*'

How long halt ye between two opinions? We must take one side or the other. When the division-bell rings in the House of Commons, the Ayes must go to the right, and the Noes to the left. A man must choose which he will take! *If* Jehovah ... *If* Baal ... We cannot be neutral without being stultified.

Who, then, is prepared to take sides, and to come out to Christ, without the camp, bearing his reproach? (Hebrews 13:13.) To be on the Lord's side is to acknowledge him as our King as well as Saviour. It is to render to him our reverence, obedience, love and devotion. It is to abandon all refuges and resorts to our own works and ways, and to strive for heart, mind, and life to be assimilated to his will and character. This is what our Saviour expects and asks of each of us! We are to belong wholly to God, to give him all that we are capable of giving, to choose his cause, and to find in him the beginning and ending, the first and last.

Prayer: O Lord, we acknowledge thy dominion over us; our life, our death, our soul and body, all belong to thee. Grant that we may willingly consecrate them all to thee, and use them in thy service. Amen.

Jesus Christ possesses an unimpeachable and absolute right over us - the right of *Creator*, 'it is he that hath made us, and not we ourselves'; the right of *Benefactor*, not only in the realm of temporal but of spiritual existence; the right of *Redeemer*, and this is the greatest claim of all.

Our decision demands declaration. Christ will not have his followers live in secret. In the days in which we live, when there are so many temptations to compromise between the disciples of Jesus and the votaries of the world, there is overwhelming reason why we should take his side. And in that great day, he will take *our* side and acknowledge us before his Father and the holy angels!

In the Beginning God
December 12

Genesis means *Beginning*. Here we discover the source of many streams, some crystal, some turbid, which are still flowing through the world. It tells us of the beginning of the heavens and the earth; of the human race; of sin and redemption; of marriage and the institution of the home; of the sciences and arts that have built up the fabric of our civilisation; of the existence of the Hebrew race, and of the division of the human family into the various nationalities of the world. All of these cannot be attributed to the originating of God, for with regard to the sin and pain and sorrow of the world, it must be conceded that 'an enemy hath done this'.

'In the beginning God created the heaven and the earth' (Genesis 1:1).

'In the beginning was the Word... all things were made by him' (John 1:1-3).

In Hebrew the word for *God* is plural, the verb conjoined to it is singular, indicating that God is One, but the noun is plural, indicating the mystery of the Holy Trinity. In his earthly life, our Lord asked the Father to glorify him with the glory that they had together before the world was.

Let us make God in Christ our beginning - the beginning of the book of our life - of our heaven, with its prayer, meditation, and devotion; of our earth, with its practical daily business; of our marriage and home; of our interests and pleasures. Here is the chief corner-stone in which alone the whole building of life can be fitly framed together. Here is the chord of harmony, with which the subsequent oratorio must be consistent. Here is the perfect circle of happiness, in which all that is fairest, sweetest, and strongest must be found.

God is a Faithful Creator. What he begins he finishes. He fainteth not, neither is weary. You may exhaust the dearest human love, but you can never wear out God. If you have never entered on the divine life, begin with putting God in his right place, as Alpha, *the First*. If we cry, 'Create in me a clean heart, O God, and renew a right spirit within me,' he will answer, 'Behold I make all things new.' Listen to the divine assurance: 'I am Alpha and Omega ... the First and the Last, the Beginning and the End. He that is athirst, let him come: he that *will*, let him take the water of life freely.'

Prayer: O God, my Father, supremely Good. Beauty of all things beautiful. To thee will I entrust whatsoever I have received from thee, so shall I lose nothing. Thou madest me for thyself, and my heart is restless until it repose in thee. Amen.

God's Thought of Me
December 13

'Thou art a God that seeth me' (Genesis 16:13 RV marg).
'How precious also are thy thoughts unto me, O God' (Psalm 139:17).

Hagar was an Egyptian slave-girl, who had been brought up amid the idolatries of Egypt, and had no sort of idea that the gods had any personal interest in so insignificant a human atom as she was. Probably in Abraham's encampment she had heard of Jehovah, but would doubtless think of him as being equally outside the limits of her little life. What care should the God of her master and mistress have for her, as she fled from the harsh treatment of Sarah, and was in danger of perishing in the lonely desert! Then, suddenly, in her despair, she heard the voice of the Angel-Jehovah speaking to *her*, and she called him 'The Living One who seeth me'.

To her the thought was an inspiration and comfort, enabling her to return and submit herself to Sarah. But to many these words have been a note of fear and judgment. They have thought of God as spying upon their evil ways, and have shrunk from the thought of his eye seeing them. That thought, however, is not the significance of these inspiring words, but that we can never wander into the far country, or take one weary step in loneliness without the tender notice of God our Father, who notices even the sparrow that falls to the ground.

The Psalmist had the same thought when he wrote the 139th Psalm. When he says that God knows his downsitting and uprising, that his thoughts and ways are all open to his Almighty Friend, it is in a tone of rapturous gladness. It is the prerogative of friendship to love the presence and thought of a friend, and the crowning characteristic of Christianity is that we are admitted into personal friendship with our Lord. He knows *our thoughts* afar off. With an instant sympathy he enters into our anxieties and discouragements. Wherever we go he precedes and brings up the rear; we are *beset* by his care behind and before. Let every reader open the door to this great Friend, remembering that his one test is obedience: 'Ye are my friends if ye do whatsoever I command you.' Thus you will find his presence the delight of your life (Revelation 3:20).

Prayer: We thank thee, O God, that thou hast been about our path, considering all our ways, and encompassing us with blessing. Thine eye has been upon us to deliver our soul from death, and to be our help and shield. For all thy gracious care we thank thee. Amen.

Communion and Transformation
December 14

Moses, as he returned from the mountain of vision, where he had beheld as much of God's glory as seems possible to man, caught some gleam of the Light which he beheld. There was a strange radiance on his face, unknown to himself, but visible to all. He remained long enough in the presence of God to become saturated with the light and glory of the Lord. What wonder that he sparkled with it and was compelled to cover his face with a veil!

'Moses wist not that the skin of his face shone while he talked with him' (Exodus 34:29). 'We all, with unveiled face reflecting as a mirror the glory of the Lord, are transformed into the same image' (2 Corinthians 3:18).

St Paul refers to this incident, and shows that the light which shone upon the face of Moses is the symbol of the lustre of character which shines from those who behold or reflect the glory of the Lord. As we behold the glory shining in the face of Jesus Christ, we are changed into his likeness.

There are two laws for Christian living: keep looking at Jesus until you become like him, and beholding are changed into the same image; then reflect him to others, and as you endeavour to reflect him, the work of transformation goes on. 'Tell me the company a man keeps, and I will tell you his character,' so runs the old proverb. We might go further and say, tell us what are the subjects of his habitual consideration - art, literature, theology, law, commerce, philanthropy - and we shall be able to anticipate the expression that will come upon his face.

If we desire to be pure and good, Christ-like and Godlike, we must live in fellowship with Christ; beholding and reflecting his glory, even the lowliest and most sinful may become changed into his image. How different to Moses is the unveiled glory of Christ. Let us beware of anything that might bring a veil between him and us, and nothing will so soon do this as sin, and inconsistency. Moses wist not that his face shone, and Samson wist not that the Lord had departed from him (Judges 16:20). There is a tragic as well as a blessed unconsciousness. Let us see to it that we watch and pray, that we may not be taken unawares, and deprived of our purity and strength whilst wrapt in unconsciousness.

Prayer: We long to be holy as thou art holy; to love as Christ also loved us; to be patient and unmurmuring as he was, and so to resemble him that men may love him for what they see of his likeness in us. Amen.

'If we say that we have no sin, we deceive ourselves. If we confess our sins, he is faithful and just to forgive us our sins, and to cleanse us from all unrighteousness' (1 John 1:8, 9).

To sin is to *miss the mark*! Such is the meaning of the original word. When the prodigal returned, his first words were: 'Father, I have missed the mark.' Are we not always missing the mark, coming short? Sin is negative as well as positive. The Confession of the Church of England and the Shorter Catechism both agree in this: 'We have done the things that we *ought not*; we have left *undone* the things that we ought to have done.' Sin consists, not only in the positive transgression of the law of God, but in the want of conformity to his will. It is needful to use this two-pronged fork. A number of men are on their way to the recruiting-station, and the standard is to be exactly six foot; they are all under that height, but the tallest of them glories in the fact that he is a clear two inches above the rest of his fellows; it may be so, but he will be as certainly rejected as the shortest, because even he comes below the standard. You may be better than scores of people in your circle, but you will need Christ's forgiveness and salvation equally with the worst!

In dealing with sin, therefore, there must be *confession*. 'Do not hide, nor cloak them before the face of your Heavenly Father, but confess them with a patient, meek and contrite heart.' Do not wait for the hour of evening prayer, nor even for the opportunity of being alone, but in the busy street, in the midst of daily toil, lift up your heart to Christ if you have done wrong, and say: 'I have gone astray: seek Thy servant'.

It is not enough to confess to Christ, if you have sinned against another, you must first go and be reconciled to him, and then come and offer your gift at the altar. Confess, and make good! It is not enough to be extraordinarily pleasant, or suggest a solatium; you must definitely ask *forgiveness*!

When God forgives he forgets (Isaiah 43:25). As David puts it, and he had reason to know, 'He restoreth my soul.' Remember that he delighteth in mercy. He is faithful and just to forgive and cleanse. Through the Sacrifice of Calvary God can be absolutely just, and at the same time the Justifier of them who believe in Jesus.

Prayer: Heavenly Father, I thank thee for thy forgiving, pitying love. I gratefully realise that my sin cannot alter thy love, though it may dim my enjoyment of it. But I pray thee to set me free from the love and power of sin, that it may not intercept the light of thy countenance. Amen.

Ambassadors for Christ
December 16

It is a wonderful thing to hear these words from the lips of our Lord, when we remember what the Devil said to him at the beginning of his ministry (Luke 4:6). Evidently the sceptre had been wrested from the hand of the prince of this world. Our Lord is supreme in heaven, and equally so on earth. He has authority over winds and waves; over the natural world with its laws and elements; over gold mines and harvest fields; over the minds and souls of all men who have been purchased by his precious blood. It would greatly facilitate our obedience to his command if we realised that the whole world is his by creation and redemption, and that wherever we go throughout its vast territory we are within his domains.

'Ye have not chosen me, but I have chosen you' (John 15:16). 'All power is given unto me in heaven and in earth. Go ye therefore and make disciples of all nations. And, lo, I am with you all the days, even unto the end of the age' (Matthew 28:18-20 RV).

Notice the care with which Christ insists that those who were disciples should be taught to observe all his commands (verse 20). He chose the apostles that they might receive his commands, not for their own obedience alone, but that they might impress them upon others. Obedience is the law of spiritual growth and blessedness. Let us resolve, first to observe whatsoever the Master has appointed; the second, to teach others to do the same. Whenever the task seems too great for our strength, let us remember the precious promise that he is with us always, as the margin puts it - 'all the days'. Never a day can come with its demands, its call for dutiful obedience, but he will be at hand to bear our burden, to help us by the right hand of his strength, to inspire us by the light of his face.

Prayer: Help us to abide in our calling with thee, to detect thy presence in every place. May we realise that every place may be a temple, every duty a service, and that we are part of thy great host, who do thy bidding, hearkening to the voice of thy word. Amen.

Christian life, after all, comes to this - how much will you obey Christ? If you refuse, you shut yourself out of his best, for he can do nothing for you or with you. But if you surrender yourself to obey, there is no limit to the usefulness and blessedness that must ensue (Genesis 18:18-19). To live like this, we must abide in him, and allow his words, by meditation and prayer, to abide in us. Then obedience ceases to be an effort, but it is the fruit of an exuberant life.

Quiet Resting Places
December 17

'My people shall dwell in a peaceable habitation, and in sure dwellings, and in quiet resting places' (Isaiah 32:18).

Isaiah's conception of these quiet spots in our lives is set forth in verse 2 of this chapter, as also by the Psalmist in the 23rd Psalm. It is scorching noon. The glare from the limestone rocks is almost unbearable. The sunbeams strike like sword-blades. Every living creature has fled for shelter from the pitiless heat, with the exception of the little green lizards that dart to and fro in play, or searching for food. The shepherd has led his panting flock down into the valley, where great rocks cast dark shadows. Listen to the musical ripple of the brown-hued brook, as it glides lazily between the mossy banks, and breaks against the little pebbles that line its bed! These are the green pastures and the water of rest!

Have they not their counterpart in our lives! The happy days of childhood, when as yet we hardly knew temptation, and had not felt the unceasing strain of life's tasks; perhaps it is the Sunday rest, with its blessed pause from the fever of activity, the calm and restful atmosphere of the House of God, the quiet stillness of worship and meditation; perhaps a period of convalescence after long illness, when we come slowly back to health and strength; or, it may be the annual holiday, when we spend long happy days by the sea, or in the country, amid the Alps or on the Broads. For physical, mental, and spiritual well-being we need days and weeks when the machinery of life has time to cool and the water to drop its silt.

Prayer: O God, may there be a pause in the busy rush of daily life, not only in outward seeming, but in our inward temper. May our anxieties and cares be borne by thyself on whom we cast them, that there may be nothing to break the repose and serenity of our hearts. Ordain peace for us, because thou hast also wrought all our works in us. Amen.

But if we would have an entrance to this peaceful habitation, we must fulfil the conditions. We must make Jesus our King, and put the sceptre of our life absolutely into his hands. We must hide under the shadow of the crucified Man of Nazareth, who offers himself as a hiding-place from the scorching sirocco, and a covert from the tropical tempest (verses 1, 2). Isaiah says this quietness and confidence rest on Righteousness and Justice. They are not the gift of caprice or arbitrary choice. 'God is faithful and just to forgive us our sins,' because in the person of his Son all possible claims have been met (Romans 5:1).

A New Name!
December 18

Throughout the Bible, name stands for nature. In those wise old days, names were not given because of their euphonious sound, but as revealing some characteristic trait. Shepherds are said to name their sheep by their defects; in some cases Old Testament names seem to have been given on the same principle. It was so with Jacob. When the Angel said: 'What is thy name?' he answered, 'Jacob', *supplanter*! Never shrink, in your dealings with God, to call yourself by your own specific title, whether it be the least of all saints, the chief of sinners, or the dissembler and cheat!

'Thy name shall be called no more Jacob, but Israel' (Genesis 32:28). 'He that over-cometh ... I will write upon him mine own new name' (Revelation 3:12).

The first condition of losing our old nature is to confess to its possession; the next is to yield to God. Be conquered by God, yield to him, submit to his will, especially in that one point where his Spirit presses thee hard. Life is full of the approaches of the wrestling Angel, only we rebut instead of allowing ourselves to be vanquished by him. Each time we allow God to have his way in some new point of our character, we acquire the new name. In other words, a new phase of character is developed, a new touch of the divine love passes into our being, and we are transformed more perfectly into his likeness, whose Name comprehends all names. Jacob becomes Israel; Simon becomes Peter the Rock-man; Saul becomes Paul the apostle.

When God calls us by a new name, he communicates to us a new Name for himself. In other words, he gives us a deeper revelation of himself. He reveals attributes which before had been concealed. The apostle in the Apocalypse tells us that every time we overcome, God gives to us a white stone, in which his new name is written, in evident reference to the pure diamond of the Urim and Thummim, by which he spoke to Israel, and on which *Jehovah* was engraved (Exodus 28:29-30; Revelation 2:17). Each victor over sin has his own stone of Urim, knows God's will at first hand, and has revelations of God's character, which only he knows to whom they are made (Matthew 11:25).

Prayer: Give unto us, O God, the white stone with the new name written on it, that he only knows who receives it. Manifest thyself to us as thou dost not to the world. Amen.

The Elder Brother
December 19

Of the two, I think the prodigal attracts more interest and affection than his elder brother. Esau seems a more attractive character than Jacob; the publican than the pharisee, who rejoices that he is not as others! Probably it is because we are conscious of a closer affinity to the life of sense and passion, than to that of outward decorum and respectability.

The elder son had a goodly heritage. He had his father's companionship in all the changing seasons of the year, and all the following years of his life; he had the comfortable assurance that he had never at any time transgressed the commands and direction which his father gave, so that he was saved from the inward canker of bitter remorse; he was at liberty to help himself, not only to a share of all that his father possessed, but to it all - *all that I have is thine.*

This is our heritage also, as the sons and daughters of the Lord God Almighty. We may live always in the presence and with the companionship of God, talking over with him all that concerns our lives and his work; we, too, are at liberty to draw on his vast resources, for whatever we require, since all that he has is ours in Christ, to be claimed by constant faith.

How loveless and selfish was the spirit of the elder brother! He was jealous of the welcome accorded to the prodigal, and complained that so much should be lavished on one whose conduct had been so great a contrast to his own. His selfish spirit alienated him from his father, who had to go out and intreat him to come in, for selfishness always isolates. The spirit which magnifies itself for its own virtues is not the spirit of true religion, however correct the exterior life may be.

Let us each ask ourselves: Can God our Father address us in such words as these? Can we be regarded with his grace and heavenly benediction, the sons of God without rebuke? If not, we are really as much prodigals as our brethren, for we are throwing away opportunities which angels covet. Let us arise and come back to our Father. Let us enter into his joy; let his joy enter our hearts, that we may make merry and be glad.

Fidelity to our Pledges
December 20

The Psalmist had been brought very low by the sorrows of death, but God had mercifully intervened to deliver him in answer to his cry, and he now walked before him in the land of the living. It seemed as though the cup of salvation had been put into his hand, overflowing with blessing. He tells us that God had loosed his bonds, as though he had been some wild creature of the woods, who had been entrapped, but was now set free and able to realise its former glad buoyancy of life.

'For thou, O God, hast heard my vows: thou hast given me the heritage of those that fear thy Name.' 'I will pay my vows unto the Lord now in the presence of his people' (Psalms 61:5; 116:18).

Under such circumstances, it is natural to ask, 'What shall I render to the Lord for all his mercies toward me?' The first and most reasonable thing is to pay the vows which we promised when we were in trouble. Nothing so deadens the heart as to vow and not to pay.

We ought to fulfil our vows for many reasons. First, because it is dishonouring to God to play fast and loose with him; second, it deteriorates character to resolve and not to do, for such failures render the next resolutions still more brittle; third, it is a great hindrance to those who may have heard us make our vows, when we go back on them; fourth, the vow which is not kept shows that we have failed, both in vowing and performing, to rely on the grace and power of the Holy Spirit. When a deed, from the inception of the first thought to its ultimate performance, is wrought in God, there can be no fear that it will not become permanent (John 3:21).

If you have vowed to be God's servant, see that you are as you have vowed; if you have promised service, money, gifts, amendment, or life-long devotion, be sure that your promise is kept. What a glorious affirmation is in Psalm 116:16: 'O Lord, truly I am thy servant.' The reduplication of the sentence is very significant, especially when joined to Psalm 118: 27. Do we not need to be tied by the cords of faith and hope and love of the mercies of God, and by the keeping grace of the Holy Spirit. Our own resolutions and pledges are so frail and uncertain, but God's grace is sufficient to make us what we long to be in our best moments (Romans 12:1, 2).

Prayer: Defend us, O Lord, from the treachery of our unfaithful hearts. We are exceeding frail and indisposed to every virtuous and gallant undertaking. Grant that we may bring our vessel safe to shore, unto our desired haven. Amen.

The Promise of Resurrection
December 21

'The third day he will raise us up, and we shall live in his sight' (Hosea 6:2). 'For as in Adam all die, even so in Christ shall all be made alive' (1 Corinthians 15:22).

Death is the precursor of life, and we cannot truly reach Easter unless we first descend into the grave. Blessed are they who descend thither in hope; their soul shall not be left in the land of shadow, nor will God permit his holy ones to see corruption. God will revive them, and they shall live. On the third day, our Lord Jesus rose from the dead, and this is the foundation-hope for the world.

Come, let us return unto the Lord. There is always resurrection, hope, and joy for those who repent of their sins. True repentance is a humble return to God; and as we draw nigh to him, he meets us with healing and salvation. The result of his coming is like the dawn, or as the spring-rains. Light and joy, fertility and beauty are the immediate response of the soul to his advent.

Do you find yourself in the dark grave of circumstances? Be of good cheer. One of God's angels is on his way to roll away the stone. Though our Lord was crucified, yet on the third day God raised him up, and he lives and reigns at the right hand of God; and we also may live with him, by the same power, not in the other world only, but in this. God will raise you up, and you shall live in his sight. The best is yet to be!

Prayer: May our self-life be crucified with Christ, that his life may be manifest in us; and out of the grave may there spring a more complete resemblance to our Risen Saviour, so that all may see in us daily evidence of the Resurrection of our Lord. Amen.

Let us follow on to know the Lord. We may always count on him. If there is any variation in our relations with him, it is on our side, not on his. Just as surely as we return to him, we shall find him coming to meet and greet and receive us with a glad welcome. When the prodigal was a great way off, his father saw him, and ran to meet him! Is there any doubt about our reception? No, there cannot be! God our Father is always waiting for us. In him there is no variation, neither shadow that is cast by turning. As certainly as we count on the day-spring may we count on God. Let your soul move towards him out of the grave of doubt and despair, and on the third day - the Day of Resurrection - he will be revealed.

Praising the Lord
December 22

It is a comely and befitting thing for us to blend praise and prayer. There is a difference between praise and thanksgiving. We thank God for what he has done for us; we praise him for what he is in himself. In praise we come nearest to the worship of Heaven, where the angels and the redeemed find the loftiest exercise of their faculties in ascribing praise, and honour, and glory to God. In my private devotions, I find nothing more helpful than to recite the *Te Deum* before asking for any gift at the hand of God. It seems to put God in his right place, and to bow the soul before him in the attitude of adoration and praise. 'It is good to sing praises, and praise is comely.'

Let us praise his condescending love (verses 1-6). He counts the number of the stars as a shepherd tells his sheep. The Psalmist likens the constellations to a flock of sheep, which their shepherd is driving through space. What a sublime conception of suns, planets, and asteroids! Yet this wonderful and infinite God can bend over our little lives, and take special notice of the outcasts, the broken-hearted, the sorely wounded, and the meek. None are too small and insignificant for his notice. Just as a mother is most careful and thoughtful for the smallest and most ailing child in her family, so God's tenderest, strongest, and most efficient help is displayed towards the neediest and most helpless of his children. He always seeks the lost sheep and the prodigal child.

Let us praise God's work in providence. Notice the present tenses in this Psalm. The Psalmist felt that God was always working in nature, and that everything was due to the direct action of his Providence. And Jesus confirmed this when he said that no sparrow fell to the ground without the Father's notice. The pure in heart, the child-like, and the meek, have this prerogative of seeing God's hand in all things. God is; God is everywhere active and energetic; and therefore there is no point of space, and no moment of time, in which he does not operate. 'Let us offer the sacrifice of praise to God continually, that is, the fruit of our lips, giving thanks to his Name' (Hebrew 13:15).

'Praise ye the Lord; for it is good to sing praises unto our God' *(Psalm 147:1).*

Prayer: We beseech thee, give us that due sense of all thy mercies, that our hearts may be unfeignedly thankful, and that we shew forth thy praise, not only with our lips, but in our lives; by giving up ourselves to thy service, and by walking before thee in holiness and righteousness all our days; through Jesus Christ our Lord. Amen.

'It shall be said in that day, Lo, this is our God; we have waited for him, and he will save us ... we will be glad and rejoice in his salvation' (Isaiah 25:9).

This song of praise was composed by Isaiah to be sung when the proud city of Babylon, which for so many years had menaced the liberty of the Hebrew people, should be overthrown. The prophet is so certain that the oppression of evil will ultimately come to desolation, and that the world shall be relieved of the awful incubus of its tyranny, that he prepares the song which was presently to break out in joyful thanksgiving. As certainly as the torrid heat of the meridian sun is reduced by the interposition of the shadow of a cloud, so should the pride and boast of the terrible ones be brought low.

The full significance of this song of praise will be realised only in Heaven, when we sit down at the Marriage-Supper of the Lamb (verses 6-8). All the Babylons which have menaced the well-being of mankind will have been destroyed then. The veil of unbelief and uncertainty, which now lies so heavily over the world, will have been torn from top to bottom. Death will have been swallowed up in life; tears will have been wiped away, and our reproach will be over. What abounding joy will be our portion then. Let the anticipation of it excite our thanks.

Are you poor? Make God your stronghold. Are you needy and in distress? Make him your hiding place. Does the storm beat on you? Flee to him for refuge. Are you scorched by the heat of temptation? Stand beneath his shadow. God your Father will not leave you alone. Your need is your best argument; your helplessness an all-sufficient plea. For you, too, there shall be song and feasting (verses 4, 6).

Prayer: O Lord, thou art my God. I will exalt thee, I will praise thy Name; for thou hast done wonderful things for my soul. Thy counsels of old are faithfulness and truth. Amen.

Praise is our highest exercise. In prayer we often approach God for more or less selfish reasons; in praise we adore him for what he is in himself. However tired and weary you may be, see to it that the morning hour of devotion begins with the key-note of thanksgiving and adoration. It is marvellous how this quickens the pulse of the soul, and reacts upon every moment that follows. 'Awake, psaltery and harp,' said the Psalmist; 'I myself will awake right early.'

Christian Courtesy
December 24

It would be a marvel to find in any community under heaven a complete embodiment of the injunctions contained in this and the following verses. Yet nothing less than this is the Christian ideal, and it would be well if, without waiting for others, each one would adopt these precepts as the binding rule and regulation of daily life. This would be our worthiest contribution to the convincing of the world, and to the coming of the Kingdom of our Lord. Does not the apostle's use of the word *finally* teach us that all Christian doctrine is intended to lead up to and inaugurate that life of love, the bold outlines of which are sketched in these words?

The general principle. 'Be ye all of one mind, having compassion one of another.' This oneness of mind does not demand the monotony of similarity, but unity in variety. We shall never be of one mind in the sense of all holding the same opinions; but we may be all of one mind when, beneath diversities of opinion, expression, and view, we are animated by a common devotion to Christ.

Note the specific applications.

Love as brethren. Love is not identical with like. Providence does not ask us whom we would like to be our brethren - that is settled for us; but we are bidden to love them, irrespective of our natural predilections and tastes. Love does not necessarily originate in the emotions, but in the will; it consists not in feeling, but in doing; not in sentiment, but in action; not in soft words, but in unselfish deeds.

Be pitiful. Oh, for the compassion of our blessed Lord! How often it breaks out in the Gospel narrative to the weak and erring, to the hungry crowds, and to the afflicted who sought his help!

Be courteous. Be ready to take the least comfortable seat, or to let others sit while you stand. Let the manners of your Heavenly Father's Court be always evident in your daily life, so that the world may learn that Christianity produces not simply the heroism of a great occasion, but the minute courtesies of daily living.

'Finally, be ye all of one mind, having compassion one of another, love as brethren, be pitiful, be courteous' (1 Peter 3:8).

Prayer: Blessed Lord, I beseech thee to pour down upon me such grace as may not only cleanse this life of mine, but beautify it a little, if it be thy will ... Grant that I may love thee with all my heart and soul and mind and strength, and my neighbour as myself. Amen.

The Glory of Christ
December 25

'The Word was made flesh, and dwelt among us, and we beheld his glory, the glory as of the Only-Begotten of the Father, full of grace and truth' (John 1:14).

The glory of Christ is apparent, as we study the titles which are given to him in the first chapter of St John's Gospel.

The Word (verse 1). As the words we speak reveal our character, so Jesus is the speech of the invisible God. He has uttered or declared God (John 14:9). The Psalmist said that the heavens declare the glory of God, and the firmament showeth his handiwork to the ends of the earth, but in the fairest panorama of the starry heavens, or sunset clouds, there was never such a presentation of God in nature as we have in Jesus.

The Creator (verses 2, 3). In the strongest language he could command, the apostle inscribes the Name of Jesus on all things that are in heaven above and in the earth beneath. The iron of which the nails were made that transfixed him to the cross, the wood of which it was composed, the thorns which composed his crown, all were due to his creative fiat.

Life and Light (verse 4). It pleased the Father that life should reside in his human nature, as its cistern and reservoir, so that from him we should derive eternal life, communicated through faith. In his life is light.

The Messiah (verses 10, 11). 'He came unto his own.'

The Shekinah (verse 14). Now and again, during our Lord's earthly career, the curtain of his human nature seemed to part and to emit some gleams of the radiant splendour of his Being. It was so on the Transfiguration mount, and again in his Resurrection and Ascension. The glory was full of grace and truth.

The Only-Begotten Son (verses 12, 14). We may be sons, thank God, but he was *The Son*. Whatever is implied in that phrase 'Only-Begotten', he is separated from the noblest of the children of men by a measureless and impassable chasm. Yet how wonderful it is, that he is not ashamed to call us brethren. Let us give glory and homage to him.

Prayer

Love infinite, love tender, love unsought;
Love changeless, love rejoicing, love victorious!
And this great love for us in boundless store;
God's everlasting love! What would we more.

Amen.

A Comforting Letter
December 26

We have much to learn from the good advice given in this letter. These exiles were unwilling to settle in the land to which they had been transported. They were always fretting and planning; talking of the past and contriving plans for returning to their own land and to the inheritance which they had forfeited. Therefore this letter was sent, not only to them, but to all in similar circumstances.

Are you in captivity? Your circumstances are the restraint and fetters that hold you. No prisoner in a cell could be more helpless than you are. You cannot *do* as you would, but you can *be*. Be the best you can where you are, and wait the Lord's leisure. It is by fidelity in discharging present obligations that you become fitted for better work.

Consider the needs of those around you (verse 7). In this the story of Joseph is a remarkable example. When he was cast into prison, he set to work to minister to the prisoners there. What a light and comfort emanated from him, as he went to and fro among them, taking a personal interest in each - 'Wherefore look ye so sadly today?' (Genesis 40:6, 7). In the peace of those to whom we minister, we shall find our own peace.

Words of comfort and hope were spoken to the captives. Hard though their outward lot seemed, God was thinking thoughts of peace, not of evil, with respect to them. So with us; we may be having a bad time; it may appear as though everything were against us, hard, comfortless, uninviting. But in his holy heaven God is thinking about you, and his thoughts are those of peace, and not of evil. Therefore the horizon is flushed with hope. There is a good time coming, and you will forget this present, as waters that pass away. There is an allotted time to your present trouble. God will surely visit you, and perform his good word towards you.

In the meanwhile, *we must live a life of constant prayer.* 'Ye shall call upon me, and I will hearken unto you; ye shall seek me, and I will be found of you' (verses 12-14). We must live in a spirit of prayer and faith and converse with God. For all these things God will be enquired of, to do them.

'I know the thoughts that I think toward you, saith the Lord, thoughts of peace and not of evil, to give you an expected end' (Jeremiah 29:11).

Prayer: For all thy gracious care of us we reverently thank thee, and if thou hast permitted things to happen which have tried us sore and filled us with bitterness, help us to believe in thine infinite love which chastens us, that through the discipline of our life we may be made partakers of thy holiness. Amen.

The Lord Reigneth!
December 27

'Rejoice in the Lord, ye right-eous; and give thanks at the remembrance of his holiness. Clouds and darkness are round about him; righteousness and judgment are the habitation of his throne' (Psalm 97:2, 12).

Behind all clouds is the clear pure ether of God's love. We are not dismayed by the storms that sweep the earth's surface, for beneath them are unfathomed depths of stillness. God sees his way through them, and is using them to fulfil his great purpose. Difficulties are nothing to him. He weighs the mountains in scales and the hills in a balance. He is our Father, and we need not fear. The children who are snugly ensconced in the car which their father is driving are not afraid of the hail-storm that rattles on the window and the wild winds that sweep the earth. It is enough for them that their father is with them, and knows his way, and is making swiftly for home. And if we are following hard after God, then his right hand will uphold us, and we can leave all the rest with him.

None of them that wait for him shall be ashamed. Revolution and anarchy may devastate the land. Storms of deluge may sweep the world. The savings of a life-time may disappear, but we shall be kept in perfect peace. The Lord reigneth, and he will ever be mindful of his covenant. We shall not want for sustaining grace. If we cleave unto God, we shall be upheld by his right hand, and no man is able to pluck us from the Father's hand. God, not selfish ease, nor human confederacies, is our end and aim; and he will not, cannot, fail those who have left all for his companionship. Although the fig-tree shall not blossom, and the labour of the olive shall fail, and the flock shall be cut off from the fold, yet we will rejoice in the Lord; for the Lord God shall supply all our need, and will make our feet, like hind's feet, to walk even on the edge of the precipice.

The world is full of tumult. The floods have lifted up their voice, but above the noise of many waters, the Lord on high is mighty; and he must reign till he hath put all enemies beneath his feet. Remember that when he was mocked in Pilate's hall, his enemies placed a reed in his hand. They were nearer the truth than they knew, for he who opens the sealed book of destiny is the Lamb that was slain. He rules with the reed as the symbol of his government.

Prayer: Our Father, let us hear thee say to us, as we step forth into the untried day, that thou art with us, holding our right hand. Keep us in the midst of the storm, and guide us by the untrodden path. Amen.

Jesus as King
December 28

Our Lord's Royalty is suggested by the opening paragraphs of St Matthew's Gospel, which emphasises his descent from David; the wise men asked for him who is born King of the Jews, and Herod feared his rivalry. All through the Gospel narrative, stress is constantly laid on the fact that he was King of the Jews and King of Israel, and it ends with the regal claim that all power and authority in heaven and earth had been entrusted to him. Jesus never abated his claim to Kingship, but always made it clear that his ideal was very different from that which was current among the Jews. His conception of Royalty was borrowed from Psalm 72, where the King is said to judge the poor of the people, and save the children of the needy. It was the collision between his idea of Kingship and that of the Pharisees, which brought him to the Cross.

'Pilate therefore said unto him, Art thou a King, then? Jesus answered, Thou sayest that I am a King' (John 18:37).

For us the lesson is clear. We must begin with the recognition of the royal claims of Christ to our homage and obedience. He only becomes Saviour, in the fullest meaning of the word, when he has been enthroned as King in our hearts. With invariable precision he is described, first as Prince, then as Saviour, and that order cannot be altered without injury to our soul-life (Acts 5:31; Romans 10:9; Hebrews 7:2). The whole content of the New Testament is altered when we view the Royalty of Christ as the chief cornerstone, not only of that structure, but of the edifice of character.

Let us not be afraid of Christ as King. He is meek and lowly, and full of understanding of the problems of our life. He shared our life, and was so poor that he had to trust in the kind offices of a friend to supply his physical needs, and in the palm branches of the peasant crowd for his palfrey and the carpeting of his royal procession; but as we watch it pass, the lowly triumph swells in proportions until it represents the whole race of mankind; and the generations that preceded his advent, and those that follow, sweep down the ages of human history, proclaiming and acclaiming Christ as King (Revelation 15:3, 4 RV).

Prayer: O God, may our hearts indite good matter, that our mouth may speak of our King. Whilst we adore him as Wonderful may he become to us the Prince of Peace. Enable us to put the government of our lives upon his shoulder, and of his government and of our peace let there be no end. Amen.

The March of God's Progress
December 29

'Then cometh the end, when he shall have delivered up the Kingdom to God, even the Father; when he shall have put down all rule and all authority and power. For he must reign' (1 Corinthians 15:24).

Whither is God moving? When we speak of the eternal progress of the Almighty, it must be remembered that we are adopting human speech, because God lives in the eternal present. He is Jehovah - '*I AM*'!

God is moving to the supreme exaltation of our Saviour. Christ must and will reign, and the Father's power is even now engaged in putting all things under his feet. He has given him the heathen for his inheritance, and the uttermost parts of the earth for his possession. It is true that we see not yet all things put under him, but God is even now engaged in hastening the fulfilment of his eternal plan. The rise and fall of rulers and kingdoms within the last few years; the clamour for new methods of government has menaced the ancient order; the vortex of elections; the Babel of voices; the rivalry of statesmen and parties! What of these? They are the clouds of his feet, the movement of his pieces on the board, the successive stages in the unfolding of his plan. Watch the Divine strategy! God raises up one, and puts down another; there is not an item in the newspaper, nor a change on the map, nor a revolution among the people, however obscure, that is not contributing to that final scene, when the Son of Man shall come to the Ancient of Days, and there shall be given him dominion and glory, and a Kingdom, that all people, and nations, and languages shall serve him!

Prayer: Hasten the coming of thy Kingdom, O Lord, the fulfilment of thy purpose. Keep us watchful and alert, that at any moment we may discern the movement of thy hand, and detect thy will and guidance in the providence of little things. Amen.

There is need for us all to know God's movements, especially in this momentous era, because only so can we enter into his Rest. We can look out calmly on a world in confusion when once we have learnt to understand the divine programme of gathering up all things in Christ, who is the Head. To the careless world his way is in the sea, and his paths in the deep waters, and his footsteps are not known. But to those who love and follow him, the heavens may depart, the hills be removed; but his kindness shall not depart, neither shall the covenant of his peace be removed.

Mortality Swallowed up of Life
December 30

This chapter begins with *We know*. There is no shadow of uncertainty. From first to last is saturated with unwavering conviction. When it was written Faith and Hope had almost faded out of the world. Men and women were groping in the wilderness of atheism, with no star in their sky, and no oasis in their march. In the midst of a decadent civilisation and vanished hope, Paul, and others who stood with him, dared to avow that there were certain facts of which man might be absolutely sure. They were not proved by argument or analogy, but discerned by the Spirit's intuition, and proved by the Resurrection of Jesus Christ.

We must always distinguish between *theories*, which change with the various moods of human thought, and the eternal *facts*, which are established on solid testimony, and are as steadfast as the throne of the Eternal. '*We know*' - there was an accent of certainty in those words, which changed the outlook of the world!

God's Objective. It is an immense help in this human life to know the direction in which God's fiery cloud or pillar is leading us. If only we can get a clue to what God is meaning in our life, it will smooth out many perplexities and disentangle many a ravelled skein. What is God doing for you and me? The apostle answers - he is endeavouring to bring it about that our mortality may be swallowed up of life. God wants to wipe out in each of us all traces of the Fall. It is his purpose to eliminate everything which brands us as members of an exiled race, so that our mortality, whether of spirit, soul, or body, may be swallowed up by Life - 'the life of which our veins are scant, the life for which our spirits pant, more life and fuller'! Think of it! For thee, and me, and all who have been translated from the region of darkness, and brought into the Kingdom of the Son of his Love! Mortality engulfed in Life! We cannot fathom it! We know not what we shall be, we only know that we shall be like him, for we shall see him as he is. Such is God's objective. He is working for us and in us, for this very thing!

'For we know that if the earthly house of our tabernacle be dissolved, we have a building from God, a house not made with hands, eternal, in the heavens' (2 Corinthians 5:1).

Prayer

Carry me over this last long mile,
Man of Nazareth, Christ for me!
Speak to me out of the silent night,
That my spirit may know, as onward I go,
That thy pierced hands
Are lifting me over the ford.

Amen.

Light in Darkness
December 31

'What I tell you in darkness, that speak ye in the light' (Matthew 10:27).

Christ is often speaking - in the secret of the heart; in the darkness of the night, 'when deep sleep falleth upon men'; there the Master tells us things in the darkness! To listen and obey will save us many a bitter hour.

We may question if it be *his* voice, but we are rarely wrong in detecting that voice, when it reminds us of duties we have omitted, and calls on us to take up the cross which we have shunned.

There is music, tenderness, love-notes in these dark sayings, like those upon the harp, of which the Psalmist sings (Psalm 49:4); the voice that utters them is not harsh and strident, but tender and gentle. They are intended to teach us how to teach, to enable us to help others who could not understand these hidden things. We have to be taken into the dark, as sensitive paper, to receive impressions that will give pleasure and help to hundreds who could never pass through our experiences.

Prayer

Lord, speak to me, that I may speak
In living echoes of thy tone;
As thou hast sought, so let me seek
Thy erring children lost and lone.

Amen.